Asian Ethnology

Asian Ethnology (ISSN 1882–6865) is published by the Nanzan Anthropological Institute, Nanzan University, Nagoya, Japan, and is produced in cooperation with Boston University's Department of Religion. *Asian Ethnology* is an open access journal and all back numbers may be viewed through the journal's website http://asianethnology.org/. Hard copies of the journal may be purchased through Amazon.com.

Asian Ethnology publishes formal essays and analyses, research reports, and critical book reviews relating to a wide range of topical categories, including

- narratives, performances, and other forms of cultural representation
- popular religious concepts
- vernacular approaches to health and healing
- local ecological/environmental knowledge
- collective memory and uses of the past
- cultural transformations in diaspora
- transnational flows
- material culture
- museology
- visual culture

Editorial correspondence should be addressed to

Editors, *Asian Ethnology*
18 Yamazato-cho, Showa-ku
Nagoya 466–8673, Japan

TEL: (81) 52–832–3111
email: dorman@nanzan-u.ac.jp

INFORMATION FOR CONTRIBUTORS

Manuscript submissions should be sent as email attachments, in Microsoft Word to the editors. All submitted manuscripts should be double-spaced throughout and limited to 10,000 words, including notes and references. Include an abstract of up to 150 words, along with 5 key words.

The format should follow the articles contained in the present volume. For more detailed information, please consult the style guide found on the journal's website:

Please be advised that submissions accepted for publication are subject to editorial modification. Submitted manuscripts should not have been published elsewhere nor currently be under consideration by another journal. Unsolicited book reviews will be considered, though there is no guarantee of publication. In principle, book reviews should not exceed 1500 words.

Asian Ethnology is indexed in: Arts & Humanities Citation Index; ATLA Religion Database; Bibliography of Asian Studies; Current Contents/Arts & Humanities; International Bibliography of Book Reviews; International Bibliography of Periodical Literature; International Bibliography of the Social Sciences; Religion Index One Periodicals; and Scopus.

Asian Ethnology

Volume 76, Number 2 · 2017

Editors' Note

WE ARE PLEASED to present this latest issue of *Asian Ethnology*, the second since the journal returned to the Nanzan University Anthropological Institute. This completes volume 76 of the journal. From next year, *Asian Ethnology* will be published as a single-volume yearbook until further notice. In order to maintain production of the journal at a consistent level of quality, we felt it was necessary to reduce the number of issues and focus on developing the quality of the articles, reviews, and other aspects of the journal.

The journal has a new webpage <http://asianethnology.org/> which will, from this volume, feature both downloadable PDFs and versions of the journal's content that are viewable in your browser through different devices. If you wish to purchase a print copy of the journal, it will be available through Amazon in various countries.

We also announce the launch of Asian Ethnology Podcast, which can be accessed via iTunes, the Podcast webpage <http://asianethnology.libsyn .com/> or from the journal's webpage. This podcast features interviews with scholars who have contributed to, or published in *Asian Ethnology* or *Asian Folklore Studies*. It also introduces scholars and individuals whose work aligns with the topical categories of the journal. Please check out the podcast series, as this is a feature we wish to develop more extensively as we move forward.

As is normal with scholarly journals, people come and go. David White served the journal for a number of years as associate editor, but has now departed. We wish him well in his future endeavors. From this issue onward we welcome John Balch, a doctoral student of religion and science at Boston University. He will be serving as an editorial assistant. Paul J. Capobianco, a PhD candidate in anthropology at the University of Iowa, joins us as book and film reviews editor. Paul is currently a lecturer at Kyushu Sangyo University's Language Education and Research Center, while he is completing his dissertation on how demographic changes are affecting constructions of Japanese identity and the positionality of foreigners in

Asian Ethnology Volume 76, Number 2 · 2017, 211–12
© Nanzan University Anthropological Institute

Japan. He is fluent in Japanese and his research interests include East Asia, transnational migration, and intercultural communication.

We also welcome our new associate editor, Harmony DenRonden, an independent scholar who also specializes as an academic editor. She has Sanskrit and Tibetan language skills and her research interests are primarily in Tibetan and early Indian Buddhism, gender issues in Buddhism, and Madhyamaka philosophy.

We hope that you, our readers, will enjoy our newly structured journal online, and we look forward to your continued support and guidance. We are always open to new suggestions on how to improve the journal and how we operate. With the end of the year approaching rapidly, let us wish all of you our sincerest greetings for a prosperous new year

Benjamin Dorman
Nanzan University Anthropological Institute

Frank J. Korom
Boston University

24 November 2017, Nagoya

SUDIPTA SEN
University of California, Davis

Betwixt Hindus and Muslims

The Many Lives of Zafar Khan, Ghazi of Tribeni

This essay explores the legends surrounding the enigmatic figure of Zafar Khan Ghazi, whose tomb still stands at Tribeni (West Bengal, India), a major Hindu pilgrimage spot on the River Ganga. Zafar Khan has been seen variously as the spearhead of the Turkish conquest in late thirteenth-century Bengal, a harbinger of early Islam, and a founder of one of the first Sufi lineages in the region. It illustrates the conflicted nature of the *ghāzī pīr* figure, idealized as a Muslim warrior and martyr, but also remembered as a champion of the poor, a composer of odes to the river Ganga in Sanskrit, and a historical bridge between Muslims and Hindus. Examining the architecture of Zafar Khan's mosque and tomb built on the ruins of a Vishnu temple, along with iconic portrayals of the *gājī* in contemporary Bengali *maṅgalakābya* verse poetry, the paper locates Zafar Khan as an interstitial and contradictory figure at the margins of what is commonly understood as Hindu devotional worship and iconoclastic Islam.

KEYWORDS: Tribeni—Ganga River—Zafar Khan Ghazi—architecture of *spolia*—*ghazā*—syncretism

Asian Ethnology Volume 76, Number 2 · 2017, 213–34

O F THE MANY odes written to the Ganges in various Indian languages, this is one of the most poignant and memorable (CHATTOPADHYAYA 1962):

> O River, daughter of Sage Jahnu, you redeem the virtuous
> But they are redeemed by their own good deeds—what is your credit there?
> If you can grant me salvation—I, a hopeless sinner—then I would say
> Here is your greatness, your true greatness.
>
> Those who have been abandoned by their own mothers,
> Those that friends and relatives will not dare touch,
> Those whose very sight makes a passerby gasp and take the Lord's name:
> You embrace these living dead in your own arms
> O Bhagirathi, you are the most compassionate mother of all.[1]

These are translations from Sanskrit *śloka*s that appear in an eight-stanza poem dedicated to the Ganges. These memorable odes entered the repertoire of hymns, recitations, and ritual offerings to the river among the Brahmins of Bengal sometime during the medieval period, and many people knew them by heart just a generation ago. They were composed—surprisingly—not by a Brahmin, not even by a Hindu, but by an author who went by the popular name of Darap Khan Gaji. The noted Bengali linguist Suniti Kumar Chatterji identified "Darap Khan" as "Jafar" Khan Ghazi, credited with daring military exploits during the first major phase of Islamic expansion in Bengal toward the end of the thirteenth century, after the Turkish Sultanate had been established in northern India around Delhi as the new capital. How did Darap Khan or Jafar (Zafar) Khan Ghazi come into the possession of such knowledge of Sanskrit? And how did his compositions acquire such popularity? And most importantly, what does the figure of the Ghazi and his associations with the pilgrimage of Tribeni tell us about the relationship between history, folklore, and myth around the advent of Islam in medieval Bengal?

This essay is based on a close reading of primary and secondary sources in Bengali along with a number of surveys conducted during the period of British rule in India. Accounts such as those of William Wilson Hunter or Henry F. Blochmann examined here contain snippets of oral history and first-hand observations that I believe are particularly valuable in any attempt to recreate the historical milieu in which the iconic figure of Zafar Khan might have taken shape. There are, of course, both promises and pitfalls in using such secondary narratives, even though they happen to be the only first-hand accounts at our disposal. Many of the stories that the British colonial archeologists were presented with appear in their accounts translated and digested from accounts in native Bengali dialect, whose denotations and nuances are now lost. There is often no way of determining what kinds of questions were put to informants, or what kinds of responses such inquiries were met with. However, despite their inconsistency and variance, by comparing multiple accounts over a period of time, it is possible to locate the essential elements of the overall narrative that has been passed down, including sequences of memorable events. There are, of course, further problems posed by the ambition, bias, and idiosyncrasies of early colonial and early nationalist accounts that are often steeped with antiquarian and archaic views of the emergence of Islam in Bengal as an inevitable result of conquest, forcible conversion, and sectarian conflict. At the same time, they present a valuable record of past inquiries.

While I have attempted in this essay to find a definitive historical context for the origin of the story of Zafar Khan as one of the harbingers of popular Islam in thirteenth-century Bengal, I have also tried to keep in mind Dell Hymes's well-known caution that no ethnography, including historical ethnography, can be reduced to a preconceived set of determinants (MOORE 2015, 11–12). In this regard, in every version of the Zafar Khan story that has been recorded, one would find disparate and contradictory elements, not to mention the whims of the narrator and the slant of the recorder being brought to bear upon the narration.[2] While all traditions of oral transmission rely on continuity, nothing persists unchanged. Storytellers impart their own experience and sense of form, influencing the ways in which audiences make sense of their own relationship with both history and genealogy (HYMES 2003, x). If there are residues of historical evidence to be found in these stories, they are not accessible in any direct way. The history of Zafar Khan is fused together with moral precepts and hagiography that have been passed on for centuries by many communities of believers. To that end, this essay is less occupied with the empirical veracity of the received histories of Zafar Khan, or the exact nature of Islamic "conquest" along the Bengal frontier, as it is with the range of possible inferences that can be drawn about the Ghazi myth in Bengal from a concerted study of history, epigraphy, archeology, and literature.

To find what remains of the memory of the Zafar Ghazi one must travel to Tribeni, now a small nondescript town in Hugli in West Bengal on the banks of the Bhagirathi, which is the name by which the Ganga is known there. Tribeni has been venerated as a sacred place by Bengali Hindus for a very long time, a spot where the Ganga once branched off into three streams: the river Saraswati flowing southwest beyond the reputed port of Saptagram, the Jamuna flowing southeast, and the Bhagirathi proper coursing through the present Hooghly channel all the way to Calcutta. This meeting point, known as the *muktabenī saṅgama* or the "unbraided confluence," was once one of the most frequented pilgrimage sites of ancient Bengal. This was also a major center of trade and commerce, ever since the time of the Pala and the Sena dynasties, and especially during the period of Turkish conquest in the thirteenth century (RAY 2004, 198–99).

FIGURE 1. Zafar Khan Ghazi's mosque in Tribeni. **All photos by author.**

Tribeni was located two miles away from the bustling port of Saptagram (also referred to as Satgaon or Satgan). We can glean from the travel accounts of Arab and European travelers that by the end of the thirteenth century this port-city had effectively replaced Tamralipti or Tamluk, which had begun to dry up as a port from the eighth century onwards, as the most important *entrepôt* of trade in deltaic lower Bengal (CHATTOPADHYAYA 2003, 59). Saptagram was located on the banks of the Saraswati river, which flowed southwest and joined up with the distributaries Damodar and Rupnarayan before debouching into the Bay of Bengal. These waterways were part of an extensive network of trade. Saptagram rose to great prominence during the Pala and the Sena periods, and after the Turkish incursions, it became a major administrative center for the Sultans of Bengal (GHOSH 1957, 496–97). Arabic and Persian inscriptions from the year 1298 CE as well as the account of the renowned Moroccan traveler Ibn Batuta confirm that Saptagram flourished as a major city and boasted of at least seven major villages and many large markets (GHOSH 1978, 13–17). Bipradasa's *Manasabijaya*, written in praise of the goddess Manasa of the serpents, further confirms the flourishing state of contemporary Saptagram (SEN 1953, 142–43; GHOSH 1957, 505). Even after the renegade Turkish *māliks* led by Bakhtiyar Khalji seized Saptagram from local chieftains during the late thirteenth century, the place continued to flourish. It soon became the site of a major Turkish stronghold in Bengal.

Changes in the course of the Ganga eventually affected the fortunes of Tribeni, located on its right bank. The river Saraswati, which had once been the main channel for drainage of the Ganga basin, dried up sometime during the fifteenth century CE. Saraswati was also a river distinguished by its sacred waters. According to legend its waters ran in a discernibly separate current within the main channels of the Ganga and the Yamuna rivers. Saraswati's waters were deemed particularly propitious for the cleansing of earthly sins, which is why the stretch between the spot where it emptied into the Ganga, beginning with the first confluence of the Ganga at Prayag in Allahabad, and the spot where it supposedly flowed out at the second confluence at Tribeni (HUNTER 1885, 480), was seen as ideally suited for ritual ablution. This is why Tribeni was especially venerated as a pilgrimage site.

The closed mouth of the old river at Tribeni could still be seen a hundred years ago, its former course outlined by lakes and marshes (COTTON, BURN, and MEYER 1908, 173). By this time the Bhagirathi had become the main branch of the Ganga. Satgaon continued as the official port and the main commercial hub of Bengal, at least until the sixteenth century during the period of the advent of the Portuguese, even though the main channel of the Saraswati had become obstructed with alluvial deposits and was no longer fit for the navigation of Portuguese maritime caravels. However, the port of Tribeni did not lose its ritual sanctity and status. Observers noted its importance as late as the early twentieth century. During the celebration of the festival of Makara Sankranti in the month of January, when the sun enters the house of Capricorn, Tribeni typically recorded a gathering of eight thousand or more pilgrims (HUNTER 1885, 282). Similar crowds of bathers thronged the *ghāṭs* of the Ganga leading to the water during the celebration of Dasahara in June, in honor of the descent of the river from heaven to earth to bless the ashes of the fallen sons of King Sagara. According to H. Blochmann, who visited the shrine of Tribeni in the 1860s, there was a well-maintained set of steps leading down to the main bathing area on the banks of the Ganga built by the last Gajapati ruler of Orissa, Raja Mukund Deo, who exercised his sway over this part of Bengal during the latter half of the seventeenth century (BLOCHMANN 1870, 282).

It was this legendary status of Tribeni, especially its trade, pilgrimage, and shrines that must have attracted the attention of the Sultans of Delhi. If local history is any indication, Zafar Khan Ghazi—along with his fellow Turkish invaders—was supposed to have struck terror among the local Hindus, attacking their temples and idols. He fought valiantly and conquered the port of Saptagram, apparently destroyed a large and ancient temple in nearby Tribeni, and used the spoils to build an imposing mosque. He was conferred the title of Ghazi, and established one of the first schools for Quranic and Arabic learning (*madrasā*) and a charity (*dār-ul-khairat*). Epigraphic evidence, however, suggests that there was a commander also by the name of Shihabuddin Zafar Khan who was deputed by the Sultan of Lakhnauti to administer Saptagram, and who *also* founded a school and charitable endowment in Tribeni. Not only is it difficult to determine with any certainty whether these two are the same person, disparate histories seem to have converged in the overall legend of the Ghazi. This is hardly surprising considering the centuries over which these narratives have been shaped, not to mention the diverse communities of believers who have memorialized Zafar Khan in their own demotic ways.

WHO WAS ZAFAR KHAN GHAZI?

When the British official and archeologist D. Money of the Bengal Civil Service went to study the mausoleum attributed to the Ghazi in 1847, the custodians (*khādim*s) of the building produced an authentic historical document or *kursīnāmā* (MONEY 1847, 395). This record stated that Zafar Muhammad Khan had indeed traveled all the way from western India with his nephew Shah Sufi to lead the infidels of Bengal toward recognition of the Islamic faith. He converted a local raja, Man Nripati, to Islam, and then fought against the powerful Raja Bhudeb near Hugli. In this second battle he was decapitated, and his torso buried in Tribeni. The Ghazi's son, Ulugh Khan, followed in his footsteps and eventually defeated the king of Hugli, converting his subjects to Islam and eventually marrying the Hindu king's daughter. Money also found a second narrative, suggesting that a certain Sultan Firuz Shah had dispatched Zafar Khan and his nephew to Bengal to avenge the death of a Muslim subject of a Hindu kingdom whose son had been killed by the Raja as a punishment for cow slaughter. This king was also known as Raja Bhudeb. In this version of the story, Zafar Khan killed Bhudeb in battle in a place called Mahanad near Saptagram. This second narrative, as we shall see, connects the exploits of Zafar Khan with the feats another Sufi saint, Shah Safiuddin of Chota Pandua.

H. Blochmann was among the first British Indian officials to study the Arabic inscriptions preserved on the interior walls of Zafar Khan's tomb. He deciphered a part of the second inscription (AH 698, CE 1298) which describes Zafar Khan as a Turk, a "lion of lions," and a builder of benevolent edifices in the manner of conquerors of yore, smiting infidels with sword and spear and lavishing gifts on the faithful (BLOCHMANN 1870, 286). Almost four decades later, in a report on the relics of Satgaon and Tribeni submitted to the *Journal of the Asiatic Society of Bengal,* the noted Indian archeologist Rakhal Das Bandyopadhyaya put this epigraphic evidence in the larger context of the Muslim conquest of Bengal (BANDYOPADHYAYA 1909). After the first forays of Bakhtiyar Khaljik, the Turks ruled the area between Deokot in the north to Lakhnaur in the south, but the entire Bhagirathi delta was not under their immediate command. Zafar Khan's advance to the region of Saptagram and Tribeni, according to Bandyopadhyaya, was thus a particularly significant event. Zafar Khan, originally of Turkish descent, had been appointed by the Sultan of Delhi as the governor of Deokot before the expedition, and his full name—found in another contemporary inscription from Dinajpur—was "Ulugh-i-Azam Humayun Zafar Khan Bahadur Bahram Tigin." Another inscription from the same site (also noted and translated by H. Blochmann) states that an Islamic institution of learning was built at Tribeni by Khan Muhammad Zafar Khan in CE 1313 during the reign of Shamsuddin Firuz Shah in Delhi. Bandyopadhyaya suggested that this was the same Zafar Khan, the conqueror of Tribeni. He had not really courted martyrdom, but was well and alive fifteen years after the conquest of Tribeni (BANDYOPADHYAYA 1909, 248).

Years later, the eminent Bengali historian Jadunath Sarkar studied these three Arabic inscriptions found in Tribeni for his voluminous history of Bengal. Sarkar came to the conclusion that Zafar Khan was indeed sent on a mission of conquest to Saptagram by the ruler of Lakhnauti, Ruknuddin Kaikaus, grandson of the Delhi Sultan Ghyasuddin Balban, during which he courted martyrdom (SARKAR 1973, 77–78). Shamsuddin Firuz Shah, who succeeded Kaikaus as the ruler of Lakhnauti, dispatched the fallen Ghazi's son, Ulugh Khan, from the stronghold of Munger in Bihar to Bengal to resume the siege of Saptagram and Tribeni. He too might have died in battle. After this, Firuz Shah appointed Shihabuddin Zafar Khan as the administrator of Saptagram, who set up a school and a charity. Sarkar's account clearly suggests that there might have been more than one Zafar Khan associated with Tribeni.

There seems to be no particular agreement among historians about the exact identity of this Ghazi. Was he truly the first spearhead of Islam in lower deltaic Bengal, as many have claimed? Was he the founder of the oldest Sufi order in the region? Was he the first Turk or Muslim to have worshipped the Ganga? These are pointed questions that illustrate the problem of casting the Islamic "conquest" of Bengal as a singular historical event. This is a problem that is common to both colonial and nationalist accounts. For a more realistic and variegated historical account, we have to disaggregate these tangled histories of Turkish raids, the establishment of Sufi lineages, and the appropriation of certain facets of Islam in Bengal. The history and legend of Zafar Khan Ghazi, however, deserves much more scholarly attention than it has received so far. It holds a key to an important question that can only be addressed partially within the space of this brief essay: how far did the military ventures undertaken by the first founders of Sufi lineages result in the extension of the Delhi Sultanate's political writ into frontier territories that it claimed as the *arzi-bangāla* (the country of Bengal), based on its new stronghold in Lakhnauti, especially after Sultan Ghyasuddin Balban routed the forces of the rebel Mu'izz al-din Tughral? Right after this victory Balban appointed his own son, Bughra Khan, as the commander of Lakhnauti, who took charge from CE 1281, an event that some historians have seen as especially significant (KARIM 1992, 8). Bughra Khan was recalled to Delhi shortly before Sultan Balban died. The rule of Lakhnauti passed to Ruknuddin Kaikaus, who ruled from CE 1291 to 1301, and then to Shamsuddin Firuz Shah, who ruled till CE 1322. Ruknuddin and Shamsuddin ruled virtually as independent governors while the Khaljis were attempting to consolidate their power in northern India. This is exactly the period during which most of the early historical legends of military conquest, martyrdom, and establishment of Sufi lineages seem to appear in lower deltaic Bengal.

THE GHAZI AS EMISSARY OF EARLY ISLAM IN BENGAL

The interwoven nature of local accounts and apocryphal lore make it difficult to determine with any degree of accuracy which historical actor was the original inspiration behind the figure of the conquering saint who fought against tyrannical Hindu kings and brought the message of Islam to the interior of Bengal. There are two key contentions here. First, it is possible to argue from surviving inscriptions of the Tribeni memorial that "Zafar Khan" was simply a title bestowed by the Sultan of Delhi on the Turkish commander Bahram Tigin. It is most likely that the same title was also given to Shihabuddin, founder of the aforementioned school of learning. Second, there are at least two other stories of Sufi saints whose life histories have become fused with the legend of Zafar Khan Ghazi in the oral narratives.

One of these is the story of Shah Safiuddin, who is credited to have introduced the first tenets of Islam to the area known as the Chota or "Little" Pandua in the district of Hughli during the early fourteenth century (HANIF 2000, 334–35). One of the first colonial reports on the living legend of Hazrat Shah Safi was submitted in 1824 by an unnamed correspondent and can be found in the old periodical, the *Calcutta Asiatic Observer*.[3] Reverend James Long later furnished a similar account in the *Calcutta Review* in 1846 (LONG 1846). Safiuddin was the son of a Turkish *āmir*, a nephew of the Sultan Firuz Shah Khalji, and according to some accounts also a nephew of Zafar Khan Ghazi, who migrated to Bengal and settled down in the region of Pandua (LONG 1846, 404–405). This was the time during which a Hindu king, known as the Pandu Raja, had just banned the slaughter of cows in the nearby region of Mahanad (or Mahanath) in Hugli. Safiuddin hosted a large feast during the circumcision ceremony of his son, for which he also killed a cow. The Raja of Hugli came to know of this act and seized Safiuddin's son, and later offered him as a human sacrifice at the altar of a temple of the Goddess Kali. In a different version of this story recorded by the British civil servant and statistician W. W. Hunter, the king had to sacrifice one of his own children, who was born on the day of the cow-slaughter (HUNTER 1876, 313). Hearing of the misdeeds of the Raja, the Sultan of Delhi sent a large army under the leadership of Zafar Khan. Safiuddin volunteered to accompany this army and was killed in the encounter that took place between the army of the Turks and the Raja of Hughli. He was buried in Pandua and became known by the title of Shahid, or martyr. Before the expedition Safiuddin had sought the blessings of the famous Sufi elder Bu Ali Qalandar at Panipat near Delhi. After his martyrdom his followers gave him the title of Shah, and a new Sufi lineage traced to Bu Ali began in Hugli. Local residents of Pandua believed that there were traces of a large battlefield called the Jang Maidan where Shah Safi had fallen, and there had been a water tank dug up after the victory of Zafar Khan's army, known as the Fateh Allah (victory to God) tank (CRAWFORD 1908, 434–35). Some believed that the Pandu Raja had a miraculous tank called the Jivat Kunda, whose waters were an elixir that could bring fallen soldiers back to life. This was the reason why he could not be defeated. The soldiers of Zafar Khan succeeded in defiling the tank with cow remains and were able to overcome him. Other versions of the same story ascribe the tank and its healing powers to the Raja of Hugli at Mahanad, an ally of Pandu Raja, who was also defeated in battle by Zafar Khan (LONG 1850, 128–29). A very similar story can be traced to the founding of the renowned Sufi lineage of Shah Jalal in Sylhet (WISE 1873, 279–80).[4] In this case a Muslim man had slaughtered one of his cows to celebrate the birth of a son. A kite flew away with a piece of flesh and dropped it on the house of a Brahmin. Much aggrieved by this, he complained to Raja Gaur Govinda, who not only persecuted the man but murdered his son. Once again, Sultan Firuz Shah intervened and sent a military expedition under the command of his nephew, Sikander Khan Ghazi, resulting in a battle that led to the conquest of Sylhet.

The fact that the legends of Shah Safi and Shah Jalal resemble each other so closely, not to mention their historic association with the figure of Zafar Khan, points to the possibility of one dominant narrative strain converging around the tropes of militancy, iconoclasm, and martyrdom. This is not only evident in the basic sequence of events narrated by these tales, such as a tyrannical Hindu king punishing innocent Muslims for butchering cows, but also in certain striking details. One example of this is a popular insignia of Zafar Khan the warrior, now a popular relic. Near one of the main entrances to his tomb, there is a stone with a piece of iron attached. This is known as the handle of the axe with which he supposedly combated his enemies (*gājīr kuṛul*). The saying goes in Bengali: "the Ghazi's axe moves but does not fall down" (*gājīr kuṛul noṛe coṛe kintu poṛe nā*). The axe is thus not just a weapon but an emblem, a reminder of Zafar Khan's resilience and endurance. According to Rakhal Das Bandyopadhyaya, this so-called "Ghazi's axe" referred to one of the two iron hooks that were used to fasten the chains by which the entrance of the original Vishnu temple was once secured (BANDYOPADHYAYA 1909, 246–47). Over time the tomb itself came to be known as the Ghazi's axe. A remarkably similar relic is associated with the Pandua Minar, which is supposedly the tower of victory erected to commemorate the success of the Turkish forces led by Zafar Khan in Chota Pandua, right next to the tomb of Shah Safi. There is an iron rod that runs all the way to the top of the structure that is known as the Shah Safi's "walking stick" (HUNTER 1876, 313).

Scholars are still attempting to piece together fragments of evidence to determine the historical authenticity of Zafar Khan's military exploits in the cities of Lakhnauti, Debkot, Tribeni, and Hugli.[5] From the standpoint of folklore, however, it seems that a composite, overarching figure of the Ghazi looms over these discrepant histories, whether or not his character can be definitively identified with the Turkish military commander, or indeed the poet who originally composed the hymns in Sanskrit dedicated to the river Ganga. However, it is not difficult to imagine that as the figure of the Ghazi of Tribeni gained popularity over time, prayers at his mosque and adjoining tomb overlooking the flight of steps to the Ganga became customary among Hindu pilgrims as the *āstānā* (hermitage) and *dargā* (tomb) of Ghazi Sahib (BLOCHMANN 1870, 282). Eventually, the venerated confluence at Tribeni became tied to his name as well. Reverend Long, during a tour of the Bhagirathi River in the early nineteenth century, noted the frequency with which the tomb received offerings from Hindus and was told by his informants that although he was a devout Muslim, Zafar Khan had indeed "worshipped the Ganges" (LONG 1846, 404–405). In the version of the story related by locals to D. Money, Zafar Khan sat in prayer to receive the blessings of the Goddess Ganga. When she actually heard the Ghazi's prayers, she rose from the surface of the water and appeared before him in all her heavenly glory (MONEY 1847, 396). The Ghazi quickly became her ardent devotee. He abjured the Quran and Persian and turned to the study of the Hindu scriptures. His daughter-in-law, a Hindu princess, was buried in the same precinct which, according to Money's account, was another reason why during the yearly memorial of the Ghazi Hindu pilgrims visited his tomb. Zafar Khan's odes to the river in Sanskrit became part of this legacy, not only for Hindus, but Muslims as well. One of the oldest Bengali Shi'i texts, for instance, has this praise for the Ghazi (CHATTOPADHYAYA 1962, 161):

> On the quays of Tribeni pay respect to Daraf Khan
> Whose water for *wazu* (ritual ablutions) came from the river Ganga.

And the following lines in simple Bengali rhyme attributed to the resident poet of Shantipur, Mahiuddin Ostagar, run thus (GHOSH 1957, 490):

> *jāphar khān gāji roila tribenī sthāne*
> *gaṅgā jāre dekhā dila ḍāka śuni kāne*
> Jafar Khan was the Ghazi in the place called Tribeni
> to whom Ganga revealed herself after having heard his call.

These incarnations of Zafar Khan, first as a warrior of Islam, then as a martyr, and finally as a devotee of the Ganga, have all endured. They are inextricably tied up with the aura and reputation of Tribeni itself as a site, which in the local Bengali parlance can be summed up in the word "*sthānamāhātmya*," which translates as "greatness of place." The sanctity of the river Ganga at Tribeni in this manner has attached itself to the memory of the Ghazi as a savior of the downtrodden and the benighted, a truly great man (*buzurg*) who laid down his weapons, donned the humble robes of a spiritual leader, and earned the love and respect of the local community. For Bengali nationalists of the nineteenth century, Zafar Khan as a devotee of the Ganga became emblematic of the much-sought-after harmony between Hindus and Muslims. The noted Bengali critic, novelist, and historian Bhudev Mukhopadhyay, writing in the latter half of the nineteenth century in his utopian *Svapnalabdha Bharatabarsher Itihas* [History of India revealed in a dream], imagined a country where all Indian Muslims would happily pay obeisance to the river by singing the hymns of Darap (Zafar) Khan (MUKHOPADHYAY 1995, 224).

THE GHAZI'S MOSQUE

BLOCHMANN, when he wrote about Zafar Khan Ghazi's mosque in 1870, noted that almost half of the existing structure was "filled with stones and rubbish" (1870, 280). When Joseph David Beglar of the Archeological Survey of India took a photograph of the interior of Zafar Khan Ghazi's tomb at Tribeni in 1872, he found it overgrown with trees and vegetation, and in a state of imminent ruin.[6] Beglar stated in a subsequent report that the structure was most likely built by material taken from Hindu temples, especially their carved stones for lintels and doorposts. Basing his observations on previous reports filed by Blochmann and Money, he noted that the temples over which Zafar Khan's shrine had been built were most closely reminiscent of the style of temples built by the Kalachuri kings in Janjgir during the eleventh century, known for their elaborate sculptures of Hindu deities and scenes from the great epics engraved on the walls (BEGLAR and CUNNINGHAM 1878, 206). During his visit to the monument in the early nineteenth century, D. Money had seen remnants of an entire cluster of dilapidated temples in the courtyard of the mosque complex (MONEY 1847, 398). He had also observed that near the northern and eastern entrances to the structure there were images from the Hindu pantheon still standing, including the various incarnations (*avatāra*) of Vishnu: Narasimha, Varaha, Rama, Krishna, and also of the goddess Lakshmi.

Stones with Arabic inscriptions had been planted directly below the partial remains of some of the deities, some of which were defaced and some almost destroyed. Money concluded that the building was once a former Hindu temple dedicated to Vishnu that overlooked the confluence and pilgrimage site.

The present-day public notice at the mosque issued by the Archeological Survey of India (ASI) describes this multi-domed structure built by bricks and stones as a "rectangular mosque" and as the earliest known "mausoleum" in eastern India, built in 1315 CE. A prominent inscription in Arabic appears over the central *mihrāb* (prayer niche) of the mosque. The main vaulted chamber rests over five stone arches and rows of ornamental stone pillars. It is possible that some of these are the pillars of the Vishnu temple whose ruins had been observed by Blochmann, Money, and Beglar. Even today, not only can one see partially effaced images of the ten avatars of Vishnu, but also carvings that have survived from the original temple illustrating episodes from the Hindu epics. At the same time, it appears that some of the masonry was brought to the site from elsewhere. A report by the Archeological Survey written in the 1930s mentions nine inscriptions on the walls of the western tomb. It suggests that the stone slabs and plinths bearing these carvings once formed part of some "Hindu buildings" whose spoils were "utilized" in the construction of the tomb and the mosque (FABRI 1936, 212–13). Written in Sanskrit with early Bengali characters below the bas-relief, they describe popular scenes from the Ramayana and the Mahabharata such as the marriage of Sita and Rama or the fight between Dhrishtyadumna and Duhshasana.

Some of the keenest insight into the origins of the mosque complex can be found in the report on the relics of Satgaon and Tribeni in BANDYOPADHYAYA

FIGURE 2. Basalt plinth showing the original structure of the building.

(1909) mentioned above. Bandyopadhyaya noted that the clutch of temples noticed by earlier observers had all but disappeared by the time he visited the edifice. However, the plinth of black basalt on which the main structure stood was still recognizable as the foundation of the original temple. He also saw remnants of deities, some defaced, and scenes from the Hindu epics carved on pillars. Within the mosque itself, he saw the impression of four images stuck on the walls between the *mihrāb*s, one of which was clearly of the main deity Vishnu recognizable by his main weapon, the mace. Bandyopadhyaya came to the conclusion that while the main part of the building complex was indeed a Vishnu temple, it also contained fragments of older Buddhist and Jain monuments.

He found a row of four Buddhas on some of the pillars seated in the *bhūmisparśa* or the "earth-witness" position, and also parts of a statute of the twenty-third Jain emissary Parshvanatha, the one who came before Mahavira (BANDYOPA-DHYAYA 1909, 247). The feet of the statue were still intact, as were coils of the giant *śeṣanāga* serpent whose hood must have adorned the head of the figure.

Bandyopadhyaya's detailed field notes raise a further set of doubts about the purpose and symbolic value of the Zafar Khan complex. What kind of ambience or authority did the mosque try to claim in its day? Perched atop one of the holiest and most frequented riverside pilgrim spots, what kind of message did it convey to idolaters and iconoclasts? The history of the construction of these early mosques in Bengal during this period of Turkish incursion remains largely unknown. One of the more authoritative chroniclers of the period, Minhaj Siraj Juzjani, mentions in his *Tabaqat-i Nasiri* that after the conquest of the capital of Bengal Lakhanawati (or Lakhnauti) and the dissolution of the Sena Dynasty, Muhammad Bakhtiyar Khalji built mosques there (JUZJANI 1881, 560). Khalji *māliks* or military commanders, such as Husamuddin Iwaz, also erected mosques that did not survive, including a large Friday mosque (JUZJANI 1881, 583). Fragments of an inscription ascribed to another governor of Bengal, Jalaluddin Masud Jani (CE 1241–51) were found by Alexander Cunningham on the back wall of a nondescript mosque on the bank of the river Ganga half a mile to the east of the village Gangarampur, in district Malda (CUNNINGHAM 1882, 45).[7] The inscription indicated that Masud Jani erected the mosque during the reign of Sultan Nasiruddin Mahmud Shah of Delhi. Since none of these mosques stand today, Zafar Khan Ghazi's tomb may very well be the earliest mosque still standing in Bengal from this period. Later mosques built in Saptagram during the fifteenth century have been found with similar remnants along with broken or defaced idols marked with inscriptions in Arabic (GHOSH 1957, 502).

However, for reasons discussed below, Zafar Khan's house of prayer may not quite fit the description of what some architectural historians might label a "conquest-mosque," heralding the triumph of Islam over Hinduism. The main schools of devotees in Saptagram during the early fourteenth century would have been the worshipers of Vishnu, the supreme god of preservation, and Surya, the sun god. Bṛndāban Dās, the famous biographer of Caitanya in his *Caitanyabhagabata*, describes the Turks as defying the authority of Vishnu (*biṣṇudrohī yabana*).[8] In this regard the history of Zafar Khan's mosque needs to be located in the context of the protracted power struggle between the Turks and the rajas of Saptagram as patrons of temples to these two deities, and not simply viewed through the customary paradigm of an inevitable clash between Hindu idolatry and Muslim iconoclasm.

The legend of the Lal Masjid (also called the Ranga Masjid) or the "red mosque" of Pir Gorachand (Syed Abbas Ali) of Gorai Gaji in Haroa-Balanda in the 24 Parganas, present-day West Bengal, is instructive in this context.[9] Local folklore has it that the solar deity Surya, very pleased by the devotion of the Muslims, asked Pir Gorachand to build a mosque. There was one condition, however. The entire mosque had to be built while he was away. In other words, Gorachand and his followers had to begin construction of the building at the start of sunset and finish the work before the sun rose the next morning. They tried their best to please the

Sun God, and almost finished building the structure overnight. However, as they were putting the roof in place a crow called and announced the arrival of the first rays of the sun. Gorachand and his men had to abandon their almost-finished project. This particular fragment of "Gorai Gaji" lore makes two key concessions: first, that Gorachand was prepared to acknowledge the authority of the sun deity, and second, that his mosque could not be completed. Some archeologists suggest that the floor of the Red Mosque was actually erected on the site of a ruined Buddhist *stūpa* dating to the late Gupta or the early Pala period.[10] In the case of Zafar Khan Ghazi's tomb and mosque complex, not only do we have fragments of Buddhist and Jain structures, but broken pieces of sculpture from many ancient Hindu temples. At Pandua, close to Tribeni, debris from images, most likely from a Sun temple, were discovered by Rakhal Das Bandyopadhyaya (BANDYOPADHYAYA 1909, 247). One of the fragments, bearing a much later inscription of Sultan Shamsuddin Yusuf Shah from the fifteenth century, had most likely been relocated from the original mosque where it belonged and was found lying near the grave of Shah Safi. On a close inspection of these remnants, Bandyopadhyaya concluded that the piece was the lower portion of an image of the sun god Surya, which had once been adorned with seven horses and the charioteer Aruna. It seems that the Surya idol was also accompanied by an image of Saturn and other planetary deities.

F. B. Flood, in his suggestive study of early Indo-Islamic architecture in the frontier regions of the Ghurid Empire in Sind and Rajasthan, points out that mosques that incorporated material from Hindu and Jain temples have long been misread as an architecture of conquest and defeat, and seen as assemblages of "mutilated fragments" (FLOOD 2009, 159). Such a simplistic view, Flood argues, glosses over the incongruent signs inherent in any architecture of *spolia* (spoils), which should be seen as an extended commentary on the processes of confrontation, incorporation, and translation. In the case of the Tribeni mosque, the presence of Hindu deities, albeit partially defaced, not to mention the ubiquity of ornamental temple motifs, suggest a similarly unfinished text, akin to an incomplete exercise in political and cultural appropriation. Not only are there remnants from older temples fixed into the bases of walls, some upside down, but the basalt slabs on which the temple once stood are the visible foundations of the mosque itself. Panels abound with decorative motifs composed of the nine planets (*navagraha*), and vegetal patterns (*kalpalatā*).

The Ghazi's tomb located at the entrance of the mosque complex is composed of two unroofed rectilinear chambers. Here are the graves attributed to Zafar Khan Gazi, his sons, grandsons, and a daughter-in-law. A carved temple portal frames one of the main entrances to the tomb. Figures at the base of this doorway have been largely removed except for full-vase (*pūrṇaghaṭa*) and miniature curvilinear (*rekha deul*) motifs (HASAN 2007, 62). The architecture and layout of the mosque and the tomb present an architectural palimpsest that seems to have added to the elusive and legendary appeal of the Ghazi.

The available evidence makes it difficult to support the contention that this was indeed the earliest commemorative mosque—built by Bahram Tigin and his troops who arrived in Tribeni—as a definitive monument to the Turkish conquest in Bengal. It was Blochmann again who first noticed that the inscription in black

FIGURE 3. Floral motif from inside the mosque.

basalt affixed to the right of the northern *mihrāb* of the Tribeni structure, which records the deeds and exploits of Zafar Khan dating to 1298 CE, also mentions a congregational mosque or Jami Masjid that must have already been in existence (BLOCHMANN 1870, 285). The slab in question appears to have been reinserted from this or some other contemporary mosque. Another inscription, which is in essence a laudatory *qaṣīdat* in Arabic that appears near the second *mihrāb*, also seems to have been brought in from elsewhere. The exact origins of these inscriptions can no longer be determined with any accuracy. Blochmann, quite perceptively, described Zafar Khan's tomb as having been turned into "a sort of museum" of older artifacts over the course of centuries (BLOCHMANN 1870, 281). A few scholars have speculated whether some of the pillars of the present structure might have belonged to the original mosque that Zafar Khan built after the conquest of Saptagram (ALI 1979, 83). In other words, the Tribeni memorial was not only built out of the ruins and spoliation of Hindu, Jain, and Buddhist monuments, but also out of the fragments of older mosques.

RECONFIGURING THE *GĀJĪ*

The latter-day veneration of Zafar Khan Ghazi, to be sure, is not based on the architectural integrity or the historical authenticity of the mosque, but the perceived sanctity of his final resting place. He is remembered during the annual commemoration (*'urs*) of his passing, when pilgrims gather to adorn his grave with votive blankets, and troops with *tablās* (drums) and harmoniums perform their obeisance through devotional singing (*qawwālī*). After their ritual ablution in the Ganges, Hindu pilgrims stroll into the *dargā* and make a wish. Zafar Khan Ghazi's enduring place in folk memory is not only a testament to the sacredness of Tribeni, or to the reassuring trope of conciliation and mutuality among Hindus and Muslims. It is also a reminder of the iconic figure of the ideal Ghazi (*gājī*) in rural Bengali folklore. In Bengal a Sufi saint is often known by the same name. The history of Zafar Khan provides an early example of the creation of a legendary figure in the form of the Sufi acolyte, who combines the roles of an iconoclastic crusader, philanthropist, and worker of miracles.

In a landmark essay on holy war and the foundations of Ottoman rule in Turkey, Linda Darling suggests that *ghāzī* was a much-contested title whose contenders varied widely at different points in time (DARLING 2000, 142). A *ghāzī* could be the title of a military adventurer seeking religious sanction, prestige, and territory. It could also be a distinction conferred upon *'ulamā* (Muslim clerics) who wanted to put their own stamp of orthodoxy over religious institutions and subjects far away from the writ of the state. It was often an honorific bestowed on Sufi saints who wanted to test their faith among non-believers. Soldier-adventurers seeking spoils during frontier raids also sought this status (KAFADAR 1995, 90). Darling finds this to be as true in Ghaznavid Afghanistan as in Sultanate Delhi. What might be the salience of a designation shared equally among tribal raiders, orthodox clerics, aspiring rulers, and anti-establishment Sufis? (DARLING 2000, 157). It is worth noting, as Ali Anooshahr has shown in the context of Babur's frontier campaigns in Afghanistan and India, that the duty of raiding and marauding also fell equally upon the humblest soldier and the most powerful sultan to uphold the cause of justice (ANOOSHAHR 2008, 11). It is this very indeterminacy of the *ghāzī*'s spiritual quest and physical journey, along with the wider latitude given to the task of bringing the message of Islam to non-believers, that seems to have inspired and animated the popular, retrospective genealogies of Islam that emerged in early Turkish Bengal. In such narratives, which have taken shape over centuries, the controversial question of how subjects were diverted from idolatry to iconoclasm cannot be answered in any simple way, especially as instances of violence occur right alongside acts of beneficence, conciliation, and acknowledgement of extant forms of Hindu devotion, often without any outward or obvious contradiction.[11]

Divinely inspired militancy, marvelous deeds for the edification of infidel rulers and their subjects, and the punishment of unjust tyrants are all forms of a praxis very much at the center of historical narratives chronicling the exploits of early Sufis who brought popular forms of Islam to the interiors of Bengal (EATON 1993, 77). Their journeys and their quest for virtue, routinely celebrated in the hagiographic accounts of other prominent Sufi groups in India, were an essential part of their disciplinary practice. As Richard Eaton has pointed out, such Sufi pioneers were not necessarily self-proclaimed emissaries of the Islamic faith who actively sought to convert infidels (EATON 1974, 126–27). The pilgrimages and privations of wandering Sufi mendicants—encapsulated in the terms *jihād* and *ḥajj*—were seen as the obligatory means of self-purification (ERNST 1992, 159). Similar stories of long and arduous journeys are attributed to the great Sufi leaders of Bengal discussed above, such as Hazrat Shah Jalal of Sylhet, or Pir Gorachand, who died from his wounds fighting the evil brothers Akananda and Bakananda near the village of Haroa-Balanda.[12] One is also reminded of the struggles of Bara Khan Ghazi in the *Raimangal* epic, who ultimately subdued the fearsome forest deity Dakshinarayan and his tigers to establish his preeminence (RAHMAN 2013, 241).

There is not enough space in this essay to discuss the rise of the tradition of verse poetry exclusively dedicated to the veneration of the figure of the Ghazi in Bengali Sufi saint literature (*pīrsāhitya*). One can easily see how closely the heroic feats of the fear-dispelling, tiger- and crocodile-battling Ghazi, who emerges victorious through all trials and tribulations, resemble the deeds and miracles performed by local deities, such as Chandi or Manasa, typically described in medieval Bengali *mangalakābya* verse poetry.[13] These portraits are consistent in texts such as the *Gaji-Kalu-Champabati* story, the *Raimangal*, or the *Banbibi-Jahurnama*. Considering all the known texts of this genre, the legends of Gaji, Kalu, and Champabati prove to be the most relevant in placing the figure of Zafar Khan Ghazi in the proper context of Bengali Muslim folklore.

This is a long and winding tale of which only an outline can be presented here.[14] Gaji (Bengali for *ghāzī*) was the son of Sikander Shah, ruler of the kingdom of Vairat, and Queen Ajupa. Gaji and his foster brother Kalu were inseparable. Because of his father's tyranny, he left his family and renounced his kingdom and traveled far and wide with his brother Kalu. During their many wanderings they tamed crocodiles and tigers, converted King Sriram to Islam and erected a golden mosque in his capital, and finally defeated King Mukutrai and his fabled military chief Dakshinarai, also converting their courtiers and subjects. Most notable in this text are the frequent references to the Ganga as a goddess. Gaji's mother Ajupa is described as her sister, and in times of danger Ganga turns up to help him. When a destitute woodcutter gives Gaji and Kalu shelter in his hut in the great forest, and cannot feed them, Ganga sends one of her serpents (*nāga*) with lavish gifts and provisions (RAHIM 1961, 16). Toward the end of the story Gaji and Kalu travel to the shore of an ocean where they disturb the meditation of three hundred powerful yogis (RAHIM 1961, 77). Enraged by this intrusion they prepare to attack the two. Asked about the object of their penance the yogis tell Gaji and Kalu that they are also worshippers of the Ganga. The Gaji then summons Ganga, and she appears in person seated on the leaf of a lotus. Witnessing this, the yogis are overwhelmed:

> *yogīgaṇa bale dhanya dhanya śāha gājī*
> *jāhar adhīn gaṅgā morā jāke pūji*
> *yabaner tulya ār nāhi āche jāti*
> *jāhāke karen mānya gaṅgā bhāgirathi* (RAHIM 1961, 78)
>
> The yogis said praise be to Shah Ghazi
> Who commands the Ganga that we worship
> There is no other race of people like the Muslims
> Even the river Ganga-Bhagirathi pays respect to them.

Thereafter the yogis embrace Islam as their faith, and a new mosque is established on that spot. Note that Muslims (*yabana*) here are entirely represented by the Ghazi and his disciples.

There is yet another detail embedded in this narrative that is worthy of attention here, and it can be traced back to the oral histories recorded in nineteenth-century British accounts of the exploits of Shah Safi and Zafar Khan. When the Ghazi attacks Raja Mukut Rai and his army of tigers, he is able to fight back with the help of a special water-well described as the *mṛtyu jība kūpa*, or the "well that restores life"

(RAHIM 1961, 66). The miraculous waters of this reservoir are able to bring back to life the Raja's elephants, horses, and soldiers that have fallen in battle, and they are ready to fight again. The Ghazi is able to put an end to this marvel by sending his tigers and angels to defile the Raja's tank with a piece of cow's flesh, so that he is no longer able to replenish his forces after each skirmish. In this instance, is the *Gaji-Kalu* narrative simply an embellished retelling of the history of Zafar Khan Ghazi's conquest of Tribeni, as some local scholars have suggested (ALI 1979, 5)? This is impossible to ascertain. More significantly, the blessings of the river Ganga and the familiar narrative plot of military conquest, the performance of miracles, building of mosques, and the spread of Islam, precipitate an iconic agent who is able to reconcile and ultimately rise above discrepant forms of authority and devotion. There are, of course, standard descriptions of the *gājī* figure in Bengali verse poetry and folklore. He has a shackle around his waist, wooden clogs on his feet, and carries a formidable cudgel (*āsā*).[15] Parts of his composite image still circulate through the ubiquitous Ghazi scrolls (*gājīr paṭ*) carried by the scroll-painters (*paṭuā*) of the Bengal countryside (KOROM 2006), where a copiously bearded Ghazi is typically depicted as sitting atop a giant tiger. The stories sung in praise of this figure are generally faithful to the overall genre of traditional *pīr* literature, where the Sufi saint must fight with oppressive kings and disbelievers, perform miracles, and bring new hope to the downtrodden and the destitute. It is in the context of these historical fragments and ambient mythmaking that we must explore Zafar Khan Ghazi's complex legacy. He is not only an embattled icon from the early period of the advent of Islam in Bengal, but a figure whose history is overgrown and intertwined with legend and apocryphal lore, samples of which have already been discussed above. The significance of this Ghazi-like figure, located at the margins of prescriptive forms of religious practice, cannot be understood within the typical explanatory device of syncretism, which treats the categories of "Hindu" and "Muslim" as given and stable.[16] Similarly, straightforward models of cultural synthesis, heterodoxy, or populism that have often been applied in the study of Sufi figures in rural Bengal, do not help explain the conflicting elements in the life story of Zafar Khan Ghazi. There is no equivalence or easy reconciliation between the figure of the destroyer of temples and the ardent devotee of the river Ganga. It is the virtuosity and resilience of folklore that allows these acts of violence, piety, and compassion, told through conflicting narratives, unruly metaphors, and partial translations, to live on within the overall allegory of the Ghazi's long and difficult adventure of suffering and redemption.[17]

NOTES

1. My translation. The ode is known by its opening words "*jahnavī munikanye*."

2. These observations are based on the idea of ethnopoetics, developed by the eminent folklorist and linguist Dell Hymes, which is still being debated and tested by contemporary scholars (MOORE 2015, 11). For a spirited discussion of the problems of trying to locate an authentic voice in oral texts see HYMES (2003, x).

3. See the essay "Traditional Account of the Minaret at Pandua," originally published in the *Calcutta Asiatic Observer* in 1824, which was later excerpted in an essay by Reverend LONG (1850).

4. J. Wise's essay was based on the hagiography of Shah Jalal. The text is known as the *Suhail-i Yaman*, composed in 1859 by Maulvi Muhammad Nasir al-Din Haidar. His account was based on two earlier eighteenth-century texts now lost, the *Rawzat al-Salihin* and the *Risala-yi M'uin al-Din Khadim*. Details of these lost texts have been discussed by EATON (2009, 384) and KHAN (2013, 25).

5. Some commentators have suggested that Zafar Khan was almost singlehandedly responsible for the conquest of Bengal and the spread of Islam. See the preface to Momammad Ali's work (ALI 1979, xxvi).

6. A copy of this is available at the British Library, UK.

7. Jalaluddin received the governorship of the province of Lakhnauti after the death of Tamar Khan Qiran in 1246 (KARIM 1992, 32).

8. The phrase appears in the *ādikhaṇḍa, tritīẏa adhyāẏ* (first part, third section) of the text (DĀS 1928, 94).

9. Recorded in my 1992 field notes written during the festival of Pir Gorachand in Haora-Balanda, North 24 Parganas district. See also O'MALLEY (1914, 240–41).

10. For a discussion of the Buddhist architectural remains found near Haroa, 24 Parganas, see the reports of the ODISA SAMSKRTI PARISADA (1995, 57).

11. ERNST (1992, 156–58) has provided a succinct summary of the major scholarly debates around the question of conversion.

12. For an account of Shah Jalal's exploits in Sylhet, see ROY (1986, 110). For the stories surrounding the martyrdom of Pir Gorachand or Gorai Gaji, see MITRA (2001, 482).

13. Asim ROY has discussed the basic contours of the *pīr* ballads in Bengal in a recently revised book (2014, 235).

14. The summary given here is based on RAHIM (1961).

15. In the *Gaji Kalu* story these symbols of the *gāji* are all made out of gold (RAHIM 1961, 8).

16. For a succinct discussion of some of the problems encountered in the use of the term syncretism in the history of Indian Islam, see Carl W. Ernst and Tony Stewart in MILLS, CLAUS, and DIAMOND (2001, 586–88). Syncretism remains a controversial category of analysis, subject to differing interpretations. Some critics have pointed out its pejorative connotations in describing aspects of religious practice that are either inauthentic or innovative, where the mélange of symbols and meanings drawn from incompatible traditions also implies a corruption of original forms of the religious traditions in question (STEWART and SHAW 2003, 1–3). Asim Roy, an early exponent of the idea of Hindu-Muslim syncretism in Bengal (ROY 1982), has recently defended the idea of a "syncretistic tradition" arguing that it best describes the nature of the interaction between religious traditions set in motion by cultural mediators. Such a tradition, according to Roy, developed in medieval rural Bengal where an external and relatively alien Arabic-Persian tradition of orthodox Islam ultimately failed to transform the world of Bengali-speaking Muslims, who cultivated their own idioms and practices of piety and devotion in intimate proximity to local Hindu traditions (ROY 2014, xvi–xvii). Tony Stewart, one of the foremost critics of this idea of synthesis, drawing on the study of devotional practices associated with the Satya Pir tradition in Bengal, has argued that this version of syncretism, in the way it poses "Hindu" and "Muslim" as relatively monolithic formations, fails to account for distinctive, local forms of identity manifest in both oral texts and architecture (STEWART 2002, 28). Syncretism in this regard is a modern concept that does not elucidate the problems of religious identity or overlapping categories of religious affiliation in medieval Bengal (STEWART 2003, 63). More importantly, it does not help explain how power and authority were claimed and expressed in the narratives dedicated to the life-stories of eminent Sufi saints.

17. STEWART (2001) provides a stimulating discussion of translation and language as the site for a critique of the Hindu-Muslim "encounter" in histories concerning the advent of Islam in Bengal.

REFERENCES

ALI, Momammad
1979   *Puṅthi Sāhitye Baṅga Jayer Itihās o Gājī-Kālu-Campābatī* [History of the Conquest of Bengal in Chapbook Literature and Gaji-Kalu-Champabati]. Bāgurā: Bāgurā Jelā Pariṣad.

ANOOSHAHR, Ali
2008   *The Ghazi Sultans and the Frontiers of Islam: A Comparative Study of the Late Medieval and Early Modern Periods.* New York: Routledge. doi: 10.4324/9780203886656

BANDYOPADHYAYA, Rakhal Das
1909   Saptagrama or Satganw. *Journal and Proceedings of the Asiatic Society of Bengal* (New Series) 5: 245–61.

BEGLAR, J. D., and Alexander CUNNINGHAM
1878   *Report of a Tour through the Bengal Provinces of Patna, Gaya, Mongir, and Bhagalpur, the Santal Parganas, Manbhum, Singhbhum, and Birbhum, Bankura, Raniganj, Bardwan, Hughli: In 1872–73.* Calcutta: Archaeological Survey of India.

BLOCHMANN, H.
1870   Notes on Arabic and Persian inscriptions in the Hugli district. *Journal of the Asiatic Society of Bengal* 39: 280–303.

CHATTOPADHYAYA, Brajadulal
2003   *Studying Early India: Archeology, Texts and Historical Issues.* New Delhi: Permanent Black.

CHATTOPADHYAYA, Sunitikumar
1962   Darāpa Khān Gājī. *Sanskrtiki* 1: 156–74.

COTTON, James Sutherland, Richard BURN, and William Stevenson MEYER, eds.
1908   *Imperial Gazetteer of India.* Oxford: Clarendon Press.

CRAWFORD, D. G.
1908   Pandua and the Pandua Minar. *Bengal Past and Present* 2: 431–38.

CUNNINGHAM, Alexander
1882   *Report of a Tour in Bihar and Bengal in 1879–80.* Calcutta: Office of the Superintendent of Government Printing.

DARLING, Linda
2000   Contested territory: Ottoman holy war in comparative context. *Studia Islamica* 91: 133–63. doi: 10.2307/1596272

DĀS, Bṛndāban
1928   *Śrīśrīcaitanyabhāgavat: Ādikhaṇḍa Mūl* [Lord Chaitanya's Sacred Story: First Section]. Kalikātā: Gauḍiya Maṭh.

EATON, Richard
1974   Sufi folk literature and the expansion of Indian Islam. *History of Religions* 2: 117–27. doi: 10.1086/462718

1993   *The Rise of Islam and the Bengal Frontier, 1204–1760.* Berkeley: University of California Press.

2009   Forest clearing and the growth of Islam in Bengal. In *Islam in South Asia in Practice*, ed. Barbara D. Metcalf, 375–89. Princeton: Princeton University Press.

ERNST, Carl W.
1992   *Eternal Garden: Mysticism, History and Politics at a South Asian Sufi Center.* Albany, NY: State University of New York Press.

FABRI, C. L., ed.
1936   *Annual Reports of the Archaeological Survey of India for the Years 1930–31, 1931–32, 1932–33 and 1933–34.* Delhi: Manager of Publications.

FLOOD, Finbarr B.
2009   *Objects of Translation: Material Culture and Medieval "Hindu-Muslim" Encounter.* Princeton and Oxford: Princeton University Press.

GHOSH, Binay
1957   *Paścimbaṅger Saṃskṛti* [The culture of West Bengal]. Kalikātā: Pustak Prakāś.

GHOSH, Pranabendra Nath, ed.
1978   *Ibn Batutah's Account of Bengal.* Calcutta: Prajna.

HANIF, N.
2000   *Biographical Encyclopedia of Sufis: South Asia.* New Delhi: Sarup.

HASAN, Perween
2007   *Sultans and Mosques: The Early Muslim Architecture of Bangladesh.* London: I. B. Tauris.

HUNTER, W. W.
1876   *A Statistical Account of Bengal,* vol. 3. London: Trubner.
1885   *Imperial Gazetteer of India,* vol. 5. London: Trubner.

HYMES, Dell H.
2003   *Now I Only Know So Far: Essays in Ethnopoetics.* Lincoln: University of Nebraska Press.

JUZJANI, Minhaj Siraj
1881   *Tabaqat-i Nasiri,* trans. Major H. G. Raverty. London: Gilbert and Rivington.

KAFADAR, Cemal
1995   *Between Two Worlds: The Construction of the Ottoman State.* Berkeley: University of California Press.

KARIM, Abdul
1992   *Corpus of the Arabic and Persian Inscriptions in Bengal.* Dhaka: Asiatic Society of Bangladesh.

KHAN, M. M.
2013   *The Muslim Heritage of Bengal.* Leicestershire, Kube Publishing.

KOROM, Frank J.
2006   *Village of Painters: Narrative Scrolls from West Bengal.* Santa Fe: Museum of New Mexico Press.

LONG, Reverend James
1846   The banks of the Bhagirathi. *The Calcutta Review* 6: 398–448.
1850   Early Bengali literature and newspapers. *The Calcutta Review* 14: 124–61.

MILLS, Margaret, Peter J. CLAUS, and Sarah DIAMOND, eds.
2001   *South Asian Folklore: An Encyclopedia.* New York: Routledge.

MITRA, Satish Chandra
2001   *Jaśohar Khulanār Itihās* [History of Jessore and Khulna], vol. 1. Kolkata: Dey's Publishing.

MONEY, D.
1847   An account of the temple of Tribeni near Hugli. *Journal of the Asiatic Society of Bengal* 16: 393–401.

MOORE, Robert
2015   Reinventing ethnopoetics. In *The Legacy of Dell Hymes: Ethnopoetics, Narrative Inequality, and Voice*, Paul V. Kroskrity and Anthony K. Webster, eds., 13–39. Bloomington: Indiana University Press.

MUKHOPADHYAY, Bhudev (trans., Sujit Mukherjee)
1995   India's history revealed in a dream. *Indian Economic and Social History Review* 32: 119-244.

ODISA SAMSKRTI PARISADA
1995   *Studies in Buddhism*, Bubaneshwar: Institute of Orissan Culture.

O'MALLEY, L. S. S., ed.
1914   *Bengal District Gazetteers: 24-Parganas.* Calcutta: Bengal Secretariat Book Depot.

RAHIM, Abdur, ed.
1961   *Gājī Kālu o Campābatī Kanyār Puṅthi* [The Chapbook of Gaji, Kalu and the Maiden Champabati]. Dhaka: Hamidiya Library.

RAHMAN, Muhammad S. N.
2013   Intercommunity relations in medieval Bengal as reflected in contemporary Bengali vernacular literature. In *Society, Representation and Textuality: The Critical Interface*, Sukalpa Bhattacharjee and C. Joshua Thomas, eds., 235–56. New Delhi, India: Sage.

RAY, Nihar Ranjan
2004   *Bāṅgālīr Itihās: Ādiparba* [The History of Bengal: Part one]. 6th ed. Kolkata: Dey's Publishing.

ROY, Asim
1982   The Pir tradition: A case study in Islamic syncretism in traditional Bengal. In *Images of Man: Religion and Historical Process in South Asia*, ed. Fred Clothey, 112–41. Madras: New Era Publications.
2014   *The Islamic Syncretistic Tradition in Bengal.* Princeton: Princeton University Press. doi: 10.1515/9781400856701

ROY, Atul Chandra
1986   *History of Bengal: Turko-Afghan Period.* New Delhi: Kalyani Publishers.

SARKAR, Jadunath, ed.
1973   *The History of Bengal: Muslim Period, 1200–1757.* Dacca: History of Bengal Publication Committee.

SEN, Sukumar
1953   *Manasa-Vijaya: A 15th Century Bengali Text.* Calcutta: Asiatic Society.

STEWART, Charles, and Rosalind SHAW, eds.
2003   *Syncretism/Anti-Syncretism: The Politics of Religious Synthesis.* New York: Routledge. doi: 10.4324/9780203451090

STEWART, Tony
2001   In search of equivalence: Conceiving Hindu-Muslim encounter through translation theory. *History of Religions* 40: 260–87. doi: 10.1086/463635
2002   Alternate structures of authority: Satya Pir on the frontiers of Bengal. In *Beyond Turk and Hindu: Rethinking Religious Identities in Islamicate South*

Asia, David Gilmartin and Bruce B. Lawrence, eds., 21–54. New Delhi: India Research Press.

2003　Surprising bedfellows: Vaisnava and Shia alliance in Kavi Ariph's "Tale of Lalmon." In *Surprising Bedfellows: Hindus and Muslims in Medieval and Early Modern India*, ed. Sushil Mittal, 55–88. Lanham, MD: Lexington Books.

WISE, J.

1873　Note on Shah Jalal, the patron saint of Silhat. *Journal of the Asiatic Society of Bengal* 42: 278–80.

DEEPRA DANDEKAR
Max Planck Institute for Human Development, Berlin

A Narrative of *Saṭvāī* Affliction in Rural Maharashtra

This article contextualizes a narrative of ritual affliction from rural Maharashtra within women's experiences of gendered, clan, and caste oppression. A case study of affliction demonstrates and exemplifies how women are socially and ritually categorized as failures in their marital duty (*dharma*) of being good mothers and wives across caste, through the worship of a popular village goddess, known as the *saṭvāī*, an ambiguous figure who presides over childbirth in large parts of Maharashtra. *Saṭvāī* worship produces two social categories of women: 1) mothers of sons, an identity that places women in an esteemed position within patriarchal hierarchy, and 2) the subaltern position of an impure and "child-eating witch," a social condemnation and ritual diagnosis that childless women come to share. The article seeks to question the postcolonial discourse, which describes native religious rituals as healing and foregrounds women's micro-narratives of affliction that subvert ritual descriptions as restorative, revealing these to be located within dominant caste interests and clan consensus.

Keywords: affliction—caste—goddesses—healing—Maharashtra—motherhood—*saṭvāī*

Asian Ethnology Volume 76, Number 2 · 2017, 235–59
© Nanzan University Anthropological Institute

THE HEALING potential of South Asian rituals is often theoretically described, explained, and bolstered with thick ethnographic descriptions. What is usually not described or is viewed only in terms of what it represents for healing rituals, is affliction itself. This interested me because I was engaged in exploring community health and how healing at rural shrines was contingent on a diagnosis that located the cause of illness in forces outside of human control: in the victim's village, or her entire body politic, with all its interlinked social and political networks. Deities were said to assume control over evil afflictions and illnesses as a force other than the victim. They provided social recognition to the sufferer and thus accorded her with victim status that served to vindicate her.

However, as I undertook fieldwork with women in reproductive-health distress in various villages of Pune district (especially around Ambegaon), my notions about healing were to undergo drastic change. In my field area, being diagnosed as "afflicted" (socially excommunicated) for child-loss after suffering reproductive crisis, or being declared non-afflicted or "healed" (socially reintegrated into marital clans) after conceiving pregnancies depended on women's social and personal status. Therefore, inhabiting the two social categories for women of "mothers" or "witches" depended on how they personally fared within their marital clans and according to patriarchal and agrarian caste rules in the village that were upheld by goddess rituals and diagnostic paradigms. This led to questions of whether they could or should be accorded victim status (blamelessness) for childlessness at all, as many who fared badly in their inter-relationships with marital clans received ritual affliction diagnoses at the very first instance of reproductive health crisis, and could never be vindicated or healed even after they became mothers. Women therefore often played a secondary role in relation to their marital clans, which played the decisive role in according them victim status based on intra-clan dynamics, the birth of sons, and dominant caste-consensus in the village. The village in turn interpreted the village goddess's verdicts about affliction and healing, with the help of goddess mediums, who inhabited lower feudatory positions in the village. Before healing actually commenced, therefore, the social and personal status of those women ritually diagnosed as afflicted had to be first identified as important enough to be accorded victimhood.

The village goddess, who presides over reproductive crisis and both childbirth and child-death in most parts of rural Maharashtra, is known as the *saṭvāī*. I will provide a brief overview of the *saṭvāī* goddess below. This will be followed by a narrative of *saṭvāī* affliction that is posited here as an example of how women's accounts of affliction do not necessarily constitute an understanding of ritual healing, but rather question it. This narrative will be followed by an ethnographic account of how *saṭvāī* affliction is diagnosed and a concluding segment that analyzes afflictions as being discursively different from ritual healing.

THE *SAṬVĀĪ*

I was familiar with the popular childbirth goddess, the *saṭvāī*, even before my research with afflicted women in rural Maharashtra began. References to the *saṭvāī* are widespread in the Marathi language, wherein she is mentioned as inauspicious, being sometimes referred to as unmarried or without paramour, and the writer of children's fates on the fifth night/sixth day after childbirth. She is also foregrounded in the grey literature as a malevolent presence, accompanying the auspicious goddess Jīvantikā (cf. ŚARMĀ 2012, 475–78). The prevalence of the *saṭvāī* as a rural goddess presiding over reproduction in Maharashtra has been pointed out by many other scholars, such as FELDHAUS (1995a), KOSAMBI (1962), and DHERE and FELDHAUS (2011), even as the goddess has been associated with many varieties of childbirth and fertility goddesses, such as the *maulyā*, the *bhivayyā*, and the *sātī āsrā* in Maharashtra. These figures preside over women's fertility, childbirth, and water-bodies that are conceptually interlinked with tantric notions of female reproductive fluids (FELDHAUS 1995a; 1995b; GORDON-WHITE 1996). At a popular level, the *saṭvāī* has further been associated with the *mātrikā*, Ṣaṣṭī, the *saptamātrikās*, *yōginī* worship, and disease goddesses such Śītālā, who is a very popular village goddess in Maharashtra. She is also associated with other deities, such as Marī-āī, Renūkā-āī, and Yellammā.

Besides all these associations, the view of the *saṭvāī* in the area where I researched her cult demarcated her primary nature into that of an ancestral spirit. In contrast to her reputation as a goddess that rebelled against husbands, paramours, and marriage (and was therefore somehow a-marital and a-reproductive), women in my field area described her as a collective of married women's ancestral souls, who had died while in labor to save their newborn sons, thus upholding their childbirth duty to their marital clans.[1] When I asked my village respondents about this contrast, they complained of how the *saṭvāī*'s reputation of being an unmarried and wild goddess was a Brahmin allegation, meant to denigrate non-Brahmin rural goddesses and women worshipping them as women whose motherhoods were aggressive and whose marriages were unchaste. My respondents, on the other hand, reiterated that the *saṭvāī* goddess was married and valorous, just like her followers, who despised menstruation only because the goddess felt that women should be pure and abhor witches and witchcraft in the village, since witches were considered to manipulate menstrual blood, known to contain malevolent powers. But the goddess was also considered to be malevolent and angry, and it was believed that she made women give up their possessive love for children, constructing this kind of motherhood (possessive love) as impure, because she herself could not enjoy motherhood and had died in childbirth. The *saṭvāī*, therefore, represented a type of reproductive function as a goddess whose shrines were located at physical village boundaries.

Each clan in the village near Ambegaon where I collected most of my data had its own *saṭvāī* and performed its childbirth rituals on the fifth night and twelfth day in her name, facing the direction of the main regional shrine[2] that organizes the village and the region into many spatial hierarchies (Dandekar and Dandekar 2011). Clan members also undertake a pilgrimage to her shrine in order to dedicate the first hair of their newborns to the goddess or sometimes dedicate this hair to the village *saṭvāī* in the name of their own clan *saṭvāī*, whose shrine may be located far away. Although the *saṭvāī* represents a spatial relationship simultaneously suggesting female motherhood duty and childbirth, it is a relationship established by rural dominant-caste agrarian clans with an influential rural deity whose clan tutelage they accept. There are, however, certain specific features that distinguish a village goddess as the *saṭvāī* as well. While she is known to consist of multiple numbers (usually an entourage of pairs of seven sisters), as well as many forms typifying various castes inhabiting and representing various eco-zones, her most important criterion is her role as a boundary sentinel separating the dominant agrarian castes from the village's lower castes. The *saṭvāī* shrine therefore marks the dominant-caste boundary of the village and produces caste and gender relationships across it by embodying its purity divide against the lower-caste inhabitation at the village periphery, and afflicting dominant-caste women, who physically cross this purity line with reproductive crisis and childbirth failure. Dominant-caste women who cross the purity divide suffer miscarriages as a result of their indiscretion and "impure" action of having frequented the goddess's shrine at the village's physical boundary during menstruation, and are thereby punished for adulterating their caste purity by exposing themselves to lower-caste spaces and thereby endangering the chastity of their marital clans. Their actions are considered to be tantamount to witchcraft, which is understood as women's crimes against their marital upper-caste clans and castes. They are accused of consorting outside the village periphery with lowly castes that are associated with cremation grounds, garbage heaps, and dead bodies, which also exposes them to contaminating bodily fluids, such as menstrual blood near goddess shrines.

Shruti and Aparna

I originally began my research in villages around Ambegaon, Pune district, where I organized group discussions about the goddess *saṭvāī* with women. These snowballed into a series of group discussions in various surrounding villages, including the village where I was staying (Ghodegaon). I soon realized that neither the women within these groups, nor the goddess I was researching, were static. Neither was the concept of region. Rather, the women, the goddesses, and the region of my research had extremely fluid boundaries that were mobile and dynamic. Marriage in Maharashtra (like most other places in India, as shown by Palriwala and UBEROI 2008) is virilocal. Marriage was thus one of the greatest reasons for women's migration into and within the region of my research.

Women within my initial discussion groups were mothers who brought their children along. These women were more interested in performing fertility rituals and projected themselves as normal, as they discussed domestic duties and child-rearing matters while playing with their babies. Asking me if I had had a child, they instructed me to have one child as soon as possible, instead of writing my dissertation on goddesses and childbirth. They warned me about the perils of childlessness, then provided me with interesting information about taboos concerning the *saṭvāī* and her rituals. But this group gradually grew disinterested in me as time passed, and they did not have much more to contribute thereafter. They only intermittently asked me if I had conceived a baby, when I would ask them whether I could attend *saṭvāī* rituals in their homes when someone in their clans gave birth (most of them declined outright or accepted, but then misinformed me about the time). This confused me initially, but I realized later that this was because I was childless and considered inauspicious myself.

The exclusion described above turned out to be a blessing in disguise, since it provided me with the opportunity for a more intense set of group discussions in and around the villages I was researching. These were groups of women, who after understanding that I was childless myself, included me by default in their groups. When they met, they recounted their affliction diagnoses, personal narratives, and stories of child-loss, assuming that I would participate and recount my experiences of the same. While being included in these ritual groups was interesting for me in the beginning, women soon asked me to perform *saṭvāī* rituals as well (DANDEKAR 2014; 2016). I primarily performed rituals to equalize power with my respondents and not seem too distant as a Brahmin researcher from an urban area. These group exchanges catapulted me not only into a world of their personal stories of domestic violence suffered at the hands of marital clans for having suffered child-loss, but also into their dreams that they believed were being sent to them by the goddess through mechanisms of ritual affliction. These dreams became infectious within various sharing circles and marked the afflicted status of women who were under the goddess's ritual control, though not every woman had these dreams (the women in the case studies I am sharing here did not, for example), which were often very traumatic. This sharing in smaller groups often introduced newer members such as relatives or visitors (like myself) to the group. Some went visiting to other villages with relatives and friends, who were women that had married and migrated to the region from other areas. Sharing dreams and affliction stories and accompanying each other on ritual sojourns became ways for women to recognize each other's stages within the prototypical affliction narrative.

The groups and discussions about affliction narratives and the goddess, therefore, existed before I entered the scene, and every childless woman like me entered their circle just as I had. I had simply been included within their group naturally, as one among other childless and afflicted women, which soon disabused me of my sense of power about forming any discussion group of my own about my research. My writing about it, instead of having a child or being able to have a child, was simply viewed as a further expression of my affliction, and because I performed *saṭvāī* rituals too, my inclusion in the group was confirmed. During the time I worked on the goddess, I did not just conduct fieldwork; my relationship with women inhabited a certain gendered domain characterized by affliction, as I was considered by countless women to share their status as they casually discussed affliction symptoms and dreams with me, assuming that I belonged, even though I held a pen and paper in hand. However, I also received a considerable amount of friendship from afflicted women, but only as an afflicted woman myself (though I was never subjected to a ritualist). This allowed me many personal invitations to women's homes to talk about their stories. I also tried to dissuade the women against the goddess's ritual diagnosis narrative, but I had to be careful about not antagonizing their clans. Many personal stories were, however, fragmented or ended badly, and I spent less time in my field area toward the end of my research to decrease my personal fear about the goddess and her affliction dreams. I did, however, honor many personal invitations extended by my respondents to visit their natal villages in Marathwada, to study shrines and goddesses and record narratives at a later date. But these private discussions that took place with friends later were more concerned with gossip about other village women and allegations about their falsehood in various ritual sessions, both public and private. Personal narratives were only further shared when women fell very ill or when clans required some help out of me, such as in the case of this article's narrative. In terms of ritual relationships, it took me a long time to extricate myself from the shared world within which afflicted women's friendship had presented my own childlessness.

Sharing and group discussions mostly took place under the pretext of singing devotional songs, as some women even knew some traditional dance steps that were typical of their rural natal regions. None of them would have ever accepted these group discussions as being defined as spaces for sharing stories about afflictions, dreams, domestic violence, or *saṭvāī* rituals. Nor would they accept them as giving advice to others whose symptoms were discussed. A fair number of women belonged to different parts of Maharashtra, such as Marathwada (including Latur, Parbhani), Northern Maharashtra (Khandesh, mostly Bhusawal, Jalgaon, and Nandurbar), and the more western parts of Vidarbha, such as Nanded, Jalna, and Nagpur. The majority, however, belonged to closer regions such as Satara, Sangli, Kolhapur, Nasik, Solapur, and the Pune district itself. Many of them returned to their natal village to perform goddess rituals because, according to ritual diagnosis, the symptoms for their affliction had manifested only after marriage; this required them to return home to undo the original affliction knot, even if their repeated returns to far off natal villages were a constant bone of contention in their marital families.

Goddesses were even more mobile. Not only did they follow their devotees from their main shrine to the devotee's village, crisscrossing the village's own *saṭvāī*'s region and territory (Dandekar 2009), but the goddess also responded to her devotee's worship across great spaces, as devotees only had to construct an impromptu shrine on the village outskirts, facing the direction of the main shrine, while performing the goddess's rituals (this was mostly restricted to non-affliction rituals). I was told by an older woman (she was an afflicted woman's mother-in-law) that though she was from a village near Yavatmal, and had never returned home in forty years since her marriage, the *saṭvāī* had never failed her, allowing her to have four sons successfully. She was disgusted that her daughter-in-law, on the other hand, needed to run home constantly because she was afflicted. But not all women were healthy enough to travel home. Women like Shruti, who were in the middle of reproductive crisis, were sent back to their natal families only as a last resort.

Shruti and Aparna shared their personal, very physical, and emotional family experiences with me, when Shruti was undergoing an intense phase of reproductive crisis, family breakdown, and *saṭvāī* diagnosis. These narratives also provide accounts of how they consciously negotiated with their village, marital clan, and caste during difficult times. I have treated their strategic negotiations as empowering, even if these may not formally fit classic definitions of feminism from a Western perspective.[3] As will become evident from the narrative, Shruti and Aparna were not merely my research subjects but had the power to understand, reflect on, and analyze their own situations. Neither do their narratives constitute a single interview, written out in one instance. I knew them both, their families, and husbands for a long period, and the narrative provided below is constructed out of a range of mutual interactions with them that were not always smooth. I have shielded their personal identities at the expense of sharing very little quantitative detail about their village, family statistics, or monetary status, since my data reveals how many afflicted and childless women, despite caste difference and status-disparity, share similarly oppressive diagnostic experiences once they are childless. Also, since I cannot provide multiple case studies to compare how social and economic contexts transform women's micro-narratives of affliction, which in any case is quite outside the purview of my research, I have instead retained my focus on the narrative of Shruti and Aparna as conscious personal journeys of affliction, to foreground their crisis that resists inclusion into typical narratives of ritual healing.

The Narratives

Shruti and her family belonged to the Maratha caste (considered a dominant and upper caste in the village). When I first met her, she introduced herself to me as a graduate and told me that she was working before her marriage in a small rural bank, but had later left her job after marriage, when she had a child. At the time I had the impression that Shruti wanted to communicate important information about her background as a woman who was not just modern and educated, but who was intelligent and worldly-wise enough to understand that her commitment to family constituted a worthwhile and conscious priority for her. This was a common attitude that many younger village women projected at the outset of my research. I felt this to be a way in which they indicated their empowerment to me. They were asking me through these mechanisms to not treat them as hierarchically lower, just because they were part of larger rural clan-caste networks. As modern and educated women, they wanted to evaluate my own work and life decisions in return for my research about affliction diagnosis.

I was to encounter Shruti's affliction diagnosis later, after another village respondent passed on the information to me as gossip. When I went to Shruti's home, she told me that she had developed *saṭvāī* affliction symptoms after she had conceived a child for the second time. She already had one somewhat mentally disabled son (though I am not certain whether he was ever medically diagnosed with mental disability). She had not wanted any more children immediately and therefore had had an intra-uterine device (IUD), known in India as a "copper-T," inserted within her uterus free of cost at the government hospital, after much discussion and argument with her husband and in-laws. This device was ideally supposed to have functioned as a contraceptive device, but since she conceived again, the IUD had failed. Shruti reported that she "knew" that she became pregnant again and also "knew" about having miscarried thereafter, even though there was no medical confirmation of this.

Even as she became very ill, she was diagnosed with *saṭvāī* affliction by a ritualist living in the nearby town, who enjoyed a wide reputation in the region for being very busy, rich, and famous as a result of her healing talents. Though the ritualist hailed from the village itself, she had begun living in a nearby town that was closer to the highway, due to its accessibility to her clientele. She had the reputation of possessing an important list of clients hailing from Pune, Mumbai, and even Delhi. Though she visited the local and older *saṭvāī* village temple, most daily temple duties were performed by her younger sister-in-law during the time I was in the village, while she herself, as the main ritualist, was playing the instrumental part in building a bigger and modern goddess temple in the town. Consequently, she had also become powerful in the village, even though she could hardly spare much time for local patients who were not members of a few important clans (Shruti's being one of them). Since the healer was of lower caste (*dhor*) with extended family still in the village, the upper castes said that she could not afford to disappoint the really important families, and she would have to serve them even without payment.[4] The healer herself was compelled into obsequious behavior, which, I suspect, was intended to deflect upper-caste attention from her fame, money, and importance, so that her stature would not cause offense and expose her extended and economically weaker family living in the village to reprisal in the form of caste-violence. She kept repeating how Shruti's family was her *āī-bāp* (mother-father) at every ritual diagnosis occasion and that she would never disappoint them. She would even "roll at their feet."

According to Shruti, there had been continuous bleeding and abdominal pain ever since the copper-T had been inserted. Sudden copious and painful bleeding, which Shruti said was unbearable and felt like a miscarriage, took place one morning when she had gone to the fields to relieve herself soon after the copper-T insertion. The nurse and midwife at the dispensary could not say anything of diagnostic importance about the pregnancy and miscarriage but identified the bleeding and pain to be caused by a prolapsed copper-T obstructing Shruti's cervix. The nurse removed the copper-T and advised Shruti to rest and generally sympathized with her condition, but also expressed amazement at an event as rare as copper-T expulsion. She asked Shruti to return after three months for a new IUD refit.

Even though many slightly older women in the neighborhood, who themselves had IUDs, by then had tried to reason with Shruti, her painful physical experiences of the IUD (lower abdominal pain and bleeding) and its expulsion were so unfathomable and traumatic for her that she could only compare her suffering to a miscarriage. But a miscarriage obviously involved other problematic questions that included sexual relationships. When she kept insisting that she had suffered a miscarriage and pregnancy, however, her mother-in-law told me and a group of other women that Shruti and her husband had been asked about their sexual relationship to ascertain whether a real pregnancy could have taken place at all. But while Shruti had displayed confusion and had been unable to answer any questions (about the sexual relationship with her husband), Shruti's husband had denied having had sex with her. I was furthermore given the embarrassing task of interrogating Shruti on the matter of her sexual encounters "one final time," since Shruti's mother-in-law believed that Shruti, as an educated woman, would somehow confide extra details to another educated woman.

I tried to tell Shruti that whatever had happened to her was normal and was not the *saṭvāī*'s punishment; she would soon feel better. Moreover, if she had had the IUD insertion according to proper medical rules, within two to three days after menstruation, how could she have been pregnant and miscarried? But she remained adamant, with her doubts, fears, and her experience of how it had all "felt" different taking precedence in the conversation. As she began speaking about the divine existence of the child, and of the goddess having detected her sin of rejecting and resisting impregnation by using the IUD, I began feeling doubtful too. There was, after all, the small and marginal chance of ectopic pregnancy, despite the IUD. When I asked Shruti whether the baby she had miscarried belonged to her husband, she stared at me blankly, saying that the baby belonged to the goddess *saṭvāī* and that the goddess had taken it from her as a punishment for using the IUD. I could not bring myself to ask her any more pointed questions about sex thereafter, and I left her house feeling unable to recognize the old Shruti, who had questioned me so closely on my research.

Shruti's husband had already denied having had any sexual relationship with her in the recent months before the IUD, and this had intensified suspicion around her, transforming her illness into impurity, immorality, and affliction. Shruti had expressed that she had had a reproductive experience, wherein she had physically felt pregnant after the IUD and felt that she had miscarried when the IUD prolapsed. Shruti also felt afflicted by the loneliness effected on her by her husband, when he abdicated responsibility and participation in her experiences of a failed IUD.

The affliction diagnosis was made thereafter. The place where the affliction was supposed to have taken place, namely the fields where Shruti had gone that morning when the "miscarriage" took place, conveniently faced the back wall of the *saṭvāī* shrine, even though at a considerable distance. The use of an IUD as "weaponry" (*śāstra-prayog*) against conceiving children was viewed as the reason for angering the goddess. Hence, the *saṭvāī* had to be ritually appeased. Once, upon meeting the healer on a six-seater ride from the village to her town near the highway, I asked whether the ritual intervention would really help Shruti. The healer made hand gestures that told me that it was only due to her ritual diagnosis that Shruti was alive at all. It was good that she was only ill, since it showed that the rituals had worked enough to stave off death. I thought the ritualist was incensed by my questions, because she invited me to her home to view the boils and lesions that she had developed on her body due to having absorbed Shruti's illness. She began extracting various visiting cards from her blouse to demonstrate the range of her clientele while I was visiting her. I realized that though it was easy for me to be skeptical of ritualists, they themselves were equally powerless and oppressed as those who faced ceaseless caste violence, especially in states such as Maharashtra.[5]

Shruti's husband, mother-in-law, and sisters-in-law blamed Shruti. They were angry with her for introducing *saṭvāī* affliction into their family as a stigmatized inheritance, so took the stance of being righteous victims who had lost a potential heir (*kuladīpak*) because of Shruti's willful desire for an IUD. It was now said that the IUD had always been intended to facilitate immorality, but the goddess had revealed Shruti's sins (*pāp*) and taught the family a lesson to never trust their daughters-in-law again and give in to their wishes. There were lots of discussions about the lost son, even though his whole existence was in question, and this plunged Shruti into deeper depression and illness. Since Shruti herself feared the *saṭvāī's* retribution and believed in the ritualist's affliction diagnosis, it became convenient for everyone in her clan not to return to the doctor for further medical diagnoses or confirmation. Taking on the mantle of primary victimhood, they all continued to blame Shruti.

With the pretext of bringing iron and calcium tablets for Shruti every week, I visited her regularly during this time, and it was then that her mother-in-law told me that her son (Shruti's husband) was also depressed, grieving the loss of his "son," due to which he had taken to drinking. I asked Shruti's husband to accompany me to the dispensary for Shruti's tablets the following week and asked him about his drinking. While looking at the pictures of various social leaders on the clinic's waiting room wall (Gandhi, Nehru, Ambedkar, etc.), he tried to answer me by pointing out how all the country's leaders would not have been born if their mothers had all been using IUDs, and how they would not have been born either if their mothers had conceived them outside of marriage. I realized that Shruti's husband had taken her at her word, deciding that she had actually confessed to having a sexual liaison outside of marriage, which he thought had always been her actual aim when being fit for an IUD. The goddess had revealed her immorality to the village and punished her through a miscarriage, despite her IUD. But now the clan had been forced to bear the brunt of the victimization effected upon them by Shruti. It made no difference to them at all that she was ill.

Both Shruti's affliction and illness progressed as she withdrew socially (due also to excessive hair loss). She was gradually unable to eat, digest her food, or sleep. She continued to suffer from gynecological problems and fainting spells and was soon bedridden. She also developed discolored patches on her face and neck, which were all diagnosed as a part of affliction as well. Shruti's mother-in-law told me not to come to their house, since the affliction was at its peak and could also infect me if I had my periods. I was to learn later that Shruti's father and uncle had come to fetch her, taking her back to her natal village.

When I asked about Shruti's *saṭvāī* rituals, I was told that Shruti had been too ill to perform them. Her younger sister-in-law Aparna had to perform these rituals in her stead, since she ran the danger of inheriting Shruti's affliction too. Shruti's narrative therefore remains that of reproductive illness and family breakdown diagnosed as affliction, after which she suffered collapse and left the village. I did not see Shruti return to the village but heard much later from the village grapevine that she had joined her husband in Aurangabad; they had both left the village.

Aparna was Shruti's younger sister-in-law and according to gossip, she had grown angry with Shruti for introducing the affliction stigma into their clan. It had now become extended to her own person and children. She was also angry with Shruti for having initiated an environment of suspicion and distrust against the daughters-in-law in the family, wherein every demand made by Aparna after Shruti's illness-affliction was first viewed as immoral and examined for its potential danger to the clan's reputation by her in-laws. Every discussion about Aparna's life had grown to become a comparison with Shruti's, and she had also been instructed to perform Shruti's rituals along with her own preventive ones in order to protect from the goddess's affliction being visited upon the clan children. When I met Aparna at a mutual friend's house, she was reflective and analytical about Shruti's situation from the very beginning, which I believed was a conscious effort on her part to separate herself from Shruti and the way the latter had collapsed. Aparna was making it amply clear to me that she was not afflicted and that she had an "academic" opinion, even if she was not educated and modern like Shruti. She was also resentful about being identified with Shruti's affliction by me and recounted how she had increasingly begun to answer solicitous or curious questions about Shruti with angry answers of "I don't know!"

Performing *saṭvāī* rituals (Aparna had not started with the rituals yet, when we were talking, but had received instructions and directions) would require Shruti (or in this case, Aparna on her behalf) to accept the ritualist's affliction diagnosis at the goddess's shrine located outside the village. This entailed apologizing for Shruti's mistake/misconduct that had resulted in transgressions, and would prevent the mistake occurring in the future for Aparna as well. After this, food and offerings of fertility (bangles, vermillion, turmeric, a comb, flowers, and a blouse-piece) would be made repeatedly at the shrine every week for five weeks. After every sojourn to the shrine to see the chosen representatives of the goddess—five virgin pre-pubescent girls, an old widow, and a *saṭvāī* ritualist or a midwife—ritual food would be consumed at home. Women without menstruation, women without reproductive capacity, and women who perform cleaning tasks occupationally are considered immune to the *saṭvāī*'s affliction and are therefore culturally considered her agents.[6] The ritual at the shrine is usually witnessed by the entire network of the afflicted woman's clan in the village, constituting her caste along with the ritualist.

The most important aspect of *saṭvāī* rituals was the undertaking of a strict fast by Aparna (on behalf of herself and Shruti), wherein she would abstain from all the foods and ritual articles that were offered to the goddess during the five-week ritual period (consisting of bread, sweets, rice, fries, certain vegetables, milk products, and rich foods). This fast acknowledged that women returned to the *saṭvāī* a claim over their food and fertility as something that was not rightfully theirs. In so doing, they marked their motherhood duty as part of a bargain that they had not fulfilled (or were fearful of leaving unfulfilled) in return for their claims to be wives in marital clans, with the accompanying rights to food and gifts. Shruti (and Aparna on her behalf) was forbidden to eat outside her home during the ritual period and hence declined all invitations lest she felt tempted to eat foods that she was supposed to ritually renounce to the goddess. This also protected her from eating at the hands of secretly menstruating women, since there was always the fear of contracting contagion. Aparna was hence publicly ritually quarantined due to Shruti's "faults." People said that she felt angry about the public quarantine.

To my surprise, Aparna's opinions about Shruti's affliction, on the other hand, remained reflective, pragmatic, and sympathetic, yet analytical. I was a little heartened to discover that Aparna was not angry with me for having helped Shruti and that she too considered herself to be ultimately in Shruti's camp, since they were both co-daughters-in-law. She considered the extending of affliction to herself irritating, however. She said that Shruti had been impulsive and foolish (*mūrkhapaṇā*) to carry on in the miscarriage vein, when they, Shruti and *dā-jī* (Aparna's brother-in-law/Shruti's husband) had obviously had no sexual contact. According to Aparna, it was this that had antagonized *dā-jī* considerably and left the clan with no other option but affliction diagnosis, since Shruti herself believed in it. Shruti's own belief in turn had led to the intense gossip. Emboldened by Aparna's preparedness to analyze Shruti's situation sympathetically along with the small steps she herself was taking in everyday life to negotiate with her marital clan's sudden heavy-handedness with its daughters-in-law, I asked Aparna her opinion on Shruti's IUD decision and the ritualist's verdict of the *saṭvāī* affliction.

Aparna said that Shruti had been hasty about the IUD decision because she had only one son, who was, moreover, mentally challenged. Aparna felt that Shruti could have waited and allowed the birth of another one or two children before taking the contraceptive step. After all, many village women had a copper-T, and IUDs were free at the hospital. Even if subsequent children had been daughters, the clan would have surely given in to a contraceptive. According to Aparna, Shruti should have satisfied the clan and her husband's expectations of a *kuladīpak* first before drawing attention to her own demands so openly. Once they were satisfied, she could have deflected attention from herself and followed her own wishes more quietly. Aparna went on to tell me how many people in the family and neighborhood had advised Shruti along similar lines: to delay the contraceptive decision, since she had only one child and was as yet only in her mid-twenties. But Shruti had remained adamant, and it had become a matter of winning an argument against the family for her. So she won in the end and the IUD was fitted. I asked Aparna the reason for Shruti's sudden capitulation after she got the IUD from a state of excitement about winning a family argument into narratives of punishment, *saṭvāī* affliction, and miscarriage, even though she knew that there had been no sexual contact between herself and her husband. Aparna did not know, but said that she could hazard a guess about Shruti's tragedy, based on what she knew about her.

According to Aparna, the fact that IUDs were not always comfortable was well-known, and although many women who had copper-Ts themselves tried to comfort Shruti with information about their own uncomfortable reproductive health experiences, this did not help Shruti because the side-effects in Shruti's case were probably much worse, unbearable, and unexpected. Moreover, getting the IUD was associated with Shruti's victory. The fact that it disagreed so vehemently with her might have disappointed Shruti more than others understood. This could have made Shruti feel that she had done something wrong and was punished for it. Aparna pointed to how both affliction and illness came together for Shruti, who perhaps hid behind an affliction diagnosis, since she was perhaps too proud to accept her mistake and get the IUD removed as many women do. Later, she hid behind illness to escape her husband's and clan's anger about the immorality accusations that always accompany *saṭvāī* affliction diagnosis. Finally stuck between both illness and affliction, she collapsed and was sent back to her father.

Aparna's opinion of the ritualist remained caustic and negative. According to her, the ritualist's riches in the nearby town did not change her lower caste and vulnerable status in the village. In fact, it made her more vulnerable because she had to counterbalance her individual power with village upper castes even more carefully, since she had more to lose by growing rich. Members from upper castes could confiscate her money whenever she displeased them. The ritualist would have to forever remember that her capital, riches, and fame rested on her own caste occupation that cleaned reproductive impurity and affliction from upper-caste women.

AN OVERVIEW OF *SAṬVĀĪ* AFFLICTION AND DIAGNOSIS

What I understood with nearly every *saṭvāī* diagnosis case that I encountered was that it was not afflicted women but their marital clans that were ritually recognized as the "real" victims in cases of child-loss. Mothers were held culpable and guilty for having caused these afflictions to their clans, even when they fell very ill. Moreover, *saṭvāī* ritual diagnoses were not just judgments that indicted individual women who were already suffering reproductive crisis, but a systemic and patriarchal diagnosis that established the clan as the primary, innocent victims. Since the clan's body politic in the village had the status of insiders, they required and deserved healing that restored their rights to an heir from the goddess. In many cases, wherein afflicted (and sometimes very ill) women were unable to conceive children, even after performing rituals, they were sent back to their natal families as failures, while their marital clans retained a wounded and righteous pride about their own innocence. From the perspective of the *saṭvāī* paradigm, therefore, afflicted women suffering child-loss were not primary victims but secondary and ambivalent victims-cum-perpetrators who needed to be exorcised in order to heal primary victims (i.e., the marital clan), so that the "othering" and evil illness besieging their clans and their fertility could be removed.

Afflicted women were therefore viewed as potential others and a weak link in the marital clan's fertility, and it was therefore the afflicted woman who had to repeatedly inhabit the boundary spaces of the goddess's shrine (that was always located outside the village boundary) in the *saṭvāī*'s rituals, while making ritual offerings in order to publicly demonstrate the danger she constituted to her marital clan in the village. It was she, when suffering child-loss and unable to provide her marital clan with children, who had to bear accusations of either being associated with or influenced by a witch[7] or herself being a "child-eating witch," even if her own child had died. When and if these women were ultimately able to have sons, a history of child-loss, if diagnosed as *saṭvāī* affliction, would continue to stigmatize them as women who possess dangerous witchcraft potential. This required their sisters-in-law, daughters, and daughters-in-law to follow *saṭvāī* rituals in a preventive form in order to appease the goddess and evade inheriting the affliction.

This placement of women as ambivalent, secondary, and guilty victims served to divest them from claiming their reproduction, motherhood, and children as their own. Instead, the birth of children, especially sons, was viewed as beneficial for a woman's marital clan inclusion, since their legitimacy was considered a form of "purity" that would ultimately contribute to their longevity and the woman's valor as an auspicious mother. Children were rightfully to belong to their fathers, patriarchal clans, and village castes. Childbirth and motherhood were hence viewed as a woman's marital duty and labor provided to clans, since child-loss was blamed on them. Those who failed their motherhood duty, therefore, faced a severe breakdown in their social relationships and emotional well-being. Consequently, they had to confront physical illness, neglect, and sometimes domestic abuse.

The *saṭvāī*'s ritual paradigm of affliction therefore assumed larger and more complex proportions than just a form of healing evil illnesses through exorcism. It progressed into a form of bodily discipline and fear among women, wherein evading punishment became a normative way of leading life under ritualized forms of law.[8] Child-loss within this context prevented women from grieving[9] and presented them instead as people facing public disgrace, culpable, and subaltern among other women, especially among auspicious mothers of sons, who occupied an upper social strata in rural communities that spanned across caste. Mothers of sons in my field area, who claimed to be fertile, auspicious, and to have never been associated with child mortality, stigmatized and discriminated against childless women or those mothers who had suffered child-loss in the past and had been ritually diagnosed as afflicted by their families. This stigma remained even if these afflicted women had been later successful in having children of their own. The stigma of being marked by child-loss continued as a sign of being inauspicious for many women, who, like Aparna, had to continue performing preventive rituals periodically but were also increasingly excluded from social invitations due to shared affliction diagnosis. Two categories of women, viz. mothers and witches or those subjected to witchcraft, were therefore produced across caste in many rural areas where the *saṭvāī* held sway. The boundary between women who were condemned as witches and women who claimed bewitchment was often so blurred that women claiming victimhood and bewitchment, who sought healing and clan reintegration, often turned against or pitied those who were caught out by the goddess and condemned as immoral or as having witch-like potential. All afflicted women were, however, stigmatized through mechanisms of social ostracism that included not being invited to social occasions, celebrations, and festivities in the village. Their food utensils were separated, destroyed, or given away, even if they were from important families in the village and had to be invited.

APFFEL-MARGLIN (2008) describes how the smallpox goddess in Orissa induced disease as a form of discipline among her worshippers. This motif also becomes very popular in the worship of other disease goddesses (described in the *maṅgalkāvyas* by scholars such as CURLEY 2008) that act as village deities (described in South India by scholars such as BRUBAKER 1978 and MASILAMANI-MEYER 2004). A gendered analysis demonstrates the importance of moral discipline especially among women and subalterns, as upholders of *dharma* (duty). Women and subalterns are marked as guilty and culpable of the crime of non-adherence and immorality, especially when those suffering its repercussions are identified as innocent sufferers and are proven to be victims. Many women in my field area referred to their motherhood duty as *dhamra*. I first thought that *dhamra* was an instance of mispronunciation, but when I noticed that *dhamra* co-existed with *dharma*, I began questioning my respondents. Though articulation of conscious definitions remains an academic preoccupation, many among my respondents explained the meaning of *dhamra* to me with the help of body language that involved first pointing in the direction of the *saṭvāī* shrine and then shaking their fists in the air to indicate her punishment and discipline.

Since *saṭvāī* afflictions are complex, with layers of primary victims and ambivalent, secondary afflicted-perpetrator layers, *saṭvāī* ritualists play a complex role in diagnosing and healing as well, since their priority and loyalty lies with upper caste clans in the village. Research on childbirth rituals and birth attendants (CHAWLA 1994; 2002) has already pointed to the perceived impurity of midwifery, due to its association with women's menstrual fluids and childbirth-related vaginal secretions that are also considered impure and dangerous in beliefs prevalent across South Asia (BENNETT 2002; RAHEJA and GOLD 1994). Midwives are therefore linked to the management of what is culturally understood as female forms of danger, since menstrual fluids are simultaneously considered to be extremely potent when deployed within witchcraft (especially by my respondents). Therefore, the management and cleaning of these fluids by midwives made many midwives ritual agents of upper-caste village clans in my field area, in what many of them expressed to me was a form of caste-based *balutedāri* (occupational tasks such as pottery, weaving, etc. performed for upper castes, especially on ritual occasions, in exchange for payment in kind and patronage, similar to the *jajmāni* system).[10] Clans retained a primary interest in cleaning female danger and witchcraft-inducing impurity that might cause their women affliction and them victimization through child-loss as well, and they therefore patronized lower-caste ritualists from the perspective of being the primary victims of afflicted women. Many midwives acted as *saṭvāī* ritualists in my field area too, though not all *saṭvāī* ritualists were midwives. Midwifery, as SADGOPAL (2009) has amply demonstrated, is also a skill.

Even as the healing rituals of upper-caste afflicted women necessitate physical contact with lower-caste ritualists, this association in my field area is completely controlled by the afflicted woman's clan members. All conversations at ritualized moments between afflicted women and *saṭvāī* ritualists are heavily monitored, remain limited, and are hardly subject to the ritualist's own terms. The ritualist is immediately made aware of her service-provider station if she tries to counter the clan's narrative. In *saṭvāī* worship, therefore, the primary interaction for afflicted women at the shrine does not take place between her and the *saṭvāī* ritualists at all, but between her own afflicted position and the *saṭvāī*, via the prescribed ritual that charts her personal journey from being afflicted to making ritual offerings that signify her possessive motherhood to the goddess.

The *saṭvāī* always recruits her own ritualists (often inter-generationally and often by sending miraculous dreams) from among Hindu lower-caste women (mostly of the mātang caste). The *saṭvāī* provides ("blesses") them with the auspicious valor of motherhood and the ritual power to clean the contaminating affliction from upper-caste women's bodies. Since rituals that rid women of reproductive contamination (known as *viṭāḷ*) are performed by afflicted women at *saṭvāī* shrines, ritualists only perform a diagnosis of affliction and describe its nature and the location of its occurrence to the afflicted woman's clan members.[11] They further attend the ritual performances made by afflicted women at the shrine and at the home of the afflicted to accept food offerings and gifts. Their ritualized cleaning services are therefore specifically characterized only by their physical presence at shrines and at rituals, not by any specific healing rituals undertaken.

When I asked my respondents about the role *saṭvāī* ritualists play in the healing of afflicted women, they told me of how their lower-caste presence was of utmost importance at rituals, since the actual ritual was performed only by the afflicted woman or by mothers who wanted to prevent affliction. The ritual was supposed to open a door or a communicative avenue (*pān*) between afflicted women and the goddess, and it was through this door that already afflicted and potentially afflictable women returned "whatever was not rightfully theirs" (i.e. their fertility, thereby counteracting possessive motherhood) to the goddess. Women in preventive rituals always laid their newborns in front of the *saṭvāī* as well. During such dedications, women's affliction and *viṭāḷ* (even if withheld secretly) seeped out of her, positing a threat to other pure clanswomen, who were her witnesses, for this vow. The lower-caste ritualist's body, therefore, had to be present at the ritual to absorb this seeping *viṭāḷ* into her own body and thereby prevent affliction and contagion to other upper-caste clanswomen present at the ritual. In return for this, she was made gifts and included as a recipient for ritual offerings. *Saṭvāī* ritualists became important among women of upper-caste clans as they were often invited for a meal when a child fell ill, so that her lower-caste absorbing presence, rewarded by food, could help to absorb the child's mother's own *viṭāḷ* and rule it out as a reason for the affliction causing the child's illness. When I asked my respondents about why lower-caste ritualists were never afflicted by *viṭāḷ* themselves, I was told that they were immune to any upper-caste impurity and affliction, reproductive or otherwise, since undertaking cleaning operations was part of their caste-based occupation and *balutedāri*, just as motherhood was women's. Indeed, those whom the *saṭvāī* had specially chosen definitely encountered affliction, according to my respondents, in cases where they ignored the *saṭvāī*'s dream-commands to become ritualists at shrines or if they disrespected their *balutedāri*, just like married women became afflicted if they disrespected their *balutedāri* of motherhood.

But there were obvious problems here. While some *saṭvāī* ritualists I spoke with did consider themselves lucky to enjoy village patronage and the goddess's blessings despite being poor and of low caste, almost all of them spoke of reproductive illnesses (such as menstrual cramps that kept them in bed, a swelling ball-like feeling in their stomach while urinating and defecating during menses, white and red discharge, blood-loss, and exhaustion) they had contracted out of the physical absorption of *viṭāḷ* from upper-caste female client bodies, almost as an occupational hazard. Any suggestions of seeking medical aid made them retort with exclamations of how the goddess would curse and afflict them with child-loss if they did so, and of how these illnesses were part of their job and the payment in return for enjoying the goddess's blessings.

Trance was a difficult subject too. Although most of them admitted to beginning their journey as *saṭvāī* ritualists with an ability to diagnose afflicted women in trances (and I attended many ritualist trances during fieldwork myself), many said that trances troubled them later, making them ill (*trās hōtō*). So, they used divine powers from trances gained by them in the initial stages of their jobs as *saṭvāī* ritualists to continue with their diagnostic work later.

There were obvious problems with the *balutedāri* of motherhood as well, because even after having children, mothers had to continue with preventive rituals, since the reproductive impurity of their *viṭāḷ* continued, which would socially produce them under affliction diagnosis as witch-like child-eaters, even after their motherhood duties were fulfilled.

In terms of caste, therefore, the subjectivity of being afflicted by the *saṭvāī* becomes revealed as one wherein women, who are defined by caste, lose their caste purity, which in turn results in child-loss. This is rather significant, since the child, who would have otherwise been of pure caste, alive, and part of its father's clan if its mother's afflicting contamination were absent, implies the nature of the mother's *viṭāḷ* to be of a sexualized variety. The contamination of caste through reproduction that produces the mother as the sexualized and immoral other becomes reminiscent of many village goddess narratives in the Deccan and Maharashtra, such as Mari-ai, Renuka-ai, and Yellamma (HILTEBEITEL 1988).

Even the unintentional sexual indiscretion of upper-caste women is a familiar story, which forms the basis for their condemnation as impure, the dismemberment of their motherhood from their own selves, and the conjoining of their bodies with lower-caste women to ward away excommunication by being redeemed both as goddesses and by goddesses. The making of ritual offerings to the *saṭvāī* encompassing "what does not rightfully belong to women" also confirms the conceptual dialectic observed by DONIGER (2009) that differentiates the passive female fertility and the active masculine sexuality in literature. Women seek a restoration to their passive and fertile feminine form, which would help them in their motherhood duty, even as their *viṭāḷ* is cleaned by ritualists.

CAN NARRATIVES OF AFFLICTION REPLACE RITUAL HEALING?

The final discussion can be divided into three topics. The first relates to the different meanings that could be read in Shruti's IUD expulsion in terms of critiquing the Indian state's medical contraceptive policies. The second topic that is interrelated with the first explores how women's narratives of affliction can form a separate category within discourses of ritual healing. The third concerns hierarchies and associations formed by conflations between gender, caste, and clan, which lead to the debacle of the lost child.

Supporters of tradition as healing may prefer me to read Shruti's affliction narrative in other ways, since alternate readings are always possible. Alternate readings of Shruti's story would focus analysis on her body's expulsion of the IUD as an almost somatic rejection of modernity, as Shruti chose to believe in the traditional diagnosis of *saṭvāī* affliction. But such readings would also reduce Shruti's narrative, forcing it to fit into predetermined structures, glorifying tradition as healing rather than letting it remain what it was: an affliction narrative. Though I knew Shruti was ill and was diagnosed as afflicted, I still do not know whether she was ever healed. Besides, reading her story thus would selectively obliterate a very important aspect of Shruti's self-projected identity: a woman who prided herself as modern and educated, who chose to assume control over her reproductive body against her marital clan's wishes, who participated in government programs for rural women's reproductive health, who once worked in a bank, and finally, who used all these attributes as empowerment, someone who consciously chose to settle into family life and motherhood. Shruti's narrative was obviously more complex and layered as within the affliction diagnosis her marital clan received the primary position of victimhood (in contrast to her herself), and in the process, her independence as a modern woman who argued for her own will failed. Her narrative demonstrates her secondary and ambivalent position as victim-cum-perpetrator, which is a classic situation within *saṭvāī* afflictions. Neither does the *saṭvāī*'s ritualist posit any traditional or alternative knowledge for scholars apart from an understanding of how lower-caste bodies are used as labor, when ritually introduced into upper-caste clans, to clean their women of *viṭāḷ*.

As far as the second aspect is concerned, the postcolonial praise of tradition as healing (KAKAR 1982; NANDY 1989; SAX 2010) posits intensely written narratives of rituals that heal, rituals that are performative and educational, including ritualists who go into trance, ritual texts, different techniques, strategies, processes, and contextual relationships. In academic descriptions, ritual healing and efficacy is theoretically located critically at the juncture of a failed, colonialist, and inadequate modernity, where it develops lacunae. Redemption is also scripted in thickly described collective spaces and the intricacy of social relationships in accompaniment with comforting images of deities and traditions. Narratives about ritual healing are written, however, almost entirely at the expense of individual women's narratives of oppression and negotiation, while many afflictions that cause the family to take center-stage as primary victims of women's afflictions are gifted by the same deity, who is constructed by these narratives as a healing agent. It is only closer examination of individual case studies that reveals afflictions to be a source of patriarchal discipline and punishment for married women. Afflictions serve to place women in a position secondary to patriarchal clans. Discourses of ritual as healing almost always locate redemption within traditional collectives of clan, caste, or village, collectives which assume consensus and a shared and linked subjectivity, using paradigms of "dividuality" (MARRIOTT 1990) as being the primary cognitive and experiential framework for South Asians. This limits discursive opportunities for understanding women's affliction that describe selfhood within contexts of excommunication, wherein individual experiences of an ambivalent boundary are generated. Women's sharing is often a conscious choice, based on their individual sexual, reproductive, and clan relationships. Their negotiations are personal and often strategic.

It is often expected that affliction narratives will tell only half the story. It is almost always taken for granted that the entire narrative will only be complete when affliction is a precursor to ritual healing. KAKAR's book on India's healing traditions (1982), for example, remains influential among many South Asian social scientists, psychologists, medical doctors, and psychiatrists. It demonstrates examples of various afflictions and maladies in ways that showcase the power of Indian mysticism in being capable of healing patients through magico-religious techniques, which become metaphorical for demonstrating the power of tradition to heal the illnesses generated by modernity itself. Affliction is thus utilized only to tell the healing story, which unfolds in the latter part of a case-story to engulf affliction and obliterate it. It is expected for ritualists to engage with the afflicted to complete the healing, and culturally contain the affliction in ways that are alternative to the methods of modernity. These exchanges are then thickly described in different ethnographic contexts to prove a certain point as scientific: that ritual is universally healing.

Although this might indeed be true even of many cases, ritual healing does not fit women's affliction narratives of reproductive health and childbirth crisis so easily, when most of them are diagnosed as witches. *Saṭvāī* affliction narratives are not success stories. Neither are these stories ever really complete, nor do women ever become totally healed or receive enough closure, since afflicted women continue to remain stigmatized as impure once accused of witchcraft and immorality. They remain hovering around the periphery of their marital clans, who are established as the primary victims in their diagnosis. Afflicted women do realize that ritual diagnosis is a form of punishment and suffering, since they also live within modernity, however fragmented its institutional execution may be. Even if they are able to have children, they remain vulnerable to a fear of affliction diagnosis due to their personal history with it. Neither do the ritualists play too important a role, because they serve marital clans as well. My research on afflicted women as exorcized elements, condemned as impure and sometimes as child-eaters, could be viewed as narratives of ritual affliction that therefore resist being subsumed into the category of ritual healing.

Arriving at the last point of my discussion, gender and caste in Aparna's narrative is conflated as she speaks of clan negotiations. She denigrates the ritualist for the same strategy she recommends Shruti to use. This seems contradictory.

In Aparna's estimation, Shruti should have first fulfilled her husband's and marital clan's reproductive demands in order to deflect attention from herself to later fulfill her own contraceptive agenda (a step-by-step negotiation that Aparna was herself undertaking). It was this strategy that the lower-caste ritualist was also employing. The ritualist had built and earned her own fame and money, but had always fulfilled the wishes of upper-caste clans in the village, too, remaining careful to always prioritize while never antagonizing them. While this strategy for Shruti, in Aparna's opinion, would have gained the former freedom, empowerment, and respect, she viewed the same strategy that the ritualist employed as a cunning ploy to subvert her low-caste station. Aparna further pointed to how Shruti would gain clan support and motherhood with patience and strategic planning, but she also pointed out how the same strategic planning and patience left the ritualist exposed, at the mercy of upper-caste clans, as the ritualist had more to lose now and could be attacked by upper castes at any time.

First, Aparna was obviously demonstrating a hierarchy between two forms of motherhood-related *balutedāri* by the discrepancies in her attitude toward Shruti and the ritualist, wherein the actual provision of motherhood to upper-caste clans through marriage defines a higher rank for women in comparison to the ritual aiding of upper-caste motherhood by the absorption of *viṭāḷ*. Second, what Aparna was expressing more vitally was a competitive desire for power over her clan in comparison to the ritualist, which she felt went missing in Shruti's case, only because the latter had antagonized her husband. Aparna was constructing two hierarchical rungs of power around her clan through her narrative. While she was intensifying the inner ring of mothers (Shruti and herself) as its strong wives and mothers who could negotiate with the clan with patience and strategy, she was competing with the outer rung (traditional service-providers of rural clans such as ritualists) by trying to distance them from the clan. More important than knowing whether Aparna was casteist was to understand that she was using caste discrimination as a means of controlling her marital clan and husband.

The question I often posed to my respondents during Shruti's illness was this: whose child was it? Shruti said that the child she miscarried belonged to the *saṭvāī*. If this was the case, how was it that her marital clan claimed victimhood for her miscarriage? Since her husband had taken no responsibility for being the father, how was Shruti's marital clan wounded? How could Shruti's miscarriage be discussed by them as their bereavement? If she had been accused of immorality (and then the child had no father), didn't this make it her own child? And hadn't the *saṭvāī* taken the child away, precisely because a fatherless child was disallowed from living in a morally patriarchal society according to *dhamra*? Even if Shruti was guilty of immorality, why could she not grieve the death of her own (even if illegitimate) child? This question was never really answered.

I asked Aparna this question too. Her answer was equally non-specific. The mutual friend at whose house we met to discuss Shruti concluded the discussion by rebuking me. She said I asked too many "why" (*kāran*) questions, when I actually knew the answer for these, in my heart. Since I could not answer questions myself, however, I wanted them to spell things out for me. She said with finality that marital families owned the bodies of women so that they could do whatever they liked with them, even kill and abandon them. They were thus offended with everything that these owned bodies did according to their own free will. The dead babies were only a way of exposing and shaming the free will (*svēcchā*) of women, who existed within bodies that were owned. There was no dead baby!

NOTES

1. The story of ancestral women has also been noted by RAIRKAR (2007) in her research with midwives in rural Maharashtra.

2. FELDHAUS (2003) and DANDEKAR (2009) each document how both the *saṭvāī* and Janai goddesses followed their devotees to their villages, on the promise that their devotees wouldn't turn to look at them. They turned to stone at the very place their devotees broke their promise and turned to look, which was usually at the village boundary.

3. DAVIS's (2014) research on Maithili women's stories is an excellent example of women's small and meaningful victories, even when they are often pitted against each other, in negotiating complex and moral battles, interwoven together in narratives. Also VANASHREE's research (2010) on Mahasweta Devi's play titled *Bayen*, concerning witchcraft accusation, analyzes the text within postcolonial feminist frameworks that present subaltern women as resistant and empowered.

4. *Dhor* is officially supposed to be of a tanner *jāti* (caste), administratively considered a scheduled caste in Maharashtra. The family of the healer in question, still living in the village, said that they were of the Valmiki caste, which is synonymous with Dalit. Many from the Valmiki caste followed the Ambedkar movement and had joined neo-Buddhism. Some, however, like the healer's family, were as yet Hindu and performed their caste duties, such as goddess healing and midwifery that were considered impure, since they also earned from it. When I asked about neo-Buddhist conversion plans for the future, they seemed optimistic, saying that they would consider conversion if the future generation secured good jobs and caste reservation. Till then, they were dependent on ritual cleaning tasks that paid more than the actual cleaning of gutters, streets, or toilets.

5. QUACK (2012) has conducted a detailed ethnography of the anti-superstition movement in India, and located the movement within a trajectory of debates about modernity.

6. CHAKRAVARTI (1995), in her research on widowhood in South Asia, demonstrates how Brahminical prescriptions of sexually "castrating" widows include injunctions for them to avoid the "anomaly" of female asceticism, since women are considered as inherently lascivious. While these prescriptions lead systemically to *sati* (widow-burning), Chakravarti's description of Havik Brahmin widows from South India reveals the social condemnations and stigma they face, wherein widows are held responsible for the death of their husbands, receive no sympathy, and are accused of cannibalism or eating up their husbands. I suggest there is a deeper stratum of witchcraft accusation embedded within these accusations. I also suggest that all *saṭvāī* ritual recipients represent systemic anomalies in the context of ritual feasts: midwives and ritualists, who are auspicious despite being impure, and prepubescent girls. The latter are an anomaly because they are legitimate clan children, without being boys and heirs of their patriarchal-clan. Because they are pre-menstrual, they cannot be wives and mothers to begin their destined function of clan *balutedāri* (occupational duty).

7. Although general anthropological literature on sorcery and magic exists (cf. e.g. NABOKOV 2000), very few accounts on witchcraft allegations and witch-hunting are available, apart from examples that analyze and document Adivasi regions. To name a few, CHAUDHURI's (2012) research explores witch-hunts among the Adivasi tea-plantation workers of West Bengal; MULLICK's (2000) research explores witch-hunts in Jharkhand; SKARIA's (1997) research explores witchcraft accusations among the Dangs of Western India, while SUNDAR (2001) analyzes witchcraft accusations in Bastar. While this creates disputed opinions about witchcraft, such as it resulting from superstition, or witch-hunts being an Adivasi problem, or

witchcraft being a product of poverty or a lack of education, it also demonstrates an absence of focus on the part of the researching self that leaves upper-caste society unmarked.

The theoretical understanding of witchcraft emerging from such research is also borrowed from western theories that are better suited to understanding witch-hunts in Europe or America: eliminating socially dominant women by accusing them of witchcraft to claim their property. This hardly fits South Asia. Research on witchcraft accusations based on *saṭvāī* afflictions firstly demonstrates that witchcraft is definitely expressed as popular practice among dominant, upper castes, as well as among educated members of society, who are completely aware of debates about rationalism and superstition, live within a modernity, and are far from being poor. Neither are accused and afflicted women more or less dominant than other women, they are not eliminated, and no-one's property is grabbed. Women are themselves owned. Desai's research (2008; 2009), even though set among the Gond in Chhattisgarh and Maharashtra, is more nuanced, dealing with questions of Hindu nationalism, witchcraft allegations as ways of understanding Maoist insurgency, intra-community friction leading to witchcraft allegations, subaltern vegetarianism, and the adoption of Hindu deities for healing, such as *mahānubhāv* saints.

8. One of the most interesting facets of Foucault (1995) of relevance to this study was his theorization of punishment that transforms punishment into a culture, wherein its prevention turns into normative discipline, culture, and tradition. Connerton (1999) further adds to this theory by pointing to how these historical cultures of law are memorized within the body discursively.

9. Scheper-Hughes (1992) points to cultures of motherhood, contextualized within the poverty and slums of the Alto, Brazil, where women become disinvested from motherhood as soon as their children suffer malnutrition and become sickly. But there is also a stark difference between the women of Brazil, described by Scheper-Hughes, and the upper-caste women of Maharashtra, since the latter suffer impoverishment due to motherhood roles and duties imposed on them within patriarchal systems, and not malnutrition and poverty.

10. There is not much specific research on *balutedāri* as a system of interaction between *jāti*s that ran parallel to the *jajmāni* system, in early modern Maharashtra, apart from Anand (2005). *Balutedār*s have now become organized according to a new awareness of four castes that are linked to reservation.

11. I have described *saṭvāī* rituals in detail elsewhere, for example in Dandekar (2016).

References

Anand, Mily Roy
2005   *The State and the Village Community in Medieval Maharashtra (Seventeenth–Eighteenth Century AD)*. New Delhi: Rajat Publications.

Apffel-Marglin, Frèdèrique
2008   *Rhythms of Life, Enacting the World with the Goddesses of Orissa*. New Delhi: Oxford University Press.

Bennett, Lynn
2002   *Dangerous Wives and Sacred Sisters: Social and Symbolic Roles of High-Caste Women in Nepal*. New York: Columbia University Press and Kathmandu: Mandala Book Point.

Brubaker, Richard Lee
1978   *The Ambivalent Mistress: A Study of South Indian Village Goddesses and Their Religious Meaning*. PhD diss., University of Chicago.

Chakravarti, Uma
1995   Gender, caste and labour: Ideological and material structure of widowhood. *Economic and Political Weekly* 30: 2248–56.

CHAUDHURI, Soma
  2012   Women as easy scapegoats: Witchcraft accusations and women as targets in tea plantations of India. *Violence against Women* 18: 1213–34. doi: 10.1177/1077801212465155.

CHAWLA, Janet
  1994   *Child-Bearing and Culture: Women Centred Revisioning of the Traditional Midwife; The Dai as a Ritual Practitioner.* New Delhi: Indian Social Institute.
  2002   *Hawa, gola* and mother-in-law's big toe: On understanding *dais'* imagery of the female body. In *The Daughters of Hārītī: Childbirth and Female Healers in South and Southeast Asia,* Santi Rozario and Geoffrey Samuel, eds., 147–62. London: Routledge.

CONNERTON, Paul
  1999   *How Societies Remember.* Cambridge: Cambridge University Press. doi: 10.1017/CBO9780511628061

CURLEY, David L.
  2008   *Poetry and History: Bengali* Maṅgal-Kābya *and Social Change in Precolonial Bengal.* New Delhi: Chronicle Books. doi: 10.1017/S002191181000358X

DANDEKAR, Deepra
  2009   Satvai and the lives of women in Ghodegaon. In *Liebe, Sexualität, Ehe und Partnerschaft. Paradigmen im Wandel: Beiträge zur orientalistischen Gender-Forschung,* M. R. Roswitha Badry and Karin Steiner, eds., 281–92. Freiburg: Foerdergemeinschaft wissenschaftlicher Publikationen von Frauen.
  2014   Childlessness and empathetic relationships. *The Oriental Anthropologist* 14: 123–39.
  2016   *Boundaries and Motherhood: Ritual and Reproduction in Rural Maharashtra.* New Delhi: Zubaan Books.

DANDEKAR, Deepra, and Abhijit DANDEKAR
  2011   The Satvai and settlement pattern in rural western Maharashtra. *South Asian Studies* 27: 221–24. doi: 10.1080/02666030.2011.614430

DAVIS, Coralynn V.
  2014   *Maithil Women's Tales: Storytelling on the Nepal-India Border.* Urbana-Champaign: University of Illinois Press. doi: 10.5406/illinois /9780252038426.001.0001

DESAI, Amit
  2008   Subaltern vegetarianism: Witchcraft, embodiment and sociality in central India. *South Asia: Journal of South Asian Studies* 31: 96–117. doi: 10.1080/00856400701874734
  2009   Anti-'anti-witchcraft' and the Maoist insurgency in rural Maharashtra, India. *Dialectical Anthropology* 33: 423–39.
          doi: 10.1007/s10624-009-9135-4

DHERE, Ramchandra Chintaman, and Anne FELDHAUS
  2011   *Rise of a Folk God: Vitthal of Pandharpur.* New York: Oxford University Press. doi: 10.1093/acprof:oso/9780199777594.001.0001

DONIGER, Wendy
  2009   *The Hindus: An Alternative History.* New York: Penguin Press.

FELDHAUS, Anne

1995a   Types of river goddesses in Maharashtra. In *Folk Cultures, Folk Religion and Oral Traditions as a Component in Maharashtrian Culture*, ed. Günther-Dietz Sontheimer, 31–47. New Delhi: Manohar.

1995b   *Water and Womanhood: Religious Meanings of Rivers in Maharashtra*. New York: Oxford University Press.

2003   *Connected Places: Region, Pilgrimage, and Geographical Imagination of India*. New York: Palgrave Macmillan.

FOUCAULT, Michel

1995   *Discipline and Punish*. New York: Vintage Books.

GORDON-WHITE, David

1996   *The Alchemical Body: Siddha Traditions in Medieval India*. Chicago: The University of Chicago Press.

HILTEBEITEL, Alf

1988   *The Cult of Draupadi 1: Mythologies: From Gingee to Kurukshetra*. New Delhi: Motilal Banarsidass.

KAKAR, Sudhir

1982   *Shamans, Mystics and Doctors: A Psychological Inquiry into India and its Healing Traditions*. Chicago: The University of Chicago Press.

KOSAMBI, Damodar Dharmananda

1962   *Myth and Reality*. Bombay: Popular Prakashan.

MARRIOTT, McKim

1990   Constructing an Indian ethnosociology. In *India through Hindu Categories*, ed. McKim MARRIOTT, 1–39. New Delhi: Sage Publications. doi: 10.1177/006996689023001003

MASILAMANI-MEYER, Eveline

2004   *Guardians of Tamilnadu: Folk Deities, Folk Religion, Hindu Themes*. Halle: Verlag der Franckeschen Stiftungen zu Halle.

MULLICK, Samar Bosu

2000   Gender relations and witches among the indigenous communities of Jharkhand, India. *Gender, Technology and Development* 4: 333–58. doi: 10.1177/097185240000400301

NABOKOV, Isabelle

2000   Deadly power: A funeral to counter sorcery in south India. *American Ethnologist* 27: 147–68. doi: 10.1525/ae.2000.27.1.147

NANDY, Ashis

1989   Shamans, savages and the wilderness: On the audibility of dissent and the future of civilizations. *Alternatives* 14: 263–77.
doi: 10.1177/030437548901400301

PALRIWALA, Rajni, and Patricia UBEROI

2008   Exploring the links: Gender issues in marriage and migration. In *Marriage, Migration and Gender*, Rajni Palriwala and Patricia Uberoi, eds., 23–60. New Delhi: Sage Publications. doi: 10.4135/9788132100324.n1

QUACK, Johannes

2012   *Disenchanting India: Organized Rationalism and Criticism of Religion in India*. Oxford: Oxford University Press. doi: 10.1093/acprof:oso/9780199812608.001.0001

RAHEJA, Gloria Goodwin, and Ann Grodzins GOLD
    1994   *Listen to the Heron's Words: Reimagining Gender and Kinship in North India.* Berkeley: University of California Press.

RAIRKAR, Hema
    2007   Midwives: A tradition on the move in Maharashtra. In *Communication Processes, Volume 2: The Social and The Symbolic*, Bernard Bel, Jan Brouwer, Biswajit Das, Vibodh Parthasarathi, and Guy Poetevin, eds., 413–72. New Delhi: Sage Publications. doi: 10.4135/9788132101178.n15

SADGOPAL, Meera
    2009   Can maternity services open up to the indigenous traditions of midwifery? *Economic and Political Weekly* 44: 52–59.

ŚARMĀ, Paṇḍit Kisanlāl
    2012   *Āplā sampūrṇa cāturmās* [*Your Complete Four Holy Months*], 4th ed. Mumbai: Manoramā Prakāśan.

SAX, William S.
    2010   Ritual and the problem of efficacy. In *The Problem of Ritual Efficacy*, William S. SAX, Johannes Quack, and Jan Weinhold, eds., 3–16. Oxford: Oxford University Press. doi: 10.1093/acprof:oso/9780195394405.003.0001

SCHEPER-HUGHES, Nancy
    1992   *Death Without Weeping: The Violence of Everyday Life in Brazil.* Berkeley: University of California Press.

SKARIA, Ajay
    1997   Women, witchcraft and gratuitous violence in colonial western India. *Past & Present* 155: 109–41. doi: 10.1093/past/155.1.109

SUNDAR, Nandini
    2001   Divining evil: The state and witchcraft in Bastar. *Gender, Technology and Development* 5: 425–48. doi: 10.1177/097185240100500305

VANASHREE
    2010   Witchcraft: Pain, resistance and the ceremony of punishment—Mahasweta Devi's Bayen. *Indian Journal of Gender Studies* 17: 223–47. doi: 10.1177/097152151001700202

MUHAMMAD A. Z. MUGHAL
King Fahd University of Petroleum & Minerals, Saudi Arabia

Time in Flux

Daily and Weekly Rhythms in Rural Pakistan

This paper aims to highlight that daily and weekly rhythms, being a part of the social organization of time, mediate people's responses to social change in rural Pakistan. Indigenous ways of measuring different stages of the day have recently been replaced by clock time as a consequence of industrialization and urbanization. Further, changing socioeconomic circumstances have given rise to a new temporal rhythm, which unfolds in daily time allocation for different activities. The debate regarding whether Sunday or Friday should be the weekend in Pakistan points to the contested notions of time that can be explained on the basis of temporal identity, religion, and urbanization. By using an ethnographic example, this study also discusses how daily and weekly rhythms are maintained in rural Pakistan through the socioeconomic realities of everyday life.

KEYWORDS: day—leisure—Pakistan—social change—time allocation—week—weekend

Asian Ethnology Volume 76, Number 2 · 2017, 261–87
© Nanzan University Anthropological Institute

EVERY CULTURE has its own ways of measuring and managing time through calendars, clocks, and other formal and informal temporal markers to regulate social and economic activities. The social organization of time is connected with other elements of social organization such as religion, economics, and politics (cf. GEERTZ 1966, 360–411; GOODY 1968; GINGRICH et al. 2002; HERZFELD 1990; MUSHARBASH 2007; SCHIEFFELIN 2002). Cultural models of time such as calendars and clocks are thus socially constructed. People perceive time through physical phenomena such as the alternation of days and nights, phases of the moon, seasonal variations, and biological changes in the human body throughout the life cycle. In other words, time and change are interrelated in human experience. I have discussed elsewhere that the social organization of time, as that of space, links different aspects of social organization, for example politics, religion, and economics (MUGHAL 2014a, 2014b, 2015a).[1] Therefore, temporal orientation underscores noticeable changes in the overall system of social organization that negotiates and reshapes social relationships.

Rural communities in Pakistan arguably have been said to be more "traditional" and "conservative" than their urban counterparts. They are considered as such because of certain norms and values, traditional authority patterns, the lack of modern education, and traditional gender roles, among other reasons, that prevail in rural areas. Rural communities in Pakistan, I argue, have experienced social change over centuries and have adapted to inevitably changing socioeconomic conditions while maintaining their specific way of living. In recent decades, industrialization and urbanization have taken place in rural Pakistan due to ongoing contact with cities through modern modes of transportation and temporary labor migration (ALI 2003; GARDEZI and MUMTAZ 2004; HAIDER 1981; HASAN 2009; QADEER 2006; WEISS and MUGHAL 2012). An inadequate supply of land available for agriculture coupled with population growth and rapid urbanization has resulted in a gradual shift from an agricultural and seasonal economy to a market economy. Indigenous temporal models, like the stages of the day, have seen shifts amid these changing socioeconomic circumstances, which has resulted in people overwhelmingly adopting clock time in rural areas. This paper offers an anthropological analysis of daily and weekly rhythms in rural Pakistan by drawing on an ethnographic example. I will show that there are certain temporal markers apparent in rural life and identify the cultural models of time linked with mundane activities that have undergone changes due to overall social change.

Different qualities and quantities of time, such as tempo and timing through which people perform their activities, are like the articulation of time between different notes while playing music, giving rise to a rhythm (GABRIELSSON 1986; YOU 1994). By analogy, people's management of time and their experience of change mark the daily flow of life. People regulate their daily lives by allocating specific amounts of time to specific activities. Anthropological analyses have demonstrated that people allocate time for different activities with certain social intervals interspersed between them (e.g., tea break, lunchtime). These culturally constructed intervals follow each other in an orderly fashion. The description of the time spent by individuals for different activities is one of the fundamental tasks of ethnography, but the "ethnographic estimates of time inputs" are rarely quantified (JOHNSON 1996). With the increase in the diversity of occupations and other alterations in rural social organization in Pakistan, the quantified estimates of time inputs may assist us in the study of how social change occurs.

The weekly rhythm of activities in Pakistan is anchored and maintained by the concept of the weekend, which is conceived to be either Friday (the Muslim day of communal prayer) and/or Sunday. Since Friday is the grand prayer day, it functions as a temporal marker for Muslims, whereas employing Sunday as the weekly holiday has been contested politically. During the colonial era, Sunday was the official holiday, however, Friday always remained an important day for Muslims. After the end of the British Raj, Sunday and Friday have alternated as weekly holidays during different periods in Pakistan (ESPOSITO 1998, 175). In 1947, Pakistan adopted Sunday as the weekend due to its colonial legacy. Under the 1956 constitution, however, Pakistan adopted the title Islamic Republic to make it more compatible with the idea that Islam was the basis of its national identity. Later on, the government also declared Friday as the weekend, but in 1997 the government announced Sunday as the weekend in order to allow for the maximum benefits of the international market and to promote business with the West. The use of Sunday as the weekend in the cultural context of Pakistan thus points to the effects of globalization. In big cities, the weekend as a weekly holiday when the worker gets a day off is observed because of fixed schedules employed at offices, factories, and other industries. The extent to which the "weekend" matters for people living in rural areas is not as straightforward as we might imagine.

I have explained elsewhere that three different calendars have been used in rural Pakistan, albeit to varying extents and for different activities (MUGHAL 2014b). These include a lunisolar agrarian calendar, the Islamic lunar calendar, and the Gregorian calendar. The use of the local agrarian calendar is declining and is limited to the older generation only. However, the names of months in this calendar, as well as the seasonal reckoning that is done mainly through this calendar, are still a part of cultural memory. The Islamic calendar is still being practiced as it has been used for centuries, because it marks all of the numerous religious festivals practiced locally and nationally. Over time, the use of the Gregorian calendar has increased in rural areas, as it was mainly practiced in cities until fairly recently. The changing use of these calendars highlights people's adaptation to social change. Similar to the changing use of these calendars, I will now explain how globalization and urbanization shape the daily and weekly rhythmic cycle in rural Pakistan. I will discuss the decreasing use of the indigenous way of dividing the day as a result of the increase in the use of clock time, indicating the shift away from an agricultural economy in the direction of a market economy. I will also highlight that despite being the official weekend, Sunday is less effective in rural areas for two reasons. First, Friday is an important day in Muslim culture no matter what day is considered the official weekend. Second, a weekly "day of rest" is absent in rural social organization, at least partially if not fully.

Before discussing the ethnographic details of daily and weekly rhythms, I wish to detail how anthropologists study time. While doing so, I do not intend to discuss in much detail the methodological or theoretical debates on the study of time that have occurred over the years in the discipline; rather, I focus on two main points that concern the research presented here. First, anthropological analyses of time have provided us with the understanding that there are no fixed ways of approaching time, mainly because of the complexities of the nature of time across human cultures. Second, time and change are two interconnected concepts, so studying the social organization of time also provides us with insights into the transformations that occur in the overall social organization.

THE ANTHROPOLOGY OF TIME

Time reckoning appears to be a universal phenomenon and many anthropological studies show that every society has a peculiar system of time reckoning, which "circumscribes" their existence (GINGRICH et al. 2002, 3). Time as a part of social organization interacts with other components and conditions of social complexity (BURMAN 1981, 266). In other words, time is a source for "co-ordinating relationship[s]" (EVANS-PRITCHARD 1940, 108). Therefore, we can come closer to understanding the worldview of a community by studying its social organization of time (MUNN 1992, 123).

GOODY (1968, 30–38) has explained that the social organization of time includes three main components. First, it includes systems of time measurement based upon the "cosmic cycle" and the "human cycle." The cosmic cycle includes such divisions of time as day, night, week, month, season, and year. It also involves two types of rites of passage: religious (e.g., shrine festivals) and non-religious (e.g., national holidays). The human cycle complements the cosmic cycle by including the categorization of biological life into various stages such as childhood, adolescence, and old age. It also involves rites of passage to celebrate these stages. Second, the allocation and scheduling of time by individuals is also an element of the social organization of time. People allocate different amounts of time for different activities. Lastly, people's attitudes toward time are also a part of the social organization of time. These attitudes are based on the aforementioned cycles, resulting in the categorization of time as past, present, and future. Calendars and clocks help people regulate their activities, keep track of their past, and plan for their future. Similarly, the categorization of time into various stages of human life, such as childhood and old age, holds different social, economic, and moral connotations associated with these stages.

Numerous anthropological studies in different cultures have highlighted the importance of time in social structure. For instance, while explaining his theory of practice, BOURDIEU (1977, 6) indicated that the "delayed exchange" duration between giving and reciprocating gifts provides information about obligations involved in the gift exchange. GLUCKMAN (1977, 271–75) found that the lineage system has a fixed stretch of time, from the origin of humans to their "present-day descendants" in tribal societies. For each type of group and social relationship, there is a specific "time-scale" in these societies. ROBERTS (1982) found that people in Zaire differentiate between heroes based on their deaths in either wet or dry seasons. Such a differentiation of heroes reveals the preferences for some seasons over others defined by the group's socioeconomic structure. In the same way, differential notions of time for both men and women in Sri Lanka, along with the power of time in the mythical aspect of Sinhalese astrology, also indicate the correlation between time and social structure (KEMPER 1980).

There is a good deal of anthropological literature to show how rituals and ceremonies are organized and celebrated through temporal organization (cf. EL GUINDI 2008; EVERS 1972, 48–60; GEERTZ 1966, 30–85). RAPPAPORT (1999, 169–235) not only described the performance of rituals with reference to time but also explained the rationale of the temporal organization to fit the social order of any particular case study. For instance, Friday, Saturday, and Sunday for Muslims, Jews, and Christians, respectively, are a religiously defined expression of identity. He also explained that people take "time out of time" from some activities, when time is symbolically suspended (RAPPAPORT 1999, 190). Such temporal bearing, by individuals or society as a whole, indicates people's preference for an ordered way of structuring activities in a pattern of flow.

The differential use of time for different activities is key to making distinctions between work and leisure. Work is seen as an economic category through which humans earn their living whereas leisure is defined in terms of a surplus economy where it is an additional and valued amount of time freed from wage labor (COOPER 1984; WELTFISH 1979). Leisure has become an economy in the form of sports, tourism, the cinema industry, and many more activities (MUGHAL 2014c). However, anthropologists generally tend to study leisure through locally perceived notions in individual cultural contexts. For instance, DEEB and HARB (2013) noted that Shi'i Muslim youth in Lebanon have developed new forms of leisure in which morality and piety are being debated due to the introduction of a capitalist economy.

The use and analysis of time is, of course, not limited to the aspects mentioned above. Anthropologists approach time in a variety of ways. FABIAN (1983, 21–33) categorized three uses of time in anthropology. The first category is "physical time," which is a parameter describing sociocultural processes and demographic or ecological changes. The "mundane" and "typological" times he discusses lie in the second category. The former describes the working of natural laws and the latter differentiates between the traditional and modern, rural and urban, and other such dichotomies. The third category is "intersubjective" time, which refers to human actions and interactions. The problem of distance between an anthropologist and the community being studied is common to all these uses. During fieldwork, anthropologists typically identify themselves with or become "coeval" with the communities they study. However, they typically organize their writings according to physical or typological time so that their ethnographies may not be regarded as poetry, fiction, or political propaganda. This issue of distance between the anthropologist and the target community has taken on new dimensions as more and more anthropologists have started to research their own cultures, which some investigators have labeled "anthropology at home" (cf. JACKSON 1987; MUGHAL 2015b; PEIRANO 1998). Anthropology at home, which is what I practice in the context of this study, allows the discipline to reconsider the way it constructs "other."

ADAM (1994), a social theorist of time, argues that studying time turns out to be complicated because it is concerned not only with the "subject" of anthropology but also with the lives of anthropologists. Further, it is "curiously invisible." It is therefore important to understand the meaning of time and its various expressions in language. Adam has also described various uses of time in English as "timing," "temporality," "time frame," and "tempo." Timing is related to "when time" in everyday English communication. Temporality forms a central component of time. Time frame is the conceptual space within which people organize, plan, and regulate their daily existence, whereas tempo is the speed of time passing. All these terminologies have become pertinent to anthropological writings about time.

LEACH (1961, 124–36) has also contributed three experiences of time. First, time-interval and duration always begin and end with the same thing. Leach recognized this experience as "repetition." Second, experience can be "aging," which involves birth, maturation, and death, through a process of irreversible change. Another experience is the "rate at which time passes." This third experience is the passing of time at a different speed during different stages of life. He offers a pendulum view of time as "a repetition of repeated reversal, a sequence of oscillations between polar opposites" (ibid.) For Leach, "we create time by creating intervals in our social life" (ibid.), whereas intervals are marked as repeated opposites. OHNUKI-TIERNEY (1969) analyzed the Ainu's time reckoning to show that the Ainu and Super-Ainu dichotomous concepts of time were, in fact, a "repeated contrast" operational at several levels in their time structure.

BARNES (1974) has preferred the term "cycle" over "oscillation," while arguing that in the yearly ceremonies of Kédang the sequence of events returned to its original state when it was completed. RAPPAPORT (1999, 169–215) argues that stages of life are not "irreversible" because "recurrence" is undoubtedly embedded into them. He quoted the example of EVANS-PRITCHARD's (1940, 94–138) study of the Nuer to support his argument, where the death of the grandfather and the birth of the son were found to be associated. Anthropologists tend to denote the cyclical expressions of time to experiences that involve repetition. These cyclical expressions of time are observable in the monthly or yearly celebrations of rituals, the division of seasons, and, in a physical sense, in the coming of day and night. On the contrary, BAILEY (1983, 167–68) and RAMBLE (2002, S84) argued that since time is perceived through events, it is one-dimensional or linear and asymmetrical, flowing irreversibly from past to future. Although different anthropologists would argue in favor of one model of time against the other (cf. MUNN 1992; GELL 1996, 2000), this points to the complicated nature of time and its varied experiences within and between different cultures. Keeping this diversity of opinions in mind, let me now move on to related concepts of time and social change.

TIME AND SOCIAL CHANGE

Change is linked with time in many respects. The nature and extent of the transformations depend upon which part of the social organization of time, and that of space as well, has been triggered to induce further changes in social organization. Economic change may bring about transformations in the ways of measuring time and space. For example, people experience the scarcity of time and space because of industrialization, which results in certain readjustments in the allocation of time and space in order to maximize productivity (cf. LOW and LAWRENCE-ZÚÑIGA 2003; SMITH 1982; THOMPSON 1967). Demographic change, technological change, migration, religious conversion, and other types of change will have similar corresponding effects on the social organization of time and space, which will eventually transform the overall social organization of the collective group.

GEERTZ (1966, 360–411) has noted that whenever there is a change in the experience of time, it will alter the greater part of culture. Similarly, ERRINGTON (1974, 264–65) analyzed social order in Karavaran as being highly desirable, and people achieved social order during their rituals. Errington argued that a cargo movement contains symbols of social change toward becoming like Europeans. Therefore, the cargo movement is "an effort to instantaneously acquire a European level of social order" (ibid.) through the way local people perform their traditional rituals. In many studies, anthropologists found that new authority patterns, formed as a consequence of social change, mediate new forms of the social organization of time (e.g. BIRTH 1996; BURMAN 1981; GILSENAN 1996; GINGRICH et al. 2002; SMITH 1982). Due to this interconnectedness of time and social change, BARTH (1967, 662) suggested studying the latter by calculating people's time allocation for different activities. People allocate different amounts of time to different activities based on their preferences, needs, and beliefs. Information about the difference in amounts of time allocated for different activities between different social groups helps analyze the direction of social change. For instance, EMBER (1983) noted that due to technological change, agricultural intensification has increased to yield more production. Technological advances result in a reduced need for human input; therefore, women previously engaged in agricultural activities started allocating more time to their household activities.

Anthropologists view change as an inevitable phenomenon in every human culture. Analyses of social change thus account for such change in ways that draw on the available local evidence. In recent theories of social change that consider it a globalized phenomenon associated with modernity, time and space are core concepts. Societies and cultures are coming closer to each other, with a higher intensity and pace than ever before, due to "time-space compression" (HARVEY 1990) or "time-space distanciation" (GIDDENS 1986) through modern ways of transportation, migration, the media, and international trade.

There has been a justifiable emphasis placed on globalization and urbanization in theories about social change because they would appear to be applicable to almost every culture today (see FORTE 1998; MAZZARELLA 2004; RANKIN 2003; SMART and SMART 2003). Such ubiquity should not be overstated, however. Different societies respond differently to the effects of globalization and urbanization. It is my contention that any explanation or interpretation of social change must make sense of the phenomenon on the ground (see MUGHAL 2014a; INDA and ROSALDO 2008; NONINI 2013). Both internal as well as external factors cause some sorts of changes in the overall social organization of a community. Both these factors may trigger, augment, or even oppose each other. A teleological explanation of their interplay is contingent upon the factors or the nature of social change. However, local socioeconomic circumstances, politics, and ideologies may pose a challenge to some of the external or global factors that bring about change. This negotiation between local realities and external or global factors of social change are often be mediated by the social organization of time and space in any given culture (BURMAN 1981; FRIEDMAN 1985; SMITH 1982; ZOOMERS 2010).

THE SETTING AND METHODOLOGY

This study is based on ethnography of Jhokwala village. The village is located in Lodhran District of the Punjab province. Despite urbanization, Lodhran's economy is chiefly based on agriculture (MUGHAL 2014a; Government of Pakistan 2000). The regional language in the southern part of the province, called South Punjab, is Saraiki. The national language, Urdu, is also understood and spoken by almost everybody in the village. In addition to Saraiki-speaking people, Urdu-speaking Rajputs who migrated from Haryana, India as an aftermath of Partition in 1947 also reside in the village. These Rajputs speak Haryanvi, considered to be a dialect of Urdu.[2]

Like many villages in the region, an inadequate supply of land available for agriculture has been caused in Jhokwala as a consequence of population growth and the division of land among multiple heirs. On the one hand, this has resulted in intensified agriculture practices enabled by modern technology. On the other hand, many farmers have abandoned agriculture, and are now working as wage laborers. This has increased the trend toward education and temporary migration to cities or even overseas in search of alternative economic prospects. The location of Jhokwala near a highway junction and local market, Adda Parmat, has also augmented the pace of urbanization and industrialization in the village. Therefore, agricultural land has been gradually transforming into industrial units and shops. Most of these changes started taking effect in the last couple of decades, at least on a visible level.

The fieldwork for this research was carried out intermittently for about ten months up until 2010 (MUGHAL 2015b). In addition to conventional ethnographic methods, such as participant observation, interviews, and focus group discussions,

I conducted surveys and spot checks regarding time allocation and time reckoning. Spot checks are particularly important in documenting time allocation (JOHNSON 1996). A spot check is "snapshot-like recording of behaviour" to measure the time allocated by people for different activities (GROSS 1984, 539). Many time allocation studies solely rely on such quantitative data, but I used spot checks by directly observing people at their engagements without taking part in their activities in order to record the time they allocate for different activities. These spot checks were often pre-informed. Sometimes I also paid unannounced random visits to homes and places of employment. I recorded most of the activities of men and women outside the household boundaries while taking into account concerns regarding privacy and gender segregation in Pakistani society. There have naturally been some issues with the reporting of women's time allocation for various activities in Pakistani villages due to gender segregation (SULTANA, NAZLI, and MALIK 1994).

Some constraints in recording rural women's time allocation are thus encountered by male researchers due to lack of access. This situation is further worsened when using traditional "quantitative surveyors," a time-bound methodology that does not prove to be appropriate in rural areas. Being a male researcher, I used the questionnaire method for the women with whom I could not meet directly for an interview or conduct spot checks, given the cultural sensitivities regarding gender. Male members of the households, some of whom I trained, filled out these questionnaires with their women because I had developed rapport in the community over time.

The collective representation of time, as well as space, creates and shapes people's temporal and spatial experiences "for it seems that we cannot think of objects which are not in time and space" (DURKHEIM 1915, 22). An analysis of linguistic expressions in various cultural models explains the relative influence of different religions, nations, and political regimes that have shaped present-day Pakistani society. Since time is embedded in every aspect of culture, local terminologies used for various temporal expressions provide a comprehensive overview of the past and the present conditions of a phenomenon. In the next section I explore some important local terms in order to describe the time conceptions of Jhokwala's residents.

DAILY RHYTHM

Pahar and Clock

According to the indigenous temporal organization of the region, a 24-hour *dīhiṇ* or *din* (day) comprises eight phases—four for daytime and four for night-time. Each phase is called *pahar*. The average length of each *pahar* is approximately three hours. However, the duration of each *pahar* is not uniform and varies throughout the year in relation to sunrise and sunset. The measurement of *pahar*s is by no means through formal tools. The movement of the sun and other celestial bodies, such as *tāre* (stars), marks the beginning or end of a *pahar*. In the past, people used to calculate *pahar*s through various methods. Elderly people in the village still have some knowledge of these methods. One man in the village described the local concepts of astronomy in the following way:[3]

> *Tāre* rise from here [points eastward in the sky]. They are [visible] in winter, not [visible] in summer. They disappear. In winter, the wells used to run according to these [*tāre*]. The wells used to start running after watching the *taraṅgaṛ* (a specific group of stars). Three *tāre* are together, these were called *taraṅgaṛ*. When the *taraṅgaṛ* rose in the east, it was the first *pahar*. There are four *pahars* in a night. Then the *taraṅgaṛ* came in the middle [of the sky]. It was midnight. This was the second *pahar*. Then the *taraṅgaṛ* start setting. Then it became the later *pahar*. Then the *taraṅgaṛ* kept coming in this direction. As the *taraṅgaṛ* continued setting, time moved further ahead. We calculated time accordingly. In the day, we used mark lines. Look! If the shadow of the sun was at this line [he marked on his hand], it was this *pahar*. If it was at that line, it was that *pahar*. [We] measured the shadow by erecting poles at appropriate distances on the ground. People were able to reckon it easily. Even the bulls [running on the well] could reckon it. Upon their turn, they used to stop. They used to stamp their feet hard the ground [to mark a *pahar*]. Then they used to start moving. When it was their turn, they stopped automatically. In addition to the *taraṅgaṛ*, there were [some other stars] the *munnī* and *chiṭhīyāṉ*. The *munnī* are [located] below the *taraṅgaṛ*, which are two thick stars. The *chiṭhīyāṉ* are just like this [he joins the tips of his two index fingers together]. They are also more visible in winter [but] less visible in summer. Now you see, *Sāvaṇ* (a month of the local agrarian calendar) has started. After *Sāvaṇ*, the *taraṅgaṛ* will be visible.
>
> (KHUDA BUKHSH, 75)[4]

The system of *pahars* is, therefore, an indigenous way of measuring time throughout the day by the length of the shadow of anything such as a twig or a tree. The night *pahars* are measured through the movement of *tāre* in the sky. Only literate people use different terms for stars and planets (i.e., *sīyāre*). The *pahars* system was linked with agriculture before the use of modern technology, until the middle of the twentieth century. This system also helped in regulating social activities and maintaining the overall rhythm of the day. Elderly people told me some basic points regarding why farmers needed to divide the day into *pahars*, or in other words, the importance of time measurement in order to maintain the daily rhythm of activities. Firstly, people used shared wells to irrigate their lands. Therefore, farmers used *pahars* to determine their turns to use the well. Second, there were more than two brothers or partners who had to irrigate the same land. In such cases, they allocated *pahars* among each other for a just division of time between their bulls to let the animals take some rest after appropriate intervals. Another villager explained to me in the following manner:

> We used to run the well [with the help of bulls]. When the two bulls [of one brother or partner] were tired then he asked the other one to run his bulls for the next *pahar*. We used to calculate *pahars* according to the position of the *tare*, just as we say it is 8 o'clock now, so it was 8 o'clock according to the position of the *tāre*. Therefore, the other [brother] might reply that his turn had

not come because the *tāre* were not at the specific position of the next *pahar*. (Muhammad Akbar, 49)

Third, women at home used *pahar*s to estimate the time of their men's returning from fields in order to find out the exact time to prepare food for them. Fourth, people who had to start work early in the morning could get prepared before dawn by reckoning the night *pahar*s. Fifth, dividing time into *pahar*s helped knowing the timings of different prayers, as each *namāz* (prayer) is offered at a specific time. The synchronization of *pahar*s with the five daily prayers helped reckoning *pahar*s. However, with the passage of time, recognizing *pahar*s with their specific names started to decline. Nowadays, specific phases of the day are referenced by prayer timings. A major factor behind the decrease in reckoning *pahar*s is the use of clock time. TABLE I shows the day and night *pahar*s along with their temporal markers and corresponding activities in Jhokwala.

One night, I was making a video of people watching a movie at a tea stall in the village where men and boys socialize and spend their free time as leisure. The light went off suddenly because of a rolling blackout that is common in the country these days due to energy shortages and load shedding. It became difficult for us to

	Stages of a Day	Western and Clock Equivalent	Temporal Marker	Activities
1	*vaḍā vīlā* (big time) or *ṣubaḥ kāzib* (pseudo morning)	very early morning 03:00-06:00	first *azān* (crow) of cock	*tahajjud* prayer
2	*fajar* (morning) or *ṣubaḥ sādiq* (true morning)	dawn or morning 06:00-09:00	*sijh ubhār dā vīlā* (sunrise; twilight); second crow of cock	fajar prayer; *saharī* (morning meal) time ends during the fasting month of *Ramzān*; people leave for their businesses
3	*dhammī dā vīlā*	the perfect morning 09:00-12:00	sun is in the center of the sky	economic/agricultural activities
4	*dūpahar* or *pīshīn*	noon 12:00-15:00	the shadow of things is visible	*zohr* (noon) prayer; *kailūlā* (daytime nap)
5	*dīghir*	afternoon 15:00-18:00	the shadow of things is doubled	*'asar* (afternoon) prayer
6	*namāshīn dā vīlā*	evening or sunset 18:00-21:00	evening or twilight	*maghrib* (evening) prayer
7	*rāt*	dusk 21:00-24:00	the *taraṅgaṛ* (a group of stars) are visible in the sky	*'ishā* (night) prayer; go to bed
8	*adhī rāt*	midnight 24:00-03:00	the *taraṅgaṛ* disappear and the *chiṭhīyān* (a group of stars)	sleeping

TABLE I: *Pahar*s (note: clock times in hours given in the table are not exact, for they only indicate a rough estimation of time)

see each other for a while. Out of the dark, I heard forty-year-old Saleem say the following:

> Come at seven o'clock early in the morning. I am going into the fields to spray [pesticide] in Basti Fateh Rasheed (a nearby village). Make your video there. Take my photograph too.

The next morning, around seven o'clock, I arrived at the designated spot and saw Saleem coming along with his two friends. We went to a nearby village, Basti Fateh Rasheed, a few miles from Jhokwala. They had obtained some land on tenancy there, where I shot the video of them spraying pesticides in the fields. I was told that they had a plan to return home at twelve noon. I could not stay there for the whole time because I wanted to meet someone else at another location. I returned to Jhokwala with one of them who was returning early too. The very next day, I saw them going to the fields in the morning at seven o'clock. I was curious if Saleem managed his entire timetable according to clock time. After some days, I asked him about *pahar*s. He told me his elders used to count *pahar*s but he did not because he used clock time only.

More than half of the village population wore watches, according to a survey that I conducted during the fieldwork, and almost every home and shop had a clock. The use of clock time indicates the need to reckon time more precisely in shorter durations. This is because their jobs, television program schedules, and even the prayer timings strictly follow clock time. In the mosque, the time for each prayer is written on a board describing hours and minutes for *jamā't* (congregation) timings. As the day length and the shadow of the sun changes during different seasons within a given year, the prayer timings are managed accordingly. These days, *pahar*s are named after the names of the daily prayers. For instance, at sunset, the commonly used term for expressing this *pahar* is not *namāshīn dā vīlā*; instead, the word *maghrib* (evening prayer that is performed at sunset) is used to express the time of sunset. People schedule their meetings by taking the prayer timings as reference.

TIME ALLOCATION

The daily rhythm of an individual's life in Jhokwala is maintained through different activities. I broadly categorize these activities into religion, economy, leisure, personal care, household, and education, instead of providing more detailed references like sleeping, bathing, and so on. In some anthropological studies, a detailed categorization is made if the community is comprised of a homogeneous population with respect to their occupations and a collective involvement in group activities. For example, SAHLINS (1972) categorized the details of hunting and gathering activities into traveling, hunting, and meat distribution, because the concerned population was all hunters and gatherers. In Jhokwala, people have different occupations and their economic, household, and social activities may not always overlap. I refer to the five daily prayers, the recitation of *Qur'an*, and other such rituals as religious activities. Economic activities include all types of agricultural labor, selling, buying, trading, wage labor, brokering, and salaried jobs. I also calculated the time required to travel to the workplace as a part of the respective activity. Household activities range from child caring to preparing food and cleaning the house.

I have categorized leisure into sports, watching TV, gossip, and listening to music. These activities are gender and age specific. For example, boys play cricket and some traditional games like *gīṭī ḍanā* or *gillī ḍanḍā* (a game similar to tip-cat) and *piṭhū garam* (a game similar to seven stones). Some sports are specific to girls like *ṣṭāpū* (hopscotch). Others are played both by girls and boys like *ludo* (a board game) and *chuppan chupāī* (hide and seek). Similarly, men play volleyball, *ludo*, and snooker. During leisure time, men gather at tea stalls or at a *ḍīrah*, a place where men meet to gossip, smoke a water pipe, and discuss important community matters.[5] Women play *ludo*, but for a majority of them, chatting with peers and watching TV are the main or only forms of leisure as a result of restrictions against movement outside of the home without familial supervision. Most elderly men and women smoke *huqqah*s (water pipes), which I have categorized as leisure. I present other activities like sleeping and bathing as personal care. There are certain social activities that are not performed regularly; for example, attending birth, marriage, death, and other such ceremonies are periodic rites of passage rather than regular activities. I have categorized them as other, which also includes activities like *tīmārdārī* or *ʿayādat*. *ʿAyādat* refers to visiting patients, inquiring about their health, bringing fruit or gifts, and spending some time with them. *Tīmārdārī*, on the other hand, refers to taking care of the patient.

The amount of time allocated to and timing of different activities varies from one individual to the other, even within the same age and occupational group. I present here an average of all the people included in the sample of about fifty individuals. These people belong to different occupations, genders, and age groups. All the activities vary throughout the year, month, and week. For example, during the fasting month, people change their routine accordingly (MUGHAL 2014b). Some people have a different routine on the weekend. Farmers are busy during some months and are relatively free during the others when they are not cultivating or harvesting. Seasonal variations cause change in the day-length, which affects the timing of various activities in different months of a year. For example, the duration between the five-time daily prayers is greater in summer than it is in winter. I have included the calculation of time allocation for different activities on an average basis. I have also shown the schedule of these activities through clock time for simplicity's sake, but this does not mean that people follow a strict timing, except for prayers and some activities like going to and returning from their offices and schools. For instance, cooking may last for fifteen minutes to an hour, depending on the complexity of the dishes being prepared. Similarly, some children go to the mosque for reciting *Qur'an* in the morning while others go in the afternoon.

The civil day in Jhokwala starts just before sunrise with the time of the morning prayer around five a.m. in summer and six a.m. in winter. The *aẓān* (call to prayer) calling the faithful to the morning prayer is the first activity noticed in the village, though some people offer *tahajjud* (early morning prayer) before the *aẓān* at their homes. The day ends around midnight in summer and earlier in winter.

Season	Time	Activities		
		Men	**Women**	**Children**
Summer	04:30 - 06:00	morning prayer	morning prayer	learning of how to recite Qur'an
Winter	06: 00 - 07:00	morning prayer	morning prayer	sleep
Summer	06:00 - 08:00	preparing for work + breakfast	preparing food + breakfast	preparing for school + breakfast
Winter	07:00 - 09:00	preparing for work + breakfast	preparing breakfast + eating breakfast	preparing for school + breakfast
Summer	08:00 - 13:00	work	visit neighbors and relatives + preparing lunch	school
Winter	09:00 - 14:00	work	household activities + visit neighbors and relatives	school
Summer	13:00 - 14:00	lunch + afternoon prayer + nap	lunch + afternoon prayer + nap	lunch + afternoon prayer + nap
Winter	14:00 - 15:00	lunch + afternoon prayer	lunch + afternoon prayer	lunch
Summer	14:00 - 17:00	nap + 'asar prayer	nap + 'asar prayer	nap
Winter	15:00 - 17:00	visit friends and relatives + 'asar prayer	household activities + 'asar prayer	learning how to recite
Summer	17:00 - 19:00	visit friends/relatives + evening prayer	household activities + evening prayer	play + homework for School
Winter	17:00 - 21:00	visit friends and relatives + evening and night prayers + dinner	household activities + evening and night prayers + dinner	play + homework + TV + dinner
Summer	19:00 - 23:00	dinner + night prayer + TV + sleep	dinner + night prayer + TV + sleep	play + homework + TV + dinner + sleep
Winter	19:00 - 22:00	TV + sleep	TV+ sleep	TV+ sleep

TABLE 2: Daily Rhythm

TABLE 2 shows a rhythm of mundane activities in Jhokwala. It represents a typical daily schedule of an adult man, woman, and a child.

Now I present the daily time allocation for various activities specific to different genders and ages. TABLE 3 shows an average time allocation for different activities by men, women, and children. It clearly demonstrates that all of the activities differ according to people's gender and age. There is also a difference of time allocation between married and unmarried people. The unmarried adults, for example, are also engaged in educational activities. I present here only an average time allocation by adult men and women regardless of their marital status. Negligible differences for time allocation in different seasons have been rounded off. For instance, during certain seasons, farmers allocate a greater amount of time to their economic activities like cultivation and harvesting than they do during usual months when they are waiting for the right time to do these activities. This affects the amount of their time allocated for other activities, such as leisure.

Men and women allocate one and eight hours, respectively, for household activities. Children allocate two hours for household activities. Girls spend more time at

Activities	Men		Women		Children	
	Hours	%	Hours	%	Hours	%
Religious activities	1.5	6.25	1.5	6.25	1	4.17
Economic activities	4.5	18.75	1	4.17	0.5	2.08
Household activities	1	4.17	8	33.33	2	8.33
Education	3	12.50	2	8.33	5	20.83
Leisure activities	4	16.67	1	4.17	5	20.83
Self-care activities	9.5	39.58	10	41.67	10.5	43.75
Other	0.5	2.08	0.5	2.08	0	0.00
Total	24	100	24	100	24	100

TABLE 3: Time Allocation of Men, Women, and Children

home than boys do and help their mothers with household activities like cooking. Children do not offer prayers regularly but they learn how to recite the *Qur'an*, which makes their time allocated for religious activities almost equal to that of men and women. Men allocate more time (4.5 hours) for economic activities than women do (one hour). Children's time allocation for economic activities shows that they help their parents in agriculture, shops, and other businesses. For example, if a shopkeeper has to visit some friend or buy something from the city, he asks his son to take care of the shop for that period instead of closing it. Farmers, shopkeepers, laborers, and those doing jobs in offices allocate different amounts of time for various activities depending upon their occupations.

Farmers allocate five hours to their economic activities at various stages of the agricultural cycle from cultivation to harvesting and marketing. Shopkeepers and laborers allocate 9.5 and six hours to their economic activities, respectively. Similarly, farmers have a different time allocation for household activities and leisure than that of other occupational groups because they allocate a lesser amount of time to their economic activities when they are not cultivating or harvesting. All the men, irrespective of their occupations, allocate an approximately equal amount of time for religious and childcare activities. TABLE 4 compares the time allocation of men in different occupations. This table also indicates that an average farmer finds more time for leisure activities than men in other occupations.

WEEKLY RHYTHM

According to most scholars, the historical evidence of practicing a seven-day week dates back to the sixth century BCE, to Jews who adopted the seven-day week framework from Babylonians during the Babylonian Captivity (SENN 1997). This means that Babylonians might have been using a seven-day week earlier than this period. Similarly, according to ancient Sanskrit sources like the Rig Veda, the practice of the seven-day week has a millennia-old history in South Asia. However, the concept of a seven-day week is not universal. For instance, Romans used an eight-day week based on a market week or nundinal cycle adopted from Etruscans, and they also adopted a seven-day week during the first or second century (PINCHES

Activities	Farmers		Doing Office Jobs		Shopkeepers		Laborers	
	Hours	%	Hours	%	Hours	%	Hours	%
Religious activities	1.5	6.25	1.5	6.25	1.5	6.25	1.5	6.25
Economic activities	5	20.83	6	25.00	9.5	39.58	7	29.17
Household activities	1.5	6.25	2	8.33	0.5	2.08	1.5	6.25
Leisure activities	5.5	22.92	4.5	18.75	3	12.50	4.5	18.75
Self-care activities	9.5	39.58	9	37.50	9	37.50	9	37.50
Others	1	4.17	1	4.17	0.5	2.08	0.5	2.08
Total	**24**	**100**	**24**	**100**	**24**	**100**	**24**	**100**

TABLE 4: Men's Daily Time Allocation in Different Occupations

2003). There is also evidence to show the use of a seven-day week in China as early as the fourth century. The Basque people in Spain have a reference to a three-day week in their language (BAUSANI 1982). The Igbos of Nigeria and Javanese in Indonesia still use four-day and five-day weeks, respectively (MANUS 2007). Similarly, there are examples of use of a six-day week in West Africa by some communities such as the Nchumuru (AGORSAH 1983). This implies that the calculation of weekdays and the weekend within the week varies in different cultures and is informed through indigenous knowledge of astronomy, and is influenced by social practices as well as economic modes.

A week consisting of seven days in all three calendars is practiced in Jhokwala. One of the words in Saraiki for welcome is *sat bismillah*. This is an indication that one is happy to meet the other again, or in other words, "you are always welcome!" One of its literal meanings is "seven [times] in the name of Allah." In fact, it means you are welcome on any of the seven days of the week. Therefore, the idea of a seven-day week is very much embedded in local time reckoning. The term used for the week is *haftah* and stands for the week as well as Saturday. It is a Persian word for the numerical *haft* (seven). *Navāṉ* or *nayā haftah* (new week), *pichlā haftah* (last week), *agle hafte* (next week), and *āunde hafte* (coming week) are used to refer to a week. When *haftah* is used for Saturday, it refers to the seventh day. Since Friday has been, and still is, the weekend in the indigenous time reckoning, Saturday has been numbered as the seventh day. There are also specific names for Saturday in both Saraiki and Urdu, which are *chaṉḍ chaṉḍ* and *sanīcar*, respectively. However, *haftah* is also used in everyday communication. The apparent ambiguity of referring to *haftah* as either a week or Saturday can only be understood according to the situation. People usually specify in their conversation to which *haftah* they are referring. For instance, *hafte ālī ḍihīṉvār* or *hafte vāle din* (the day of *haftah* [Saturday]) and *navāṉ haftah* (the new week) are self-explanatory expressions.

The Saraiki and Urdu names of the days of the week are of Sanskrit origin except for *khamīs* or *juma'rāt* (Thursday) and *juma'h* (Friday), which are of Arabic and Persian origin.[6] The names of the rest of the days of the week are in Sanskrit and do not have any association with the Islamic beliefs, as shown in TABLE 5.

These names have religious significance in Hinduism but their continued use in Pakistani society, which is largely Muslim, is now simply a part of a previously

English	Local Terms	Meaning/Association	Origin
Saturday	*chaṇḍ chaṇḍ/sanīcar/haftah**	Saturn	Sanskrit
Sunday	*āḍit/itvār*	Sun	Sanskrit
Monday	*sunvār/somvār/pīr*	Moon	Sanskrit
Tuesday	*maṇgal*	Mars	Sanskrit
Wednesday	*budh/budi*	Mercury	Sanskrit
Thursday	*khamīs/jum'rāt**	Fifth [day]/Friday Night	Arabic/Urdu
Friday	*juma'h*	Friday Prayer	Arabic

Table 5: The Days of the Week (Note: The first local term is in Saraiki while the second one used as an alternate is in Urdu. An asterisk [*] suggests that the designated terms are used equally in both languages.)

shared naming practice that is relegated to cultural memory. Local names for Friday and Thursday signify the religious importance of these days for Muslims. Friday is the day of the communal weekly prayer. Hence, the day is called *juma'h* (literally meaning congregation) after the prayer offered on that day by Muslims. *Juma'h* is an Arabic word that connotes the congregation of worshippers who gather together in a mosque for communal prayer. The significance of *juma'rāt* is primarily because the lunar Thursday starts on the eve of the solar Friday according to the Islamic calendar. Therefore, the solar Thursday enters into lunar Friday. *Jum'rāt* literally means Friday night. For Western observers this concept of Friday night may be somewhat confusing. The names used for Thursday and Friday, *jum'rāt* and *juma'h*, respectively, mark religious identity and show the importance of these days in the religion, such as during death rituals (cf. PHILIP 1921[1911], 30; RAPPAPORT 1999, 169–235). The use of older names in new traditions is common to almost every culture. For instance, the modern English names of the days of the week continue those of the ancient Romans and Greeks (Brown 1989; RICHARDS 1998). *Sunvār* or *somvār* (Monday) is also sometimes symbolized as a sacred day in Jhokwala because many *'urs* (death day) commemorations of saints are celebrated on this day. Hence, it is named *pīr* (saint), as in the expression "*sunvār, pīren dā vār*" (Monday [is] the day of the saints).

In addition to *jum'rāt*, the Saraiki term for Thursday is *khamīs*. *Khamīs* is Arabic for the fifth [day]. This meaning indicates Saturday as the first day of the week, which suggests that Friday is the weekend. However, Sunday is the official weekend in Pakistan now, as mentioned earlier. Some people in Jhokwala believe that Friday should not be celebrated as a holiday and there is no concept of a weekend in Islam. One villager, for example, told me the following:

> There is no weekly holiday according to Islam. The *Qur'an* says close your shops, and buying, and selling when you hear the *azān* calling the *juma'h* [prayer]. Then spread in the earth for earning. (Hayat, 27)

Some people in Jhokwala support the official weekly holiday on Friday. For them, Friday is a sacred day and an important symbol of Islamic identity. Therefore, they believe that the weekly holiday should be on Friday. In fact, the weekend is partially practiced, be it on Sunday or Friday, by farmers. No school in Jhokwala remains open on Sunday, and those working or studying in Lodhran City take Sunday off, though markets in the city are also fully or partially closed on Friday. However, not all people take their day off on Sundays. For instance, the tailor's shop in the village is also closed all day on Friday. Many people, especially some farmers, consider Friday as the day of rest, since this is the day they offer the grand congregational prayer as a major event of a usual week. It is important to clarify here that in the usual cycle of agricultural activities there is no consistent weekly holiday. Farmers work on any day that suits them and carry on their activities as needed. For instance, in harvesting season, they rent a harvesting machine on an hourly basis, so much depends upon the availability of the machine on the days when it is required. Therefore, farmers have to carry on their activities regardless of Fridays and Sundays to complete the task within the period they can use the harvester or any other machinery rented for the period. Their routine is thus scheduled according to other service providers, such as offices, markets, and shops. Similarly, women at home, who also work in the fields, work on all the days of the week.

The local market, Adda Parmat, remains open seven days a week though some shops are closed on Friday. Farmers and shopkeepers, who work on Fridays, take a break during the Friday prayer while others may not work on Friday at all. Many shops close at *juma'h* prayer time but reopen as soon as the prayer finishes. Since the Adda Parmat market is a highway bus stop and traffic runs 24/7, some shops and hotels are open from early morning until late at night. Similarly, this market is at the junction of several villages, so there are several mosques nearby where people may offer *juma'h* prayers at different timings. This means that if shop A closes for *juma'h*, shop B might remain open at that time. I mentioned earlier the ambiguity inherent in the term *haftah*. The ambiguity increases regarding whether *navān haftah* starts from Saturday or Monday. Therefore, no fixed weekend is practiced in rural areas.

Discussion and conclusion

I have discussed the indigenous method of dividing the day into different stages called *pahar*s, once an essential element of agricultural activities in rural Punjab. For better or for worse, they have been replaced by clock time, due to pressure from the cosmopolitan areas to keep time with global economic flows. In the *pahar* system, the day is divided into longer phases in contrast to smaller units like hours and minutes. The use of the clock indicates the scarcity of time in the industrial economy, caused by, and expressed through, technological change (see Ingold 1995; Smith 1982; Thompson 1967). Further, in the *pahar* system the temporal markers are natural phenomena, such as the movement of the sun. Therefore, *pahar*s are automatically adjusted with seasonal variations, without any need to adjust them for daylight saving time, in contrast to clock time that is unable to coordinate with climatic changes (Bastian 2012). Pakistan started practicing, though intermittently, daylight saving time in 2002 for some years in order to regulate its energy needs, but it has been a hotly debated practice since then. The issue is whether the country needs to practice it at all, given the largely rural nature of the national economy (e.g., DAWN 2009). In rural areas, despite following clock time, people did not practice daylight saving time whenever it was announced by the government. The reason for this was because villagers' daily rhythm is maintained through prayer timing and a partial reckoning of *pahar*s. Regulating day timing with prayer timing also points to people's attitudes toward time as well as religion.

Time allocation data shows that men, women, and children allocate different amounts of time for various activities. People perform their activities according to their specifically ascribed roles, depending upon their age, gender, and socio-economic conditions. Men spend most of their time outside of their homes, be it for economic or leisurely reasons. Women take care of their homes, and because of restrictions on movement outside of the home their leisure activities are mainly inside the household's boundaries. However, female time allocation also shows that rural women are involved in economic activities along with household care. The data also show that shopkeepers spend more time on their economic activities. This indicates the nature of activities they perform as part of their occupation. For instance, markets are open until late in the evening and even over the weekend. On the contrary, wage laborers and farmers spend less time on their economic activities than shopkeepers do. Therefore, farmers and wage laborers have more time for leisure activities. However, people from all these occupations spend almost an equal amount of time on religious activities.

The Islamic names for religiously significant days like *juma'rāt* and *juma'h* represent religious identity in a society where Muslims have lived with Hindus, Sikhs, and other religious groups for centuries. Continuity in the use of the names of other days like *mangal* provide a trace of cultural memory echoing a multi-religious past. Muslims offer their great congregational prayer on Friday and it is the most venerated day of the week in Muslim cultures all over the world for religious reasons (BÖWERING 1997; EICKELMAN 1977; EL GUINDI 2008, 130–31; GOITEIN 2007). The weekly holiday has become a matter of debate in some Muslim countries. People argue in opposition to or in favor of celebrating Friday or Sunday as a weekly holiday, taking into account the significance of Friday from a religious perspective and that of Sunday for international business (cf. ARAB NEWS 2007; BRITISH BROADCASTING CORPORATION 2009; BLEY and SAAD 2010; GULF NEWS 2006). The debate is ongoing, with seemingly no resolution in sight. Despite the fact that Sunday is the official weekly holiday in Pakistan, Friday is still an important day of the week because of the grand prayer held on that day. However, the concept of a weekly holiday is partially practiced in villages, mainly because farmers organize their social lives according to the seasonal cycles that regulate agricultural activities.

The effects of globalization and urbanization in rural Pakistan can be observed through shifts in the market economy, nuclear household units, modern education, and the availability of more pervasive communication, like mass media and the Internet. However, certain norms and values are still a vital part of rural social organization, and they highlight people's resistance to some aspects of social change. As I have shown, there are some aspects of the social organization of time that seem to have resisted transformation, such as the centrality of prayer timings in the categorization of day phases. Moreover, Friday still remains a quintessential day of the week. These two aspects of culture are indicative of a cultural response toward social change in Jhokwala. In order to understand how rural people adapt to social change, therefore, the study and analysis of daily and weekly rhythms can provide us with keen insights into what is changing and what is not in the local lives of rural villagers. For instance, the aspects of time that are essentially religious in nature seem to continue, but even they are being transformed gradually for utilitarian purposes, although their underlying religious or moral reasoning still appears to be the same. Similarly, cultural memories and the continuity of centuries-old traditions as expressed in indigenous cultural models of time highlight religious and ethnic co-existence in rural Pakistan. On the contrary, transformations in what is called the "secular" or economic domains of society are also occurring. Jhokwala is no exception, for similar situations exist in most Pakistani villages, albeit at different rates of social change with different intensities, depending upon the local context of rural economy and demography. Villages that are close to cities or have good access to roads and transportation, as Jhokwala does, have experienced industrialization and urbanization at a considerably higher pace, bringing about more rapid sociocultural and economic transformations.

The centrality and continuity of religious aspects of the social organization of time must not be confused with Islamization or religious fundamentalism, however. Since there are so many diverse opinions on what Islamization is and means, we need to be cautious in using this term in the context of my research on time calculation. In a country with diverse cultural traditions (e.g., peasantry, tribalism, urbanism), diverse ethnicities, and, most importantly, multiple schools of thought or sects, the extent and strength of Islamization varies across Pakistan. In some parts, for example the tribal areas of Pakistan, specific geopolitical conditions have played a decisive role in shaping the response toward urbanization and "modernity."[7] In two neighboring countries, Iran and Afghanistan, Islamization took place after the religious revolution in 1979 and under the impact of the Taliban in the 1990s, respectively. However, as opposed to the condition of "post-Islamization," where the relationship between religion and the state has been contested after the experiences of Islamization, such as in Iran (BAYAT 1996, 2005), rural Pakistanis have not been as deeply influenced by national policies of Islamization, such as those carried out during the 1980s. As KURIN (1985) concluded in his study of the peasantry, rural Pakistanis consider the nation as a state that was formed to uplift the political control and economic conditions of the Muslims of South Asia. He noted that while rural Pakistanis assert their Islamic identity, when required, in the context of India-Pakistan relations, U.S. policies, Israel, and Pakistan's nuclear technology, they also define themselves as Islamic by being "part of a larger human community that is indeed moral" (KURIN 1985, 862). The resistance in rural Pakistan to certain aspects of "cultural globalization" (MAZZARELLA 2004) or urbanization, I argue, should be analyzed by taking into account the people's worldview and local socioeconomic realities. Studying the temporal and spatial aspects of a community's worldview, as I have done, is one way to begin understanding the degrees of sociocultural change that impact rural communities in Pakistan and elsewhere in South Asia.

ACKNOWLEDGMENTS

This paper is based on my doctoral research at the University of Durham. I am thankful to my supervisors, Dr Stephen M. Lyon and Dr Iain R. Edgar, for their guidance and support during this project. I am indebted to the support of the people of Jhokwala and the District Agriculture Department, Lodhran during the fieldwork. I also thank the anonymous reviewers for their comments. The editors of the journal also assisted generously in the final preparation of the manuscript. The University of Durham supported the research (Durham Doctoral Fellowship), as did the Royal Anthropological Institute (Sutasoma Award), and the Charles Wallace Pakistan Trust, UK (Doctoral Bursary).

NOTES

1. Since time and space are two interrelated concepts, reference to one automatically implicates the other. There is a great deal of anthropological literature to support the idea that both play important roles in social organization (MUGHAL 2014a).

2. Both groups share most of the local terminologies regarding time. In this paper, I will use the terminologies from both languages, if separate terminologies are used in either of those languages spoken in the area. Subsequently, only the Saraiki terminology has been used for the concept for the sake of simplicity. Most local terminologies for different stages of the day are Saraiki, as these were collected only from Saraiki-speaking people, but are mutually intelligible in both the languages. If two alternative terms are given in the text, the first one is Saraiki. Some terminologies are of Arabic and Persian origin but their spelling and transliteration is given as colloquial in Pakistani languages.

3. No differentiation is made between stars and planets in local terminology and a single term *tāre*, is used for both.

4. Some names are pseudonyms to protect the identities of local residents who wish not to be named.

5. Although it is a place where men meet and gossip, enjoy smoking a pipe, and other leisure activities, it is also used for various other purposes. For instance, depending upon circumstances, it is also used a place where local disputes are settled (LYON 2004).

6. The spellings of Arabic and Persian terminologies are not standard but are closer to the colloquial use in Pakistan.

7. Different definitions and expressions of modernity exist in various academic and political discourses. A reference to any particular form of modernity is not intended here. Instead, I intend here to refer to all those expressions of "modernity" that are presumed to be opposites of so-called traditional norms and values, religious extremism, and traditional gender roles.

REFERENCES

ADAM, Barbara
    1994   Perceptions of time. In *Companion Encyclopedia of Anthropology*, ed. Tim INGOLD, 503–26. London: Routledge.

AGORSAH, Kofi E.
    1983   Archaeology and resistance history in the Caribbean. *The African Archaeological Review* 11: 175–96.

ALI, Mina Zulfikar
    2003   Agrarian Society in Transition: Modernization, Development and Change A Case Study of the Potwar. PhD dissertation, Quaid-i-Azam University.

ARAB NEWS
2007   Kuwait adopts Friday-Saturday weekend. *ARAB NEWS*, 28 May. http://www
        .arabnews.com/node/298933 (accessed 14 October 2015).

BAILEY, G. N.
1983   Concepts of time in quaternary prehistory. *Annual Review of Anthropology*
        12: 165–92. doi: 10.1146/annurev.an.12.100183.001121

BARNES, Robert H.
1974   *Kédang: A Study of the Collective Thought of an Eastern Indonesian People.*
        Oxford: Clarendon Press.

BARTH, Fredrik
1967   On the study of change. *American Anthropologist* 69: 661–69. doi: 10.1525
        /aa.1967.69.6.02a00020

BASTIAN, Michelle
2012   Fatally confused: Telling the time in the midst of ecological crises. *Journal
        of Environmental Philosophy* 9: 23–48. doi: 10.5840/envirophil2012913

BAUSANI, Alessandro
1982   The prehistoric Basque week of three days: Archaeoastronomical notes. *The
        Bulletin of the Center for Archaeoastronomy* 2: 16–22.

BAYAT, Asef
1996   The coming of a post-Islamist society. *Critique: Critical Middle Eastern
        Studies* 5: 43–52. doi: 10.1080/10669929608720091
2005   What is post-Islamism? *IsIM Review* 16: 5.

BRITISH BROADCASTING CORPORATION
2009   Algeria switches weekend, again. *BBC News*, 14 August. http://news.bbc
        .co.uk/2/hi/africa/8198365.stm (accessed 14 October 2015).

BIRTH, Kevin K.
1996   Trinidadian times: Temporal dependency and temporal flexibility on the
        margins of industrial capitalism. *Anthropological Quarterly* 69: 79–89. doi:
        10.2307/3318035

BLEY, Jorg, and Mohsen SAAD
2010   Cross-cultural differences in seasonality. *International Review of Financial
        Analysis* 19: 306–12. doi: 10.1016/j.irfa.2010.08.004

BOURDIEU, Pierre
1977   *Outline of a Theory of Practice.* Cambridge: Cambridge University Press.
        doi: 10.1017/CBO9780511812507

BÖWERING, G.
1997   The concept of time in Islam. *Proceedings of the American Philosophical
        Society* 141: 55–66.

Brown, Cecil H.
1989   Naming the days of the week: A cross-language study of lexical accultura-
        tion. *Current Anthropology* 30: 536–50. doi: 10.1086/203782

BURMAN, Rickie
1981   Time and socioeconomic change on Simbo, Solomon Islands. *Man* 16: 251–
        67. doi: 10.2307/2801398

COOPER, Eugene
1984   Mode of production and anthropology of work. *Journal of Anthropological
        Research* 40: 257–70. doi: 10.1086/jar.40.2.3629575

DAWN
2009   Daylight saving: Are we really saving anything? *Dawn*, 26 April. http://www.dawn.com/news/884605/daylight-saving-are-we-really-saving-anything (accessed 14 October 2015).

DEEB, Lara, and Mona HARB
2013   *Leisurely Islam: Negotiating Geography and Morality in Shi'ite South Beirut.* Princeton: Princeton University Press. doi: 10.1515/9781400848560

DURKHEIM, Emile
1915   *The Elementary Forms of the Religious Life.* London: George Allen & Unwin Ltd. First published 1912.

EICKELMAN, Dale
1977   Time in a complex society: A Moroccan example. *Ethnology* 16: 39–55. doi: 10.2307/3773102

EL GUINDI, Fadwa
2008   *By Noon Prayer: The Rhythm of Islam.* Oxford: Berg. doi: 10.5040/9781474214537

EMBER, Carol R.
1983   The relative decline in women's contribution to agriculture with intensification. *American Anthropologist* 85: 285–304. doi: 10.1525/aa.1983.85.2.02a00020

ERRINGTON, Frederick
1974   Indigenous ideas of order, time, and transition in a New Guinea cargo movement. *American Ethnologist* 1: 255–67. doi: 10.1525/ae.1974.1.2.02a00030

ESPOSITO, John L.
1998   *Islam and Politics.* New York: Syracuse University Press.

EVANS-PRITCHARD, E. E.
1940   *The Neur: A Description of the Modes of Livelihood and Political Institutions of a Nilotic People.* New York: Oxford University Press.

EVERS, Hans-Dieter
1972   *Monks, Priests and Peasants: A Study of Buddhism and Social Structure in Central Ceylon.* Leiden: E. J. Brill. doi: 10.1017/S0026749X00013111

FABIAN, Johannes
1983   *Time and the Other: How Anthropology Makes its Object.* New York: Columbia University Press.

FORTE, Maximilian C.
1998   Globalization and world-systems analysis: Toward new paradigms of a geo-historical social anthropology (A research review). *Review* 21: 29–99.

FRIEDMAN, Jonathan
1985   Our time, their time, world time: The transformation of temporal modes. *Ethnos* 50: 168–83. doi: 10.1080/00141844.1985.9981301

GABRIELSSON, Alf
1986   Rhythm in music. In *Rhythm in Psychological, Linguistic and Musical Processes*, J. Evans and M. Clynes, eds., 131–67. Springfield: Charles C Thomas Publishers.

GARDEZI, Hassan N., and Soofia MUMTAZ
2004   Globalisation and Pakistan's dilemma of development [with comments]. *The Pakistan Development Review* 43: 423–40.

GEERTZ, Clifford
1966   *The Interpretation of Cultures*. New York: Basic Books, Inc., Publishers.
GELL, Alfred
1996   *The Anthropology of Time: Cultural Constructions of Temporal Maps and Images*. Oxford: Berg Publishers.
2000   Time and social anthropology. In *Time in Contemporary Intellectual Thought*, ed. P. Baert, 251–68. Amsterdam: Elsevier. doi: 10.1016/s1387-6783(00)80016-1
GIDDENS, Anthony
1986   *The Constitution of Society: Outline of the Theory of Structuration*. Berkeley: University of California Press.
GILSENAN, Michael
1996   *Lords of the Lebanese Marches: Violence and Narrative in an Arab Society*. Berkeley: University of California Press.
GINGRICH, Andre, Elinor OCHS, and Alan SWEDLUND
2002   Repertoires of timekeeping in anthropology. *Current Anthropology* 43(Supplement): S3–S4. doi: 10.1086/339564
GLUCKMAN, Max
1977   *Politics, Law and Ritual in Tribal Society*. Oxford: Basil Blackwell.
GOITEIN, S. D.
2007   The origin and nature of Muslim Friday worship. *The Muslim World* 49: 183–95. doi: 10.1111/j.1478-1913.1959.tb02369.x (originally published 1959).
GOODY, Jack
1968   Time: Social organization. In *International Encyclopedia of the Social Sciences*, ed. D. L. Sills, 30–42, vol. 16. New York: Macmillan.
Government of Pakistan
2000   *District Census Report of Lodhran 1998*. Islamabad: Population Census Organization, Statistics Division, Government of Pakistan.
GROSS, Daniel R.
1984   Time allocation: A tool for the study of cultural behavior. *Annual Review of Anthropology* 13: 519–58. doi: 10.1146/annurev.an.13.100184.002511
GULF NEWS
2006   Friday-Saturday weekend in UAE from September. *GULF NEWS*, 17 May. http://gulfnews.com/news/gulf/uae/general/friday-saturday-weekend-in-uae-from-september-1.237326 (accessed 14 October 2015).
HAIDER, S. M.
1981   *Social Change and Development in Pakistan*. Lahore: Progressive Publishers.
HARVEY, David
1990   Between space and time: Reflections on the geographic imagination. *Annals of the Association of American Geographers* 80: 418–34. doi: 10.1111/j.1467-8306.1990.tb00305.x
HASAN, Arif
2009   *The Unplanned Revolution: Observations on the Processes of Socio-Economic Change in Pakistan*. Karachi: Oxford University Press.
HERZFELD, Michael
1990   Pride and perjury: Time and the oath in the mountain villages of Crete. *Man* 25: 305–22. doi: 10.2307/2804566

INDA, Jonathan Xavier, and Renato ROSALDO
2008   *The Anthropology of Globalization: A Reader*. London: Blackwell Publishing Ltd.

INGOLD, Tim
1995   Work, time and industry. *Time & Society* 4: 5–28. doi: 10.1177/0961463x95004001001

JACKSON, Anthony
1987   *Anthropology at Home*. New York: Tavistock Publications.

JOHNSON, Allen
1996   Time allocation. In *Encyclopedia of Cultural Anthropology*, D. Levinson and M. EMBER, eds., 1313–16, vol. 4. New York: Henry Holt and Company.

KEMPER, Steven
1980   Time, person, and gender in Sinhalese astrology. *American Ethnologist* 7: 744–58. doi: 10.1525/ae.1980.7.4.02a00090

KURIN, Richard
1985   Islamization in Pakistan: A view from the countryside. *Asian Survey* 25: 852–62. doi: 10.2307/2644114

LEACH, Edmund R.
1961   *Rethinking Anthropology*. London: The Athlone Press.

LOW, Setha M., and Denise LAWRENCE-ZÚÑIGA, eds.
2003   *The Anthropology of Space and Place: Locating Culture*. Malden, MA: Blackwell.

LYON, Stephen M.
2004   *An Anthropological Analysis of Local Politics and Patronage in a Pakistani Village*. Lampeter: Edwin Mellen Press.

MANUS, Ukachukwu Chris
2007   The sacred festival of Iri Ji Ohuru in Igboland, Nigeria. *Nordic Journal of African Studies* 16: 224–60.

MAZZARELLA, William
2004   Culture, globalization, mediation. *Annual Review of Anthropology* 33: 345–67. doi: 10.1146/annurev.anthro.33.070203.143809

MUGHAL, Muhammad A. Z.
2014a   Time, Space and Social Change in Rural Pakistan: An Ethnographic Study of Jhokwala Village, Lodhran District. PhD dissertation, Durham University.
2014b   Calendars tell history: Social rhythm and social change in rural Pakistan. *History and Anthropology* 25: 592–613. doi: 10.1080/02757206.2014.930034
2014c   The play of time in sports. *Recreation and Society in Africa, Asia and Latin America* 5: 1–4. https://journal.lib.uoguelph.ca/index.php/rasaala/article/view/3157/3368 (accessed 14 October 2015).
2015a   Domestic space and socio-spatial relationships in rural Pakistan. *South Asia Research* 35: 214–34. doi: 10.1177/0262728015581287
2015b   Being and becoming native: A methodological enquiry into doing anthropology at home. *Anthropological Notebooks* 21: 121–32.

MUNN, Nancy D.
1992   The cultural anthropology of time: A critical essay. *Annual Reviews in Anthropology* 21: 93–123. doi: 10.1146/annurev.an.21.100192.000521

MUSHARBASH, Yasmine
  2007   Boredom, time, and modernity: An example from aboriginal Australia. *American Anthropologist* 109: 307–17. doi: 10.1525/aa.2007.109.2.307

NONINI, Donald M.
  2013   The local-food movement and the anthropology of global systems. *American Ethnologist* 40: 267–75. doi: 10.1111/amet.12019

OHNUKI-TIERNEY, Emiko
  1969   Concepts of time among the Ainu of the northwest coast of Sakhalin. *American Anthropologist* 71: 488–92. doi: 10.1525/aa.1969.71.3.02a00090

PEIRANO, Mariza G. S.
  1998   When anthropology is at home: The different contexts of a single discipline. *Annual Review of Anthropology* 27: 105–28. doi: 10.1146/annurev.anthro.27.1.105

PHILIP, Alexander
  1921   *The Calendar: Its History, Structure and Improvement.* Cambridge: Cambridge University Press. First published 1911.

PINCHES, T. G.
  2003   Sabbath (Babylonian). In *Encyclopedia of Religion and Ethics*, J. Hastings and J. A. Selbie, eds., 889–91, vol. 20. Whitefish, MT: Kessinger Publishing.

QADEER, Mohammad Abdul
  2006   *Pakistan: Social and Cultural Transformations in a Muslim Nation.* New York: Routledge. doi: 10.4324/9780203099681

RAMBLE, Charles
  2002   Temporal disjunction and collectivity in Mustang, Nepal. *Current Anthropology* 43 (Supplement): S75–S84. doi: 10.1086/341106

RANKIN, Katharine N.
  2003   Anthropologies and geographies of globalization. *Progress in Human Geography* 27: 708–34. doi: 10.1191/0309132503ph457oa

RAPPAPORT, Roy A.
  1999   *Ritual and Religion in the Making of Humanity.* Cambridge: Cambridge University Press.

RICHARDS, E. G.
  1998   *Mapping Time: The Calendar and its History.* Oxford: Oxford University Press.

ROBERTS, Allen F.
  1982   Comets importing change of times and states: Ephemerae and process among the Tabwa of Zaire. *American Ethnologist* 9: 712–29. doi: 10.1525/ae.1982.9.4.02a00060

SAHLINS, Marshall
  1972   *Stone Age Economics.* London: Tavistock.

SCHIEFFELIN, Bambi B.
  2002   Marking time: The dichotomizing discourse of multiple temporalities. *Current Anthropology* 43(Supplement): S5–S18. doi: 10.1086/341107

SENN, Frank C.
  1997   *Christian Liturgy: Catholic and Evangelical.* Minneapolis, MN: Fortress Press.

SMART, Alan, and Josephine SMART
  2003   Urbanization and the global perspective. *Annual Review of Anthropology*
         32: 263–85. doi: 10.1146/annurev.anthro.32.061002.093445

SMITH, Michael French
  1982   Bloody time and bloody scarcity: Capitalism, authority, and the transfor-
         mation of temporal experience in a Papua New Guinea village. *American
         Ethnologist* 9: 503–18. doi: 10.1525/ae.1982.9.3.02a00040

SULTANA, Nargis, Hina NAZLI, and Sohail J. MALIK
  1994   Determinants of female time allocation in selected districts of rural Paki-
         stan. *The Pakistan Development Review* 33: 1141–53.

THOMPSON, E. P.
  1967   Time, work-discipline, and industrial capitalism. *Past and Present* 38: 56–97.
         doi: 10.1093/past/38.1.56

WEISS, Anita M., and Muhammad A. Z. MUGHAL
  2012   Pakistan. In *The Berkshire Encyclopedia of Sustainability*, Louis Kotzé and
         Stephen Morse, eds., 236–40, vol. 9. Great Barrington, MA: Berkshire
         Publishing.

WELTFISH, Gene
  1979   The anthropology of work. In *Toward a Marxist Anthropology: Problems
         and Perspectives*, ed. S. Diamond, 215–56. New York: Mouton Publishers.

YOU, Haili
  1994   Defining rhythm: Aspects of an anthropology of rhythm. *Culture, Medicine
         and Psychiatry* 18: 361–84. doi: 10.1007/BF01379231

ZOOMERS, Annelies
  2010   Globalisation and the foreignisation of space: Seven processes driving
         the current global land grab. *Journal of Peasant Studies* 37: 429–47. doi:
         10.1080/03066151003595325

Mu Li
Southeast University, Nanjing, China

Performing Chineseness
The Lion Dance in Newfoundland

This article attempts to explore how individuals of Chinese descent maintain, negotiate, and re-create their multiple and often competing ethnicity of being "Chinese" through the Chinese lion dance as a cultural performance in the multicultural context of Newfoundland, Canada. My findings suggest that individuals of Chinese descent in Newfoundland, due to their regional, generational, and other categorical differences, perceive of the role of lion dance as a cultural marker in various ways, so that the cultural performance often serves as an open and multivocal forum for the discussion of ethnicity. During this intensive negotiation, a new diasporic identity and culture emerge.

KEYWORDS: lion dance—cultural performance—Chinese diaspora—ethnicity

Asian Ethnology Volume 76, Number 2 · 2017, 289–317
© Nanzan University Anthropological Institute

THE LION DANCE is a popular Chinese drama-like folk dance that often involves two players, one positioned in front as the lion's head and the other in the back as its body. Wearing a stylized lion-like costume, two performers move like a lion by following rhythmic music with a changeable melody to the accompaniment of some Chinese instruments, such as a drum, gongs, and cymbals. Overseas, the lion dance is brought along by Chinese immigrants to their new settlements, where the tradition is kept, performed, reshaped, or even rejected.

Newfoundland and Labrador, the easternmost province of Canada, is one of those places where lion dancing occurs at the juncture of the social and the performative. With less than 2000 members, the Chinese community of Newfoundland and Labrador represents the province's largest non-aboriginal visible minority[1] (LI 2014). The Chinese have had a commercial presence since 1895, but their cultural impact has been less visible. According to the findings of my fieldwork (2009–2015), the local lion dance is a key aspect of Chinese Newfoundlanders' multiple and often competing constructions of identity.

This article is an ethnographic examination of Chinese lion dancing, which illustrates cultural processes of retention, adaptation, and invention within Newfoundland's Chinese community. In this article, I explore how the performative practices of lion dancers and the perceptions of audience members of Chinese descent conceptualize the ideas of historical authenticity (recovering the details of the original/traditional performance of specific historical periods) and personal authenticity (presenting performers' own internal feelings and understanding when performing), and reflect their various and sometimes competing understandings of their cultural identities, which are emergent in the various sociocultural occasions when the lion dance is performed. In particular, I adopt Andriy Nahachewsky's concept of "New Ethnicity," which refers to "later generational persons and groups who consciously choose to claim this ethnicity and both privately and publicly incorporate ethnically defined cultural practices" (NAHACHEWSKY 2002, 177), to look at generational differences in understanding how the lion dance shapes later generations' various senses of Chineseness.

In Newfoundland, Chinese diasporic identity and culture are constructed, presented, negotiated, and renegotiated through multiple folkloric practices, such as lion dancing, in various sociocultural circumstances and through the multivocal interpretations of individual participants. In many ways, the lion dance serves as an open forum for individuals of Chinese descent to strengthen or challenge their preset esoterically and/or exoterically defined notion of being Chinese and the "authentic" Chinese culture, and to develop their own version of Chineseness. Due to its role as a base for negotiating and (re)constructing identities of individuals of Chinese descent, the lion dance, even if it is sometimes not accepted as a cultural marker by some individuals, becomes an inseparable part of individual perceptions of diasporic Chineseness in Newfoundland. In this sense, Newfoundland's Chinese community is woven together through various webs through which individuals relate themselves to the lion dancing, which is neither simply remote (Chinese) nor vernacular (Canadian), but a new form of cultural performance both in between and beyond. The Newfoundland case echoes Juwen Zhang's observation of the emergent and creolized Chinese diasporic identity and culture, which cannot be seen "as a simple combination of the group's home country culture and so-called American culture," but develops "its own tradition and cultural traits, which, in turn, are expressed through new markers to reinforce the group's new identity" (ZHANG 2015, 468).

LION DANCE AND CHINESE DIASPORIC IDENTITY

The lion dance is frequently the most explicit and important marker of Chinese culture in overseas (southern) Chinese communities (FELTHAM 2009). Because of its close association with Chinese festivals and other sociocultural events, it has not often been an independent research focus. For example, an early discussion of Chinese lion dance appears in William HOY's (1948) article on native festivals of the California Chinese, in which the lion dance is considered as "an integral part of the New Year's festivities." It has only been since the 1980s that researchers began to consider this traditional performance more seriously.

Some researchers have explored the history of the lion dance and traced its origin to either the Han Dynasty (206 BCE–220 CE) (LIU 1981) or Tang Dynasty (618–907 CE) (MATUSKY and TAN 2004) through the Silk Road from Middle Eastern countries such as Sasanian Persia (FELTHAM 2007, 2010). In addition to its history, Wan-Yu LIU (1981) and William C. HU (1995) attempt to probe other technical and cultural aspects of the lion dance overseas as it is performed in China, such as the differences between the northern and southern styles, costumes, moving steps, and performing skills.

In terms of the transnational transmission of the lion dance, some scholars look at lion dances performed in new societies where Chinese immigrants settled as a direct cultural transplantation without significant changes, especially the performances in Chinese enclaves in Southeast Asia and in major North American cities (LIU 1981; HOE 1984). The intact transmission of performance indicates a strong cultural attachment of Chinese immigrants to their homeland. Therefore, in some countries (for example, Malaysia and Indonesia), when pro-assimilationist policies were predominant, lion dance, symbolizing "the protection of Chinese culture and identity," was thought to be a cultural threat to the national identity (TAN 2007, 66). The cultural importance of the lion dance also explains why, when bans against Chinese culture were removed, "the lion dance in particular was selected for revival" (TAN 2007, 66).

Other researchers highlight distinctive vernacular elements that are added to the traditional lion dance when it is performed in overseas Chinese communities. For example, based on her studies on lion dancing in New York City, Madeline Anita Slovenz-Low argues that the lion dance is a "truly popular contemporary Cantonese American performance expression that is practiced by Chinese immigrants and fully acculturated American-born Chinese" instead of "an exotic remnant from China's feudalistic past" (SLOVENZ-LOW 1994, xiii).

Innovations and changes in the traditional Chinese lion dance in overseas Chinese communities are visible in trans-generational transmission processes. In some communities, the lion dance has been widely used as an effective approach to educate younger, mostly local-born people of Chinese descent about Chinese traditions and provide them an opportunity to experience Chinese culture in a multicultural setting (JOHNSON 2005). In a culturally diverse society, second- or later-generation Chinese dancers have various motivations. Writing of her lion dance workshops in Dallas, Texas, Mei-Hsiu Chan feels that her students are less motivated to learn the lion dance than using digital media (CHAN 2001). Even though they are interested in the dance, Feltham also finds that, "Many younger students are more concerned with the sports/martial arts aspects of lion dancing, than with cultural modes and traditional meanings" (FELTHAM 2009, 128). Therefore, Henry Johnson reminds us "how host country context can help shape cultural identity, especially a rediscovery of homeland culture" (JOHNSON 2005, 185).

The lion dance as a cultural marker of Chinese ethnicity reflects the idea of "cultural performance," coined by Milton Singer. As Singer writes, cultural performances are "taken as the most concrete observable units of the cultural structure" of outsiders and cultural insiders (SINGER 1959, xiii). Richard Bauman further explains that cultural performances "are cultural forms about culture, social forms about society, in which the central meanings and values of a group are embodied, acted out, and laid open to examination and interpretation in symbolic form, both by members of that group and by the ethnographer" (BAUMAN 1986, 133).

In addition, Victor Turner explores the reflective and reflexive aspects of cultural performances and looks at how cultural meanings are created and transmitted. As reflective, Turner argues that all senses, including vision, taste, smell, and touch, are employed in cultural performances to communicate the content of culture (TURNER 1981, 158). Turner explains reflexivity as what "a sociocultural group turns, bends, reflects back on itself upon the relations, actions, symbols, meanings, codes, roles, statuses, social structures, ethical and legal rules, and other components that make up their public selves"; therefore, cultural performances function reflexively as "active agencies of change, representing the eye by which culture sees itself and the drawing board on which creative actors sketch out what they believe to be more apt or interesting "designs for living" (TURNER 1988, 24).

Turner's theory of reflexivity indicates that cultural performances are capable of embracing changes, new creations, and even conflicting perceptions of cultural meanings. Building on Turner's insights as well as other scholars' ideas in the same vein (CONQUERGOOD 1989; GUSS 2000; HOLLING and CALAFELL 2007), this article explores how lion dancing participants (both dancers and audience) in Newfoundland present their multiple viewpoints of being Chinese through performances and interpretations.

HISTORICAL AUTHENTICITY: CULTURAL ROOTS AND EARLY LION DANCERS

The Pearl River Delta in China's Canton Province was the hometown of a majority of early Chinese settlers in Newfoundland.[2] It is also the birthplace of southern Chinese martial arts and the Cantonese lion dance.[3] Outside of Canton, the lion dance, as a traditional and ceremonial folk dance, is also popular in Hong Kong and some overseas communities with a large Cantonese population. Feltham notes that lion dance is "at the heart of the traditional Cantonese speaking villages of Southern China" (FELTHAM 2009, 117). Feltham's observation is strongly supported by my interviewees. Kim Hong, who came to Newfoundland in 1950 from Toisan, Canton, observed the admiration of lion dancing in southern China before his arrival in Canada:

> Many Chinese who immigrated here [Newfoundland] were from the southern part of China, and they came from small towns or villages, where the lion dance was a popular event all year round. There were lessons given in those villages to teach people the lion dance and kung fu. (Kim Hong, personal interview, 18 April 2011)

Chan Chau Tam, a Hong Kong immigrant who arrived in Newfoundland in 1972, and Joseph Mo, a Cantonese newcomer who came in 2007, also report the popularity of lion dancing in the same region od southern China (Chan Chau Tam, personal interview, 26 February 2012; Joseph Mo, personal interview, 8 July 2013).

After the foundation of the Chinese Association of Newfoundland and Labrador (CANL) in 1976, the southern lion dance was immediately introduced to the community upon the request of many Cantonese-speaking members (Kim Hong, personal interview, 18 April 2011). The first lion puppet and corresponding musical instruments were bought in Hong Kong. The drum, gong, and cymbals currently used in lion dancing are still the same set of instruments bought in the 1970s. The whole set of equipment arrived in Newfoundland in May 1977 and it was first displayed in public at the post-Flower Service garden party in August of the same year (FIGURES 1 and 2).[4]

The first lion costume in Newfoundland was a rainbow lion with a variety of colors (FIGURE 3). Many scholars associate the color difference of lion costumes with the warriors in a popular Chinese historical novel named *The Romance of the Three Kingdoms*, which was first printed in the sixteenth century (CHAN 2001; HOE 1984; MATUSKY and TAN 2004; SLOVENZ-LOW 1994). For instance, MATUSKY and TAN explain the symbolism of the costumes as follows:

FIGURE 1: Lion Puppet at the 1977 CANL Garden Party at the Beaconsfield High School's gym (Kim Hong holding megaphone). Courtesy of Kim Hong.

FIGURE 2: Instruments at the 1977 CANL Garden Party at the Beaconsfield High School's play ground (Ming Hong—Drum, Yin Hai Gin—Gong, Jim Mah—Cymbals). Courtesy of Kim Hong.

A head colored yellow and black with a white beard depicts Liu Bei, who is remembered as a kind and generous person, while a head colored red and black with a black beard depicts Guan Ti who is known for his honesty. The black and white lion head with a black beard is associated with Zhang Fei, a general who is famous because of his braveness, and a multi-colored lion head with a white beard is associated with Zhao Zi Lung, famous for his cleverness and wisdom. (MATUSKY and TAN 2004, 152–53)

It seems that the first lion puppet in Newfoundland represents the image of Zhao Zi Lung. To decode the symbolism of the rainbow costume, I also consulted a Toronto lion dancing master, Lat Yip, who challenged the above system and

FIGURE 3: The CANL's rainbow lion. Courtesy of Kim Hong.

considered the connections between historical characters and the colors of lion costumes as flexible and sometimes arbitrary (Lat Yip, personal interview, 20 September 2012). In my fieldwork, I realized that many lion dancers have little knowledge of the symbolism of the lions.

The basic frame of the lion's head was made of bamboo and the surface was made of materials like cloth, satin, and paper-mache. The lion's head was round-shaped with a big mouth and big eyes. In terms of the shape, traditionally there are two major types of mask in Cantonese lions: Buddha mountain style and crane mountain style. The Buddha mountain style features "its round-shaped head, big mouth, big eyes and pointed horn root"; the crane mountain style is characterized by "its oval-shaped head, small mouth, long eyes and fat-rounded horn root" (LIU 1981, 61). My observations indicate that Newfoundland's lion masks can be categorized as the Buddha mountain style. The lion's body looked like a satin cloak with the same patterned design as the head in color and texture. In addition to the lion puppet, a mask of a teaser was also purchased, which is a human character with a big Buddha head, used in lion dancing to "play" with the lion.[5] The mask was an oversized roundish paper-mache head that was able to completely cover the dancer's head. It was designed as a smiley obese face with a big nose, large black eyes, and blue hair (FIGURE 4).

The introduction of the lion dance is intended to "show people, especially those who were born and raised here, what Chinese culture is about" (Kim Hong, personal interview, 18 April 2011). The availability of costumes and accompanying musical instruments called for experienced dancers and musicians to perform. In the 1970s, dancers were mostly involved in the restaurant business, such as David Chiu and Chung Lem, with a few exceptions such as Daniel Wong (engineer) and Jim Mah (student). Some of these dancers were entrenched in Cantonese tradition and had opportunities to become familiar with the cultural meanings of the lion dance. For example, Daniel Wong is the fifth-generation direct disciple of Wong Fei Hung, the most famous grand master of Chinese kung fu. Chung Lem learned

FIGURE 4: The Big Head Buddha (left). Courtesy of Kim Hong.

his kung fu in Hong Kong in his earlier years. However, other performers who were not professionally trained, such as Chan Chau Tam, had limited knowledge of the performance.

Daniel Wong says, the lion dance in Canton is not only a set of choreographic movements, but it is also a form of art, highlighting some basic principles in relation to the traditional Cantonese society (Daniel Wong, personal interview, 29 August 2013). Joseph Mo agrees:

> I learned that things like respect, intelligence, and loyalty to your village and neighborhood are the core of lion dance....It tells us the boundaries between "us" and "others," it requires people to follow social order, and it encourages us to improve ourselves. That is the culture of lion dancing in my hometown. (Joseph Mo, personal interview, 8 July 2013)

Lion dancing is also a form of storytelling because all the movements are based on the story of a lion's daily life:

> At first, the lion in the story wakes up but it does not just jump up. Just like human beings, it opens its eyes slowly, yawns, rubs its eyes, and touches its hair and ears....After the lion gets up, it starts to get ready to go out of its cave for food. But it is always cautious, so it checks if any traps or other kinds of dangers are around its cave. When it feels safe, it begins to seek food. On its way, it might pass bridges or go through some other challenging places so it has to figure out how to overcome those difficulties. When it sees food, again, it has to find out if there are any traps or dangers, so it checks carefully to make sure that everything is okay. Then it starts to eat its food. When it finishes, it might burp and touch its belly. Then, it might feel tired and go back to sleep again. In some cases, there is a teaser or Buddha involved in the dance. The story is that the food is owned by a person [mostly a Buddha] but is stolen by the lion. Therefore, the Buddha has to chase the lion to get his food back. When he finds that the food has been eaten up by the lion, he sets various difficult tasks as revenge. As you

can see, the whole dance is a terrific story. (Daniel Wong, personal interview, 29 August 2013)

During the dance, movements are all guided by the music, which is provided by three percussion instruments: a drum, cymbals, and gongs. Among them, Daniel Wong looks at "drumming" as "the spirit of the dance" (ibid.). In my interview with Wong, he used his desk as a mock drum to explain the drum beats:

> In the lion dance, there is only one drum. All parts of the drum—the drumhead, the edges of the drum, and even the drumsticks—are used to make melodic and tonal changes. We have some basic beats in lion dancing. They are three-star beat, five-star beat, and seven-star beat[6]....The three-star beat is basically two beats, but the first beat is divided evenly into two shorter beats. The five-star beat is three beats, but the first two beats are divided evenly into four shorter beats, and the seven-star beat is four beats, but the first three beats are all divided evenly into six shorter beats. (ibid.)

Wong continues:

> To match these beats, there are three basic steps called three-star step, five-star step, and seven-star step. Three-star steps are used when the lion is checking stuff, waking up, and doing things around the original spot it stands. Seven-star steps are used when the lion is doing a long walk. Five-star steps are the most commonly used in lion dancing, and they are used in all other occasions. Of course, there are more variations other than these three steps, but all other steps are based on these three basics. (ibid.)

Wong comments, "If you don't know all these basics, you can't do the lion dance and you can't understand it" (ibid.).

To improve dancers' skills and enhance their understanding of the culture, in February 1984 Wong drew on his personal connections and invited Luk Gan Wing, who was a third-generation direct disciple of Wong Fei Hung and then lived in Toronto, to come to Newfoundland to train local dancers (FIGURE 5). According to Wong, thirty to forty people attended the series of workshops and a majority of them were Cantonese-speaking restaurant workers. In this two-week workshop, as Wong says,

> He [Luk] taught everything about lion dance starting from basic martial arts drills to basic lion dance steps and the meaning of each step. He also tried to explain the culture of lion dancing as much as possible in this series of intensive workshops. He trained different people in different roles based on their talents. Some people were trained in drumming and some others were learning how to dance. (ibid.)

Many participants noticed the substantial improvement of their skills after the intensive training. Chan Chau Tam comments,

> Luk was a terrific teacher and a lot of misunderstandings about the lion dance in my mind were completely corrected. I was learning drumming with him. In Hong Kong, I had a lot of opportunities to listen to the beats but couldn't

FIGURE 5: The group photo of Luk's workshop in 1984. Courtesy of Chan Chau Tam.

understand. He explained to me and taught me the real drumming techniques. (Chan Chau Tam, personal interview, 26 February 2012)

Wong adds,

> He taught us the right way of performing the traditional Chinese lion dance. After the workshops, our performance was much better than earlier. We could do the whole set of the dance including waking up the lion, lion's jumps, walking through bridges, picking/eating greens, and stacking at the height of three times as tall as a person. We can play more than an hour without any breaks. (Daniel Wong, personal interview, 29 August 2013)

"The right way" in Wong's words refers to the way that people who are affiliated with Wong Fei Hung's kung fu school in Cantonese-speaking areas learn and perform the lion dance, which has been transmitted for generations without major changes. However, Wong's school is only one of many kung fu styles in southern China. Luk's visit was crucial to Newfoundland's Chinese lion dancing group, which therefore was able to claim their lineage in the lion dancing tradition. In that tradition, lineage "is important in martial arts, where every performance refers back to one's teacher" (SLOVENZ-LOW 1994, xi). While in Newfoundland, this martial arts tradition is not strictly carried on and the absence of this conservative restriction encourages any individual interested in the lion dance to practice and perform, whereas in other places, people's affiliations often determine if they are allowed to perform the lion dance.

In addition to lineage, individually, many people reconnected to the Cantonese culture and traditions and some of them refreshed their earlier memories of the old world's heritage by attending Luk's workshop. Because of the workshop, lion dancing as a living tradition returned to their community, Daniel Wong says:

> I was born in the culture of the lion dance and I was so happy to see that the association brought *Sifu* [Master] Luk to Newfoundland. He was the one who made me feel that I had never left the culture. (Daniel Wong, personal interview, 29 August 2013)

More importantly, Luk's workshop attempted to recover every performative detail and recreate the lost culture behind the performance including the tradition of kung fu linkage; as a result, it allowed Chinese lion dance in Newfoundland to regain some of its "historical authenticity." The quest of "historical authenticity," which is thought to be substantial to various kinds of performances, echoes the debate in the Early Music Revival movement, in which performers are encouraged to restore the original performances of masters like Bach and others in specific periods on period instruments, which are instruments corresponding to the periods that those pieces of music were first played (HASKELL 1988; KENYON 1988). Likewise, Luk's workshop also attempted to lead the lion dancing in Newfoundland to return to the original Wong Fei Hung style.

Daniel Wong observes that after Luk's workshop, the period from the late 1980s to the mid-1990s was the peak time of lion dancing in Newfoundland. He says,

> At that time, all people [Cantonese-speaking individuals] wanted to participate in lion dancing, especially those people who were working in Chinese restaurants. Many of them were in their 30s or early 40s. It was quite easy to get thirty to forty people to do regular practice. (ibid.)

In addition to those names mentioned earlier, regular lion dancers also included "Sing Lang Au, Anthony Tam, Wing Yuen Au, Jim Lam, Wing Hui Hong, Rennies So, and many others" (Kim Hong, personal interview, 18 April 2011). It seems that Luk's visit not only reconnected Chinese individuals to their homeland by the restoration of "historical authenticity" in lion dancing, but also reconnected them as a culturally united Chinese community, which was loosely bound by shared ethnicity in earlier days.

PERSONAL AUTHENTICITY: NEW-GENERATION LION DANCERS

In the late 1990s and early 2000s, some dancers moved out of St. John's to smaller communities to open businesses or to bigger metropolitan areas after their retirement. For example, Chung Lem relocated to Harbour Grace (a community in Eastern Newfoundland), Sing Lang Au and Wing Yuen Au moved to Toronto, and Jim Mah left for Ottawa. In addition to relocation, many active lion dancers such as David Chiu and Rennies So, who were getting into their 50s, were reluctant to take part in the actual performance.

These changes called for a new generation of lion dancers to take over the tradition and keep it going. Peter Wong recalls,

> Before us, there were also twin sisters, Ni Chu-Chen and Ling Chu-Chen, and their brother Ping performing lion dance and they were taught by Jim Mah. They carried on performing through 8 or 10 years….After their graduation from here, they all left for Toronto. (Peter Wong, personal interview, 7 April 2011)

The current leader of the CANL lion dancing team, Justin So, was also trained by Jim Mah (Justin So, personal interview, 3 February 2014). However, without professional lion dancing masters, the training of the younger dancers was slow and limited.

In 2006, upon the request of some local Chinese in Newfoundland and with funding from Canadian Heritage to celebrate the Canadian Government's apology to Chinese head tax and the CANL's thirtieth anniversary, Lat Yip, a Cantonese-speaking Vietnamese Chinese, was invited by then CANL president Betty Wong to Newfoundland from Toronto. For the workshop, two new lions were purchased: one of them was flaming red and the other golden yellow (FIGURE 6). Different from the older lions owned by the association, "these two lions have tails and pants which come with the lions' heads, matching the patterns of the other parts of the costumes in the same fabric and design to symbolize lions' legs" (Daniel Wong, personal interview, 29 August 2013). In traditional Cantonese lion dancing, the players' pants were either plain martial arts pants or gym pants (ibid.). The differences in the older and newer costumes somewhat reflect the generational differences in lion dancing.

Yip's one-week workshop was attended by nine people, who were trained two hours per day (FIGURE 7) (Peter Wong, personal interview, 7 April 2011). After Yip's workshop the current lion dance group formed with fourteen regular dancers under the leadership of Justin So (FIGURE 8). Different from the older-generation lion dancers, who were mostly first-generation Cantonese, members of this new lion dance team are from more diverse cultural backgrounds. A majority of them, such as Peter Wong, Teresa Wong, Joshua Lau, Gabriel Lau, Justin So, Matthew So, Joshua Wong, and Catherine Shek, are still from Cantonese-speaking families. Among them, Joshua Wong was born and raised in Hong Kong, and Catherine

FIGURE 6: Lions at the 2008 CANL Family Fun Day, Gower Street United Church, St. John's. Courtesy of Alick Tsui.

FIGURE 7: The workshop of Lat Yip. Courtesy of Lat Yip.

FIGURE 8: Some Members of the CANL Lion Dance Troupe at 2011's CANL Family Fun Day, Gower Street United Church, St. John's (left to right: William Ping Jr., Matthew So, Teresa Wong, Justin So, Jerry Xie, Andrew Leung, Joshua Lau, and Gabriel Lau). Courtesy of Alick Tsui.

Shek is a third-generation Chinese born in Calgary, Alberta. Some members have strong associations with non-Cantonese Mainland China. Jerry Xie was born to a northern Chinese couple and Emma Cole was born in western China but adopted by the Newfoundland Cole family. Some were born and raised in intermarriage families between individuals of Chinese descent and British Newfoundlanders, such as Andrew Leung, William Ping Jr., and Cerith Wong. In addition, Tzu-Hao

Hsu was born in Taiwan but raised in Newfoundland. All the current members of this team are fully acculturated into local culture and, except Joshua Wong, have had little exposure to the Cantonese version of Chinese culture, even though many of them have Cantonese parents. They come together under a united identity of "second-/later-generation Chinese in Newfoundland." Sometimes people with "new ethnicity" confront difficulties as they try to balance loyalty to their ancestral heritage and to the mainstream values. Therefore, because participants are drawn to the lion dance for diverse reasons, it may be misleading to emphasize the second- or later-generation Chinese dancers' motivation to reconnect with their heritage. People in the lion dance group actually have different perceptions and visions of their involvement in the performance.

Justin So has participated in the lion dance group for a long time, since he was eight years old, and is a very self-motivated lion dancer (Justin So, personal interview, 3 February 2014). He takes on much of the responsibility for locating educational materials from various sources, encouraging members to share their own information and dancing experience, and organizing regular practices and pre-event rehearsals. So says, "I feel responsible to educate other people about my culture" (Justin So, personal interview, 3 February 2014).

Nevertheless, other dancers in the group do not usually attempt to research aspects of either the lion dance performance or its history. Jerry Xie, whose parents had no cultural attachment to Cantonese lion dance before their immigration, commented that "I joined the lion dance when I was younger because I thought it was going to be really fun, which it still is, and because of how amazing a lion dance looked" (Jerry Xie, personal interview, 7 September 2012). A secondary consideration was "the history behind it" (ibid.). Like Xie, most members do not share So's deep commitment to exploring the lion dance's historical and cultural meanings. Peter Wong was recruited by the CANL executives to the lion dancing team because of the low enrolment of Lat Yip's workshop (Peter Wong, personal interview, 7 April 2011). Because of his lesser interest in the cultural part of lion dance, Wong admits,

> I am one of the type who reads technical books and manuals, but those fictions don't really interest me. I am not really motivated to read those cultural things. They are low on the list. (ibid.)

William Ping Jr. joined the team because he was invited by some members (Peter Wong) in the lion dancing group when he was watching the performance at an international show, and was encouraged by his parents to maintain at least some aspects of his Chinese heritage (Violet Ryan-Ping and William Ping Jr., personal interview, 16 April 2011).

Partially because of the lesser interest of members in the cultural part of lion dancing, the improvement of skills is often the main focus of the members in their occasional practice or pre-performance rehearsals. Joshua Lau says, "when we practice we don't usually talk about the culture unless someone asks. It's more about different routines for different occasions. That's about it" (Joshua Lau, personal interview, 6 October 2012). In many cases, the understanding of culture in lion dance performing is more optional than "critical" because, like other activities, the lion dance is only a recreational hobby, which "everybody can pick up" (Justin So, personal interview, 3 February 2014).

Sometimes, practice and rehearsal time is often too tight for the experienced members to introduce the cultural aspects of lion dance to others. Violet Ryan-Ping comments,

> These guys…don't really have too much practice. If they have a performance within the next week, they would get together this Friday and go over the routine again. They don't really have time because many of them are working full-time. If they have time, they will concentrate on how to improve. They don't care about culture in that case. (Violet Ryan-Ping and William Ping Jr., personal interview, 16 April 2011)

In this sense, on the one hand, when performing the lion dance "the youth and the group" are given "a sense of cultural identity, that this is something unique to the Chinese culture and this is part of who they are" (Tzu-Hao Hsu, personal interview, 29 January 2012). As Joshua Lau says, "You would learn a little bit about your culture. I mean I suppose it's part of my roots because I grew up Chinese" (Joshua Lau, personal interview, 6 October 2012). On the other hand, they may also experience a lack of knowledge of their own ancestral culture, which they—especially those Cantonese descendants—are told is part of them.

Because the lion dance is still foreign and exotic to many dancers who have little exposure to Cantonese culture, some strategies are commonly used in the learning process, which is different from the traditional way of training based on the understanding of the culture. In some cases, in order to simplify the drumming for the lion dance, beating is divided into smaller units. For example, in a lion dance performance for CANL's 2013 Chinese New Year celebration (FIGURE 9), the drumming beats were broken down into a sequence of the following components by Justin So (TABLE 1). Corresponding to the standardized musical playing, the dance movements are also choreographed into "separate" figures.

FIGURE 9: Lion dancing at the 2013 CANL Chinese New Year Celebration.
Courtesy of Violet Ryan-Ping.

Figure		Beat
Silver Lion 1	**Red/Gold Lion 2**	
Eye Dotting	Waiting side room	No drumming
Sleeping Lion, waking up – Flop down, snoring – Scratch ear, Flop down – Scratch eye, fall to side, kicking – Lick leg and get up	Waiting side room	Rapid rim shots – Scratches/licks (follow lion)
Hai ci	Enter room Run in with *Hai ci* finish	*Hai ci* beat
Running bow	Running bow	Running bow beat (x3) (Drum roll, drumstick beat, finishing beat on last bow)
Stationary cross steps	Stalking walks to center	Waiting beat
Notice other lion – Side hops with crouch	Standing side to stage area	Rapid gong beat
Greeting lions walk (half)	Greeting lions walk (half)	Greeting beat
Jump forward	Raise head and step to side with toe flick	Skin-rim drum roll to crash
Circle other lion – Quick turn to stance	Circle other lion – Quick turn to stance	Skin-rim drum roll to crash
Roll or skip to side – End in low stance	Head up, large jump on the spot	Skin-rim drum roll to crash
Greeting lions	Greeting lions	Greeting beat
Circle other lion, walk to crowd	Circle other lion, walk to crowd	High drum to walk
Walk and greetings (x3) – Rub – Lick – Eyes and ears	Walk and greetings (x3) – Rub – Lick – Eyes and ears	Walking beat and bowing beat
Smelling greens	Smelling greens	Rim shot to cymbals (x2) Waiting/searching combo
Searching for greens (x3)	Searching for greens (x3)	Searching for greens beat
Spitting greens (x3)	Spitting greens (x3)	Drum roll to crashing beat
Hai ci	*Hai ci*	*Hai ci*
Running bows	Running bows	Running bow beat (x3)
Ending	Ending	High drum and ending beat

Breaking down beats reduces the chance of making mistakes in a live performance, but there are also drawbacks. The music no longer needs to flow as an artistic entity and changes of rhythmic beats and smooth transitions between different chapters of music sometimes become unexpected pauses during playing. From time to time, the pauses transform the melodic stream into a mechanical combination of discrete musical segments. Music, in this sense, is directed by movements rather than leading the latter. The musical performance in the lion dance is thus transformed from an emotional expression to performative techniques for the sake of movements only. That said, these techniques make music skills easier to learn and transmit across generations.

Because they are less bound to the lion dance tradition that prioritizes cultural meanings, this new generation of lion dancers has more freedom to create their own new tradition. For example, Peter Wong recalls:

> [T]here is no gender in appearance for the lions when we do the dance. So for Mary Gin's wedding,[7] we made the red one be female and the yellow one be male. We used different actions and movements to indicate the genders. Say, when we made the routine, we made the red one more submissive, more feminine than the yellow one [FIGURE 10]. We didn't learn from anybody but we just figured it out. (Peter Wong, personal interview, 7 April 2011)

Nowadays, various online resources provide rich information on different aspects of lion dancing. Tzu-Hao Hsu says,

> YouTube is an excellent teacher. It is a good visual reference material. A lot of the time, we are doing our own research on YouTube or other websites and try to incorporate elements into our practice and training. (Tzu-Hao Hsu, personal interview, 29 January 2012)

As one of the productive consequences, at the 2013 Chinese New Year Gala on local Memorial University's campus, Jerry Xie, dressed in a panda costume instead

FIGURE 10: Lion dancing at Mary Gin's Wedding, St. John's. Courtesy of Alick Tsui.

of the traditional big-head Buddha, creatively combined the traditional Chinese lion dance with a popular pop song "Gangnam Style." Perhaps Xie's northern Chinese background allows him to freely present his idea of lion dancing. In 2014's Chinese New Year Celebration, the big-head Buddha was replaced by a panda (FIGURE 11).

The new generation of Chinese lion dancers differs from earlier Cantonese dancers, who strictly observed the lion dancing traditions as they learned them in Canton or Hong Kong, in terms of how they performed and how they perceived their performance and the associated traditions and culture. It seems that the pursuit of historical authenticity is not seen as being as important for contemporary dancers as it was for their predecessors. These performers do not consider locally performed lion dancing as a cultural survival of the ancestral country; instead, through an interplay between "here" (Newfoundland) and "there" (China), the dance is now interpreted in a more vernacular way,[8] so that the performance is distanced from the original practice. William Ping Jr. reports:

> What I am doing now [lion dancing] is a way to reconnect with what my grandfather is about. Unlike Justin, Matthew, and Peter, they are more authentic Chinese people than me so that the culture is a bigger deal to them. (Violet Ryan-Ping and William Ping Jr., personal interview, 16 April 2011)

Self-identifying as a less authentic Chinese individual, William Ping Jr. has less attachment to the Cantonese roots of the lion dance and claims a more personal sentimental connection to the performance as a symbolic presentation of his ancestral heritage. Nevertheless, the performative/perceptive variation does not suggest that the performance of the new generation of lion dancers is not authentic. The performance by the new ethnicity like Ping may not fit into the category of "historical authenticity" but falls into the rubric of "personal authenticity," which, as Peter Kivy puts it:

FIGURE 11: Lion dancing with a Panda at Memorial University's Chinese New Year Celebration at St. Augustine Church, St. John's, February 9, 2014. Courtesy of Julie Zhang.

> When we talk of a...performance that is "authentic" in the sense of being "personally authentic," we are praising it for bearing the special stamp of personality that marks it out from all others...we are making it out as a unique product of a unique individual, something with an individual style of its own—"an original." (KIVY 1995, 123)

In the case of Chinese lion dance in Newfoundland, the new generation of locally born or raised lion dancers, managing a new definition of their ethnicity, are less motivated to pursue historical authenticity as a goal for the dance, but are more interested in incorporating their personal understandings of being Chinese descendants of various cultural and regional backgrounds into their performances in ways that highlight social and cultural changes in the local society. To some degree, the performance of the new generation, representing a new and united Chinese identity within their group members with diverse cultural backgrounds, challenges the older Cantonese version of Chineseness that was established in the performance of the first-generation Cantonese dancers.

When present at their various practices and rehearsals, summer leisure gatherings, and coffee times, from how they were interacting I realized that not only was the new generation lion dancers' Chineseness negotiated and reconstructed in folkloric practice in the sense of Juwen ZHANG (2015), but also participation in lion dancing practice and performance also makes these local-born Chinese, who were/are suffering identity ambiguity, for the first time intensively experience Chinese culture outside of their families. They begin to meet people from the same ethnicity as friends and co-players rather than kids of parents' Chinese friends. Henry Johnson makes a similar comment on this social role of lion dancing groups, which first bridge the distance between co-ethnics by "forming social and cultural links with other members of the group" (JOHNSON 2005, 186), and which create a common sense of Chineseness "because of the traditional 'home' of the Chinese lion dance" (JOHNSON 2005, 179). In this sense, the new Chinese diasporic identity and culture identified with the formation of "new ethnicity" in Newfoundland emerge from the folkloric performance and social webs established in the practice.

MANY VOICES: LION DANCING AUDIENCE

The meaning of any cultural performance is created during the interaction between performers and audience members, who are not passive receivers but active participants often negotiating and/or challenging the senders' ideologies based on their own perceptions.

Since its inception in Newfoundland, lion dancing, a Cantonese tradition, has been long associated with the Chinese presence in special cultural contexts such as Chinese New Year celebrations, to serve as a cultural representation that delivers a pan-Chinese identity. In addition, lion dancing is not only reserved for relatively private ethnic spaces, but also is a part of ethnic educational programs, multicultural gatherings, and more community events. Kim Hong notes:

> Other than the garden party after the Flower Service and our traditional Chinese New Year celebrations, the lion dance was also played for a few occasions like the opening of restaurants [FIGURE 12] and St. John's Labour Day Parade, which we attended twice in late 1970s and early 1980s….We also did it a few times for some schools like the Bishop College….We wanted to show people in St. John's a bit of Chinese culture. (Kim Hong, personal interview, 18 April 2011)

Tzu-Hao Hsu also comments:

> The lion dance is the ambassador for us. We typically reserve the lion dance for pretty much Chinese Association functions, but in recent years, we perform for fundraisers, we have done it for weddings in the community, and we also started to perform for educational events to promote cultural diversity, so we have been getting ourselves in a little bit more with diversity initiatives… [FIGURE 13; Video 1 and 2] (Tzu-Hao Hsu, personal interview, 29 January 2012)

In 2013, the CANL lion dance troupe was invited to participate in the St. John's Christmas Parade (FIGURE 14).

As said, the enthusiastic participation of Cantonese immigrants in lion dancing indicates that this demographically dominant Chinese subgroup actively promotes lion dancing as a cultural representative of all individuals of Chinese descent through its festive performance both within and outside of the community. The gradually increasing involvement of lion dance in various local socio-cultural events tells that this promotion is successful and well recognized by Newfoundland's general public, who largely contribute to celebrate and, in turn, reinforce this ideology. An example is, when lion dancing was absent for some years in the early 2000s, CANL was highly encouraged by the general public to resume the tradition (Alick Tsui, personal interview, 20 January 2012).

The interest of people, especially non-Chinese, is often sparked because "the lion dance is a kind of visual performance with noise and color, which makes it

FIGURE 12: Lion dancing at the opening of Jade Garden Restaurant, St. John's. Courtesy of May Soo.

Figure 13: Lion dancing at the rooms for the event "Sharing Our Culture" in 2012, St. John's (left to right: William Ping Jr., Jerry Xie, Catherine Shek, Justin So, Tzu-Hao Hsu and Gabriel Lau). Courtesy of Violet Ryan-Ping.

Figure 14: Lion dancing at the 2013 St. John's Christmas Parade (Joshua Lau). Public website source: CBC NL: http://live.cbc.ca/Event/t_Johns_Santa_parade_2013?Page=0

more attractive than other Chinese performances such as singing and instruments" (Daniel Wong, personal interview, 29 August 2013). Wong's explanation reflects Chiou-Ling Yeh's findings in her study of Chinese New Year celebrations in San Francisco. Chiou-Ling Yeh characterizes three types of ethnic activities displayed at the Chinese New Year occasions, namely, "the first contained exotic and popular spectacles; the second was too ethnic to generate any interest; while the third was simply too foreign to be accepted" (YEH 2008, 51). Yeh categorizes the dragon dance and the lion dance in the first group because they not only embodied ethnic sentiments, but also showcased multiculturalism; on one hand, they were symbols that Chinese immigrants could relate to as they embodied good fortune, while on the other hand, they manifested a kind of American democratic practice that encouraged ethnic expression (Yeh 2008, 51–52). However, other forms of performance such as Chinese opera, folk dances, and martial arts are often preferred by Chinese immigrants, and yet Yeh notes that "mainstream newspapers publicized these activities but never discussed them at length, possibly because they only catered to Chinese immigrants" (Yeh 2008, 52). Non-Chinese audience members often express a lack of interest in esoteric expressions such as songs in Chinese languages and talk shows with many confusing cultural hints and puns. The general interest of the host society encourages event organizers "to emphasize the bicultural character or exotic Chinese traditions" as part of their major goal to "generate political and economic resources" (Yeh 2008, 52). In Newfoundland, according to my interviewees, because of the small size of the Chinese community, performances other than the lion dance, such as Peking Opera and Cantonese Opera, have never been as popular as in other Canadian cities, as discussed in some scholarly works (e.g., Cheung 2013; Li 1987; Sebryk 1995).

In addition to catering to general interests, lion dancing is also thought by some advocators like Justin So to be an effective way to educate people of Chinese descent, especially those who are "second or later generation, kids of intermarriage families, and adopted Chinese kids," about their Chinese cultural roots (Justin So, personal interview, 3 February 2014). As an ethnographer, I observed that at the annual "family fun day," an event held the day after the local celebration of Chinese New Year, when performers leave the lion costumes on the stage after the performance, many children rush to the spot of the exhibition in order to touch the lion puppets and get a good position for taking pictures. According to many children and their parents, the lions are not only treated as plush toys but also a symbol of their heritage, which, for many children, especially those Chinese children adopted by non-Chinese Newfoundlanders, is often inaccessible (Video 3). Without the lion dance, as Justin's father Peter So says, many of the younger generation of Chinese descent have limited interaction with Chinese traditions in their daily life (Peter So, personal interview with Ban Seng Hoe, 28 March 2009).

In this sense, lion dancing in Newfoundland is not only nostalgic but also educational. Consequently, memories and experiences of lion dancing at various cultural events kept in the mind of many second- or later-generation individuals of Chinese descent have a strong impact on the conceptualization of their understanding of Chineseness. Many of them, such as Chin Tan, therefore ask for lion dancing to be included at important times to represent their identity (Chin Tan, personal interview, 29 April 2012). Without lion dancing as a cultural medium in those rite-of-passage events, especially at weddings, people may feel a loss of cultural identity in the public setting. One day in early September 2010, I dropped by Bill Ping's house to bring him some Chinese wedding paper-cuttings for his daughter's upcoming ceremony. Although he cannot speak any Chinese due to his mother's Irish roots, Bill Ping self-identifies as a second-generation Chinese. He feels the deep cultural influences of his father, William Ping, and he constantly reminds his own children of their Chinese heritage. Therefore, a wedding featuring traditional Chinese cultural elements was planned for his daughter Candice. When Bill looked at the red decorations with Chinese characters and symbols, he was delighted: "At least we have these." I immediately realized that there was some disappointment hidden under his excitement. When I asked what had happened, he replied, "Oh, the lion dance team might not be able to show up at Candice's wedding." I asked if having the lion dance really mattered and whether he couldn't find some other replacement, but he responded, "The lion dance is the only thing I can think of as real Chinese stuff in Newfoundland." To Bill and his family, the lion dance made Chineseness visible. Without it at the wedding, his daughter's Chinese identity would not be well represented.

However, interest in lion dancing does not guarantee individuals' full comprehension of the performance's cultural meanings. It is unclear how many Chinese people, especially those local-born or -raised individuals, respond to the bright colors and striking movements and noise of the lion dancing, and how many have any deeper kind of knowledge of the dance so that they are able to decipher its embedded cultural symbolic codes. In this sense, Kristin Valentine argues that,

> Intensive spectators do not pretend to understand the ceremony as they think a member of that culture might. Rather, spectators try to make sense of what they experience as audience members, being their comments on extensive background research and careful observation of the public parts of the ceremonies. Knowing that ethical codes of conduct are not fixed, intense spectators necessarily live with ambiguity. (VALENTINE 2002, 281)

In Newfoundland, many individuals of Chinese descent, even some Cantonese, have a vague knowledge of the cultural meaning of the Cantonese lion dance. Kim Hong says, "I was told that the lion dance is supposed to bring good luck and chase away evil, but I couldn't go any further to explain the tradition and culture" (Kim Hong, personal interview, 18 April 2011). Many Chinese Newfoundlanders, if they are not culturally educated, are not able to interpret the traditional meanings of a performance. This does not diminish the enjoyment lion dancing can bring to audience members of all cultural backgrounds and ages and levels of Chinese cultural literacy, but these comments suggest that deep historical and cultural meanings are not accessible to all present.

At the same time, while the lion dance is well accepted as a Chinese symbol in public circumstances to reflect collective Chinese ethnicity, some individuals of Chinese descent look at it differently. Generationally speaking, almost all first-generation Chinese people recognize the Chinese cultural elements in the lion dance. However, some of them, like Shinn Jia Hwang, hesitate to accept the lion dance as a pan-Chinese cultural marker in Newfoundland because they see the local version as lacking historical authenticity. Hwang comments,

> Most performers don't know the culture and what they could do was imitating some movements and randomly hitting the instruments. That is not real Chinese lion dancing. (Shinn Jia Hwang and Ching Hsiang Lin, personal interview, 29 March 2012)

New immigrants from northern China may consider lion dance as a regional and archaic expression rather than a national and modern representation of Chinese culture. They refuse to accept this designated cultural expression as representation of their sense of Chineseness. Lili Wang comments:

> In Newfoundland, we have the lion dance every year, so in the minds of local people, it is an inseparable part of Chinese New Year. In my opinion, lion dancing itself represents the impression of older-generation Chinese about Chinese New Year. In fact, in China, we had never seen the lion dance in Chinese New Year celebrations....For people like me, we don't really have that kind of strong attachment to the lion dance. (Lili Wang, personal interview, 25 January 2012)

A few people reject the lion dance as a symbol of their ethnicity due to negative personal impressions. Katherine Huang says, "I often saw lion dancing performed there but I didn't like it at all because the lion's face looks scary to me" (Katherine Huang, personal interview, 22 February 2012). Peter Hing also says, "I am not interested in Chinese lion dance. It is foolish because it is repetitive all the time" (Peter Hing, personal interview, 8 April 2014).

Different from the first-generation Chinese who challenge the legality of lion dance as a pan-ethnic cultural marker but still consider it as an integral part of their heritage, second- or later-generation individuals usually make a clear decision on taking the tradition as a cultural marker to represent their sense of Chineseness. The current situation of lion dancing in Newfoundland suggests the refusal of many second- or later-generation individuals of Chinese descent to accept the role of the performance as an ethnic symbol.

In recent years, the population of regular participants of the local lion dancing team has dramatically decreased. According to my observation, almost half the members of the lion dance team, such as Inga Liu, Jerry Xie, Cerith Wong, and Peter Wong, have difficulties in attending regular practice (if any) and performances. The situation indicates that without new members, it will be unfeasible to maintain more advanced performances involving two lions. However, recruiting new dancers is always a challenge. Since the early 2000s, after the peak time of lion dancing, low enrollment has been a major problem, hindering the transmission and development of local lion dancing. Peter Wong comments,

> The tradition is passed to who wants to do it, but not many people want to do it. We did ask around. We tried to get more young kids to practice and we sent out emails, but didn't get back any responses. (Peter Wong, personal interview, 7 April 2011)

The unsuccessful recruitment can be attributed to a variety of reasons such as availability of time, personality, and the relatively strict age and gender requirements of traditional lion dancing (male-preferred) (Peter Wong, personal interview, 7 April 2011; Tzu-Hao Hsu, personal interview, 29 January 2012).

However, these reasons are considered to be secondary factors. I would suggest that the difficulty in recruiting new lion dancers first reflects the demographic change of the current Chinese community in Newfoundland. Nowadays, many newcomers come to Newfoundland as professional or students who are mostly from non-Cantonese Mainland China. They do not share the same cultural knowledge as older waves of Cantonese immigrants. Secondly, local-born Chinese present a distinct, modern, and vernacular identity of being Chinese, which is no longer defined by the lion dance (Daniel Wong, personal interview, August 2013). Some older-generation Chinese like Kim Hong fear the death of traditional lion dancing in Newfoundland. However, Daniel Wong seems more positive about the changes in the tradition:

> My point is, if people are still debating the issue of whether the lion dance can or cannot represent Chinese culture, or other similar cultural concerns, the lion dance won't disappear because it is a platform for people to discuss and negotiate their identities. (Daniel Wong, personal interview, 29 August 2013)

I agree with Daniel Wong that an effective functional tradition will not disappear if it is still used to achieve efficient communication for exchanging information and ideas, however, it can be replaced when a better channel is available and recognized. The current situation of the Chinese lion dance troupe in Newfoundland indicates that many second- and later-generation individuals of Chinese descent show less interest in connecting themselves to the Cantonese version of Chinese culture through performing the lion dance. As members of the "new ethnicity," they are free to choose whether and how to present their Chinese heritage, which is reflective and reflexive.

FURTHER DISCUSSION

The above description and discussion suggest that, although many people worry about the loss of tradition, lion dancing in Newfoundland is still an active and strong representation of Chineseness. In Newfoundland, the lion dance performance, whether by older-generation Cantonese-speaking Chinese in the past or new local-born or -raised dancers today, represents some historical continuity with earlier dancers forming in China; they present and celebrate Chineseness in general, but that performance carries various meanings for different individuals. Nowadays, most lion dancers and audience members do not prioritize historical authenticity of the Cantonese culture. They do not claim expertise in the ancestral culture of lion dancing, nor do they attempt to promote or understand every detail of the old cultural aspects of this Cantonese tradition. Francis Tam says,

> Now, what we want to tell people is "we are here and we can be different," but we don't really push people to accept the traditional cultural perspectives as people have done in the old country, because we are in Canada. (Francis Tam, personal interview, 28 July 2013)

It is plausible that the trivialization of traditional meanings or the historical authenticity of lion dancing is influenced by the preference of both the performers and audience, who choose to understand the lion dance in a local rather than a "foreign" way.

As a cultural performance, the lion dance in Newfoundland provides its performers and audience with "a special enhancement of experience, bringing with it a heightened intensity of communicative interaction which binds the audience to the performer in a way that is specific to performance as a mode of communication" (Bauman 1977, 43). During the communication process, dancers and audience members who are different from each other in age, region of origin, and generation, are exchanging their perceptions on the lion dance. Because of these exchanges, some participants of Chinese descent strengthen their cultural affiliation to Chineseness, some may discover or rediscover their cultural identity, and some others might choose to distance themselves from their ancestral culture but claim their new understanding of their ethnicity not associated with the lion dance, which is no longer a taken-for-granted pan-ethnic marker. At the same time, the performance itself is continuously changed due to the variations of the personal cultural perceptions of performers and audience members in their communications with co-ethnics and non-Chinese in different sociocultural settings. The current trend, from the pursuit of historical authenticity to the presentation of personal sincerity, shows that the Chinese lion dance is reflexive, shifting from a foreign invention to a local creation, which is often used to transmit a vernacular version of ethnic identity that is not simply "Chineseness" but a complex system of multivocal definitions of "Chineseness".

When Chineseness is negotiated in the geographic and cultural space where the ethnic performance—lion dance—is played, a sense of "united community" with identical self-awareness rises among all attendees, including performers and audience, beyond the social, ethnic, and cultural boundaries. A somewhat unique Chineseness becomes the "mainstream" identity in those events featuring Chinese diasporic culture and tradition, and the united diasporic identity therefore temporally transforms all individuals into one category—"Chinese"—socially and culturally. In this sense, Chinese communities are reorganized and reintegrated by a cultural performance that constructs a new identity to embrace people with different cultural origins into one. In this regard, Newfoundland's Chinese lion dance, which is a Cantonese version, to a large extent not only represents Chinese who are born in the culture of southern China, but also provides a possibility to unite all individuals of Chinese descent regardless of their regional, generational, linguistic, and other differences as "one" diasporic community with its "unique" identity and culture.

Acknowledgment

This article is supported by the Fundamental Research Funds for the Central Universities, China (Southeast University, project 2242016S20001).

Notes

1. According to Statistics Canada (2006), Chinese comprise only 0.26 percent of the province's total population.

2. For a better life and more work opportunities, many Chinese came to Newfoundland through family ties or their personal connection with people from the same regions in Canton Province, such as Toisan and Hoi Ping. In 1975, families with Cantonese origins comprised more than eighty percent of the local Chinese population. But after 1967, when Canada adopted a new immigration policy to select immigrants based on factors such as profession and education instead of race and ethnicity, more professionals started to move to Newfoundland.

Along with the emergence of new generations, the Chinese demography became more diverse and the Cantonese proportion of the population declined to less than one third (LI 2014).

3. The Cantonese lion dance (southern lion dance) is the main form performed in Newfoundland. It is also widespread in Chinese diasporic communities around the world (JOHNSON 2005; LIU 1981; SLOVENZ 1987; SLOVENZ-LOW 1991, 1994). Compared to the costume of the northern style, with less fur and no mane, the costume of the southern style is more distant from the image of a real lion. However, the abstraction makes the southern lion more aggressive (MATUSKY and TAN 2004, 152). Moreover, because the body of the southern lion is bigger and longer with more and brighter colors, it is often thought to contain more "strength, agility and power of energy" (MATUSKY and TAN 2004, 152). In addition, according to my interviewees, at present performers of both traditions mutually adopt skills and costumes from each other.

4. Flower Service is a local Chinese grave decoration practice to memorialize early Chinese settlers and family members who passed away in Newfoundland. This event is held on the Sunday following St. John's (the capital of Newfoundland and Labrador) Regatta Day, which is set on the first Wednesday in August annually. The Chinese Flower Service is often followed by a garden party with a BBQ and beverages, and sometimes includes traditional performances.

5. In the legend that Matusky and Tan's theory is based on, it is said that the lions were tamed for entertainment by a monk upon the command of the emperor (MATUSKY and TAN 2004, 152). In addition, the story also indicates that the role of the Buddhist monk is a critical part of the lion dancing. Matusky and Tan's legend thus reveals a close relationship between lion dancing and Buddhism. More specifically, lion masks are similar to the images of lions in ancient Buddhist decorations and paintings (FELTHAM 2007, 2009; LIU 1981), in which lions are generally portrayed as guardians or as mounts with wide-open mouths, fan-like ears, big eyes, and horns on the top center of their foreheads. Therefore, in consideration of the similarities between the lions in the dance and those in Buddhism, Liu confidently says that, "We can be quite sure that the later development of the lion dance mask has been influenced directly or indirectly by the appearance of the guardian tomb animals" (LIU 1981, 30).

6. The word "star" is "used to illustrate the beats caused by the touch of the drum sticks to the big drum" (LIU 1981, 63).

7. Mary Gin is a local-born, second-generation Chinese.

8. However, according to Justin So, local adaption of lion dance can fit into a new tradition of lion dancing, which is more popular in overseas Chinese communities (Justin So, personal interview, 3 February 2014). As he says, "It is not our invention. There are some other troupes who have been doing that. They take modern songs instead of traditional ones. It is a newer tradition and newer style" (ibid.).

REFERENCES

BAUMAN, Richard
  1977 *Verbal Art as Performance.* Rowley, Mass.: Newbury House Publishers.
  1986 Performance and honor in thirteenth-century Iceland. *Journal of American Folklore* 99: 131–50. doi: 10.2307/539970

CHAN, Mei-Hsiu
  2001 Transdisciplinary Multicultural Dance Education: Teaching Chinese American Students Chinese Culture through Lion Dancing. PhD dissertation, Texas Woman's University.

CHEUNG, Helen Kwan Yee
  2013 The Social Functions of Cantonese Opera in the Edmonton Chinese Community 1890–2009: From Sojourners to Settlers. MA dissertation, University of Alberta.

CONQUERGOOD, Dwight
1989 Poetics, play, process, and power: The performance turn in anthropology. *Text and Performance Quarterly* 1: 82–95. doi:10.1080/10462938909365914

FELTHAM, Heleanor B.
2007 Here be Lions: An Investigation into the Origin, Distribution, Meaning and Transformation of Lion Imagery. PhD dissertation, University of Technology, Sydney.
2009 Everybody was kung-fu fighting: The lion dance and Chinese national identity in the 19th and 20th centuries. In *Asian Material Culture*, Marianne Hulsbosch, Elizabeth Bedford, and Martia Chaiklin, eds., 105–140. Amsterdam: Amsterdam University Press.
2010 Lions, silks and silver: The influence of Sasanian Persia. *Sino-Platonic Papers* 206. http://sinoplatonic.org/complete/spp206_sasanian_persia.pdf (accessed 5 September 2012).

GUSS, David M.
2000 *The Festive State: Race, Ethnicity, and Nationalism as Cultural Performance*. Berkeley, Los Angeles, and London: University of California Press.

HASKELL, Harry
1988 *The Early Music Revival: A History*. New York: Thames and Hudson.

HOE, Ban Seng
1984 Legend of a traditional lion dance. *Journal of the Canadian Folk Art Council* 7: 12–13.

HOLLING, Michelle A. and Bernadette Marie CALAFELL
2007 Identities on stage and staging identities: ChicanoBrujo performances as emancipatory practice. *Text and Performance Quarterly* 27: 58–83. doi:10.1080/10462930601046053

HOY, William
1948 Native festivals of the California Chinese. *Western Folklore* 7: 240–50. doi:10.2307/1497548

HU, William C.
1995 *Chinese Lion Dance Explained*. Ann Arbor and San Francisco: Ars Ceramica Ltd. and Chinese Performing Arts Foundation.

JOHNSON, Henry
2005 Dancing with lions: (Per)forming Chinese cultural identity at a New Zealand secondary school. *New Zealand Journal of Asian Studies* 7: 171–86.

KENYON, Nicholas
1988 *Authenticity and Early Music: A Symposium*. Oxford and New York: Oxford University Press.

KIVY, Peter
1995 *Authenticities: Philosophical Reflections on Musical Performance*. Ithaca: Cornell University Press.

LI, Mu
2014 Wanders betwcen Cultural Boundaries: Exploring the Individual Expressions of Chineseness in Newfoundland. PhD dissertation, Memorial University of Newfoundland.

LI, P. Stephen K.
1987 Cantonese Opera in Toronto. MA dissertation, York University.

LIU, Wan-Yu
1981   The Chinese Lion Dance. MA dissertation, York University.

MATUSKY, Patricia and TAN Sooi Beng
2004   *The Music of Malaysia: The Classical, Folk, and Syncretic Tradition.* Hampshire, UK: Ashgate Publishing.

NAHACHEWSKY, Andriy
2002   New ethnicity and Ukrainian Canadian social dances. *Journal of American Folklore* 115: 175–90. doi: 10.2307/4129218

SEBRYK, Karrie M.
1995   A History of Chinese Theatre in Victoria. MA dissertation, University of Victoria.

SINGER, Milton
1959   *Traditional India: Structure and Change.* Philadelphia: American Folklore Society.

SLOVENZ, Madeline
1987   "The year is a wild animal:" Lion dancing in Chinatown. *The Drama Review: TDR* 31: 74–102. doi: 10.2307/1145803

SLOVENZ-LOW, Madeline
1991   On the tail of the lion: Approaches to cross-cultural fieldwork with Chinese Americans in New York. In *Creative Ethnicity: Symbols and Strategies of Contemporary Ethnic Life*, Stephen Stern and John Allan Cicala, eds., 55–71. Logan: Utah State University Press.
1994   Lions in the Streets: A Performance Ethnography of Cantonese Lion Dancing in New York City's Chinatown. PhD dissertation, New York University.

TAN, Sooi Beng
2007   The lion dances to the fore: Articulating Chinese identities in Penang and Medan. *Senri Ethnological Reports* 65: 63–78.

TURNER, Victor
1981   Social dramas and stories about them. In *On Narrative*, ed. W. J. T. Mitchell, 137–64. Chicago: University of Chicago Press. doi: 10.1086/448092
1988   *The Anthropology of Performance.* New York: PAJ.

VALENTINE, Kristin
2002   Yagui Easter ceremonies and the ethics of intense spectatorship. *Text and Performance Quarterly* 22: 280–96. doi: 10.1080/10462930208616174

YEH, Chiou-Ling
2008   *Making an American Festival: Chinese New Year in San Francisco's Chinatown.* Berkeley: University of California Press. doi: 10.1525/california/9780520253506.001.0001

ZHANG, Juwen
2015   Chinese American culture in the making: Perspectives and reflections on diasporic folklore and identity. *Journal of American Folklore* 128: 449–75. doi: 10.5406/jamerfolk.128.510.0449

TERENCE LANCASHIRE
Osaka Ohtani University

Izumo *Kagura*, Iwami *Kagura*, and National Intersections

Ritual, Propaganda, Tourist Attraction

Izumo *kagura* 出雲神楽 (music for the gods/to make the gods happy) and Iwami *kagura* 石見神楽 in Shimane prefecture are characterized by a mixture of unmasked *torimono* 採物 (hand-held objects) dances and masked drama. The contrast between these two types has led *kagura* scholar Ishizuka Takatoshi 石塚尊俊 to question the historical usage of the term *kagura*. This article examines the content of the theatrical pieces and considers non-ritual roles for performance. In particular, attention is drawn to pieces such as *Sankan* 三韓 (Three Koreas), the mythical conquest of the three Korean Kingdoms. Although supposedly in decline, recent performances suggest that *Sankan* remains an integral part of the *kagura* repertoire. Given friction between Japan and Korea over Takeshima 竹島, the outmost extremity of Shimane prefecture, it is difficult to ignore the propaganda potential of performances in recent times and historically. Other factors that have impacted on performance function are shifts in the performers from shrine priests to secular bodies; here the role of *seinendan* 青年団, youth groups, which came to the fore at the beginning of the twentieth century, is examined. Other impacting intersections, the emergence of folklore academia, and the use of performances for tourism are also considered.

KEYWORDS: Izumo *kagura*—Iwami *kagura*—*shinnō*—Sankan—ritual—propaganda—tourism

Asian Ethnology Volume 76, Number 2 · 2017, 319–42
© Nanzan University Anthropological Institute

THE ELDERLY MAN standing next to me shouted "One more time! One more time!" "One more time," was the response from the stage. It was past two in the morning and the assembled audience had grown thin in number. But there was still enough of a gathering to urge on the protagonist as he slayed three demons. In the theatrical *kagura* 神楽 of western Japan, demon slaying is often the clichéd denouement. But these were no ordinary demons. They were the incarnated simulacrums of Baekje (Kudara) 百済, Silla (Shiragi) 新羅, and Goguryeo (Kōkuri) 高句麗—the three ancient kingdoms of the Korean peninsula. Here, they were being harried by a large, white-masked demon, an alternative incarnation of the hero-statesman Take no Uchi no Sukune 武内宿禰 at the behest of Jingū Kōgō 神功皇后, consort of the semi-mythical Japanese Emperor Chūai 仲哀天皇. She too makes her appearance on the stage, standing in the background, bow and arrow drawn, ready should the Korean demons' resistance prove too great. But her assistance is not necessary as Take no Uchi battles each of the Korean kingdoms in turn. They have already been battled twice and, as they prostrate themselves on the stage, Take no Uchi has repeatedly demanded that they subjugate themselves to Japan. But the audience is not satisfied, and the battle is re-engaged for the third time before submission is achieved and the three kingdoms are ordered to pay tribute to their Japanese conqueror.

Sankan was just one of many dance/theatrical pieces that were performed by the Ōdochi *kagura* 大土地神楽 preservation society on the nights of the 26 and 27 October 2012 at the Ōdochi Kō *jinja* (shrine) 大土地荒神社, awkwardly located between the narrow streets of Taisha 大社 town, Izumo city, Shimane prefecture. According to a now defunct internet link for what was recorded as the Izumo kagura jōhō sentā 出雲神楽情報センター (Izumo Kagura Information Center)—a link that could be accessed at least up to October 2014), performances of *Sankan* were rare and in decline. A publication on Ōhara *shinshoku kagura* 大原神職神楽 (Ohara priests' *kagura*),[1] based in what was once Ōhara county, Unnan city, approximately twenty kilometers southeast of Izumo city, relates that, "in consideration of the content" performances of *Sankan* had ceased after World War II (Shimane ken kodai bunka sentā 2000, 29). In the early 1990s, when researching Iwami *kagura* in the neighboring western part of Shimane prefecture, a pamphlet providing brief descriptions of performances had clumsily deleted a reference to demons coming from the Korean peninsula in the equivalent piece, *Take no Uchi*

武の内, which takes its name from the protagonist. Clearly, post–World War II sensibilities prevailed, and in a climate of reconciliation in the 1990s, evidenced in the proclamation by former Korean president Kim Dae-Jung in 1998 to lift a ban restricting the import of "Japanese popular culture," references to past conflicts, semi-fictional or not, were inappropriate. Thus, in addition to noting that performances of *Sankan* were in decline, the Izumo Kagura Information Center website continued that, particularly after the War, when the piece *Sankan* was staged, it was performed in a strong atmosphere of restraint. However, the removal of this website description and performances by the Ōdochi *kagura* preservation society on both the 26 and 27 October 2012, suggest and demonstrate that the mood of "restraint" is now no longer pertinent. The baying of those gathered, and the response of the performers, made that all too apparent.[2]

To the east of Taisha town, separated by Shinji ko (lake) 宍道湖, is Sada 佐太 shrine, academically claimed by some to be the origins of the Izumo *kagura* tradition.[3] On the second day of the festival, held every year at Sada shrine on 25 September, modern time restrictions allow for the performance of only three theatrical pieces, the *shinnō* 神能 (sacred *nō* drama), out of a known repertoire of twelve. Yamatodake 日本武, the name of the protagonist in the piece, Yaegaki 八重垣 (The eight-fold fence), and Ōyashiro 大社 (The great shrine) make up the staple diet of performances, and this too is iterated in the explanation given of the *shinnō* provided by the shrine office. But, in 2012, Sada shrine too gave a performance of Sankan, all too evident for anyone to see on a YouTube upload (HIRO88641 2013). The restraint and decline in performances in the programme notes for Sankan provided by the Izumo Kagura Information Center seem to run counter to the reality of performances on the ground, or rather on the *kagura* stage.

But 2012 was not a usual year. Many celebratory performances of *kagura* in Shimane prefecture were planned for the 1,300-year anniversary of the completion of the ancient text, the *Kojiki* 古事記 (Records of Ancient Matters), the source material for much of what appears on the theatrical *kagura* stage. This could explain a bumper performance of *kagura* pieces. But even with the anniversary of a classic text, it is difficult to ignore the extra-national geopolitics of the area.

Far out in the Japan Sea, or for the Koreans, the East Sea, lies that outmost extremity of Shimane prefecture, the island of Takeshima. The Koreans call it Dokdo and the dispute over territoriality has continued since the de facto control of the island was realized through the occupation by Korean forces in 1954, under the presidential direction of Syngman Rhee.

In a pre-election stunt to boost flagging popularity figures, a later President, Lee Myung-bak, flew to Takeshima/Dokdo in August 2012, exacerbating tensions between the two countries. Prior to this, in 2005, the local government in Shimane prefecture had designated 22 February as "Takeshima no hi" 竹島の日 ("Takeshima Day"), to heighten local awareness of Japan's claim of territorial sovereignty. According to a report for the US Congress , this and territorial disputes with China have, in part, seen a rise in Japanese nationalist sentiment, and that sentiment may be evidenced in the performances of *Sankan* in Izumo *kagura* (CHANLETT-AVERY et al. 2017, 8).

Certainly, a homepage describing the piece performed by the Ōhara *kannushi* 神主 (priest) (*shinshoku*) *kagura* preservation society, the very same *kagura* group noted above that purportedly had ceased to perform *Sankan* after World War II, clearly forges a connection between *Sankan* and the territorial rancor that has arisen between Japan and Korea over the disputed Takeshima/Dokdo. The homepage states: "… The piece *Sankan* is [where] Jingū Kōgō dispatches a military force to the Korean peninsula and defeats the three Korean [kingdoms] of Silla, Baekje, and Goguryeo. The peninsula has surely gone mad. Shimane prefecture, which has established "Takeshima Day," is tremendously strong."[4] And the revival of *Sankan* by the Ōhara *kannushi* (*shinshoku*) *kagura* preservation society some time after the year 2000, when the report by the Shimane ken kodai bunka sentā 島根県古代文化 センター (Shimane Prefectural Historical Cultural Center) had claimed a postwar cessation of performance, adds further weight to the argument.

The aim of this article is not, however, to focus on expressions of nationalism but to examine the status of *kagura* itself and its reflection of and adaptation to changing historical circumstances. If *Sankan* today can mirror national sentiments, or the sentiments of the people of Shimane prefecture, then *kagura* in the past too cannot be divorced from wider national concerns prevalent in earlier periods of formation and presentation. These concerns include nationalist expressions through the Edo period into the Meiji period; early twentieth-century appropriation of the performing arts in general, and *kagura* in particular, to galavanize Japanese youth; intersections with folklore academia, resulting, in modern times, in the exploitation of *kagura*; and following centralized policies on tourism, to stimulate regional economies.

To examine the status of *kagura*, I focus on two related traditions with which I am most familiar, Iwami *kagura* in western Shimane prefecture and Izumo *kagura* to the east. *Kagura* is, by definition, a ritual. And this is where the problem lies. In the most recent study of Iwami *kagura*, Yamaji Kōzō 山路興造 emphasizes the ritual, concluding that historically there were two major performance formats: unmasked *torimono* dances (dances with hand-held objects such as *suzu* 鈴 bells and fans), collectively known as *shichi za* 七座,[5] and grander displays of theatrical performance during which spirit possession could occur (YAMAJI 2014, 52–53). The *shichi za* were performed every year as part of a shrine's annual festival, *rei-sai* 例祭. *Kagura* with spirit possession entailed greater financial and human resources and were held once every five or seven years. This was the *shiki-nen no kagura* 式 年の神楽 or, alternatively, Ōmoto *kagura* 大元神楽. Here, theatrical performances also took place. According to Yamaji, Ōmoto represented multiple deities of ancestors who could be consulted during a spirit possession ritual. Yamaji points to a survey by the nineteenth-century local Kokugaku 国学 (National Learning) scholar Fujii Muneo 藤井宗雄 (1823–1904) who, in his *Iwami no kuni jinja ki* 石見国神社 記 [Iwami province shrine records], recorded that belief in Ōmoto was widespread in the Iwami area where, for each of the six counties that made up Iwami (Naka 那賀, Ōchi 邑智, Nima 仁摩, Ano 安濃, Mino 美濃, and Kanoashi 鹿足), Ōmoto deities could number well over a hundred (YAMAJI 2014, 56; YAMAZAKI 2009).

Today, Ōmoto *kagura* survives only in the mountainous area of Ōchi county, having escaped the cultural purges of the Meiji restoration (YAMAJI 2014, 49–71).

In an act of government intervention, performances of *kagura* by shrine priests were banned. In eastern Shimane prefecture, this was the *Shinshoku enbu kinshi rei* 神職演舞禁止令 (priests' dance performance prohibition order) issued by the Matsue Domain Civil Administration Offices for Shrine 松江藩民政局神祠懸 (Matsue han minsei kyoku shinshi gakari) in the eighth month of 1870. And in the first month of 1873, although aimed specifically at *miko* 巫女, shrine priestesses, spirit possession was also abolished.[6] These bans propelled the emergence of performances given by civilian groups, already beginning to make their presence felt toward the end of the Edo period (LANCASHIRE 2006, 249).

In the eyes of some, the shift from performances by shrine priests to those by civilian groups also saw a detrimental shift from the ritual to the secular. Performances in concert halls and sports venues emphasized the intrinsic entertainment value of the *kagura*. This is particularly true for Iwami *kagura*. In 1941, local scholar Yadomi Kumaichirō wrote that Iwami *kagura* had entered an evil path (YADOMI 1941, 850). Other local scholars too were perturbed, lamenting that the *kagura* had been reduced to a mere spectacle (ŌBA 1975, 45; ISHIZUKA 1979, 22). Others recalled a seeming golden age when early performers ignored those gathered and directed their attention to the center of the stage, beneath the suspended *kumo*[7] to which the deities had descended. The *kagura* was, after all, a ritual entertainment for the gods (TAKEUCHI 1990, 4). But, in the past, was that really so? Even with Yamaji Kōzō's emphasis on the historical, ritual nature of Iwami *kagura*, he too briefly notes the predominance of battle scenes in Iwami *kagura* portraying enemies coming from foreign lands. He suggests a possible residual fear following the failed invasion attempts by the Mongols in 1274 and 1281,[8] or the comparative proximity to the Korean peninsula, naming specifically the ancient kingdom of Goguryeo (Kōkuri) and presumably the Goguryeo–Yamato War of the late fourth century and early fifth century (YAMAJI 2014, 67). Either way, the obviously political content of *Sankan* in particular, even if it portrays mythical/historical events in a very distant past, hints that the theatrical pieces possibly had an alternative agenda.

More importantly, one is inevitably led to the question, "is the theatrical *kagura* really *kagura*?" The question is by no means new. Ishizuka Takatoshi, renowned *kagura* scholar and expert on the *kagura* of western Japan, has, in a variety of publications, questioned the status of the theatrical *kagura* (ISHIZUKA 1979, 407, 443; 2005, 11–13, 41–42).

Today, at Sada Shrine, performances of unmasked *torimono* dances and theatrical performances, referred to respectively as *shichi za* and *shinnō*, sacred *nō*, take place on 24 and 25 September. For the *shichi za* today, the repertoire consists of seven pieces: *Kenmai* 剣舞 (sword dance), *Sangū* 散供 (scattered offerings), *Kiyome* 清目 (purification), *Goza* 御座 (The honorable seat), *Kanjō* 勧請 (summoning the deities), *Yaotome* 八乙女 (eight maidens), and *Takusa* 手草 (hand held grass). In reality, only six pieces are performed as *Yaotome*, what would have been the only female dance in the festival, ceased to be performed, according to the shrine offices, "in recent times" (personal communication from shrine office, March 8th 2013).

Goza is the raison d'etre for the festival, for the dances are performed as part of the central ritual, the *Goza-gae sai* 御座替祭 (Festival for Changing of the Seat). A mat, made of locally grown rush, is changed annually within the bodies of the three shrines that make up Sada in the belief that the "spiritual power" 霊威 (*reii*) of the gods will continue anew. Sada Shrine draws a parallel to the *shiki nen sengū* 式年遷宮, the rebuilding of Grand Shrines, which, for example at Ise Jingū, occurs every twenty years, and for Izumo Taisha, every sixty to seventy years (Sada-jinja 2005).

Historically, twelve dramatic pieces make up the repertoire of the *shinnō*. These are *Ōyashiro*, *Makirime* 真切女, *Ebisu* 恵比須, *Yawata* 八幡, *Yamatodake*, *Iwato* 磐戸 (The rock door), *Sankan*, *Sumiyoshi* 住吉, *Kōjin* 荒神, *Itsukushima* 厳島, *Takemikazuchi* 武甕槌, and *Yaegaki*. Five of these pieces Kirime, Ebisu, Yawata, Takemikazuchi, Kōjin take the names of deities and two, Sumiyoshi and Itsukushima, refer to major shrines.

A current pamphlet, issued by the adjacent Kashima rekishi minzoku shiryō kan 鹿島歴史民俗資料館 (Kashima History and Folklore Museum), notes that the pieces *Itsukushima*, *Takemikazuchi*, and *Kōjin* are no longer performed. *Sankan* is, however, on the list. According to oral tradition the *shinnō* were created by a shrine priest at Sada shrine, a certain Miyagawa Hyōbu no shō Hideyuki 宮川兵部少輔秀行, who travelled to Kyoto in the fifth month of 1608 to obtain a priest's license from the Yoshida family. He learnt *nō* and used the *nō* piece *Takasago* 高砂 (from Takasago bay), presumably as a template, to create the *shinnō*.[9]

The two performances types, unmasked *torimono* dances (*shichi za*) and theatrical pieces (*shinnō*), make up, in current terminology, Izumo *kagura*. They are also present in neighboring Iwami *kagura* though the same, specific nomenclature is not used.

Ishizuka's doubt about the *kagura* status of the *shinnō*, the theatrical pieces, rests on the simultaneous usage of both the words *kagura* and [*shin*]*nō* in early documentation. The *Kaikitsudan* 懐橘談 of 1653 records dramatic pieces corresponding to the repertoire of Sada Shrine, and these are simply referred to as *nō*. Separation of the terminology is evident in such statements as "…are ritual *mikagura* or otherwise *nō*…" ("…*shinji mikagura mata wa nō ari,*…" 神事御神楽又は能あり, 御神楽又は能あり) (KUROSAWA and TANIGUCHI 1914, 65–66).

Ishizuka likewise draws attention to a diary, *Masayori nikki shō* 正仍日記抄 [Annotated diary of Masayori] , penned by a certain Hatagaki Masayori 幡垣正仍, which covers a period of sixty years from 1684 to 1744. Here, specifically mentioned are the terms *kitō kagura* 祈祷神楽 (prayer *kagura*), *yaotome kagura* 八乙女神楽, *dai kagura* 大神楽 (great *kagura*), *kagura*, and *mikagura* 御神楽 (honorable kagura). And, in the same document, for an entry dated the 18th day of the 3rd month, 1700, there is a separate reference, which is unconnected to *kagura*, to three pieces that match those in the *shinnō* repertoire (ISHIZUKA 1979, 408–10, 454).

Another document referenced is the *Un'yōshi* 雲陽誌 [Journal of Un'yo] of 1717, a geography of the domain of Matsue. What is significant in this document is, despite references to *kagura* rituals that incorporate the *shichi za* ritual, there is no reference to any form of theatrical performance corresponding to the *shinnō*. In the section on Sada Shrine, only the *Goza-gae sai*, the changing of the mat, is mentioned. After this, the priests perform "rituals for one day and one night" (ASHIDA 1971, 71). What these rituals entail is unclear. Nevertheless, what is of possible significance is that the rituals occur for only one night.

This contrasts with the first known descriptions of the *Goza-gae sai* festival in a document, the *Shichi jū yodo no matsuri no na o chiji* 七十余度之祭之名ヲ知事 [Knowledge of the names of over seventy festivals] of 1512, with *shichi za* on the first night and a performance form termed *hōraku* 法楽 (Buddhist music/to make Buddhist deities happy), possibly a precursor to the *shinnō*, on the second night.[10] This concurs with current performance practice today, with the same format of *shichi za* on the first night and the *shinnō* on the second. A possible interpretation is that, in the *Un'yōshi*, the *shinnō* were not deemed to be ritual and hence only one day and one night of ritual were noted. If this is true, then again the ritual status of the *shinnō*, let alone the *kagura* status, is brought into question.

Leaping forward into more recent times, the ban issued in 1870 by the Matsue Domain Civil Administration Offices for Shrines was the *Shinshoku enbu kinshi rei* 神職演舞禁止令 (Priests' dance performance prohibition order). Here, the characters clearly indicate that what was banned was *enbu* 演舞 (dance performance), not *kagura*. And what ceased to be performed was what is now understood today as Izumo *kagura*, namely theatrical *kagura*, in Sada Shrine, the *shinnō*. And even over fifty years after the ban, the same uncertainty over the status of the theatrical pieces was evidenced when "*kagura*" performance groups travelled around the country to demonstrate their performance skills. The *Yatsuka gun shi* 八束郡誌 [A history of Yatsuka county] of 1926 records for the previous year that a group from Ōchi county, today home of the nationally designated Ōmoto *kagura*, travelled to Kyoto and Osaka to perform. Here it is noted that the performances were simply titled *Shindai geki* 神代劇 [Theater of the age of the gods] (OKUHARA 1973, 648).

In current performance practice, extant nomenclature still infers a distinction between the *kagura* dance and, simply put, all the rest. In Sada Shrine, when all the performances are over, the performers and shrine priests retire to a separate building within the grounds of the shrine and a performance of *Shin kagura* 真神楽 (true *kagura*) ensues. The dance is that of a *miko*, in reality a man dressed in women's garb, with an elaborately ornamental golden crown complementing the white, female mask that conveniently conceals the gender of the dancer.

In Iwami *kagura* too, a seemingly similar distinction can be made. Here, the only piece actually entitled "*Kagura*," the first piece listed in the repertoire, may be danced within the body of the shrine whilst the remaining, variously titled pieces are danced in an adjacent building.[11] Thus, both the pieces "*Kagura*" of Iwami *kagura*, and the "*Shin kagura*," the "true kagura" of Sada Shrine, stand in contrast to the nomenclature used for the remaining performance forms.

Ishizuka himself finally concludes that popular use of the term *kagura* for theatrical pieces such as the *shinnō*, at least in the western part of Japan today, is possibly the result of its mistaken usage in the mass media and, by implication, this usage has no real history (ISHIZUKA 1979, 407).

THEATRICAL *KAGURA*: PROPAGANDA TOOL?

The possibility that theatrical *kagura* may, in fact, not be *kagura*, and therefore not ritual, means that alternative functions are open to interpretation. As noted at the outset, with the performance of *Sankan*, the propaganda potential for theatrical pieces is clearly evident. And in the Muromachi and Edo periods, the visual display of stage performance could have served as a major form conveying the ideas of certain religious groups with invested interests in gaining popular support. Certainly, proselytizing through the performing arts is well documented. But with a piece like *Sankan*, there is undeniably a political dimension that surpasses a simple interpretation of good *kami* 神 (deities) conquering evil demons.

Documented proof of propaganda intent is, however, not available. What one can do is draw attention to the social and political environment of the time, which may have impacted on the formation and content of shrine theatre.

The oral tradition of the Sada Shrine priest, Miyagawa Hyōbu no shō Hideyuki, travelling to Kyoto in 1608 to obtain a priest's license from the Yoshida family is a starting point. Yoshida Kanetomo 吉田兼倶 (1435–1511), descendent of the Urabe 卜部 clan, vice-intendant of the Heian period *Jingikan* 神祇官 (Department of Divinities), put the Yoshida family on the religious map of Japan with the establishment of Yoshida Shintō. In a religious climate of Buddhist and Shinto syncretism, Kanetomo aimed to restore Shinto to its "original" state—Sōgen Shintō 宗源神道. In this, Japanese deities precede all. And to spread his doctrine, he taught the ancient classics of the *Kojiki* and *Nihon shoki* 日本書紀 (Chronicals of Japan) as well as the purification ritual *Nakatomi no harae* 中臣祓 (purification [rituals] of Nakatomi)[12] to a growing following of priests, monks, and social elite.[13] However, it was his licensing system that would ensure the influence of Yoshida Shinto in spreading his doctrines from the urban center to the rural periphery. By the time of Miyagawa Hyōbu no shō Hideyuki, the licensing system had been strengthened under Kanetomo's successor, Yoshida Kanemigi 吉田兼右 (1516–73). And, to further the influence of the Yoshida family, Kanemigi's sons, Kanemi 兼見 (1535–1610) and Bonshun 梵舜 (1553–1632), had affiliated themselves respectively with the great generals of Oda Nobunaga 織田信長, Toyotomi Hideyoshi 豊臣秀吉, and Tokugawa Ieyasu 徳川家康.[14] In 1665, through the edict Shosha negi kannushi hatto 諸社禰宜神主法度 [Ordinances for Shrine Priests], all shrines were effectively placed under the control of the Yoshida family. Three years prior to this, in 1662, the extent of Yoshida control may already have determined the ban of Buddhist practice including the chanting of sutras in Izumo Grand Shrine as well as the removal of a pagoda, normally the provenance of Buddhist temples, from within the grounds of the shrine (ISHIZUKA 1979, 362).

But the earlier connection between the Yoshida family and Oda Nobunaga, Toyotomi Hideyoshi, and Tokugawa Ieyasu may also be significant. When Miyagawa Hyōbu no shō Hideyuki travelled to Kyoto in 1608, this was only ten years after the death of Toyotomi Hideyoshi and the end of his military campaign on the Korean peninsula.

Hideyoshi's Korean campaign may be seen as the cumulative act following his unification of Japan, a united nation, for which he had proclaimed himself regent, or *taikō* 太閤. The mobilization of an impressive number of daimyo (feudal lords) brought together to combat a foreign land, no doubt served as a means to end internal strife by directing potentially disruptive energies overseas (FUJIKI 2005, 313). And then there was the expanding Spanish empire, which could both threaten and rival Hideyoshi's newly established regime. All this served as a potential catalyst for the early stirrings of nationalist sentiment.

Against this background, pieces like *Sankan* would easily resonate with Toyotomi's campaign. Certainly connections had been made between Toyotomi and Jingū Kōgō, as is evident from the accounts of the campaign by the samurai Yoshino Jingozaemon 吉野甚五左衛門, who invoked the mythical conquest of Korea by Jingū Kōgō as a historial precedent for justifying the attack on the Korean peninsula (ELISONAS 1991, 265). Given the military background of some shrine priests, as noted by ISHIZUKA Takatoshi (2005, 46–47), it is not inconceivable that Miyagawa Hyōbu no shōyū Hideyuki, himself of samurai status,[15] participated in the Korean campaign. Certainly, his name in part harkens back to an earlier age of military aristocracy in the Nara/Heian periods where *shōyū* 少輔 designated a high rank in the *hyōbu* 兵部, which was the erstwhile, though then defunct, War Ministry established under the *ritsuryō* 律令 legal system in the eighth century. The inclusion of Hyōbu no shōyū was not uncommon in the names of military men during the Sengoku and Edo periods.

In more modern times, against an international background of nineteenth-century nation-state formation and imperial expansion, restoration of the Meiji emperor and the establishment of a new political order followed a pattern of state formation through both the overthrow of what was deemed a disfunctioning regime, the Tokugawa, as well as the subsequent emulation of foreign, more powerful nation states (WIMMER and FEINSTEIN 2010, 769 and 785). A new political order would also demand international recognition to further legitamize its status. This was the intent of the Meiji oligarchs, but the response from neighboring countries only elicited friction due to preexisting alliances and allegiances. The refusal by Korea to recognize an alternative Imperial institution other than that of China sparked off the *Seikanron* 征韓論 (debate on subjugation of Korea), in 1873. Here too the propaganda potential of *Sankan* could easily be reworked or even revived to reflect frustration at a perceived sleight against a newly formed Japanese political institution.

In a similar vein, a connection between the Korean attack by Jingū Kōgō and nineteenth-century justifications for an attack has been examined by Richard W. Anderson, who sees a correlation between these justifications and votive paintings or *ema* 絵馬 depicting Jingū Kōgō. These were particularly prevalent during the nineteenth century and up to the beginning of the twentieth century in Yamaguchi and Fukuoka prefectures (ANDERSON 2002, 247–70). Performances of *Sankan* in the nineteenth century too could also be an alternative popular expression reflecting such debates as well as events leading to the final annexation/colonization of Korea in 1910. In prewar Japan *Sankan* had the more explicit title of *Sankan Seibatsu* 三韓征伐 (The Conquest of the Three Koreas).

But, *Sankan* is just one of many pieces that make up the repertoire of shrine theatre in Izumo and Iwami. It is also not peculiar to the Shimane prefectural area and can be found in the repertoires of other shrine theatre across the country. Nevertheless, it is unique in that it is the only piece in the theatrical repertoire where a specified country is identified as an enemy. The timing of the formation of the *shinnō* may see a correlation with Toyotomi Hideyoshi's advances into the Korean peninsula.

Toyotomi's Korean expedition was the major international concern at the end of the sixteenth century. But it was not the only one. At the extreme western end of Shimane prefecture, adjacent to the border of Yamaguchi prefecture, is the small town of Tsuwano. Sometimes referred to as a "small Kyoto," today it is a popular tourist destination, particularly famed for the annual July folk performances of the Sagi bird dance, dance of the heron. Iwami *kagura* groups too make frequent trips to the town, cashing in on the tourist trade with abbreviated performances. On the eastern side of the main street of Tsuwano is the Catholic Church, and to the west of Tsuwano station, surrounded by dense vegetation, is the comparatively recent construction of Maria *seidō* 聖堂 (sanctuary). The latter building commemorates thirty-six "hidden Christians" who, among a total of 153 individuals, were sent at the beginning of the Meiji period from Nagasaki to Tsuwano and were persuaded to change their faith. The thirty-six refused, and were subsequently tortured and then martyred (Shimane ken kankō renmei n.d.). Their persecution tragically emulates the execution of the twenty-six Christians in Nagasaki in 1597.

Miyagawa Hyōbu no shō Hideyuki's journey from Sada Shrine to Kyoto not only follows ten years on from Toyotomi Hideyoshi's invasion of the Korean peninsula but also took place at a time when restraints on Christian activity were periodically enforced. A ban on Christian activity had already been proclaimed twice in 1587 and 1597, the second resulting in the execution of the twenty-six Christians in Nagasaki. Six years on from Miyagawa's Kyoto journey, an edict was issued in 1614 under Tokugawa Hidetada 徳川秀忠, calling for the expulsion of all missionaries from Japan. The claim was that Christians "contravene governmental regulations, traduce Shinto, calumniate the True Law, destroy regulations and corrupt goodness"[16] (Elisonas 1991, 367). But, in addition, reports of Spanish control of the Philippines and Mexico raised fears that this would be emulated on Japanese soil. Either way the policy of isolationism, finally coming into force in 1639, was a clear statement of Japan's perceived threat of the foreign.

It is during this time frame of government-sanctioned xenophobia that the first references to theatrical *kagura* in Shimane prefecture find their way onto the pages of local histories and geographies of the region. At what stage individual performance pieces were incorporated in the repertoire is unclear.

The list of eleven pieces in the *Kaikitsudan* of 1653 is comprehensive, though the piece *Sankan* is not recorded. Its absence does not necessarily mean, however, that it was not present in the repertoire of other shrines. The oldest surviving script, the *Wada hon* 和田本 (The book of Wada), includes *Sankan* but dates back only to 1844, making any assessment of historical depth inconclusive.[17] And if *Sankan* does not date back to the supposed origins of the Sada *shinnō* in the early seventeenth century, its subsequent inclusion could reflect the sentiment of later generations, for *kagura* texts were always in a constant state of flux. The current text used in Iwami *kagura*, the *Kōtei Iwami kagura daihon* 校定石見神楽台本 [Corrected Iwami kagura script], for example, is a 1954 attempt to revamp a lost text, which, despite a ban on priest performances, was fabricated in the 1880s by the local, late nineteenth-century "national learning" *kokugaku* scholar, Fujii Muneo. He, in turn, incorporated songs from the *Tamahoko hyakushu* 玉鉾百首 (Hundred poems of an ancient road), penned by Motoori Norinaga 本居宣長 in 1786.

A paucity of documentation of any historical depth means that in terms of content, the nature of the pieces can only be gleaned from extant texts, which, as in Iwami *kagura*, is perhaps a greater reflection of late nineteenth-century Meiji sentiment than that of preceding generations. Either way, adversity to the foreign, the isolationist policy of the Tokugawa *bakufu* 幕府 (government, literally tent government), including similar sentiments at the end of the Edo period, is a possible interpretation for the threat of demons hailing from other lands. In Iwami *kagura*, of a total of twenty theatrical pieces, within seven of these (*Yahata* 八幡, *Chigaeshi* 道返し (returning [the demon] back on the road), *Jinrin* 塵輪, *Shōki* 鍾馗, *Yamatotakeru no Mikoto* 日本武尊, *Kumaso* 熊襲, and *Take no uchi*), the recurring phrase is a variation of, for example, that in *Yahata*:[18]

今度異国より悪王飛び来り，わが国の人民を害す
Kondo ikoku yori aku ō tobikitari, waga kuni no jinmin o gaisu

Now, a bad king from a different country is flying in and is harming the people of our country   (SHINOHARA 1972, 12)

And the response, after the inevitable victorious battle against the assailant, can be, as in *Chigaeshi*:

早や早や元つ国にと立ち帰るべし
Haya haya mototsu kuni ni to tachi kaeru beshi

"Quickly, quickly you must go back to your own country"   (SHINOHARA 1972, 28)

In the two pieces *Kumaso* and *Yamatotakeru no Mikoto* the enemy is near, for here the mission of the warrior Yamatotakeru is to attack and pacify respectively the Kumaso folk of southern Kyushu to the west,[19] and following on from this, the Emishi (Ainu) to the east. Both peoples are again causing harm against the people of our country, the land of Yamato.

The remainder of the pieces can be didactic. *Gokoku tane moto* 五穀種元 (origins of the seeds of the five crops) shows how to grow crops and thank deities for them. And the piece *Gojin* (five deities) explains the concepts of *gogyō* 五行 (five phases) with particular reference to the five seasons, Spring, Summer, Doyō 土用 (dog days), Autumn, and Winter. *Kirime* too briefly highlights the importance of *gogyō*. Then there are the expositions of the myths in the *Kojiki* and *Nihon shoki* in pieces like *Kashima* 鹿島, *Yasogami taiji* 八十神退治 (subjugation of the eighty deities), *Iwato, Ebisu, Orochi* 大蛇 (the great snake), and *Yachimata* 八衢 (eight divisions of the road). Included here too are the aforementioned *Chigaeshi, Yamatotakeru no*

Mikoto, Kumaso, and *Take no uchi.* Then there are theatrical pieces whose sole aim seems to be purely entertainment and which have corresponding versions in *nō* and/or *kabuki.* Pieces here include *Tenjin* 天神 (*kabuki*),[20] *Kurozuka* 黒塚 (black mound) (*nō*), *Kifune* 貴船 (*nō*), and *Yorimasa* 頼政 (*nō*). Recent additions to the repertoire have seemingly reinforced the entertainment value of performances.

This variety of pieces, whose functions can be variously interpreted and yet today all fall under the rubric of *kagura*, shows the degree to which the elasticity of this term has been stretched.

That the majority of pieces are sourced in the *Kojiki* and *Nihon shoki* could be directly correlated with the expanding influence of Yoshida Shinto. Some pieces warn of the external threat of the foreign. But Yoshida Shinto was also competing against alternative internal religious or thought systems within Japan, most obviously Buddhism and Confucianism, whose foreign derivation was denounced by Shinto scholars such as, for example, Masuho Zankō 増穂残口 (1655–1742) in his *Endōtsugan* 艶道通鑑 [A complete model of a beautiful way] of 1715 (MASUHO 1996).

The preeminence of Shinto, however, would come to the fore with early Meiji policies that also saw a restructuring of the Shinto establishment, including a dismantling of existing shrine networks. In the third month of 1870, the Matsue *han minsei kyoku shinshi gakari* 松江藩民政局神祠懸 (Matsue Domain Civil Administration Offices for Shrines) abolished the titles of the hereditary *heitō* 幣頭, the heads of shrine families attached to neighboring shrines, which fell under the jurisdiction of Sada. This would mean the demise of the family networks that supported the performances of the *shichi za* and *shinnō* at Sada. And the ban on performances by priests issued in the same year would spell the end of the existing format of the Sada performances. The ban did not, however, finish the tradition of priests' performances. They still remained central to the transmission of the *shichi za* and *shinnō*, although that transmission would be to civilian groups, ordinary farmers, and laborers, who, in some cases prior to the ban, had already taken on the mantle of *kagura* performers (ISHIZUKA 1979, 6–7). Signficantly, Ishizuka claims that it was in this transition from priests to civilian groups that the qualitatively and functionally distinct performance formats of *shichi za* and theatrical drama were brought together to become collectively known as *kagura* (ibid., 455).

This is the state of *kagura* today, but the survival of folk performing arts in the early part of the twentieth century owes much to the emergence of a national movement to galvanize youth, namely the formalization of youth groups, the *seinendan.*

KAGURA AND SEINENDAN

Youth groups in Japan can trace their histories back to the Edo period and beyond, where sodalities, known by such names as *waka renchū* 若連中 (young groups), ensured the continuation of both village tradition and industry. Preparation and participation in village festivals, with the shrine as the focus of those festivals, could also form a part of their duties—the carrying of *mikoshi* 神輿, portable shrines, being one example.

In the Meiji period these groups continued to perform their functions at the regional level without any central control. This changed, however, from the outbreak of the Russo-Japanese War of 1904–05.[21] In 1904, the then Home Office Minister, Yoshikawa Akimasa 芳川顕正, was ordered to survey the country and, during his travels, he met up with a certain Yamamoto Takinosuke 山本瀧之助, a school teacher in a village near Fukuyama city, Hiroshima prefecture. Yamamoto Ryunosuke had been inspirational in organizing youth groups toward the end of the nineteenth century, a time when there was much vocal concern about the sloven and careless nature of the young resulting from what was seen to be the poor results of "new era" education (TAZAWA 1934, 34). In 1896, Yamamoto published a book, *Inaka Seinen* 田舎青年 (Rural youth), (YAMAMOTO 1896), and when Yoshikawa met up with Yamamoto, Yoshikawa was impressed by the contribution Yamamoto's youth groups had made to the war effort—not only to the Russo-Japanese war but also to the previous Sino-Japanese war of 1895. Recognizing that the potential of youth groups could be tapped for local projects in peace time, the report of the Home Office Minister instigated a series of policies that saw the centralized control of youth groups, resulting in the establishment of the *Seinendan chūō bu* 青年団中央部, The Centralized Youth Group Department, following the first National Meeting of Regional Seinendan (全国地方青年団中央機関設置の議 zenkoku chihō seinendan chūō kikan setchi no gi) in Aichi prefecture in 1909. In order to stimulate and encourage youth groups across the country, awards were issued by the Ministry of Education (Monbushō 文部省), to the best youth groups at the prefectural level. The first of these was awarded in 1910.

The formalization of *seinendan* and the stimulus of the award system had a particular impact on the Japanese folk performing arts. And rural theatre, like the *shinnō* in Sada Shrine, was no exception. *Seinendan* became bearers of the *shinnō* tradition in around 1914 following the official advocation for *seinendan* groups in the area, which was timed to coincide with the exact day of the promulgation of Japan's "annexation" of Korea on 29 August 1910 (OKUHARA 1926, 96). The connection between *shinnō* and *seinendan* became almost synonymous, and for some groups participation and learning of the *kagura* was compulsory for all members of the *seinendan*. At least this is the known case for Mimiku *kagura* 見々久神楽, an Izumo *kagura* based in Izumo city, a situation that continued up to the Second World War (SHIMANE KEN KODAI BUNKA SENTĀ 2001, 41).

Compulsory participation in the *kagura* by the *seinendan* points to yet a further alternative function of the *kagura*, namely as a tool for the moral and cultural education of the local youth. Even after the era of *seinendan* had come to an end, a history of Kashima town, where Sada Shrine is located, writes that "*seinendan* were the barometer of regional society and their "cultural education" (教養 *kyōyō*) and physical state could [determine] the rise and fall of rural society…" (KASHIMA CHŌ HENSAN IINKAI 1962, 254).

As part of that cultural education, in rural Shimane Izumo *kagura* would likely have played a central role, for in 1922–23 the youth group in Sada village was selected to receive the *seinendan* award by the Ministry of Internal Affairs (*Naimushō* 内務省) and the Ministry of Education. The award was for both their "cultural" achievements and "self-improvement" (修養 *shūyō*) (ibid., 255). And here, "cultural" achievements in the small rural village of Sada could only point to performances of the *shinnō*.

The *shinnō* may have been valued for its capacity to educate culturally, but as shrine theatre—originally performed by shrine priests—its appropriation by the young meant a perceived debasement of performances. Priests, who had been actively involved in the transmission process, decried the vulgarization of the *kagura*, claiming that current performances were a farce. A contemporary document notes that priests boycotted their assistance in performance (OKUHARA 1926, 648). Yet, despite the anguish of shrine priests, it was the performances by youth groups of the *shinnō* of Sada that impressed the Shinto scholar Miyaji Naokazu (宮地直一) (1886–1949). In 1924, Miyaji became head of the *Jinja kyoku kōshō ka* 神社局考証課 (Historical Investigation Bureau of Shinto Shrines) set up within the Home Office, and during his survey of shrines in Shimane prefecture he saw a performance of the Sada *shinnō* in 1925. Miyaji Naokazu was impressed and suggested that the *shinnō* be performed in Yasukuni Shrine in Tokyo as part of the annual festivals there.

1925 also saw the opening of the first Nippon Seinenkan 日本青年館 (Japan Youth Building) in Tokyo and the subsequent presentation of national concerts of representative folk performing arts. Perhaps inspired by the support of Miyaji, representatives of Izumo *kagura* applied to perform in Tokyo, at the *Nippon Seinenkan*. They were successful and gave their first performances there in 1926. The organizers in Izumo were keen to make a good impression and examined two performance groups to decide which one should represent eastern Shimane prefecture. The result was the *shinnō* from Sada Shrine. The organizers were also careful to select performance pieces that would inspire and to avoid, in the words of one of the organizers, pieces that may be deemed vulgar (SHIMANE HYŌRON SHA 1924, 57).

This careful selection could and would be the catalyst for the modification of performance practice, an ongoing process that still is determining the nature of performance practices, as adaptations to alternative performance settings and audience invite the inevitable anathema to tradition, change.

Performance of the Sada *shinnō* in the *Nippon Seinenkan* in 1926 would transect with what could be interpreted as yet another expression of nationalist sentiment, the establishment of folkloric studies.

IZUMO *KAGURA* MEETS FOLKLORE ACADEMIA

When Yanagita Kunio 柳田国男 (1875–1962) and Orikuchi Shinobu 折口信夫 (1887–1953) were spearheading research into folkloric Japan, it was at a time of both social and cultural upheaval. If a concern with the "other" or the "foreign" could be a stimulus for the creation of some of the pieces that make up the repertoire of shrine theatre, this same stimulus could spark endeavors in the emergence of Japanese folkloric studies to seek and preserve the native in contradistinction to the imposition of the foreign. Yanagita was clearly concerned with change in folkloric customs, and although there are no clear statements to preserve folkloric customs in the face of increasing Westernization, a sense of rivalry with the West both academically and nationalistically is clarified in such publications as *Shinpojiumu Yanagita Kunio* シンポジウム柳田國男 [A symposium on Yanagita Kunio] (KAMISHIMA and ITŌ 1973). Certainly, an expression of that nationalism is all too evident in the erection of a stone monument in Takeuchi Shrine, Abiko city, Chiba prefecture, by Yanagita, his younger brother, and five others to commemorate victory in the Russo-Japanese War. And to emphasize the internationalist rivalry, the commemoration is written in English, "In Memory of the Conquest over the Russians." Conversely, for all Yanagita's extensive writings, he apparently showed little interest in neighboring China or Korea (KAMISHIMA and ITŌ 1973, 54, 61).

More generally, within the process of Westernization, a struggle for cultural survival could become manifest in encounters with the folk, recording and researching the folk culture of "our country" (*waga kuni* 我が国) against the fear that the native would be lost and forgotten. In the early part of the twentieth century, *seinendan* would play a central role in ensuring the survival of many folk performing arts.

In 1926, when the *seinendan* of Izumo gave their debut performance of the *shinnō* in Tokyo, it was the young folklorist Kodera Yūkichi 小寺融吉 (1895–1945) who would be responsible for the organization of their performance at Tokyo's *Seinenkan*. Kodera Yūkichi and Yanagita Kunio were regular contributors to the journalistic arm of the *Seinenkan*, the magazine *Teikoku Seinen* 帝国青年 (Imperial Youth), subsequently retitled *Seinen* (Youth). Their contributions to the journal reveal not only the close relationship that had formed between folk performing arts, festivals, and youth groups but also the intentions of the governing body of the *seinendan* in educating Japanese youth.

Kodera Yūkichi was occasionally requested to express opinions on various aspects of youth education including, for example, for a section entitled "On the principles of modern youth and what they should do" (KODERA 1928, 31). But, it was Kodera's activities in organizing performances at the *Seinenkan* for which he is noted, and his first encounter with the *shinnō* of Sada at the *Seinenkan* in Tokyo would be instrumental in putting the *shinnō* in particular, and *kagura* in general, on the academic map. In 1929 Kodera published his research of *kagura* as an art form, which was the first comprehensive account of *kagura* (KODERA 1929). In it he regrets that up to his publication, *kagura* had been totally ignored by academics and explains that, in comparison to the *kagura* of the imperial court, that performed in regional areas was considered to be a vulgarized form of court *kagura* and therefore not worthy of study (ibid., preface, 1–2). Even with the performances of the Sada *shinnō* at the *Seinenkan* in 1926, it is clear from the various responses of Tokyo scholars and interested parties that many had not seen this form of *kagura* before and had difficulty in understanding what it was. Theatre critic and writer Ihara Seiscien (伊原青々園) (1870–1941) likened performances to Chinese theatre from Shanghai and speculated a Chinese influence on the *shinnō* (IHARA 1926, 41–42). Takano Tatsuyuki, a specialist in the history of Japanese theatre at Tokyo Imperial University, recognized the influence of *nō* drama and thought that the *kagura* may have preserved an older form of *nō*. Takano also commented on what he perceived to be a similarity between the preceding unmasked dances in Izumo *kagura* with the *mikagura* of the imperial court—a possibly fateful comparison that may have influenced subsequent thinking postulating the erroneous speculation that the Sada *shinnō* was of great antiquity and central in the development of *kagura* across the country (Takano 1926, 45).

Yanagita Kunio was himself present and added his comments. He was circumspect when faced with the reality of the *shinnō* performance. He claimed that they were too long, should be shortened to fit in with the busy bustle of Tokyo, and that the standard of performance itself was no more than that of farm laborers taking time out during a lunch break to spend time performing *kagura* (Yanagita 1926, 44–45). Given Yanagita's lifetime work to introduce and promote folkloric Japan, faced with the reality of a performance his frank comments appear paradoxical. Yet, panel discussions held after some of the earliest Japanese folk performing arts performances given in the *Seinenkan* back in the 1920s elicited similar responses. In transcripts of the discussions published in the journal *Seinen*, Kodera, Yanagita, and Orikuchi Shinobu, amongst others, concluded that the performances in the 1929 concert were monotonous and boring. Orikuchi, who later produced his own book on Japanese folk performing arts, confessed at that time that he knew nothing about musical performance (Yanagita et al. 1929, 29–43).

Given that Japanese folklorist Hashimoto Hiroyuki 橋本裕之 has suggested that early urbanite Japanese folklorists possibly romanticized rural Japan, these statements perhaps shed a different, and possibly more honest, light on the current thinking of folklorists (Hashimoto 2006). Or rather, the romantic image embraced was jolted by the reality of performances given. This too comes out in Hashimoto's publication in a discussion of the folklorist Ushio Michio 牛尾三千夫, whose romanticist publication *Utsukushi mura: minzoku saihōki* 美しい村—民俗採訪記 [Beautiful village: Fieldwork records] concealed his less congenial experiences of village life—one, for instance, being his brief arrest for spy activity during World War II.

Today with the support of government authorities, Izumo *kagura* survives, though with rural population decline, problems of sustaining traditions prevail. A rebuilt *Seinenkan* in Tokyo is still a venue for folk performing arts concerts as well as conferences held by the Society for Folkloric Performing Arts, but although Izumo city hall has a youth section in its offices, the staff claim that *seinendan* as such no longer exists, having seen a steady decline from the 1970s. The relationship between youth groups and performing arts in particular was prevalent in the prewar years. And, although *seinendan* may have continued or been revamped in a postwar setting, according to the *Kashima chō shi* 鹿島町誌 [History of Kashima town], where Sada is located, *seinendan*, like those in Kashima town were dissolved, at least in their original form, at the end of the War following the orders of General Douglas MacArthur (Kashima chō hensan iinkai 1962, 255).

Compulsory participation in *kagura* performances for *seinendan* members, at least for the Mimiku *kagura* in Izumo city before the Second World War, may have been the norm for members of other *seinendan* too. In this respect, a staff member in the Cultural Assets section of Izumo City Hall speculated that a prewar climate and the fear of being chastised for un-Japanese activity possibly led to the compulsory participation by youth group members in certain Izumo *kagura* groups.[22]

In Shimane prefecture, and no doubt elsewhere, the moral education of Japanese youth in pre–World War II Japan seems to have been assisted by performances of shrine theatre. But along with this, there was also the recognized potential for performances to attract revenue into regions in general and shrines in particular and also to serve as advertisements for the local. In other words, the economic function of shrine theatre is yet a further dimension of performance and falls in the category of the Japanese folk performing arts and tourism, a much-discussed topic and particularly pertinent to Iwami *kagura*—arguably more so than Izumo *kagura* (THORNBURY 1997, 67–74; LANCASHIRE 2006; 2011).

TOURIST INTERSECTIONS

The implementation of the Festival Law in 1992, which saw the publicizing of folk performing arts falling into the hands of local tourist offices, only put the seal on a trend that had been long established.

Yamaji Kōzō emphasized the ritual and solemnity of pre-Meiji Iwami *kagura*, reinforcing a tendency to see the use of *kagura* as tourist attractions to generate regional revenues as only a post-Meiji, or even later modern phenomenon. Yet despite the perceived modern-era secularization of performances, the use of *kagura* and other ritual performances for alternative agendas saw *kagura* groups in pre-Meiji Japan travelling beyond their customary boundaries of activities to promote their art, or perhaps more importantly, to supplement incomes.

In the year 1715, a priest by the name of Sasaki Chikugo 佐々木筑後 from the town of Kake to the south of Masuda city in the western part of Shimane prefecture, was invited to perform Iwato kagura in Kyoto. The priest took five performers with him and performed every day for three weeks before audiences of three to four hundred people (KAKECHŌ YAKUBA HENSHŪ IINKAI 1961, 705–706).

Likewise, in a publication penned by the essayist Kodera Gyokuchō 小寺玉晁 in 1824, which records spectacles of interest ranging from living freaks to displays of perversion, there is a reference to a performance at the *shugendō* temple of Seijuin 清寿院,[23] Nagoya, of what Ishizuka interprets to be *shinnō* (KODERA, GUNJI, SEKIYAMA 1991, 48). The performances of *Shindai geki* in Kyoto and Osaka recorded in the 1920s, as noted above, are an example of this. And even the performances of the *shinnō* in the *Seinenkan* could similarly serve as a stimulus to attract tourism into the Shimane prefecture area.

The railway from Osaka to Izumo was opened in 1908, and this superseded the longer boat journey from Osaka via Shimonoseki to Maizuru set up by the merchant vessel, the Hankaku Maru 阪鶴丸. This vessel would anchor in the bay adjacent to Izumo grand shrine and let sightseers travel by smaller vessel into the town.

That performances of shrine theatre could serve to draw in additional revenue is clear, for example, in the decision made in the early Meiji period to introduce Iwami *kagura* into the northern reaches of Hiroshima prefecture. This decision was spurred on by a failure of prior attractions such as horse racing and children's *kyōgen* 狂言to draw in people, and more importantly, make financial contributions to local shrines. The entertainment value of the *kagura* here was further enhanced in 1947–48 through the creation of a new style of dramatic dance, *shinmai* 新舞 (new dance), by a middle-school headmaster, a certain Sasaki Junzō 佐々木順三, in Takada county, northern Hiroshima (Rokugō 2004, 347). In more recent history, Expo '70 in Osaka would be an additional catalyst in transforming the nature of Iwami *kagura*, in particular in terms of performance format. Such venues, involving performances on large stages, would enhance the visual display but in some pieces sacrifice the content in terms of greatly reducing the exposition of the written text and the omission of the spoken word. That tourism has become an all-important factor determining the performance itinerary of many groups is evidenced today in the wide variety of performance venues, from hotel lobbies to concert halls. Here too, the multi-varied function of shrine theatre is again re-emphasized.

CONCLUSION

What today is understood as Izumo *kagura* and Iwami *kagura* emerged against a volatile history of late sixteenth-century nationalist expansionism; Toyotomi Hideyoshi's unification of Japan, consolidated by a Korean campaign with the original, ultimate aim of controlling China; a radically contrasting period of national isolationism during which, through Yoshida Shinto, an attempt was made to place greater influence on the native religion of Japan as opposed to the foreign; the rising specter of foreign intervention from the mid-nineteenth century; and the mobilization of Japanese youth, who would play a central role in ensuring the preservation of "traditional," rural culture.

Against this background of historical change, the role and function of shrine theatre has arguably shifted, adapting to and reflecting the historical circumstances in which it was and is embroiled. Although the *shinnō* and similar shrine theatre are usually understood as a ritual entertainment, as *kagura* performed for deities, Ishizuka Takatoshi has pointed to clear historical distinctions in the nomenclature where the terms *kagura*, *shichi za*, and *shinnō* are listed as separate performance items. In so doing, he has called into question the ritual status of theatrical drama and, more importantly, its status as *kagura*. Pieces like *Sankan* suggest an alternative agenda for shrine theatre, a form of political propaganda. This at least is the implication of the Izumo Kagura Information Center, which felt an expressed need to emphasize that today *Sankan* is performed in "a strong atmosphere of restraint." And if shrine theatre was, and may still be, an expression of various forms of nationalist sentiment, such as sixteenth-century national unification, nineteenth-century state formation, or twenty-first-century chauvinistic reactionism, the emerging discipline of folkloric studies, like the object of its study, was in itself reflecting a concern to preserve the native against the intrusion of the foreign, impacting within a rapid process of Westernization.

Shrine ritual, political propaganda, moral education for prewar Japanese youth, and tourist attraction—the varied, adapting functions, or arguably simultaneous multi-functionalism, of what is understood as *kagura* today have assisted as unwitting survival strategies in the continued transmission of Izumo *kagura* and Iwami *kagura* into modern times. Thus, through the advocacy of various agencies like youth groups, the Home Office and Ministry of Education, folklorists, and tourist agencies, the final accolade of that survival strategy occurred on 27 November 2011 when continued advocacy saw the Sada *shinnō* finally achieving the ultimate accolade of United Nations-designated Intangible Cultural Heritage.

NOTES

1. Ōhara *Shinshoku Kagura* is the title of a publication on this *kagura*. The Agency for Cultural Affairs uses the title *Ōhara Kannushi Kagura* 大原神主神楽. A rendition in English remains the same, *Ōhara Priests' Kagura*.

2. An observation of a performance of "Sankan" performed by the Ōhara Kannushi Kagura and recorded by the *Tottori Kōjin Kagura Kenkyū Kai & Kagura dan* 鳥取荒神神楽研究会＆神楽団 (The Tottori Kōjin Kagura research group and *kagura* group) reported that a battle with the Korean kings was repeated five times (Tottori Kōjin Kagura Kenkyū Kai & Kagura dan 2014); or one blogger was inspired to introduce his observations of *Sankan* with the heading, "The overwhelming victory of Shimane prefecture in its fight with Korea is tremendous" 「韓国と戦う島根県の圧勝っぷりがスゴイ！」(JUNKWORLD n.d.). (http://matome.naver.jp/odai/2140370607532875701).

3. Claims for the origins of Izumo *kagura* in Sada stem from Honda Yasuji (1960, 12–14) and are repeated in encylopedias and dictionaries on Japan in general and folk performing arts in particular, e.g., Kodansha's edition of *Japan – An Illustrated Encyclopedia* (1993, 777). Doubts about origins in Sada have been been expressed by ISHIZUKA Takatoshi (1979, 449) and LANCASHIRE (2006, 56–64).

4. http://matome.naver.jp/odai/2140370607532875701. 演目「三韓」は、神功皇后が朝鮮半島に出兵し、新羅、百済、高句麗の三韓を征伐するというもので、半島の方が見たら発狂することうけあいです。竹島の日を制定する島根県は、すさまじい強さです (JUNKWORLD n.d.).This description of *Sankan* follows on from the blog title given in note 2.

5. *Shichi za* is a term more associated with Izumo *kagura* rather than Iwami *kagura*. Its usage here points to a number of unmasked dances, not necessarily seven, which usually precede the performance of theatrical pieces.

6. In Ōmoto *kagura*, individuals becoming spiritually possessed are men.

7. *Kumo* is an alternative name for *tengai* 天蓋, a square wooden lattice decorated primarily with sakaki branches and ornamental paper, and hung over the area of performance.

8. Yamaji simply states Mongolia. I have provided the years for the attempted Mongolian invasions as Yamaji can only be alluding to this threat.

9. Ishizuka Takatoshi obtained his information about Miyagawa Hyōbu no shō Hideyuki creating the *shinnō* from a document, *Shindai kagura sho* 神代神楽書 [Writing on the *kagura* of the age of the gods], by Izumo scholar Gotō Kurashirō 後藤藏四郎 (1865–1945). The *Yatsuka gun shi* 八束郡誌 [A history of Yatsuka county] of 1926 provides a similar account of the same events (OKUHARA 1926, 644).

10. HONDA Yasuji draws attention to the *hōraku* and postulates a connection to the later *shinnō* (1966, 42, 435).

11. This at least is the case for the *Tsuda kagura shachū* 津田神楽社中 (Tsuda kagura group) based to the east of Masuda City.

12. *Nakatomi no harae*, an abbreviation of *Nakatomi no harai kotoba* 中臣祓詞 was a ritual to expel sins and pollutants through the recitation of Shinto prayers, *norito* 祝詞.

13. Information obtained from the *Encyclopedia of Shinto* produced by Kokugakuin University (ITŌ 2006)

14. Yoshida Bonshun, in particular, had developed a personal relationship with Toyotomi Hideyoshi and was involved in establishing a shrine for the general, the Toyokuni Shrine 豊国神社 in Kyoto. Bonshun later gave personal instruction to Tokugawa Ieyasu on Shinto deities (Itō 2006).

15. Information obtained from a descendent of Miyagawa Yasuhide 宮川康秀 via Niwano Shōko 丹羽野輝子 of the Kashima rekishi minzoku shiryōkan 鹿島歴史民俗資料館 Kashima history and folk materials building on 8 October 2014.

16. This is a translation by Elisonas of Ōkubo et al, eds., 1963, 124–25.

17. Earlier scripts exist but only include one or two pieces. The oldest script, titled *Kagura nō no sho* 神楽能の書 [A script of *kagura nō*], dating to 1715, was destroyed in a "recent fire" (Honda 1974, 51–52).

18 The titles of the following pieces are the names of deities, demons or semi-historical characters/peoples. Yahata (deity), Jinrin (demon), Shoki (Chinese scholar and deity), Yamatotakeru, Take uchi (semi-mythical warriors), Kumaso (an ancient tribe in southern Kyushu)

19. The identity of the Kumaso remains uncertain. A connection is postulated to another group of people, the Hayato. And an article by Kakubayashi Fumio has interestingly suggested that this group may have been of Austronesian origin (1998, 15–31).

20. The *kabuki* and *ningyō jōruri* 人形浄瑠璃 (puppet) version of *Tenjin* is *Sugawara denju tenarai kagami* 菅原伝授手習鑑 [Sugawara's secrets of calligraphy].

21. The following account of the formation of *seinendan* at the national level is given in a number of publications, e.g., Kumagai Tatsujirō (1931, 28–40) and Tazawa Yoshiharu (1934, 34–40).

22. The "Japan-Korea Annexation Treaty" (韓国併合ニ関スル条約 Kankoku heigō ni kansuru jōyaku) was ratified on 22 August and officially proclaimed on 29 August.

23. The Seijuin temple was abolished following the Meiji restoration and was subsequently converted into Tsuruma *kōen* 鶴舞公園 (Tsuruma Park) in 1909.

References

Anderson, Richard W.
  2002   Jingū Kōgō "Ema" in southwestern Japan: Reflections and anticipations of the "Seikanron" debate in the late Tokugawa and early Meiji period. *Asian Folklore Studies* 61: 247–70. doi: 10.2307/1178973.

Ashida Ijin 蘆田伊人, ed.
  1971   *Un'yōshi* 雲陽誌 (Journal of Un'yō). Tokyo: Yūzankaku.

Chanlett-Avery, Emma; Mark E. Manyin; Rebecca M. Nelson, Brock R. Williams, Yamakawa Taishu
  2017   Japan-U.S. Relations: Issues for Congress.
         https://www.fas.org/sgp/crs/row/RL33436.pdf (accessed 16 October 2017)

Elisonas, Jurgis
  1991   The inseparable trinity: Japan's relations with China and Korea. In *The Cambridge History of Japan Volume 4: Early Modern Japan*, ed. John Whitney Hall, 235–300. Cambridge: Cambridge University Press. doi: 10.1017/CHOL9780521223553.007

Fujiki Hisashi 藤木久志
  2005   *Tenka tōitsu to Chōsen shinryaku Oda/Totomi no seiken no jitsuzō* 天下統一と朝鮮侵略 織田・豊臣政権の実像 [Unity under the heavens and the invasion

of Korea, the true image of the Oda/Toyotomi political administration].
Tokyo: Kodansha.

HASHIMOTO Hiroyuki 橋本裕之
2006   *Minzoku geinō kenkyū to iu shinwa* 民俗芸能研究という神話 [A myth called
        folk performing arts research]. Tokyo: Shinwasha.

HIRO88641
2013   佐陀神能10の内07 三韓 Sada shinnō 10 no uchi no 7 sankan. https://www
        .youtube.com/watch?v=oUy3BJPs5eY (accessed 16 October 2017).

HONDA Yasuji 本田安次
1960   *Zuroku Nihon no minzoku geinō* 圖録日本の民俗藝能 [An illustrated record
        of Japanese folk performing arts]. Tokyo: Asahi Shinbun Sha.
1966   *Kagura Nihon no minzoku geinō 1* 神楽、日本の民俗芸能 1 [Kagura, the
        Japanese Folk Performing Arts 1]. Tokyo: Kijisha.
1974   Sada shinnō Wada hon 佐陀神能和田本 [The Wada book of Sada shinnō]. In
        Nihon shomin bunka shiryō shūsei 1, kagura・bugaku 日本庶民文化史料集成
        第一巻神楽・舞楽 [A collection of historical materials on Japanese common
        people volume 1 kagura, bugaku], Masaaki UEDA 上田正昭, Yasuji HONDA
        本田安次, and MISUMI Haruo 三隅治雄 eds., 51–52. Tokyo: San'ichi Shobō.

IHARA Seiseien 伊原青々園
1926   Sada shinnō shokan 佐陀神能所感 (Impressions of Sada shinnō). *Shimane
        hyōron* 島根評論 [Shimane review] 3: 41–49. Kyoto: Shimane Hyōronsha.

ISHIZUKA Takatoshi 石塚尊俊
1979   *Nishi Nihon sho kagura no kenkyū* 西日本諸神楽の研究 [Research on the var-
        ious kagura of western Japan]. Tokyo: Keiyūsha.
2005   *Sato kagura no seiritsu ni kansuru kenkyū* 里神楽の成立に関する研究
        [Research on the formation of rural *kagura*]. Tokyo: Iwata Shoin.

ITŌ Satoshi
2005   "Yoshida Shintō" http://eos.kokugakuin.ac.jp/modules/xwords/entry.
        php?entryID=372 (accessed 16 October 2017).
2006   "Bonshun" http://eos.kokugakuin.ac.jp/modules/xwords/entry.php?en-
        tryID=420 (accessed 16 October 2017).

IZUMO KAGURA JŌHŌ SENTĀ 出雲神楽情報センター
n.d   http://izumokagura.jimdo.com/主な演目紹介/よく舞われる演目 (no lon-
        ger accessible.

JUNKWORLD
n.d.   http://matome.naver.jp/odai/2140370607532875701 (accessed 16 Octo-
        ber 2017).

KAKECHŌ YAKUBA HENSHŪ IINKAI 加計町役場編修委員会
1961   *Kakechō shi jō/ge kan* 上下巻 [History of Kake town first and second vol-
        ume]. Kake chō (Hiroshima prefecture): Kakechō Yakuba.

KUMAGAI Tatsujirō
1931   *Kyōdo bunka to seinendan* 郷土文化と青年団 [Regional culture and youth
        groups]. Tokyo: Yūzankaku.

KAKUBAYASHI Fumio 角林文雄
1998   Hayato: Ōsutoronesia-kei no kodai Nihon buzoku 隼人: オーストロネシア
        系の古代日本部族 [The Hayato: An ancient Japanese tribe of Austronesian
        descent]. *The Bulletin of the Institute for Japanese Culture* 3: 15–31.

KAMISHIMA Jirō 神島二郎 and ITŌ Mikiharu 伊藤幹治 eds.
1973   *Shinpojiumu Yanagita Kunio* シンポジウム柳田國男 [Symposium on Yanagita Kunio]. Tokyo: Nihon Hōsō Shuppan Kyōkai.

KASHIMA CHŌ SHI HENSAN IINKAI 鹿島町誌編纂委員会 [Journal of Kashima town editorial committee]
1962   *Kashima chō shi* 鹿島町誌 [Journal of Kashima town]. Kashima chō: Shimane Ken Yasoku Gun Kashima Chō Yakuba.

KODANSHA
1993   *Japan: An Illustrated Encyclopedia*. Tokyo: Kōdansha.

KODERA Gyokuchō 小寺玉晁, GUNJI Masakatsu 郡司正勝, and SEKIYAMA Kazuo 関山和夫, eds.
1991   *Misemono zasshi* 見世物雑志 [Magazine on public exhibitions]. Tokyo: San'ichi Shobō.

KODERA Yūkichi 小寺融吉
1928   現代青年の信条とすべきものについて [On the principles of modern youth and what they should do]. *Seinen* 13: 31–37.
1929   *Geijutsu to shite no kagura kenkyū* 芸術としての神楽の研究 [Research on kagura as a performing art]. Tokyo: Chiheisha Shobō.

KUROSAWA Sekisai 黒沢石斎 and TANIGUCHI Tameji 谷口為次 (annotated)
1914   *Kaikitsudan zengohen* 懐橘談前後篇 [Edited first and second part of Kaikitsudan]. Matsue: Hatakeinosuke.

LANCASHIRE, Terence
2006   *Gods' Music: The Japanese Folk Theatre of Iwami Kagura* (Studien zur traditionellen Musik Japans, vol. 12). Wilhelmshaven: Florian Noetzel.
2011   *An Introduction to Japanese Folk Performing Arts*. London and New York: Routledge.

MASUHO Zankō 増穂残口
1996   *Endōtsugan* 艶道通鑑 [A complete model of a beautiful way] (*Edo jidai josei bunko* 江戸時代女性文庫 A women's library of the Edo period 41). Tokyo: Ōzorasha.

ŌBA Yoshimi 大庭良美
1975   Iwami kagura zakki 石見神楽雑記 [Miscellaneous notes on Iwami kagura]. In *San'in minzoku* 山陰民俗 [Folklore of the San'in area] 22: 42–51. Matsue: San'in Minzoku Gakkai.

ŌKUBO Toshiaki 大久保利謙, KODAMA Kōta 児玉幸多, YANAI Kenji 箭内健次, INOUE Mitsusada 井上光貞, eds.
1963   Shiryō ni yoru Nihon no ayumi (Kinsei) 史料による日本の歩み（近世） Japan's course from historical documents (early modern period). Tokyo: Yoshikawa Kōbunkan.

OKUHARA Fukuichi 奥原福市, ed.
1973   *Yatsuka gun shi* 八束郡誌 [Journal of Yatsuka county]. Shimane ken: Yatsuka Jiji-Kai.

ROKUGŌ Hiroshi 六郷 寛
2004   Kinsei makki Aki no kuni hokubu chiiki ni okeru "Iwami kagura" no jyuyō 近世末期安芸国北部地域における「石見神楽」の受容 ("Iwami kagura" in the northern area of Aki province up to the end of the early modern period). In *Kinsei kindai no chiiki shakai to bunka* 近世近代の地域社会と文化 [Regional society and culture in the early modern and modern period], ed. Rai Kiichi

sensei taikan kinen ronshū kankō kai 頼祺一先生退官記念論集刊行会 (Society for the publication of articles to commemorate the retirement of professor Rai Kiichi), 318–50. Osaka: Seibundō.

SADA-JINJA
2005   http://sadajinjya.jp/?m=wp&WID=4200 (Accessed 16 October 2017).

SHIMANE HYŌRON SHA 島根評論社
1924   *Sada shinnō no Tokyo shutsuen to kenin kazoku no yū* 佐陀神能の東京の出演と縣人家族の夕 (Performance of Sada shinnō in Tokyo, an evening with the family of the prefecture). Tokyo: Shimane hyōron sha.

SHIMANE KEN KANKŌ RENMEI 島根県観光連盟
n.d.   Otometōge Maria seidō 乙女峠マリア聖堂. http://www.kankou-shimane.com/ja/spot/detail/3598

SHIMANE KEN KODAI BUNKA SENTĀ 島根県古代文化センター, ed.
2000   Ōhara shinshoku kagura 大原神職神楽 [Priests' kagura of Ōhara]. Matsue: Shimane-Ken Kodai Bunka Sentā.
2001   *Mimiku kagura* 見々久神楽 [The kagura of Mimiku]. Matsue: Shimane-Ken Kodai Bunka Sentā.

SHINOHARA Minoru 篠原 實
1972   *Kōtei Iwami kagura daihon* 校定石見神楽台本 [Corrected Iwami kagura script]. Hamada: Kusaka Yoshiaki Shoten.

TAKANO Tatsuyuki 高野辰之
1926   Sada shinnō shokan 佐陀神能所感 [Impressions of Sada shinnō]. *Shimane hyōron* 島根評論　[Shimane review]3: 41–49.

TAKASE Kōichirō 高瀬弘一郎
1977   *Kirishitan jidai no kenkyū* キリシタン時代の研究 [Research of the Christian period]. Tokyo: Iwanami Shoten.

TAKEUCHI Yukio 竹内幸夫
1990   Roku chōshi kara hachi chōshi e 六調子から八調子へ (From the six mode to the eight mode). *Furusato to gakushū shirīzu, seijin kōza, kagura hen, tekisuto* 故郷と学習シリーズ、成人講座、神楽編、テキスト [Series on homeland and study, adult course, kagura edition, text] 3: 1–8.

TAZAWA Yoshiharu 田沢義鋪
1934   *Jinja to Seinendan* 神社と青年団 [Shrines and youth groups]. Tokyo: Zenkoku Shinshokukai.

THORNBURY, Barbara
1997   *The Folk Performing Arts: Traditional Culture in Contemporary Japan*. Albany: State University of New York Press.

TOTTORI KŌJIN KAGURA KENKYŪ KAI and KAGURA DAN 鳥取荒神神楽研究会, 神楽団
2014   http://kagura.kaiz.asia/2014/06/25/oohara2/ (accessed 16 October 2017)

WIMMER, Andreas, and FEINSTEIN, Yuval
2010   The rise of the nation-state across the world, 1816 to 2001. *American Sociological Review* 75: 764–90. doi: 10.1177/0003122410382639

YADOMI Kumaichirō 矢富熊一郎
1941   *Yasuda mura hattenshi jō* 安田村発展史上 [History of the development of Yasuda village first volume] Shimane prefecture, Mino county, Yasuda village: Yasuda Mura Toshokan.

Yamaji Kōzō 山路興造

2014　Iwami kagura no tanjō 石見神楽の誕生 [The birth of Iwami kagura]. *Minzoku geinō kenkyū* 民俗芸能研究 [Research of folk performing arts] 56: 49–71.

Yamamoto Takinosuke 山本瀧之助

1896　*Inaka Seinen* 田舎青年 [Rural Youth]. Osaka: Yamamoto Takinosuke.

Yamazaki Makoto 山崎 亮

2009　*Honkoku Fujii Muneo cho "Iwami no Kuni Jinja ki"* 翻刻 藤井宗雄著「石見国神社記」 [A reprint: Fujii Muneo, Record of shrines in the Province of Iwami, vol. 1, (An-no District)]. Matsue: Shimane Daigaku Hōgakubu San'in Kenkyū sentā.

Yanagita Kunio 柳田国男

1926　Sada shinnō shokan 佐陀神能所感 [Impressions of Sada shinnō]. *Shimane hyōron* 島根評論 [Shimane review] 3: 41–49.1929. Dai yon kai kyōdo buyō to min'yō gappyoukai 第四回郷土舞踊と民謡合評會 (Fourth joint review meeting regional dance and folk song). *Seinen* [Youth] 14: 29–43.

SHENSHEN CAI
Swinburne University of Technology, Melbourne

Guo Degang

A *Xiangsheng* (Cross Talk) Performer Bridging the Gap Between *Su* (Vulgarity) and *Ya* (Elegance)

Xiangsheng 相声 (cross talk), which has been one of the most popular folk art performance genres with the Chinese people since its emergence during the Qing Dynasty, began to lose its popularity at the turn of the 1990s. However, this downward trajectory changed from about 2005, and it once again began to enthuse the public. The catalyst for this change in fortune has been attributed to Guo Degang and his Deyun Club 德云社. The general audience acclaim for Guo Degang's *xiangsheng* performance not only turned him into a *xiangsheng* master and a grassroots cultural hero, it also, somewhat absurdly, evoked criticism from a few critics. The main causes of the negative critiques are the mundane themes and the ubiquitous vulgar *baofu* 包袱 (comical elements) and rude jokes enlisted in Guo's *xiangsheng* performance that revolve around the subjects of ethics, pornography, and prostitution, and which turn Guo into a signifier of vulgarity. However, with the media platform provided via the Weibo 微博 microblog, Guo Degang demonstrates his penchant for refined taste and his talent as an elegant literati. Through an in-depth analysis of both Guo Degang's *xiangsheng* performance and his microblog entries, this paper will examine the contrasting features between Guo Degang's artistic creations and his "private" life. Also, through the opposing contents and reflections of Guo Degang's *xiangsheng* works and his microblog writings, an opaque and sometimes diametrically opposed insight into his worldviews is provided, and a glimpse of the dualistic nature of engagement and withdrawal from the world is revealed.

KEYWORDS: Guo Degang—*xiangsheng*—microblog—vulgarity—elegance—comic performing arts

Asian Ethnology Volume 76, Number 2 · 2017, 343–65
© Nanzan University Anthropological Institute

GUO DEGANG has recently emerged as the new master of *xiangsheng* (cross talk), folk performance which combines stand-up comedy with pun and poetry. This has led to a resurgence of *xiangsheng* and to an increase in its popularity. Guo is widely regarded as a contemporary reviver of this ancient Chinese art, and his contribution to saving and recovering *xiangsheng* is a cultural breakthrough. It is of particular importance and relevance, as *xiangsheng*, as a representative form of traditional performing arts and a part of the intangible cultural heritage of China, was in danger of being lost in the barrage of new entertainment mediums and the loss of interest in traditional entertainment (MOU, TAN and LIU 2010, 1). In the extremely competitive entertainment market of contemporary China, particularly with the increasing popularity of talk shows and other stand-out comic performers such as Shanghai's Zhou Libo 周立波, Guo Degang helps make *xiangsheng* (viewed in China as a distinct performing art) stand out from among the other comic performing genres. Focusing more on current affairs, social debates, and foibles of present-day China, Zhou Libo's talk show lacks vulgarity in comparison to Guo Degang's *xiangsheng* performance, which retrieves the merits of traditional *xiangsheng* works with its abundance of smutty, banal jokes.

Born in 1973 in Tianjin 天津, a historical center of performing arts in China, Guo Degang began his career at the age of nine by learning *xiangsheng*. After years of practice he was able to perform hundreds of traditional and modern *xiangsheng* pieces and he became an expert in a broad range of folk art forms, such as *pingshu* 评书 (storytelling), *jingju* 京剧 (Peking Opera), *pingju* 评剧 (a local opera of north and northeast China), *dagu* 大鼓 (drum song), *taiping geci* 太平歌词 (an old Chinese folk art similar to drum song), and *Hebei bangzi* 河北梆子 (Hebei clapper) (QIAN 2006, 51). All of these forms are also components of traditional *xiangsheng*.

Imitating other folk art forms is one of the four basic skills of a *xiangsheng* performer. The other three are *shuo* 说 (speaking), *dou* 逗 (teasing), and *chang* 唱 (singing). There exists an aesthetic tradition in the *quyi* 曲艺 (folk art) performance, called *yasugongshang* 雅俗共赏, which means the performance must suit both refined and popular tastes. This tradition explains how the *quyi* genres as a whole fascinate an extensive diversity of audience members—those who are enticed by the *ya* of the lyrics of a *dagu* piece as well as those who are interested in the *su* of a *xiangsheng* or *kuaibar* 快板儿 (rhythmic comic talk or monologue to the accompaniment of bamboo clappers) piece. Therefore, the *ya-su* dichotomy is already implied within the totality of the genres as a whole and there is a mixture of *ya* and *su* genres in a singular *quyi* performance. For example, in a traditional *xiangsheng* work, there are often mini performances of some of the other *ya* genres, such as *dagu* and *taiping geci*, embedded within it. Thus, juxtaposing *ya* and *su* is already part of the *quyi* aesthetics, in particular for the *xiangsheng* performers.

At the age of 22, without any affiliations with formal performing arts groups, Guo made a risky decision to try his luck in China's cultural center, Beijing. In order to make a living, he performed in teahouses and ran errands for film crews, because at that time he was unable to obtain admission into the formal performing arts organizations due to having no "connections" in Beijing. In 1996, Guo Degang founded his own *xiangsheng* club, originally called Beijing *Xiangsheng* Meeting 北京相声大会 (*Beijing xiangsheng dahui*), which in 2003 was renamed the Deyun Club (*deyunshe* 德云社).[1] According to Guo, his purpose in establishing the club was to bring *xiangsheng* fans back to the theatre (ZHANG 2006; XIANG 2008, 156). After almost ten years of persistent striving, Guo Degang eventually made his name a popular *xiangsheng* brand (XIANG 2008, 157; FAN 2006, 85; QIAN 2006, 52), and his popularity began to grow in earnest, especially from the end of 2005 up until the present.[2]

One reason above all others that led to Guo's great success was the social and political critique embedded in his works, which could only be voiced in live club shows and not on radio or TV. According to Moser (cited in LINK 2013, 346), the presentation of real life is an "impossibility" in the CCTV Spring Festival TV Gala as a performer could not step out of line and crack a joke about current affairs, or satirize a leader, which is very much the case of Guo Degang's *xiangsheng* performance. Clearly the authorities only allowed Guo Degang's belated appearance in the 2013 CCTV Spring Festival TV Gala because his *xiangsheng* pieces could be largely circumscribed, whereas his regular routines could not.

There are several other distinguishing features that have contributed to Guo Degang's success. For example, the rich employment of folk art forms in his *xiangsheng* works have become a distinctive trait. A good example of Guo's talent may be found in *Leining zai 1918* 列宁在1918 [Lenin in 1918] (GUO n.d.2), as it exposes the depth of skills of Guo's training in folk art forms and his talent in vividly imitating different genres, such as *jingyun dagu* 京韵大鼓 (Beijing drum song), *pingju*, and *Hebei bangzi*. In *Lenin in 1918*, Guo cleverly inserts *pingju* ballads into the plot of a classic movie from the former Soviet Union, also titled *Leining zai 1918* [Lenin in 1918] (MILAIL 1939), and achieves a farcical effect. Lenin also appears as a hilarious subject in Jiang Wen's film (WEN 1995), which proposes that Guo's caricature is part of a generational reconfiguration of the revolutionary era in an ironical, reflective mode.

Besides resurrecting folk art forms practiced in traditional *xiangsheng* pieces into his own performance, the topics and contents of Guo Degang's works also reflect the social realities of contemporary China. Guo's works focus on the concerns of the Chinese commoners and topical social problems, such as brutal competition in the employment market, unspoken rules in the entertainment industry, mistresses of the wealthy people, prostitution, and pornography. These themes of

Guo's *xiangsheng* pieces are in sharp contrast to the subject matter of the official *xiangsheng* performances. Guo calls himself an "obscure" *xiangsheng* performer, and describes characters in his works as, for example, the "non-official scientist," the "non-official professor," and the "non-official scholar." In this way, he demarcates his work from those official *xiangsheng* performers who are capable only of singing praises of the government. "Official *xiangsheng* performers" are those *xiangsheng* performers who mainly perform through the mainstream and official arts and culture channel, such as the CCTV Spring Festival TV Gala. As noted by China's famous writer and blogger HAN HAN (2010), the Spring Festival Gala, as the biggest stage, painfully presents only poor-quality *xiangsheng* works that are full of flattering, eulogizing the government, and nauseating lines. In other words, these *xiangsheng* performers have been assimilated, politicized, and ideologized by official cultural policies. Besides "official *xiangsheng* works," there are plenty other insipid *xiangsheng* works on Chinese TV. Some of these *xiangsheng* works are just boring due to the poor quality of performance or are bland, even though they are not necessarily presenting propagandistic subject matter.

Another prominent feature that contributes much to the popularity of Guo Degang's *xiangsheng* performance is its secular focus on the daily routines of the commoners and its rich employment of vulgar *baofu* and dirty jokes, which has evoked criticism and condemnation from mainstream art critics and the official media. Of particular concern to the critics are loutish *baofu* and rude jokes enlisted in Guo's *xiangsheng* performance that concern ethics, pornography, and prostitution, which turn Guo into a signifier of vulgarity and a foul-mouthed and controversial figure. Although Guo's sarcastic and vulgar sketches received scorn from government censors in 2010, they were also exalted by millions of Chinese people. Guo's vulgarization of *xiangsheng* performance restored its intrinsic nature, catered to the aesthetic pursuit of the ordinary people, and challenged the prudish tradition of the CCP government. Further, through embodying and discussing the polar virtues of the vulgar vs. the refined in his routines, Guo created more interest in these issues with the Chinese public, and this increases Guo's standing as both a comic performer of a folk art and an influential writer in the public domain. Because of his audience impact, Guo has become a target for a central government anti-vulgarity campaign (as discussed in the following sections). It seems that this campaign has backfired though, because Guo was able to turn the tables by exalting *su*—a term that implies not just vulgar (a loaded term), but also simply "popular"/"populist," which turns Guo into a revolutionary figure in the contemporary Chinese culture sphere. The Guo Degang cause verifies Geremie BARME's observation on the 1980s Chinese cultural scene that government prohibitions no longer marked the end of one's career but, when appropriately managed, could often add to the public profile of a provocative artist (1999, xviii).

However, to conclude that Guo Degang is a vulgar person based on his *xiangsheng* performance would be superficial and a misunderstanding. Guo started writing microblog posts from the end of 2010 for Sina Web, which is one of the biggest commercial online media portals in mainland China, and whose microblogging section attracted numerous celebrity bloggers.[3] In many of his microblog posts, Guo Degang demonstrates his talent as a writer with the refined taste of a traditional Chinese scholar. Guo is capable of writing traditional poetry with a half-classical and half-vernacular language style, which is identical to the Yuan Dynasty (1271–1368) *qu* verse. In addition, his microblogs show his inclination for elegant taste that is reflected in imitating the leisure activities of the traditional Chinese scholars, such as calligraphy, painting, and reading. Therefore, the interest and aesthetic appetite of Guo Degang's pastimes exposed in his microblog entries contrast sharply with that of his *xiangsheng* works and provide a completely different and alternate image of him.

Through an in-depth textual analysis of both Guo Degang's *xiangsheng* pieces and his microblog entries, this article endeavors to examine the polarizing characteristics of Guo Degang's artistic creations and his other pastimes. Furthermore, through the antithetical contents and aesthetic proclivities of the seemingly oppositional dualism of Guo's life, his worldviews and outlook on life are revealed; although, it seems puzzling and at times absurd as he oscillates between engaging with the world by criticizing the social evils of present-day China, and being transcendental and living the idyllic life of a recluse.

GUO DEGANG'S SU DEMONSTRATED IN HIS *XIANGSHENG* PERFORMANCE

Xiangsheng, as a traditional folk art performing genre, has historically featured profane topics and vulgar elements that poke fun at deteriorating ethics and pornography. In particular, before the founding of the People's Republic of China (PRC), "non-vegetarian" performances, which refers to *xiangsheng* works that contain pornographic jokes, were exceptionally popular, actually mainstream (LINK 1992, 9). Of course, not all early *xiangsheng* routines were uncultured, as many routines focus on wordplay, puns, and songs with cultured themes. In traditional China, *xiangsheng* emerged from and was designed to entertain the ordinary working person of the lower social strata. The founding of the PRC in 1949 marked the beginning of a new social system, and in 1950, with Chairman Mao Zedong as the prime mover, a group of *xiangsheng* performers, headed by Lao She 老舍, Luo Changpei 罗常培, and Hou Baolin 侯宝林, organized the Small Group for the Improvement of *Xiangsheng* (*Beijing xiangsheng gaijin xiaozu* 北京相声改进小组, hereafter referred to as "the Group"). The Group modified many old *xiangsheng* pieces and removed pornographic or risqué jokes, references to inappropriate class attitudes, and other ideological flaws that were originally part of these works (LINK 1984, 97; XUE 1985, 124; XIANG 2008, 155). The Group eradicated the "unhealthy" content of *xiangsheng* and simultaneously conserved its form, so that it could be recycled as a conduit for reaching the Chinese masses with politically and socially acceptable messages (LINK 1992, 1), and also as a propaganda tool for the government (DUTTON 1998, 49). During the Mao era and even in the immediate post-socialist era, the CCP government believed itself obliged to regulate culture in all its aspects, such as form, content, production, distribution, and canonization (HOCKX 2015, 2). Generally speaking, the cultural censoring scheme in the PRC used a narrow attitude to humor, vigorously disheartening writers, filmmakers, and performers from crafting entertainment that was not "eulogistic" (REA and VOLLAND 2008, viii). Even after the 1980s, humor, be it in slogans and officially disseminated jokes, was swiftly recognized as a practical sugar-coating for government propaganda (CHEY 2011, 19). Here, I argue the reformation of *xiangsheng* led by the Group built up a "velvet prison," the phrase employed by Perry Link when he discusses the Hungarian writers' situation in the 1950s (LINK 2013, 13), for the *xiangsheng* performers, within which the official ideology dulled their creative work.

Seen more as a political propaganda tool in the newly founded socialist state, beginning in the 1950s *xiangsheng* pieces came to be divided into *gesong* 歌颂 (praising) vs. *fengci* 讽刺 (satirical). Eulogistic *xiangsheng* works were also an important development after the founding of the PRC (XUE 1985, 145–46), and the work of Ma Ji 马季is the best example of this development, with works such as *Lao zhanzhang* 老站长 [The old station master] and *Youji xiaoyingxiong* 游击小英雄 [Little guerrilla hero]. In rationalizing his work, Ma Ji said that he was influenced by Chairman Mao's 1942 talks at the Yan'an Forum on Literature and Art. Mao's instructions to the performers were to praise the people, praise the army, and praise the party (ANON. 2009). However, this new laudatory form of *xiangsheng* failed due to its poor quality (KAIKKONEN 1990, 143), as correct revolutionary passion only was not enough for a good piece of art. While often the eulogistic variety maps on the "official" *xiangsheng*, at certain political junctures the state has welcomed *fengci xiangsheng* to repudiate previous political regimes or policies.

At the end of the Cultural Revolution *xiangsheng*'s popularity increased, particularly when it was enlisted to mock the Gang of Four (MOSER 1990, 61) such as in *Ruci zhaoxiang* 如此照相 [Taking photos], and *Maozi gongchang* 帽子工厂 [Hat factory]. Sarcastic material, which had accrued during the Cultural Revolution, and political humor thrived among the people, which together make the post-1976 period a golden age for *xiangsheng* (KAIKKONEN 1990, 101). During the 1980s, the current representatives of the official *xiangsheng* establishment, such as Jiang Kun 姜昆, rose to fame. As time went on, more and more challenging pieces surfaced that were not just anti–Gang of Four, but also taunted the very underpinnings of official rhetoric. Jiang's *Dianti Qiyu* 电梯奇遇 [Tempest in an elevator], which lampooned contemporary social ailments, such as excessive bureaucracy, is a good example of this newly found artistic risk-taking. Writers and artists competed for the honor of being the first to lampoon a particular "socialist" factory, a Party secretary, or any other taboo. *Xiangsheng* pieces during this post-Cultural Revolution period were nonconformist by nature and "particularly relieving and invigorating and therefore extra stimulating" (KAIKKONEN 1990, 156).

Just as the members of the Group shifted the social function of *xiangsheng* from entertainment to the political tool of "serving the party," Guo Degang completed the paradigm shift by turning its focus back to "serving the people" as a means of entertainment and social criticism. Guo resurrected the essence of *xiangsheng*, successfully commercialized it in a market economy, and simultaneously deconstructed the official discourse through grassroots means. For Guo Degang, the "de-vulgarizing" of the art form by the Group at an early stage of socialist China destroyed its original essence as a source of entertainment. Guo's return to the core values of traditional *xiangsheng* revives its intended purpose, which is to entertain the common people by inserting boorish baofu and jokes of a primitive nature in his *xiangsheng* performance. Most importantly, Guo Degang's xiangsheng pieces regenerate a style of one-upmanship humor between the two comedians of the *xiangsheng* that was essentially expunged from *xiangsheng* in the first decade following the founding of the PRC.

The jokes used by the two comedians empowered the *dougen* 逗哏 (joke-cracker) to offend the *penggen* 捧哏 (joke-setter) by, for instance, deriding the generation of the *penggen*, or imputations about the fidelity/chastity of the *penggen*'s mother or wife, etc. In some of Guo Degang's famous pieces, as seen in YouTube recordings, there exist an extremely high percentage of jokes that revolve around the "old-style" rivalry between the *dougen* and the *pengen* characters. Guo Degang's *su*, I contend, stems from his retrieval of the "unethical" jokes and humor that are embedded in traditional *xiangsheng* performance, which was necessitated by the state's crackdown on humor. These restrictions by the state unintentionally forced popular *xiangsheng* performers such as Guo Degang to find mileage for jokes in "filthy" material. For example, mentioning pornography and prostitution, particularly in the social context of present-day China, is a regular routine in Guo's *xiangsheng* pieces, which is also criticized and censured by the mainstream cultural critics as *su*, as they offended the Party censors for their overt earthy and bawdy content. This timely social satire, together with its political potential serves as a reason why Guo Degang is labeled as *su* by representatives of the state, although it may also be that the state is using this criticism as a subterfuge for suppressing political and social criticism. In the case of Guo Degang, although humor could not be used when censorship and social control were most stiffly enforced in China, however, when some freedom was sanctioned, humor seemed to realize a need for self-expression and acknowledgment of unspoken truths (CHEY 2011, 26). However, despite the official "crackdown," Guo Degang's renovation of *xiangsheng* caters to the demands and tastes of the contemporary Chinese who are tired of didactic lecturing found in the prudish traditions of the predominant government ideological rhetoric, and have already seen through the truth of the "manufactured" and self-endorsed harmonious society of present-day China.

The "old-style" rivalry between the *dougen* and the *penggen* characters is best exemplified in Guo Degang's performance through a traditional *xiangsheng* means of derision, *xiangua* 现挂 (improvised lines). During a performance, a performer may change or simply add a few lines to the pieces according to the particular occasion, place, and time, in order to catch the public's attention more effectively (KAIKKONEN 1990, 243). *Xiangua* is widely used by Guo Degang in his performances as he playfully mocks a performing partner or other performers and their wives, children, and other family members. The teasing usually focuses on names, age, appearance, or the subject's abnormal or immoral behavior. For instance, giving the performing partner's father a different surname than the partner indicates the partner's illegitimate birth, and hinting at affairs concerning the partner's wife puts the partner in an awkward situation. In almost all of the *xiangsheng* pieces performed by Guo and his performing partner Yu Qian 于谦, Guo routinely teases

Yu. For example, he always addresses Yu's son as Guo Xiaobao 郭小宝, thus hinting that he, Guo, has had an adulterous relationship with Yu's wife; or, Guo often calls Yu's father "brother," which automatically makes him Yu's elder. In other cases, Guo labels Yu's father as Uncle Wang, which implies that Yu is an illegitimate son. In his recent works such as *Haohao xuexi* 好好学习 (Guo n.d.1), Guo Degang improvised the name of his performing partner, Yu Qian:

> Guo: This is the famous *xiangsheng* performer *LuBian* [donkey penis].
> Yu: I must stop you here. Please say my name clearly. The way you pronounce it makes it sounds like an aphrodisiac.
> Guo: His surname is Yu, so that his full name is Yu Bian [a male fish's sexual organ].
> Yu: So it is getting smaller.
> Guo: It is a whale actually.

In the above improvised lines, Guo Degang substitutes "Yu Qian" with "Lu Bian," which factually means the penis of a donkey, as "bian" by itself refers to the male organ of an animal. Further, in Chinese medical customs and culture, an animal's penis can be used as an aphrodisiac to boost a man's sexuality. As Yu is Yu Qian's surname, Guo Degang thus changes it to "Yu Bian," which refers to a male fish's sexual organ. To overtly mention the sexual organs, whether it is veiled or not, is still very much a taboo within Chinese cultural and media domains.

Also in *Haohao xuexi* (Guo n.d.1), Guo Degang employs Japanese adult video actors as *baofu*. In his *xiangua* of his performing partner's year of birth, he says:

> Guo: In the year you were born there was a bad famine, and both the granary and the well were empty.
> Yu: You mean *cangjingkong*.

Cangjingkong is the Chinese pronunciation of the name of a well-known Japanese pornographic video actress. Japanese names are generally written in Chinese characters, and coincidently, *cang*, *jing*, and *kong* not only rhyme but they also have the same denotation as the Chinese characters "granary," "well," and "empty." Thus, the smart use of the name of a Japanese pornographic video actor in his *xiangsheng* works not only recovers the "vulgar essence" of the old-fashioned *xiangsheng* pieces but also enhances the entertainment value of the work. In the same work, Guo Degang and his performing partner Yu Qian converse:

> Guo: Let's do a role play. We are two Japanese youths now. You are the girl and I am the boy.
> Yu: Do we have names?
> Guo: Your name is "Cangjing Maliya."
> Yu: I have to complete two people's workload.
> Guo: I am your boyfriend, and my name is "without an end."
> Yu: Your physical condition fits really well.

In this conversation, Guo Degang presumes himself and Yu Qian as actors in Japanese adult videos. Cangjing Maliya is a mixture of the names of Cangjing-kong and Xiaoze Maliya (Ozawa Maria), another very trendy Japanese adult movie actress who is equally famous in China. Moreover, the name "without an end" hints that the man Guo is performing as has sexual prowess.

Overt puns and innuendo focusing on pornography and prostitution are ubiquitous in Guo Degang's *xiangsheng* pieces, which, as discussed above, are also considered and denounced by the official ideology as *su*, since they go against the prudish tradition of the CCP cultural discourse. Further, these smutty and vulgar themes and topics expose too much of the dark side and corrupt nature of the current Chinese society, which the audience can immediately relate to as they are fed up with the social malaise and moral deterioration of their society. In *Haohao xuexi* (Guo n.d.1), Guo depicts a man's experience in a nightclub:

> Guo: I went in the nightclub and said to the waiter: "Give me two and they must be under eighteen."
> Yu: You should not say such things so clearly [to be overheard].
> Guo: What do you think I am ordering? Girls? You are too lewd. I am ordering mixed fruit dishes. I want them no more than eighteen yuan.
> Yu: I also think you are ordering mixed fruit dishes.

Here, in this skit, Guo and his partner fire not-so-subtle barbs at the pornography and sex industry in contemporary China, which, although banned by law, operates broadly in KTVs (karaoke bars), nightclubs, and public baths. This pointed social satire wins applause for Guo from his fans for his deep understanding of the social reality of modern-day China, although there is little doubt that propaganda officials will see it as exposing the dark side of contemporary China.

In another work, *Niyao gaoya* 你要高雅 (GUO n.d.4), puns and witty remarks are employed to signify prostitution. Guo also makes good use of the Chinese language and words with similar pronunciations:

> Guo: I have looked at your *whoremonger* (*piaoke* 嫖客).
> Yu: Wait a moment, I think you mean *weblog* (*boke* 博客)?
> Guo: There are a lot of people who have *hired you* (*dianni* 点你).
> Yu: I do not provide a service. You should say *click* (*dianji* 点击).
> Guo: What? To *click on your weblog* (*dianni*) means to *hire a prostitute* (*dianji* 点鸡)?

Here, *piaoke* (meaning *whoremonger*) is a clever substitute for *boke* (meaning *blog*), as their Chinese pronunciation rhymes, and *dianni* has two semantic meanings in a Chinese cultural context: first, it can be understood as a computer mouse "click," as on a webpage or blog; second, in Chinese slang it means "hiring a prostitute" in the context of prostitution, as a prostitute is nicknamed *chicken* (*ji* 鸡) in Chinese slang. And *dianji* also means a mouse "click," and has an explicit connotation of "hiring a prostitute."

In *Woyao fansansu* 我要反三俗 (GUO n.d.5), Guo entwines official discourse into his plots, which most likely is the cause of the tension between himself and officialdom. It also reveals his uncooperative and antagonistic attitude toward the criticism of the official performers and critics. The "three vulgarities" refers to coarseness 低俗 (*disu*), profanity 庸俗 (*yongsu*), and obscenity 媚俗 (*meisu*), and Guo invents an Association to Counter the Three Vulgarities 反三俗协会 (*fansansu xiehui*). In this work, "counter the three vulgarities" is a slogan projected to mirror political campaigns such as Three Anti, Five Anti, the Anti-Rightist Movement, and the Cultural Revolution. For example, the fictional members of the Association of Counter the Three Vulgarities are described by Guo in his work as "people with integrity, people who have given up vulgar tastes," which were popular movement slogans in the CCP's (Chinese Communist Party) lexicon of political discourse. Besides vulgar tastes, Guo adds "people who do not eat meals that human beings eat," which is a line used to counterweight the loftiness and idealism of the official ideological propaganda and to add an element of humor.

When mimicking a character that has a wide waist, his performing partner asks what is wrong with his waist, and Guo replies: "It was wounded during the Counter the Three Vulgarities years," which again juxtaposes the fictional campaign with other factual political movements. Parallels between the Counter the Three Vulgarities campaign and historical political movements are also shown when the members of the Association go to a public bathhouse, where prostitutes are known to frequent, to complete their "mission" and to achieve "allocated quotas" of vulgar people they must catch. Here "allocated quota" is a clichéd signifier of existing political movements in the history of socialist China as there were "quotas" of the rightists and counter-revolutionaries to be caught that were allocated from the central government, and each work unit must complete them. Furthermore, when the characters are invited by the prostitutes to buy their service, they accept and say, "I will just go and fulfil the missions of the Counter the Three Vulgarities Campaign," which reveals the hypocritical nature of the CCP cadres. These innuendoes, hinting at the political movements of the previous decades under Mao's reign, are skillfully woven into Guo's *xiangsheng* performance, and these features distance and differentiate him from official entertainment.

Although there are signs designating a political thawing in the cultural and artistic spheres, Guo Degang's *xiangsheng* performances outwardly went too far for the official censor. In July 2010, the then-Chairman Hu Jintao 胡锦涛 explicitly rejected the Three Vulgarities from the cultural realm of contemporary China (ANON. 2010). In August, the CCP's Propaganda Department propelled a new cultural campaign, the Counter the Three Vulgarities campaign (this campaign was used in Guo's performance as a made-up event), at which time Guo Degang and his *xiangsheng* productions were labelled as vulgar.

On 4 August 2010, CCTV aired a program on their News Studio section condemning the representatives who were ferreted out during the state's official Counter the Three Vulgarities Campaign. Although Guo's name was not mentioned outright, the criticism below was undoubtedly directed at him: "Between the merits and trash of the profession, he chose the latter. Between healthy trends and unhealthy trends, he chose the latter….This public figure's secular and vulgar behavior is so ugly" (PENG 2010, 68). As a result of the official denunciation, two of Guo's most favorite disciples publicized their withdrawal from the Deyunshe, and many major Beijing video stores were ordered to remove videos of Guo from their shelves. All programs on local television stations in which Guo took part were replaced by alternatives. Consequently, the Deyunshe announced that it would temporarily cease performing and conduct a rectification within the club (PENG 2010, 68).

Apart from the government vilification, Jiang Kun, the celebrated *xiangsheng* performer and the current Chairman of the Association of China's Folk Art Performers, asked the Chinese People's Political Consultative Conference to pay attention to the budding vulgar tendency within little theatre performances and other cultural activities. Without mentioning Guo Degang's name, Jiang Kun covertly critiqued Guo's *xiangsheng* performance as vulgar and immodest, which caused a series of verbal skirmishes between the two. In his response to Jiang Kun's criticism, Guo Degang claims that his *xiangsheng* works contribute much in assisting to build a harmonious socialist society. Here, Guo's self-praising is in line with the Confucian humor traditions, as Confucius proposed balancing physical (or psychological) tension with entertainment and in conducting emotion toward decency through the *Rites*, a historical book he compiled. Continuous withholding of emotion was perceived as detrimental to health and perilous to society, as stifled emotions can explode and disturb personal or social life (XU 2011, 52), and this Confucian understanding of humor stems from a weighty concern for social morality, order, and harmony (XU 2011, 70). Based on my observations, Jiang Kun's caution and condemnation of Guo Degang's performance is because he, Jiang, is the so-called "*xiangsheng* master" in the post–Cultural Revolution era, during which he emerged as a hero in performing politically oriented *xiangsheng* pieces, such as those that criticize the Gang of Four. These politically informative *xiangsheng* works set themselves apart from the traditional *xiangsheng* pieces that have been reformed by the Group. However, Guo has been able to successfully retrieve the inherent characteristics of old *xiangsheng* works and consequently remove the "political function" of *xiangsheng* as a folklore and cultural propaganda tool of the Party. Jiang Kun therefore feels that it is his responsibility to monitor the development of *xiangsheng* performance in regards to guiding it down a correct political and ideological route. Moreover, Jiang Kun's public identity as a government official lends him superiority as a mainstream power that supervises and regulates the "non-official" performers, such as Guo Degang.

GUO DEGANG'S *YA* REFLECTED IN HIS MICROBLOG ENTRIES

Microblogging, which is a mutation of blogging, is an indisputably important grassroots intermediary (JENKINS 2006, 179), a new form of personal and subcultural manifestation which encompasses summarizing and linking to other sites (JENKINS 2006, 151), and it has become a popular platform for social networking in present-day China. Not only is it popular among ordinary Chinese, but also it is widely utilized by celebrities as a medium to help them keep in touch with their fans. For example, some celebrities write regular microblog entries to inform fans about selected parts of their private lives. This may include events, such as announcements of their engagement and marriage, their travels, photos, and encounters with others, all of which may be used to promote their works. Some celebrity microbloggers use this medium to exhibit their talent in writing or to promote their views on certain topics. Guo Degang's microblog functions in all the above mentioned categories, and reveals an utterly different side to the public Guo Degang. There are two noticeable aspects in Guo Degang's microblog writing that highlight his aesthetic penchant for *ya*, which is in sharp contrast with his *su* as demonstrated in his *xiangsheng* works. One of them is his gift in writing traditional poetry, which appears quite often in his microblog posts, where he uses both vernacular and classical languages and shows an artistic conception of elegance and refined taste. The other is his obsession with a lifestyle that is enjoyed by traditional Chinese literati and scholars.

Although it seems that the theatrical persona is obviously staged and the private persona is the "real" Guo, it may also be argued that the glimpses afforded to us via his blog postings are also just staged as a counter to his risqué stage performances. Whatever psycho-philosophical position we take on what is the "real" Guo, there is no doubt that both available personas are talented and complimentary. Although it is arguable that Guo's Weibo postings are not comparable in a creative sense to his performance output, they have attracted millions of fans for Guo on the virtual social networking platform. Many of Guo's Weibo postings, in particular those poems written in classical inflected verse, gained hundreds and thousands of retransmissions and likes, which gives his Weibo posts lots of influence with his *xiangsheng* fans. Through extending his creative force into online social network conduits such as Weibo, Guo Degang has revived the tradition of *quyi*, which calls for *yasugongshang*. By including a considerable part of the *ya* elements in his *xiangsheng* performance, Guo risks losing some *su* fans in the highly competitive cultural marketsphere of present-day China. Conversely, if he only did performance advertising in his Weibo posts, Guo would risk losing the opportunity to display his literary talents to his fans. Therefore, Guo's clever construction and combination of the so-called public and private personas of himself reciprocate rather than clash with each other.

Following this sense, I argue that through his microblog posts, Guo Degang provides a more balanced public image to his fans. In countering the "vulgar" nature and impression he leaves on the public stage audience, Guo has used his microblog entries to counterbalance the excesses of *su* in his *xiangsheng* performer persona. Guo has a savvy understanding of social media culture and it permits every fan to feel an instant association with the celebrity they "follow." Guo's clever use of social media exemplifies a larger trend among Chinese celebrities to use the internet to "talk back" to their audience, industry, and government. They do this to eschew being categorized in certain roles, or to elude the constrictions they face when acting in film, on television, and through other broadcast media. In today's China, celebrity's blogs and microblogs have millions of followers, which has turned social media into the most effective and wide-reaching means for celebrities to communicate with their fans. Some celebrities display talents which otherwise may go unnoticed in their on-screen roles. Others use social media to quell rumors regarding their private life and to provide information about their close friends and relationships. Social media, especially microblogging, has proved itself a functional and efficient venue for celebrities to keep in touch and promote themselves among their existing or potential fans.

Through his blog posts Guo Degang is widely recognized as a talented writer by the Chinese netizens who are playing an important role in the contemporary Chinese cultural and media spheres.[4] Guo's unique talent rests on his gift of constructing traditional poetry utilizing both classical and vernacular lexicons, a talent that may have been acquired from his years of reciting and studying the traditional folk-art texts and performances. Guo Degang endeavors to write in classically inflected verse, and that situates his writing as *ya* or elegant. Compared to the Tang 唐诗 poems, the Song *ci* 宋词 poetry, and the Yuan *qu* 元曲 verse, Guo Degang's writing is more casual in both thematic topics and versification traditions. I think that Guo Degang is trying to imitate Yuan *qu* verse in style, however that does not mean that his writing is comparable with Yuan *qu* verse. The Yuan *qu* verse is read more like the popular literature of today, however, its combination of elegance and subtlety of poetry and classical Chinese along with popular and mundane expression and theme, forms a literary genre that is humorous, unaffected, and forthright. Similar to the Tang poems and the Song *ci* poetry, the Yuan *qu* verse also follows fixed forms of versification conventions that have different combinations and choices of word numbers and lines, tonal patterns, and rhyme schemes. However, the Yuan *qu* verse enjoys more freedom than other types of classical Chinese poetry composition in regard to abiding by established patterns and versification rules.

In the case of Guo Degang, his poetry writing is similar in genre to the Yuan *qu* verse but even more casual in setting word numbers, tonal patterns, and rhyme schemes. However, it is still read, to a certain extent, like traditional verse in terms of its use of words and phrases of classical language. In particular, when compared to the popular literature written in pure vernacular language nowadays, such as modern poems and novels, Guo Degang's writing in classically inflected verse demonstrates the elegance and charm of the classical Chinese language and verse. One of his recent microblog posts (7 February 2014, MB11) is an example:

大年初八，德云社一队开箱！雷轰天地，风扫雾霾。帝里繁华巷满莺花添锦路，仙家静寂云穿虬树锁丹崖。

[On this eighth day of the new lunar year, the Deyun Club premieres its new season! Rolls of thunder fill heaven and earth;
Wind sweeps the smog away.
In the capital, bursting blossoms adorn bustling alleyways.
In the silent heavens, cloud wends its way through bending trees and envelops gorgeous cliffs.]

In this microblog entry, which was used to commemorate the opening performance of the Deyun Club in 2014, it is easy to discern the rhyme scheme and the lingering charm of the classically inflected verse. It shows Guo Degang's capacity to handle classical Chinese language and artistic conception. For example, the classical phrases *qiushu* 虬树 (bending tree) and *danya* 丹崖 (gorgeous cliff) are used by Guo in this small verse to describe the spectacular scenery of ancient China, which is full of lingering charm and magnificence. In traditional Chinese poetry and verse, depiction of scenery was frequently used to connote the emotional and artistic conception haunting the poet, and is full of subtlety and elegance that leaves room for the reader to muse and imagine. Therefore, the scenery and artistic imagery of the traditional poetry are replicated by Guo in this verse. In addition, Guo's choice of words like *qiu* 虬(bending) and *dan* 丹 (gorgeous), which belong to the classical lexicon and are no longer used in vernacular Chinese, show his familiarity with classical language and verse.

In another entry (3 November 2013, MB7), Guo Degang wrote:

一声飞鸿叫，撕破了碧天皱，秋来才知愁时候。金井锁梧桐，人比黄花瘦。疏雨滴滴，池荷添锈。几株衰柳，欲解凄凉何能够。

[The call of the flying goose tears through the blue folds of the sky.
Only when autumn arrives do we realize the time.
The phoenix tree is bound up in gold, and the people are more slender still than chrysanthemums.
Rain drips; lotus rusts.
Withered willows hope for an end to the chill.]

Similarly, in this verse Guo Degang employs typical and popular scenery and imagery of traditional Chinese poetry such as *feihong* 飞鸿 (flying goose), *wutong* 梧桐 (phoenix tree), *huanghua* 黄花 (chrysanthemum), and *shuailiu* 衰柳 (withered willow), to depict the sorrowful connotation of autumn. Flying geese migrate from the north to the south of China at the beginning of autumn, therefore in traditional Chinese it represents the change of season; the phoenix tree has a classic implication of grief in traditional Chinese writing; a withered willow acts as a metaphor of farewell; and chrysanthemum symbolizes the noble character of the ancient Chinese literati, who are indifferent to fame and wealth. Through this verse, Guo Degang shows his knowledge of traditional Chinese literature and culture, and imitates the ancient poets to express sentiment and thought via observing and appreciating the natural scenery, which is full of sophistication and delicacy. Guo expresses in this verse his identification with the noble characters of the ancient man of letters through the connotation of the chrysanthemum.

In an entry written on 27 January 2014 (MB12), Guo Degang writes:

朔风凛冽，雾霭霾霾。颠狂衰草，难分辨野店楼台。梅花片似剪裁，凄凉尽在墙儿外。冰天如玉砌，银枝似粉埋。推锦被踏雪白，开眼界少卖乖，游遍江川策蹇归来，诗成酒后天地犹嫌窄。

[The north wind is piercingly cold; fog makes haze. Ailing grass withers, and it is hard to make out any landmarks. Plum blossoms have been pruned, and the sadness is outside the wall. The icy sky is layered like jade; silver branches appear coated in powder. Emerging from an embroidered quilt, I tread on the snow outside. I must look where I am going and show off less; I roamed mountains and rivers but came back lame. When poetry is done and wine drunk, even the world seems small and narrow.]

In this post, written in the midwinter of Beijing, Guo Degang first describes the beautiful scenery of the city after a strong wind and heavy snow. He then moves on to describe his thoughts and feelings, and reveals an image of himself as an unruly literati whose profligate and unrestrained nature is exaggerated when composing poems, while drinking alcohol after travelling across the country. Here, drinking alcohol, travel for pleasure, and composing poems, are distinguished life routines of the traditional Chinese literati with natural and unrestrained temperaments, such as Li Bai 李白 (Tang Dynasty poet) and Bai Juyi 白居易 (Tang Dynasty poet), who are famous for their contempt of dignitaries and for pursuing freedom and lofty ideals. Similarly, in this verse Guo Degang demonstrates an elegant and unruly personality that mirrors the traditional Chinese man of letters. In the post above, 蹇 (pronounced *jian*) is a very rare word in classical Chinese language that means lame. Here, Guo's employment of this particular character in his verse indicates not only his level of proficiency in classical Chinese but also his unruly spirit that mirrors that of ancient Chinese literati.

Besides imitating the writing of traditional Chinese literati, Guo Degang's microblog entries also reveal his other pastimes and hobbies, which are also highly identifiable with the leisure activities of the traditional Chinese poet. When he does not perform, Guo Degang spends his time reading, practicing traditional calligraphy, painting, writing poems, and collecting antiques. He is also a collector of fan painting and calligraphy. In ancient China, fan painting and calligraphy was popular among scholars and literati, and a fan with one's own painting and calligraphy was used as a gift to friends to symbolize friendship. Fans with drawings and calligraphy of famous people are highly desirable, and in one of his 28 January 2014 (MB13) posts, Guo Degang attached a photo of a fan that he painted for his performing partner, Yu Qian, on that day. In his 16 November 2013 entry, Guo attached a photo of a fan that was offered to him by Yu Qian as a present. This fan is an antique as it was painted by the Peking Opera master Mei Laifang 梅兰芳 and was inscribed by the Kunqu Opera master Yu Zhenfei 余振飞. In another post written on 5 October 2013 (MB6), Guo showed photos of a recently purchased antique fan painted by another Peking Opera master, Zhou Xinfang 周信芳.

In one of his 22 November 2013 (MB10) microblog posts, Guo Degang wrote:

秋意甚浓。沏花茶，烫黄酒。沐手焚香，盘竹根润手串…
[The sense of autumn is strong.
I brew jasmine tea and heat yellow rice wine.
I light incense and wash hands,
Wetting my bracelet of bamboo beads…]

In his 9 January 2013 (MB4) entry, Guo said:

闻香品茗习字听曲，观窗外积雪，闻室内虫鸣，人生之快无过于此…

[There is no greater happiness in life than smelling flowers, sipping tea, practicing calligraphy, listening to folk music, gazing at the piles of snow outside, or hearing birdsong inside…]

Drinking tea and alcohol; burning incense; observing flowers, rain, or snow; listening to ancient music; and appreciating bamboo carving are common pastimes of traditional Chinese literati, and show their aesthetic sensitivity and cultured taste. For a star who is admired and supported by millions of fans and has long immersed himself in an extremely colorful and materialistic world of entertainment, Guo Degang's leisure pursuits, to certain degree, suggest a person with refined taste, which seems antithetical to the vulgarity embedded in his *xiangsheng* performance. In another entry posted on 26 May 2011 (MB2), Guo wrote:

闷坐不如品茶，品茶不如饮酒，饮酒不如吃面，吃面不如吃肉，吃肉不如吃鸟，吃鸟不如养鸟，养鸟不如放生，放生不如观棋，观棋不如弹琴，弹琴不如写字，写字不如画画，画画不如登山…

[Sipping tea is more enjoyable than sitting still, drinking wine is more enjoyable than sipping tea, eating noodles is more enjoyable than drinking wine, eating meat is more enjoyable than eating noodles, eating a bird is more enjoyable than eating meat, keeping a bird is more enjoyable than eating a bird, freeing a bird is more enjoyable than keeping a bird, watching a game of chess is more enjoyable than freeing a bird, playing music is more enjoyable than watching a game of chess, writing calligraphy is more enjoyable than playing music, drawing is more enjoyable than writing calligraphy, climbing a mountain is more enjoyable than drawing...]

In this entry, Guo uses pure vernacular language written in repeated sentence structure to explain his pursuit of the elegant enjoyments that are popular among traditional Chinese scholars. This post does not follow any versification rules of conventional poetry, however, through repeating the same syntax pattern in every sentence it becomes carefree, humorous, unpretentious, and frank. In a relaxed atmosphere created by this simple way of expression, Guo Degang voices the happiness he obtains from the cultured recreational activities of the ancient intellectuals, such as playing chess and music, and practicing calligraphy and painting.

Guo Degang also tells of his love for bamboo in his 7 November 2013 (MB8) post, with a group of photos of the bamboo handicrafts he has collected:

喜爱竹子。竹者重节，节者为信。
[I love bamboo. Bamboo is a traditional symbol of integrity, and that which has integrity is trustworthy.]

Bamboo is frequently used in traditional Chinese poetry as a symbol of the exemplary conduct and noble character of a person, and it is admired and appreciated by traditional Chinese literati. Guo Degang uses bamboo as a medium to reveal his viewpoint on the behavior of a "perfect gentleman."

GUO DEGANG'S WORLDVIEWS REFLECTED IN HIS *YA* AND *SU*

Guo Degang's *su* embedded in his *xiangsheng* performance and his *ya* reflected by his microblog entries, reveal different and sometimes even contradictory worldviews. A comparison between his *xiangsheng* shows and his microblog posts indicates that his outlook on life is ambiguous and wavers between engaging with the world through critiquing social problems and being transcendental and living like a hermit. In many of Guo Degang's *xiangsheng* works, although many of them contain *su* elements, he courageously uses satire of topical social problems and injustices that are rampant across contemporary China to reveal his cynicism and to win admiration from his fans. An example of his satire may be found in *Woyao shang-chunwan* 我要上春晚 (n.d.7), which depicts a young man wanting to use "unspoken rules" to get an acting opportunity by using the "casting couch" with the female director. However, when the director opens her bedroom door, the young man finds that the male producer is in her bed. The plot cleverly lampoons the "unspoken rules"—the dirty tricks that are rampant in the entertainment industry, as well as within Chinese society. In *Woyao naofeiwen* 我要闹绯闻 (Guo n.d.6), a girl offers herself to the male director in order to get a role in his film. Soon after they finish making love, the girl slaps the director and says, "You bastard, how come you didn't let me know in advance that you are actually a cartoon director?" Also in *Woyao naofeiwen*, Guo Degang mocks the mistress problem in contemporary China. In China today, it is a common belief that rich businessmen and government officials have mistresses, and this reflects the moral degradation of Chinese society. In one scene, Guo depicts a traffic jam on the road near a film academy. There are an unusual number of vehicles there because all the entrepreneurs of Beijing city have gathered there to pick their mistresses up when they finish school (they are pretty, young, female acting students). This plot mirrors the social reality of today's China and pokes fun at a morally declining society.

In *Lun wushi nian xiangsheng zhi xianzhuang* 论五十年相声之现状 (GUO n.d.3), Guo focuses on social paradox and injustice:

> People who have enormous knowledge may not produce books
> The knowledge in books may not be good
> Those leaders in work units may not be qualified
> Those dismissed (from work) may not be all bad
> Bookstores may not sell books
> Pharmacies may not sell drugs
> Nutritious drinks may not have nutrition
> People who go to public baths may not get a shower
> People who go to KTV may not go for the singing
> *Xiangsheng* stars may not know how to perform *xiangsheng*
> Singers may not know music
> People who love each other may not be husband and wife
> Husband and wife may not love each other.

The remarks above appear casual, but they contain candid logic and reflect the reality of contemporary Chinese society. For example, the relationship between knowledge and power reflects the inequitable competition within academic circles; the qualified and dismissed leaders reveal the unspoken rules—the under-the-table deals and games in Chinese officialdom; the services provided by the public baths and KTV disclose the growth of prostitution and the sex industry; and legal and illegal partners hints at corrupt social morals. In a certain number of his *xiangsheng* pieces, Guo specifically ferrets out the malaise and injustice in Chinese society, which reflects to some degree his outlook on life, which is to engage with the world and to combat social injustice.

However, Guo Degang's microblog entries show an utterly diverse temperament and worldview where he wants to stay away from mundaneness and social concerns and to live a pleasant life. Guo's relaxed and tranquil mood reflected in his microblog posts may be the result of his success after years of painful struggles in the *xiangsheng* circle. As he has revealed in many interviews, before he found fame and wealth he could barely support himself in Beijing and was pushed aside by the Beijing *xiangsheng* circle, until he became a disciple of Hou Yuewen 侯跃文 and the Hou School.[5] Even after his success, Guo Degang has been criticized and condemned by critics and official propaganda organs because of the vulgar elements of his *xiangsheng* performance, which has resulted in numerous verbal skirmishes and disputes between Guo and his antagonists. Media reports frequently distort the facts and smear Guo's image, and it is a combination of all these experiences that contribute to Guo's understanding of the fickleness of the world and the evolution of his outlook on life.

In a post written on 16 June 2011 (MB3), Guo said:

… 看破人生梦一度，也只好携琴揽酒观山望水纸扇长衫笑天涯！
[Seeing that life is but a dream, what can I do but don a long gown, take up a fan, zither, and wineglass, gaze into the distance, and chuckle to the ends of the earth!]

Another entry composed on 27 April 2011 (MB1) reads,

遇好晴天，好山水，好书，好字画，好花，好酒，好心情，须受用领略，方不虚度…
[When you happen upon fine weather, scenery, books, painting and calligraphy, flowers, wine, or mood, savor the experience; do not let it pass in vain.]

Also in his post written on 22 July 2013 (MB5),

书房内荷莲绽放，心情大悦。三千年读史，不外功名利禄；九万里悟道，终归诗酒田园 [6]
[The lotus [flowers] in my study are in full bloom, bringing me great delight. For three thousand years, Chinese history has recorded only matters of position and wealth. Having travelled the world and attained enlightenment, I have come to favor the simple things in life.]

In the above microblog posts, Guo Degang depicts the idyllic lifestyle of the traditional Chinese scholar, which is to read history and write poems, appreciate painting and calligraphy, play music, drink alcohol, observe flowers and natural scenery, and travel for pleasure. It seems that Guo had penetrated the mysteries of life that burden those chasing and experiencing fame, wealth, and achievement, which is despised by him as he now prefers a pastoral life where he can pursue his refined hobbies and live like a traditional Chinese intellectual. However, Guo Degang is still unable to give up his *xiangsheng* performances, as it was he who revived *xiangsheng*, and he wishes to carry on this trend.

Conclusion

By juxtaposing and examining Guo Degang's *xiangsheng* performance and his microblog entries, this paper sheds light on the *su* nature of his artistic creation and the *ya* trait in his microblog writings. Guo Degang's intentional restoration of the "immoral" jokes of *xiangsheng* serves as a journey of seeking the roots of this traditional folk art performance genre, which led to its regaining of popularity today among the contemporary Chinese audience. In doing so, Guo Degang was targeted by the government in its counter-vulgarity campaign, despite his huge contribution to retrieving this folk art form. Guo Degang himself has become a signifier of vulgarity for those people who do not like his *xiangsheng* shows. Together with the "old-style" rivalry between the *dougen* and *penggen* characters, which serves as the main source of the debauched jests, the wide engagement of themes and topics about pornography and prostitution constitute the *su* features of Guo's performance. Through the *su* characteristics of his *xiangsheng* routines, Guo Degang issues his sharp criticism of the social malaises and stigmas of today's China, but this also leads to the labeling of him as a figurehead of vulgarity and the consequent crackdown on his performances. In other words, the labeling of Guo Degang's *xiangsheng* as *su* by representatives of the state is just a subterfuge for suppressing political and social criticism.

On the other hand, Guo Degang's microblog entries on Sina Web reveal his *ya* temperament, which is reflected in his poetry (his writing style is similar to classically inflected verse) and in his refined hobbies, which are similar to those of the ancient Chinese literati. By extolling these polar virtues Guo has heightened their significance to the Chinese public, as they attest the power of a comic performer of a folk art who has also succeeded in seizing public space and influencing public discourse. Further, Guo Degang's clever enlistment of social media to work against the perception of his *su xiangsheng* performer persona suggests his savvy understanding of social media culture, which reveals a broader inclination among Chinese celebrities to employ the internet to "talk back" to their audience, industry, and government—so as to avoid being typecast in certain characters, or to escape the restrictions they face performing in film, on television, and through other broadcast media.

NOTES

1. At the outset, the Deyun Club had only three performers including Guo himself, but by 1998 there were a dozen performers, and today it has more than a hundred signed performers. From 2003, the main venue of the *deyunshe* performance was the Tianqiao Happiness Tea House (*tianqiaole chayuan* 天桥乐茶园), located at Tianqiao neighborhood in the Chongwen district of Beijing. The Tianqiao neighborhood was originally a gathering place for laborers and poor street performers of Old Beijing, however now the neighborhood represents the grassroots culture that has long been popular in Old Beijing and which is embodied in the modern *xiangsheng* revived by Guo Degang. Since the beginning of the 2000s, the Deyun Club has had tremendous success and publicity, and its audiences are broad, including not only fans of Guo from the lower social stratas, but also white-collar workers, college students, private entrepreneurs, and popular stars and celebrities.

2. From October 2005 to March 2006, he was invited to appear, or was reported on, in almost all of China's influential television shows, newspapers, and magazines. The internationally recognized director Zhang Yimou invited Guo to host the launch of his 2006 film (ZHANG 2006), *Mancheng jindai huangjinjia* 满城尽带黄金甲 (cited in ZHOU 2006, 78). In 2009, to celebrate the twentieth anniversary of his *xiangsheng* career, Guo held a successful series of special *xiangsheng* performances at The Great Hall of the People and other famous

theatres and stadiums across China. Guo appeared on the 2007 Forbes Wealth Chart, with an annual income of more than 10 million yuan (PENG 2010, 67).

3. Compared to blogging, microblogging has a word limit of 140 Chinese characters. While microblogging, Guo Degang also wrote frequent blog posts for the blogging platforms Sina Web, Netease Web, and Blog China Web from 2007 to 2012. However, he seemed to quit blogging when microblogging became the dominant online social networking platform, which enjoys more popularity among Chinese bloggers and is utilized by celebrities as a medium to update information and keep in touch with their fans.

4. Guo does not claim to be the author of all of his routines, however, he is assumed to be the author of all of his "official" microblog posts as there is no evidence suggesting that an assistant or employee in the Deyun marketing team writes them for him.

5. Hou Yuewen is the youngest son of the *xiangsheng* master Hou Baolin 侯宝林. Because of the unsurpassed reputation of his father in the industry, Hou Yuewen enjoyed great popularity and admiration among his fellow performers and audiences alike. Within the *xiangsheng* circle in Beijing, there is a deep-rooted belief that one's master is crucial for career development, and intense connections exist among different *xiangsheng* performing groups and individuals. Therefore, although Guo Degang did not learn many performing skills from Hou Yuewen, their relationship as master and disciple lent Guo authenticity as a *xiangsheng* performer. Since then, he started receiving more opportunities to perform his art and display his talents.

6. The second sentence in this posting is not Guo's original creation, however, he intelligently borrowed it from the ancient Chinese literati to express his emotions and outlook on life.

REFERENCES

ANON.
2009   Dang xiangsheng buzai fengci, zhiyou gegong songde 当相声不再讽刺，只有歌功颂德 [When *xiangsheng* stops satirizing, only praising]. *Tencent Web*, 29 July. http://news.qq.com/a/20090729/000552.htm (accessed 19 May 2012).

ANON.
2010   Hu Jintao: Tuidong shehuizhuyi wenhua dafazhan dafanrong 胡锦涛：推动社会主义文化大发展大繁荣 [Hu Jintao: Promoting the great socialist cultural development and prosperity]. *Xinhua Web*, 23 July. http://news.xinhuanet.com/politics/2010-07/23/c_12367399.htm (accessed 16 March 2014).

BARME, Geremie
1999   *In the Red: On Contemporary Chinese Culture*. New York: Columbia University Press.

CHEY, Jocelyn
2011   Youmo and the Chinese sense of humour. In *Humour in Chinese Life and Letters: Classical and Traditional Approaches*, Jocelyn Chey and Jessica M. Davis, eds.,1–30. Hong Kong: Hong Kong University Press.

DUTTON, Michael
1998   *Streetlife China*. Cambridge, Melbourne: Cambridge University Press.

FAN Suhua 樊苏华
2006   Toushi Guo Degang xianxiang 透视郭德纲现象 [Reflection on the phenomenon of Guo Degang]. *Touzi Beijing* 3: 84–87.

GUO Degang 郭德纲
Microblog (MB) entries, all on Sina Web
MB1   Posted 27 April 2011, https://www.weibo.com/guodegang?is_all=1&stat_date=201104#feedtop, accessed 19 October 2017.

MB2 Posted 26 May 2011, https://www.weibo.com/guodegang?is_all=1&stat_date=201105#feedtop, accessed 19 October 2017.

MB3 Posted 16 June 2011, https://www.weibo.com/guodegang?is_all=1&stat_date=201106#feedtop, accessed 19 October 2017.

MB4 Posted 9 January 2013, https://www.weibo.com/guodegang?is_all=1&stat_date=201301#feedtop, accessed 19 October 2017.

MB5 Posted 22 July 2013, https://www.weibo.com/guodegang?is_all=1&stat_date=201307#feedtop, accessed 19 October 2017.

MB6 Posted 5 October 2013, https://www.weibo.com/guodegang?is_all=1&stat_date=201310#feedtop, accessed 19 October 2017.

MB7 Posted 3 November 2013, https://www.weibo.com/guodegang?is_all=1&stat_date=201311#feedtop, accessed 19 October 2017.

MB8 Posted 7 November 2013, https://www.weibo.com/guodegang?is_all=1&stat_date=201311#feedtop, accessed 19 October 2017.

MB9 Posted 16 November 2013, https://www.weibo.com/guodegang?is_all=1&stat_date=201311#feedtop, accessed 19 October 2017.

MB10 Posted 22 November 2013, https://www.weibo.com/guodegang?is_all=1&stat_date=201311#feedtop, accessed 19 October 2017.

MB11 Posted 7 February 2014, https://www.weibo.com/guodegang?is_all=1&stat_date=201402#feedtop, accessed 19 October 2017.

MB12 Posted 27 January 2014, https://www.weibo.com/guodegang?is_all=1&stat_date=201401#feedtop, accessed 19 October 2017.

MB13 Posted 28 January 2014, https://www.weibo.com/guodegang?is_all=1&stat_date=201401#feedtop, accessed 19 October 2017.

n.d.1 *Haohao xuexi* 好好学习 [Study hard]. Available at https://www.youtube.com/watch?v=4wnCtNUWrl4 [time-stamp: 4:22–35] (accessed 12 October 2017).

n.d.2 *Leining zai 1918* 列宁在1918 [Lenin in 1918]. Available at https://www.youtube.com/watch?v=KitXE23YEdM [time-stamp: 34:00–36:11] (accessed 12 October 2017).

n.d.3 *Lun wushi nian xiangsheng zhi xianzhuang* 论五十年相声之现状 [Fifty years of *xiangsheng* performance]. Available at http://www.youtube.com/watch?v=FsTUQWgrmnE [time-stamp: 6:18–35] (accessed 12 October 2017).

n.d.4 *Niyao gaoya* 你要高雅 [One should have taste]. Available at http://www.youtube.com/watch?v=4ZXaAcGq55Q [time-stamp: 2:08–11] (accessed 12 October 2017).

n.d.5 *Woyao fansansu* 我要反三俗 [I will counter the three vulgarities]. Available at https://www.youtube.com/watch?v=t9Z905phvs4 [time-stamp: 20:35–22:00] (accessed 12 October 2017).

n.d.6 *Woyao naofeiwen* 我要闹绯闻 [I want to have a sex scandal]. Available at http://www.youtube.com/watch?v=fXyIS3Vo5sI [time-stamp: 13:05–10:00] (accessed 12 October 2017).

n.d.7 *Woyao shangchunwan* 我要上春晚 [I want to perform in the Spring Festival Gala]. Available at https://www.youtube.com/watch?v=RHPKovAFaxk [time-stamp: 8:26–34] (accessed 12 October 2017).

HAN Han 韩寒

2010 *Chuntian de gushi* 春天的故事 [Story of spring]. Blog post at *Sina Weibo*, 15 February. http://blog.sina.com.cn/twocold (accessed 16 September 2014).

HOCKX, Michel
2015   *Internet Literature in China*. New York: Columbia University Press. doi: 10.7312/hock16082

JIANG Kun 姜昆 and TANG Jiezhong 唐杰忠
1988   Dianti Qiyu 电梯奇遇 [Tempest in an elevator]. Cross-talk performance. China: 1988 CCTV (China Central Television) Spring Festival Gala, available. https://www.youtube.com/watch?v=apjLq-7S3aM, accessed 21 October 2017.

JIANG Wen 姜文, dir.
1995   *Yangguang Canlan de Rizi* 阳光灿烂的日子 [In the heat of the sun]. China: China Film Co-Production Corporation.

JENKINS, Henry
2006   *Fans, Bloggers, and Gamers: Exploring Participatory Culture*. New York: New York University Press.

KAIKKONEN, Marja
1990   Laughable Propaganda: Modern Xiangsheng as Didactic Entertainment. PhD dissertation, Stockholm University.

LINK, Perry
1984   The genie and the lamp: Revolutionary xiangsheng. In *Popular Chinese Literature and Performing Arts in the People's Republic of China 1949–1979*, ed. Bonnie S. McDougall, 83–111. Berkeley: University of California Press.
1992   The mum sparrow: Non-vegetarian xiangsheng in action. *Chinoperl Papers* 16: 1–27. doi: 10.1179/chi.1992.16.1.1
2013   *An Anatomy of Chinese: Rhythm, Metaphor, Politics*. Cambridge, Mass.: Harvard University Press. doi: 10.4159/harvard.9780674067684

MILAIL, Romm, dir.
1939   *Leining zai 1918* 列宁在 1918 [Lenin in 1918]. The Soviet Union: Moscow Film Studio.

MOSER, David
1990   Reflexivity in the humor of xiangsheng. *Chinoperl Papers* 15: 45–68. doi: 10.1179/chi.1990.15.1.45

MOU Yanlin 牟延林, TAN Hong 谭宏 and LIU Zhuang 刘壮
2010   *Fei wuzhi wenhua yichan gailun* 非物质文化遗产概论 (Introduction to Intangible Cultural Heritage). Beijing: Beijing Normal University Press.

PENG Fei 彭飞
2010   Guo Degang: Cong xiangsheng dashi dao "sansu" daibiao 郭德纲：从相声大师到三俗代表 [Guo Degang: From *Xiangsheng* master to representative of the "Three Vulgarities"]. *Jizhe Guancha* 66–68.

QIAN Qiang 钱强
2006   Fei zhuming Guo Degang 非著名郭德纲 [The lesser-known side of Guo Degang]. *Baixing* 1: 50–52.

REA, Christopher, and Nicolai VOLLAND
2008   Introduction to the special issue on comic visions of modern China. *Modern Chinese Literature and Culture* 20: v–xviii.

XIANG Shi 向适
2008   Lun xiangsheng chuantong de jicheng yu fazhan 论相声传统的继承与发展 [Commentary on the inheritance and development of the traditions of *xiangsheng* performance]. *Hunan Diyi Shifan Xuebao* 8: 155–57.

Xu Weihe 许为和
    2011   The classical Confucian concepts of human emotion and proper humour. In *Humour in Chinese Life and Letters: Classical and Traditional Approaches.* Jocelyn Chey and Jessica M. Davis, eds., 49–72. Hong Kong: Hong Kong University Press.

Xue Baokun 薛宝琨
    1985   *Zhongguo de Chuantong Xiangsheng* 中国的传统相声 [Traditional Xiangsheng performance of China]. Beijing: People's Press.

Zhang He 张和
    2006   Zhengyi zai jixu Guo Degang: Xiangsheng shi wo de shengming 争议在继续郭德纲：相声是我的生命 [Continuing debates, Guo Degang: *Xiangsheng* is my life], *Renmin Web*, 24 February. http://culture.people.com.cn/GB/27296/4138218.html (accessed 21 November 2012).

Zhang Yimou 张艺谋, dir.
    2006   *Mancheng Jindai Huangjinjia* 满城尽带黄金甲 [Curse of the golden flower]. China: Beijing New Picture Film Co.

Zhou Yanan 周雅囡
    2006   Cong Guo Degang xianxiang kan chuantong yishu zhenxing 从郭德纲现象看传统艺术振兴 [Resurrection of traditional arts: The Guo Degang phenomenon]. *Xiju Congkan* 4: 78.

AMBIKA AIYADURAI
Indian Institute of Technology, Gandhinagar

CLAIRE SEUNGEUN LEE
Inha University, Inchon, and the University of Massachusetts, Boston

Living on the Sino-Indian Border
The Story of the Mishmis in Arunachal Pradesh, Northeast India

In northeast India, there are several indigenous peoples who reside along the Sino-Indian border about whom there is very little academic research. Some communities are present on either side of the border, making research very difficult. The Mishmi is one such indigenous group living in the northeast region of India bordering southern Tibet. Out of four Mishmi clans, three reside on the Indian side and one on the Chinese side of the international border. After the 1962 Sino-Indian War, movement of Mishmi people across the border was restricted, impacting social ties and trade-related activities. We discuss relations between the Mishmi and the British, followed by their interactions with the Indian administration. We document how people used the borders before the war and how development on the border has impacted Mishmi lives. This research is a first attempt to document information about the Mishmis in India and China. In this article, we present our preliminary observations based on anthropological fieldwork in Arunachal Pradesh, India. Secondary information was gathered from websites, archives, and reports.

KEYWORDS: Arunachal Pradesh—China—India—Mishmi—Sino-Indian border—Tibet

Asian Ethnology Volume 76, Number 2 · 2017, 367–95
© Nanzan University Anthropological Institute

RESEARCH on ethnic minorities is particularly challenging for those living in a disputed region close to international borders. The region between India and China is strategically crucial for the two superpowers, and both are investing heavily in the development and security of their respective frontier regions. Several indigenous peoples live along the international border and are impacted by developmental policies. As India and China vie to gain the status of the next global superpower, the stories of indigenous peoples may get lost. There are several indigenous communities on either side of the Sino-Indian border (TAPP 2002; CHAUDHURI 2013).[1] One among them is the Mishmi, who live in Arunachal Pradesh (India) and Zayu County (China). In this research report, we document how the Mishmi used the borders before the war and how development on the border has impacted their lives in Arunachal Pradesh. This report is our first attempt to document ethnographic and archival data concerning the Mishmi community both in India and China.

Arunachal Pradesh (Arunachal, hereafter) is a frontier state of northeast India, also known as the "land of the rising sun." It shares a 1,126-kilometer international border with Tibet, which is claimed by China (NOORANI 2011; KURIAN 2014). Arunachal has been largely cut off from mainstream economic and infrastructural development until fairly recently. In its national policy the government of India has imagined the region to be "backward" due to a lack of infrastructure and connectivity (BARUAH 2003). Arunachal, however, is claimed by China. The dispute over the territory led to a war between India and China in 1962. Today, the region continues to remain central to the boundary dispute between the two countries (JACOB 2015).

The movement of Mishmi people across the border has been restricted since the war, thus impacting social ties and trade-related activities. Because the state of Arunachal is a border zone, even Indians require an Inner Line Permit. In China, the Deng Mishmi live in such a sensitive area that it is difficult to get research permission, even by Chinese scholars. The last time any serious investigations were conducted was probably the year 1985, when the Chinese Academy of Social Sciences sent in a team of four anthropologists from the Institute of Ethnology and Anthropology.

We begin by providing a brief account of the current situation on the Sino-Indian border. Then, we visit the archival literature to offer a glimpse of the colonial presence on the border. We provide two stories, one of Yaaku Tacho,[2] a Mishmi woman who went to China in the 1950s and worked for the Chinese government. The first author met Yaaku's daughter, who shared pages of her mother's personal diary written in Chinese. In her diary, Yaaku writes as a Chinese patriot. She praises Chinese officials for being helpful in providing education and jobs. The second story we provide is of the hunters who visit the border zone to hunt the prized musk deer. These hunters claim that Chinese hunters have started to enter deep into Indian territory, where they hunt indiscriminately, without any concern for the delicate ecological balance of the area. They also claim that the trips they make to the border help in the protection of India's territory, since they keep an eye out for Chinese intrusions. The hunters note that the military agencies are not very well versed with the landscape, leading to a demand for their service. They thus take pride in their skills and knowledge, things that are used predominantly by the military during intelligence gathering. Mishmi hunters on the Indian side of the border are thus contracted government agents of sorts, performing a duty for which enlisted Indian troops are not equipped.

The Mishmi: A transborder community

There are three sub-groups within the Mishmi cultural group residing on the Indian side of the border (Idu, Digaru, and Miju), who reside in the districts of Lohit, Anjaw, Lower Dibang Valley, and Dibang Valley. These districts are collectively termed the Mishmi Hills (see Figure 1). One sub-group, the Deng Mishmi, live on the Chinese side in the county of Zayu, which is located in the Tibet Autonomous Region (LANG and QIANGBA 2000; see Table 1). There has been little or no connection with the Deng Mishmi in Tibet since the war between India and China in 1962. The Deng never became an officially recognized ethnic group in China and were finally classified as an "unidentified ethnicity" or "others," due to the nature of a category for characterizing only a handful of people in contemporary China (LI 2008; DA 达蔚 2011).

The Mishmi ethnic community is one of the twenty-six major "tribal" groups of Arunachal.[3] Since there are four sub-groups recognized within the Mishmi fold, each addresses the members of other Mishmi groups as their brothers and recog-

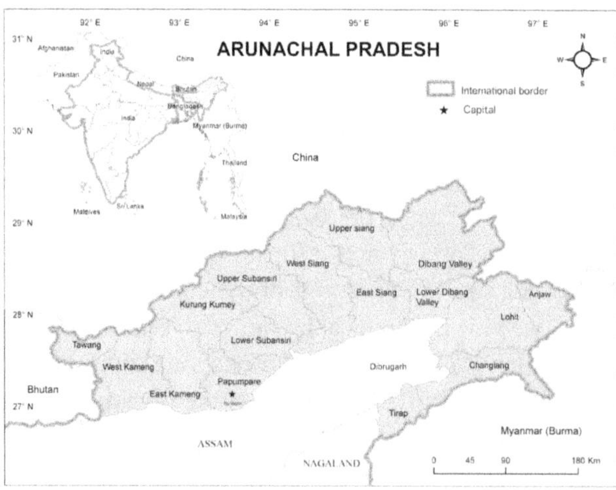

Figure 1. Arunachal Pradesh. AIYADURAI 2012.

Mishmi	Sites	Country	Population*(approx.)
Idu	Dibang valley and Lower Dibang valley	India	12,000
Miju	Lohit and Anjaw	India	----
Digaru	Lohit and Anjaw	India	----
Deng	Zayul valley	South Tibet (China)	1300

TABLE 1: Details of the four sub-groups of the Mishmi. There is no tribe-specific population data available for Miju and Digaru. It is estimated that the Mishmi population in India, including all three districts, is 50,000 (KRI 2008). According to the census of 2001, there were 9,076 Idu Mishmis and in the census 2011, their population rose to 12,000. Source: SARMA 2015.

nizes each other as belonging to one major "tribe" of Mishmi, according to those residing on the Indian side of the border. Each sub-group has several clans that are known to live along the rivers and tributaries streaming through the area. The Mishmi see themselves as a separate ethnic group from their neighbors, the Adi, who belong to the Tani group (SARKAR 1987). The Tani group consists of the Adi, Nyishi, Apatani, Tagin, and Hill Miri tribes of Arunachal, all of whom have a common ancestor, Abotani, the primal ancestor of these "tribes." Each sub-group of the Mishmi, on the other hand, have their own primal ancestors (Nani Initaya for Idus, Amik Matai for Mijus, and Jamalo for Digarus).

According to a senior Mishmi informant of ours, all Idu, Miju, Digaru, and Deng are different "tribes," whereas another Mishmi scholar, who did his PhD among the Idu Mishmi, claims that the groups are "sub-tribes." In the archives, however, Mishmi are reported to be divided into "clans" without any specific reasons for labeling them as such (MITCHELL 1883). The Mishmi themselves, however, recognize separate apical ancestors, hence the term "clan" does not seem appropriate. The Idus and Digarus have language similarities (SARMA 2015), but socio-culturally the Digarus have more affinity with the Miju and Deng Mishmis. All the Mishmi are believed to have migrated from Burma following the course of the Lohit river (BHATTACHARJEE 1983). But there are different claims about their migration routes, for according to BARUAH (1988), the Idu Mishmi migrated from Tibet. HUBER (2012) discusses the complexity of understanding the origins and migration in the region, especially in the case of the northern Subansiri hill peoples. AISHER (2012) makes similar points about Nyishi migratory routes. BLACK-BURN (2005) has written briefly about Mishmi migration history through the lens of the funeral ritual and how the journey of the soul is perceived to be through the migratory route of the Mishmi.

The ambiguous nature of the border decides identity and legality, depending on which side of the border one is present and active. People's movements across the border were common in the past, with traders bringing stories from China stating that people there had a better living standard, higher education, and more prosperous material conditions than in India. This compelled Indian Mishmi to visit China. When the Indian administration made its presence in the Dibang Valley, the Mishmi men and women who returned from China were looked upon with suspicion. The border thus became a space that defined "patriots" and "traitors," having an extreme effect on the lives of those Mishmi who had crossed from one side to the other.

Geopolitical significance

The region of Arunachal under investigation here is strategically important for both China and India (see Figure 1). There is a large amount of information on issues to do with security and political debates (Vertzberger 1982; Basu and Miroshnik 2012), but anthropological and sociological research on the local communities living on the borders is lacking. It was only after the war in 1962, when India began building infrastructure in northeast India, that the region entered a new nationalist discourse aimed at the "nationalization of the frontiers" (Baruah 2003). This process has made so-called tribal regions, such as northeast India, financially dependent on the central government. Since then, there have been tremendous demographic and socio-cultural changes with "significant social, environmental, and political costs" (ibid., 917). However, the development of Arunachal has been shaped by a concern for national security. This is why Baruah (2003) has argued that it is only in the cosmetic sense that Arunachal has witnessed development.

The rise of China and its increasing significance in the world is of great interest to scholars and policy makers the world over. But the question of its rise in terms of its immediate neighbors, borderlands, and rapid development shapes how the impacted local communities react in terms of their everyday lives, for living conditions along the frontiers are rapidly changing (Saxer and Zhang 2016). Across the border, western China has invested huge funds to develop these frontiers. China is increasingly engaging with and controlling border disputes by strengthening its defence and border security (Sharma 2014). There have been discussions about developing the border regions for mutual benefits, but China has prevented a multilateral development loan in Arunachal.[4] China even raised a concern over the use of the name "Arunachal," as it signified belonging to India, and insisted that the toponym be removed from the policy document. This action was taken because China claims the entire state of Arunachal as its own. China opposes the idea of any further infrastructure development on the border, seeing it as a threat to its own autonomy (Anon. 2014). In addition to that, China has been openly expressing disappointment with Japan because it was assisting India with infrastructure development in Arunachal. Japan's statement that Arunachal belongs to India was a source of friction between India and China as recently as 2015 (Reuters 2015).

India is investing in military power and development in the northeast region, which was neglected for years. The state-building projects have intensified in the last decade, and the government continues to expand its infrastructure and military facilities in Arunachal. The government of India plans to build a 2,000 kilometer all-weather road along the border with China (KUMAR 2014). Arunachal's first passenger railway service was started in 2014 (SINGH 2014) and a special Mountain Strike Corps was set up along the border by the Indian Army (PANDIT 2014). To fortify defences along the China border, fifty-four new Indo-Tibetan Border Police posts are being planned in Arunachal (TIMES OF INDIA 2014). The region is also currently witnessing the construction of several hydro-electric projects (DUTTA 2008). One of them is the 3000 MW Dibang Multipurpose Project, which in 2014 got clearance from the Ministry of Environment and Forests, Government of India. To raise the socioeconomic profile of the region, funds for northeast India during the eleventh five year plan (2007–2011) were 122,086 crore, which amounts to roughly 9 billion US dollars (KURIAN 2014). Other than military and infrastructural development in the region, ideas of development are reflected through the creation of national parks and biosphere reserves within the framework of "green development" and "ecological modernization" (MCAFEE 1999; YEH 2009, 2012). Rural people in the region often see such biodiversity conservation schemes as new forms of "development" with economic consequences. While local people welcome these developmental activities, environmental activists, non-governmental organizations (NGOs), and civil groups within and outside Arunachal are concerned about the unplanned development in this geo-politically, ecologically, and culturally sensitive region (BHAUMIK 2009; RAHMAN 2014).

Recent publications have been produced by the Mishmi themselves (KRI 2008; MENE 2011, 2013). In addition, there are several articles on Mishmi culture, language, and customs published within India by both the Mishmi themselves (PULU 1977; PULU 1982; DEURI 1983; LINGI 2011; RONDO 2011) as well as other scholars in India.[5]

FROM THE CHINESE SIDE

The Chinese name for Arunachal is "Afunaqiaerbang," which is simply the transliteration of "Arunachal" (or *zangnan diqu*) into Chinese, the region of south Tibet (see ARPI 2013; MAPS OF INDIA n.d.). The group of Mishmi in southern Tibet is called Deng, which is one of the fifty-seven minority groups officially recognized by the government of the People's Republic of China (LI 2008).

The Deng are known by other names as well: Dengba, Darang, Geman, Kaman, Mishmi, or Miju.[6] They live mainly in the southeast part of the Tibetan Autonomous Region in the county of Zayu, especially in the forested areas of the Hengduan Mountains at an elevation of 1,000 meters. According to LANG and QIANGBA (2000), Deng people live on the border of southeast Tibet and Myanmar (for a similar case of minorities living across national borders, see TAPP 2002). The Deng are known to be divided into at least two groups: Darang and Geman. These are related to the Miju sub-group living in the Arunachal province in India. Fei Xiaotong, one of the founders of early Chinese anthropology and sociology in China, states that the official status of the Tibetans of Pingwu County in Sichuan

Province and the Dengs of Zayu is not yet "established" (FEI 1980). The Deng, as the Mishmi, speak a language derived from the Tibeto-Burman language family.[7] From the limited image resources available on the Internet, the material culture of the Deng looks very similar to that of the Digaru and Miju Mishmi. During the first author's research in the border villages of Chaglagam and Taflagam in the Anjaw district during a 2006–08 field trip, the Mishmi there often talked about their relatives on the other side of the border.

THE BRITISH AND THE MISHMI: IMAGINING AND SHAPING PEOPLE AND TERRITORY

Arunachal was never brought under any formal administrative control by the British government during British rule.[8] Arunachal, earlier known as the North East Frontier Agency (NEFA), was administered as part of Assam during the British period. A policy of minimal interference was adopted by the British, which Guha has termed "shadowy suzerainty" (GUHA 1999). The British did not interfere too much for the fear of provoking violent rebellion, but later made visits to the Mishmi Hills for mapping and surveying. They also engaged in punitive expeditions. The British saw these border regions as promising territory for trade (i.e., tea, timber, and ivory) and thereby focused mainly on maintaining law and order to maximize the economic gains, while gaining control of this resource-rich land.

There was constant friction between the hill people of Arunachal and the so-called "civilized" valley dwellers of Assam. People in Assam paid tolls to the hill people for collection of wood or any other forest product. Mishmis (Miju) even collected tolls from Hindu pilgrims who visited the Parasuram Kund in Anjaw district. Raiding by the Mishmi prompted the British to set up an armed outpost to keep a check on the movements of the hill people.

In 1873, the British enacted a regulation known as the Inner Line Regulation of 1873, which prohibited anyone who was residing in Assam, or passing through the districts of Assam, from going beyond this line without a pass. The pass constituted a written permission from the designated authorities. The intention of the Inner Line Permit (or Pass) (ILP) was to stop poachers, moneylenders, woodcutters, traders, and missionaries in the valleys from exploiting the hill people. Arunachal continues to be a restricted area and even today an official permit is required to enter the state for all visitors except the native people of Arunachal. The ILP has been an impediment to the economic development of Arunachal state ever since. It still continues to be a contentious issue there. The first ever railway service, as mentioned above, opened in 2014, but was suspended due to huge protests by the Arunachal Pradesh Student's Union because of a fear of mass entry of non-native Arunachal people flooding in from outside the state (GAO 2015).

British relations with the Mishmi and other hill peoples were guided by a payment system called *posa* (blackmail money).[9] For efficiency of administration, the British created the special post of "political officer." These political officers were required to be intelligent in their instinct, quick in their sympathies, and have the ability to learn vernacular languages (BOSE 1979, 175). In a couple of years, these officers managed to assert some influence on the frontier people and opened friendly communication to start commerce (BOSE 1979; KINGDON-WARD 1927). The British policy with regards to the hill people was, as stated earlier, generally of non-interference—unless of course there were attacks on British subjects, violations of the "inner line," or danger to the people in the foothills and Assam. But later, the British changed their approach and entered the inner line on several occasions to survey, map, and even punish the hill tribes for various "unlawful" incidents.

For the British, Assam and the adjoining hills, including the Mishmi Hills, were important for expanding trade as well as for promoting their commercial interests (BHATTACHARJEE 2002). The British carried this policy out by exerting control over the frontier people. They needed to conquer and subdue the inhabitants to further their economic interests by, for example, planting tea in Assam (BARAL 2009). Defining the frontier was thus a key step toward identifying and classifying the people who were to become British subjects (ROBB 1997). Maintaining peace in the region was crucial for the promotion of trade, as there were conflicts not only between the hill tribes but also between the Mishmi and the Tibetan ethnic groups over incursions into the territory. Hunting issues also continued to be a constant point of tension and negotiation. Stopping feuds between these groups was therefore a major challenge for the British. One of the ambitious ideas the colonialists came up with was to establish a rail link from Sadiya to Batang in Sichuan, China through the Mishmi Hills, but this never materialized due to the fear that such a rail link would facilitate the entry of Chinese troops into Indian territory (BOSE 1979). During that time, the British controlled territory up to Zayul Chu,[10] a Chinese outpost near Rima. At the local level, however, there was trade between the Mishmi Hills, China, and Burma using the historic trade routes.

Another strategic reason to manage a frontier area was that the British were concerned that if they did not take interest in this region, the Mishmi people would end up becoming "Chinese" subjects. To win over the local native people, governmental representatives carried with them tea and cigarettes as "political presents" (ROUTLEDGE 1945). F. P. Mainprice, the Assistant Political Officer of Lohit Valley in 1945, had a long list of political presents that included iron and steel for making *dao*s (machetes), black thread for making coats, salt, tea, rum, cigarettes, and opium (MAINPRICE 1945). Tobacco leaves for Tibetan coolies and wristwatches, safety razors, torches, soap, and towels were gifts for Tibetan officials in Rima. Even guns were presented to local village headmen, if they cooperated with the British. In 1909, Noel Williamson, the Assistant Political Officer of the time presented six Mishmi (Miju) men each with Double Barrel Machine Loading (DBML) guns for assisting him in his journey in 1907–08 (WILLIAMSON 1910). Headmen who cooperated with the British and those who checked existing feuds were presented with red coats (ROUTLEDGE 1945).[11]

These political officers had multiple duties, for they were not only administrators and surveyors but also naturalists and anthropologists (see TABLE 2). Acquiring knowledge about people and places was an integral part of the colonial enterprise, as MONAHAN (1899) puts it in his letter to the Foreign Department Secretary of the Government of India.[12] In the letter he writes the following:

Year	Visitors/events	Remarks
1825	Lt. Burlton	The Mishmis were first mentioned by Lt. Burlton (British officer). He explored the upper course of the Brahmaputra.
1826	Lt. Richard Wilcox	Visited the Mishmi country and carried out a number of surveys in Assam.
1836	Dr. William Griffith	A British botanist travelled up to the Lohit river to explore the natural history of the area.
1848	Permanund Acharya	Murdered in the Mishmi Hills when he travelled to Tibet from Assam.
1873	T. T. Cooper	British explored routes for tea trade.
1854	Father Krick and Bourry	French Missionaries murdered in the Mishmi Hills.
1885	J. F. Needham	Visited Mishmi Hills and nearly reached Rima.
1911–12	Mishmi Mission	Punitive mission by Major. Dundas (British Officer).
1945	B. H. Routledge	British Political Officer posted in the Mishmi Hills.
1950	Anini outpost	Indian government set up an outpost in Anini. First ever office to be set up by Indian government.
1980	Rajiv Gandhi's visit	First and the only Prime Minister to visit Anini.
1980	Lohit to Dibang district	Dibang district carved out of Lohit district. Anini became the headquarters.
1983	Road construction	First metalled road constructed up to Anini.
1998	Dibang Wildlife Sanctuary	4,914 km² of district set up for wildlife conservation.
2001	Dibang district	Dibang district was divided into two (Dibang district and lower Dibang district with Roing as its headquarters).
2013–14	Military	Establishment of Indian Army battalion. ITBP has been present in Anini for a long time.
2013–14	Wildlife conservation	Dibang Tiger Reserve (proposal stage)

TABLE 2. Key visitors and events in the Mishmi Hills (1825–2014)

...acquiring as far as possible, an accurate knowledge of the country and of the haunts and habits of the people, and, of impressing definitely on these savage marauders that they cannot raid on our frontier, or murder, rob, and carry off unoffending British subjects with impunity (MONAHAN 1899, 1).

Acquiring knowledge about the residents and landscape was not the only aim in reaching out to these frontier people, since the idea was to gain control over locals. For example, the murder of Noel Williamson (a political officer) and Dr Gregorson (a tea planter and doctor) changed the approach of the British from non-interference to direct confrontation. There were several incidents during which British troops extracted fines, arrested "criminals," and even destroyed Mishmi villages. An expedition was carried out in 1853 when two French Missionaries, Fathers Nicolas Michael Krick and Augustine Etienne Bourry, were killed by a Mishmi headman named Kaisha in Anjaw district (HERIOT 1979). Kaisha was later arrested and hanged in Dibrugarh. One of the best-known expeditions into the Mishmi Hills in 1911 was "the Mishmi Mission" led by W. C. M. Dundas, the Chief Political Officer, to subdue and settle three groups: the Abors (Adis), Mishmis, and Miris. The Mission was undertaken particularly to punish those who had murdered British officials. The military strength of this mission was 750 troops, made up of 350 Naga Hills military police, 150 Dacca military police, 200 sappers,[13] as well as 1,200 Naga coolies who acted as porters (HAMILTON 1912).

In addition to trade and maintaining law and order, the earlier European visitors were intrigued by the magnificent landscape and fascinating wildlife. Some of the junior officers, like Ronald Kaulback, a British explorer and geographer, wrote several letters to Francis Kingdon-Ward, the well-known British botanist and explorer, asking his advice and suggesting that he visit this region. Kaulback later took the position of an assistant for Kingdon-Ward's botanical survey (KAULBACK 1935). Kingdon-Ward visited the region, and came to be known as the last of "the greatest plant hunters" (LYTE 1989). William Griffith, a British doctor and naturalist-cum-botanist, travelled up the Lohit river to explore the natural history of the area.

Writings by these visitors created an image of "untouched" hills waiting to be explored. These explorers saw the frontier Himalayas as a natural laboratory for documenting plants, insects, mammals, and birds. On the one hand their writings exposed the natural heritage of the region, the majestic mountains, rivers, and waterfalls, while on the other hand they also wrote about the hill people, their behavior, cultures, and customs. They wrote of the region's people as "dangerous" and "barbaric." Such negative descriptions stand in contrast with the mesmerizing beauty and magic of the landscape. The British perceived the Mishmi as dangerous, dirty, unfriendly, and wild. The views of earlier visitors toward them were equally negative, not at all sympathetic toward understanding the locals. The Mishmi, in 1882, were seen as "untouched by any civilizing influences" (WALLER 1990), and the description of all the so-called natives "as less than human and abominable" was a common characteristic of colonial ethnographies written about northeastern India (BARAL 2009).

The Mishmi controlled the trade routes in the area between Tibet and Assam. They regularly refused the entry of outsiders into their territory and were thus labelled as a "ferocious tribe" (STEWART 2006, 79). The Mishmi country was regularly reported to be dangerous, and because it was not properly explored until the early twentieth century, it was seen as "a place not for an outsider." Some reports about the Mishmi held that they were a friendly yet uncultured race from the point of view from the British. For example, the British intelligence officer F. M. Bailey's account, noted that the "Mishmi were whole friendly but a very ill-mannered race, troublesome and unpleasant" (BAILEY 1945; KINGDON-WARD 1927, 287). According to KINGDON-WARD (1913, 1), "…though they would not ordinarily murder an intruder, they would willingly leave him stranded without food and porter."

HAMILTON[14] (1912) observed that the tribesmen were of uncertain temperament and frequently at war among themselves. After 1826, intense fighting among Mishmi factions prevented the entry of visitors from outside the region for approximately five years (HAMILTON 1912). T. T. Cooper reported that the Mishmi (Idu) were "war-like and predatory," and that at one time they were such trouble that they were forbidden to visit Sadiya (COOPER 1873, 180–81). The Mishmi in Lohit Valley were reported to be "uncooperative with each other and with strangers," and they were disliked and not trusted (MILLS 1952). COOPER (1873, 189) again writes the following about Mishmi houses:[15]

> The interiors of the Mishmee houses more resemble a cowshed than human habitation, while from the outside they might be mistaken for fowl house. The most striking feature of the interior is the number of skulls of mithuns, bullocks, buffaloes, tigers, bears, deer, monkeys, and takin.

In spite of the skewed representations by visitors, writings by Europeans left behind a rich source of archival information about the material culture and lives of the Mishmi. For example, J. P. Mills, administrator-cum-anthropologist, gave a detailed account of the Mishmi of the Lohit Valley (MILLS 1952). But one has to be careful when reading what the Europeans wrote about the Mishmi, given the prejudice and unequal power relationships between the colonial administration and the local Mishmi. ELWIN (1959), who was known for his relentless defense of India's indigenous people, was probably one of the few scholars who had positive views about the Mishmi as being friendly, colorful, and beautiful. He was surprised by the negative views of previous visitors, writing in his autobiography that they seem to have something wrong with their eyesight:

> …all the previous travellers had stressed how "difficult" the Mishmis were and how unpleasant and unattractive. I can only say I fell in love with them at once. Our first village was inhabited by Digaru Mishmis and the men wore their hair tied in a knot on the top of the head and the women has theirs in a fantastic piled up style which would attract admiring attention anywhere. (ELWIN 1964, 274)

The diaries written by missionaries and anthropologists provided data about the native people's way of life for effective local administration. In the absence of any text prior to the British period, one is dependent on colonial ethnography, but one should be critical of how these texts were produced and for what purposes. Mishmi people were often seen as "backward," "uncivilized," and "primitive" by the British. Similar terms were used to describe several groups in India by the colonial state. The term "tribe" emerged as a distinct category in colonial times, which continues to be used today by bureaucrats, scholars, and even by the Mishmi themselves. Among the Mishmi, like other groups in northeast India, the term is internalized and used in identity discourses as a source of pride (McDUIE-RA 2012).

THE STORY OF YAAKU TACHO AND THE HUNTERS ON THE BORDER

The first author interviewed[16] a Mishmi government official posted in Khonsa (Tirap district) whose parents lived in China for nine years in the 1950s. This is the story of her mother Yaaku, who had free school education in China and was then later employed by Chinese officials. Her daughter told the first author that Yaaku probably worked as a spy for the Chinese government. She and her husband went to China with a small group of people from Dibang Valley. Most of the Mishmi people who went to China received education for eight to nine years. They saw the Chinese as very kind and believed that communists are nice people. They spoke of the Chinese army as being good. Yaaku's daughter remembered what her parents told her about the time they reached China:

> When we reached, we were welcomed. It was very nice. We were taught patriotism for China. We were told that China is the best. Boys and girls were kept in separate hostels. We were kept in a military school. We were always trained by military officers and we received weapons training.

Yaaku's diary also reflects that Mishmi were well treated and taken care of by the Chinese. They were influenced by the Chinese propaganda of India as their enemy and China as their good friend. Along with education, Mishmi received weapons training. Some of the Mishmi even participated in the 1962 Sino-Indian war and fought against India. Based on Yaaku's writings, it seems that the Chinese Liberation Army aimed to liberate the Mishmi from India.

> Uncles—the Liberation Army on the border is defending our motherland, please liberate Luoda region! …I am one of China's sons and daughters.

The meaning of "motherland" (*zuguo* 祖国) in her diary refers to China and not India. Thus, the Mishmi people were considered to be part of the territory of China. This feeling is reflected in Yaaku's diary (see FIGURE 2 and translation below). This certificate (see FIGURE 3) of "ethnic harmony" was issued by the Government of China in December 1960 to Yaaku Tacho. The certificate has a picture of Mao Zedong on the top with the flag of China on either side with an official seal. The text in the certificate reads:

> This is to certify that Yaaku Tacho (student from Aidabo village, district…, Luo Yu ethnic group[17] (20 years old) has graduated from the Mandarin class four in Department two.

The war broke out in 1962, and Yaaku's husband and brother-in-law[18] fought with China in Kibithoo against India. After the war, the Indian officials on the border arrested them, imprisoned them, and reportedly tortured them for several days. The story of their escape from Tezpur prison is popular in the Dibang Valley even now. Even after returning to their respective villages, the intelligence officials in India continued to monitor their activities to check if they continued to have links with China. They were suspected of being Chinese citizens and spies.

现在中国人民和洛瑜族人民团结起来打倒印度军队吧。现在民族都得解放了，我们洛瑜人民是没有得解放的民族，中国人民解放军和洛瑜族人民一定要团结起来打到印度军人。我是一个中国儿女________同志。我永远等着中国共产党，我没有望（忘）记毛主席和中国共产党，我永远跟着走中国共产党！

Text and Translation of Yaaku's diary
(Original in Chinese)
(Chinese Pinyin by the second author)

FIGURE 2: Yaaku's diary. This was provided Mishimbu Miri, whom the
first author met during fieldwork on 29 April 2014.

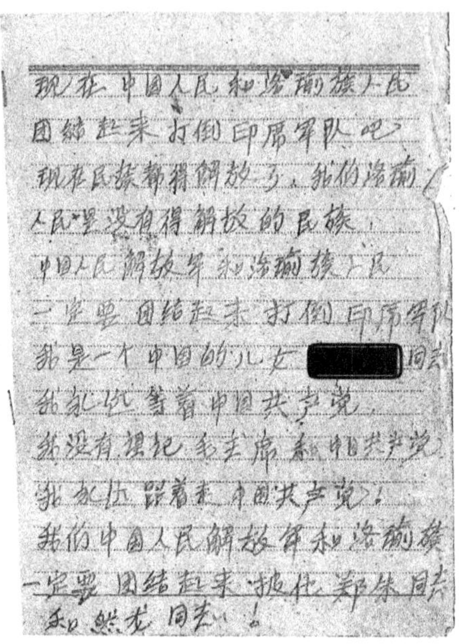

*Xianzai Zhongguo renmin he Luoyuzu renmin tuanjie qilai dadao Yindu jun-
dui ba. Xianzai minzu de jiefang le, women Luoyu renmin shi meiyou jiefang de
minzu, Zhongguo renmin jiefangjun he Luoyuzu renmin yiding yao tuanjie qilai
dadao Yindu junren. Wo shi yi ge Zhongguo ernv________tongzhu. Wo yongyuan
dengzhe Zhongguo gongchandang, wo meiyou wang (wang)ji Mao zhuxi he Zhongguo gongchandang, wo yongyuan gen zhe zou Zhongguo gongchandang!*

Let us Chinese and Mishmi peoples, unite and overthrow Indian army. Now all
the other minorities have liberated, but we Mishmi have yet to be liberated. The
Chinese Liberation Army and the Mishmi people should unite to overthrow
Indian army. I am one of China's sons and daughters. Yakku comrade [referring
to herself] will wait for the Chinese Communist Party forever. I will never forget
Chairman Mao and the Chinese Communist Party. I will always follow the Chinese Communist Party.

These stories evoke the ambiguities of border spaces that have witnessed years
of isolation, followed by independence and the creation of a nation state which
made people like Yaaku Tacho and others who went to China at that point of
time "for all practical purposes, both Indian and Chinese nationality" (BARUAH
2003). For the security forces, such ambiguities of identities and geographic spaces
are seen as dangerous, and therefore nationalizing such spaces becomes urgent
and crucial for the government. Although the government shifted its focus to the
frontier region only after the war, the ambiguities of the border regions continue
to become suspect, as reflected in the tales hunters tell. Mishmi men who visit
the borders frequently for hunting musk deer bring back current stories of China
or about the people in China. The commonly heard narrative from hunters is,

FIGURE 3: Certificate of "ethnic harmony" issued by the Government of China

"If we don't go to hunt, the Chinese will end up at our doorsteps. Our going to the borders is a way to check on the Chinese intruders." Mishmi hunters claim that they are protecting not only the nation's boundary but also protecting wildlife from Chinese hunters. "Chinese[19] hunt everything, they come with AK-47s and advanced weapons, they don't spare any animal or bird," the hunters asserted, citing examples of how Mishmi follow taboos so they do not hunt every animal that comes their way but the Chinese hunt indiscriminately. The reliance of the Indian military and paramilitary on Mishmi knowledge gives the hunters a sense of importance, so they take pride in this. Similarly, Mishmi knowledge of the wildlife and the trails up in the mountains make wildlife researchers completely dependent on the Mishmi.

After the war, the borders were militarized and army bases were set up at Walong and Kibithoo, which were key sites during the war. Dibang Valley has had the Assam Rifles[20] and Indo-Tibetan Border Police since the 1950s. The Indian Army is currently taking over the border patrols. The Dibang Valley is witnessing a rise in military activities as the Government of India is investing in military infrastructure there. A new settlement close to Anini has army offices and quarters. Though there is limited interaction between the Army and the local people, during the Long Range Patrols (LRPs)[21] Mishmi men are hired as guides and also as porters. Two to three trips lasting 14–15 days are carried out every year during the summer close to the international borders. Other than the Long Range Patrols, men of the Special Information Bureau (SIB) and Special Branch (SB) visit the borders. They often work in close collaboration with the Mishmi men who work as porters and informers. Hunters and the local villagers are also often hired by the Indian military agencies for intelligence gathering. These are all welcome activities for the local Mishmi people, who make substantial amounts of money in a short period of time. Thus they look forward to these activities every summer. In the early nineteenth century, spies known as "pundits" were sent by the British to these borders (STEWART 2006). In the 1880s, for example, one of the famous pundits was A. K., whose real name was Kishen Singh. He visited Tibet and came in contact with Mishmi people. These frontier regions continue to be explored by modern spies (intelligence officers) who work for the Indian government. The first author met a Mishmi man in 2008 in Chaglagam (Anjaw district) who was hired by the Special Branch to plant hidden video cameras on the Sino-Indian border. She asked him, "Don't you feel scared, it's a risky job. What if the Chinese catch you?" He proudly answered, "There are Mishmis on the other side so they don't harm us because we also look like Chinese." He jokingly pointed out to me that, "If you go you will be shot," and laughed out loud, and continued, "for that matter any educated-looking person will not be spared."

The stories of Yaaku and the current hunters are from different periods and relate to the border differently. Yaaku's trips across the borders were facilitated by Tibetans to help her group meet the Chinese officials, who provided them access to education, trade, and jobs. Fifty years later, however, movement through the border regions is restricted to just hunting and surveillance. It was only after the establishment of the Anini in Dibang Valley outpost in 1950 that the restriction on people's movement was implemented. Similar to Yaaku's story, these men who visit the borders bring back stories of better infrastructure and talk about how advanced Chinese villages are. The roads are good, they have concrete houses, and vehicles are able to reach the border on the Chinese side.

The China-related topics are never-ending during discussions in the Dibang Valley, since the Chinese army is known to show aggression every now and then on the Arunachal border. Recently, Chinese troops reportedly crossed over the border and occupied territory twenty kilometers inside Anjaw district for nearly four days (TNN 2013). National media in India highlighted this incident that evoked public nationalist sentiments, but for the local people it is not new, as incursions have been known to happen frequently. Border problems in Arunachal continue to cause issues between the two countries. During the recent trip of Prime Minister Narendra Modi to China, the state-owned Chinese Central Television (CCTV) showed India's map without Jammu and Kashmir and Arunachal (SHARMA 2015). This made the social media and general public agitated in India and started debates over India-China relations. Such "cartographic aggression"[22] can be equated with military aggression when troops from China entered Jammu and Kashmir during Chinese President Xi Jinping's visit to India in 2014. A year earlier, in 2013, during the earlier part of the first author's field work, two young archers were not allowed to go to the Youth World Archery Championship in Wuxi (China) because they were issued stapled visas, which is not an official visa form (DIKSHIT 2013). The reason for this action was that China does not recognize Arunachal as part of India, so it did not issue standard visas; instead, they provided stapled visas that were unacceptable. One of the archers was Maselo Mihu, a girl from Kongo village where the first author was based during her fieldwork (Aiyadurai 2016). This incident was often brought up by the villagers to make a point that the Indian government is not treating people from Arunachal fairly and that the people of Arunachal are caught up in the politics between India and China.

BIODIVERSITY CONSERVATION ON THE BORDER

In addition to road building and the militarization of the borders, there is a tremendous increase in scientific activities that shapes the border for wildlife conservation on the Indian side. There are large protected areas along the Sino-Indian border that were created in the last couple of decades. In Tawang, the Tsangyang Gyatso World Peace Park was announced in 2004, with the intention to set aside 2,000 km² for setting up a biosphere reserve, on the recommendation of a conservation NGO (Mishra, Madhusudan, and Datta 2006). The creation of protected areas has often been in response to international concern and because of influential NGOs in the region. The Government of India responds to such concerns and has turned over its borderlands for biodiversity conservation. Conservation is, arguably, one of the ways to keep the territory free of human occupation, while at the same time taking such actions will win India favor on the international stage. Through such initiatives, we would argue that India is trying to represent itself as environmentally concerned in contrast to China, which often gets bad press for being environmentally reckless and destructive.

The Dihang-Dibang Biosphere Reserve was created in 1998 and spreads across an area of 5,112 km². In 2012, following the rescue of tiger cubs there, the Dibang Tiger Reserve was proposed, whose northern boundary overlaps with the international border. Half of Dibang Valley district (4,194 km²) is already under state protection in the form of the Dibang Wildlife Sanctuary. The sanctuary was officially established in 1988 (notification no: CWL/D/42/92/744-844; dated 12th March 1988). According to the Mishmis, the sanctuary was created without the people's consent and this has been a point of contestation between the state forest department and the local Mishmi. There is a Forest Range Office with just seven staff and two officers to manage the sanctuary.[23] From 2012 onward, there has been a surge of activities in the name of tiger conservation in the Dibang Valley. Although the Mishmi are unhappy about the wildlife sanctuary, they have concerns about the environment. The anti-dam protests against the Dibang Multipurpose Project from 2007 until 2011 resulted in political mobilization and environmental consciousness among the local Mishmi. In 2008, they blocked a road to prevent entry of National Hydro Power Corporation officials to resist dam-related activities. National and global environmental NGOs and reporters covered this story (Anon. 2008).

Similar to the early nineteenth-century explorers, the current scientific explorers visit these borderlands in search of "new species" of wild animals. These explorations have found meaning in the surge in ecological studies carried out by both national and international scholars with the support of NGOs, research, and conservation organizations. This has been driven in part by inclusion of the region within the Eastern Himalaya "biodiversity hotspot" (MYERS et al. 2000). A large number of public and civil society organizations are currently engaged in supporting ecological and conservation activities in Arunachal. The Mishmi Hills is emerging as a new site for conservation with the efforts of conservation NGOs to control traditional hunting practices and resource use.

Geographical Information System (GIS), remote sensing technologies, and camera trap technology are being used by scientific experts and state planners to showcase rich biodiversity that often excludes consideration of the human inhabitants in favor of a focus on dense vegetation cover and biological complexity. These new actors from the scientific community seek help from the local Mishmi as porters and guides, because they have deep knowledge of local wildlife and the landscape. Without the local knowledge of the Mishmi, the NGOs and research groups would never be able to carry out their research successfully. Hunters are often sought to record animal presence, bird sightings, and high altitude lakes. Locally known hunters become the key informants for researchers who look for potential sites to fix camera traps and to identify the footprints of animals, while also providing guidance on the most convenient ways hike up the mountainous terrain.

HUNTERS AS "BORDER PROTECTORS"?

The government of India has requested the Arunachal forest department to submit a proposal for a Tiger Reserve (DEPARTMENT OF ENVIRONMENT AND FOREST, GOVERNMENT OF ARUNACHAL PRADESH 2014). This initiative is suspected by the local Mishmi to be a mechanism to prevent their access to hunting grounds, but hunters justify their hunting trips as also having a nationalistic purpose. Hunting trips, according to Mishmi hunters, are also a way to keep a check on Chinese intrusions into the Indian territory, as was suggested earlier in this article. The proposal of a tiger reserve challenges both the Mishmi's claims to preserving wildlife and to protecting the borders. It has added another burden to the local people's concerns, because there is a possibility of curbing hunting practices and also the possibility that more military presence will be added, making even their movements to the borders difficult. Increased surveillance and increased control over the local population is what the local Mishmi fear most.

What the state considers illegitimate (illicit) could be what people residing in the region see as legitimate (licit). In the case of hunting, what Mishmi hunters are doing is illegal, because they defy the norms and rules of the forest department. But hunting is a socially acceptable, morally right, and culturally justified practice among the Mishmi. They see their actions as licit, especially those that live in the remote villages near the border, who regularly go for musk deer hunting or to protect crops and cattle from predators. One wing of the state (forest department) sees this as illegal while the other (Army, Indo-Tibetan Border Police (ITBP, below), intelligence branches, and research teams) appropriates the very act of hunting to obtain intelligence about the Chinese and gather information about wildlife, respectively. Frontier areas like the Dibang Valley are like what Tsing calls "interstitial spaces," made by collaborations among legitimate and illegitimate partners (Tsing 2005, 27).

India's Wildlife Protection Act was passed in 1972 to prohibit hunting of all wildlife without any consideration for people who live and depend on forest resources for their subsistence, especially those in rural areas. The noticeable lack of any cultural sensitivity toward the so-called "tribals" of northeast India made all those local people who hunted wildlife for subsistence, trade, or for cultural reasons, "criminals" and "poachers" overnight. The very people who appear as criminals in the official discourse of the state clearly hold a different point of view of themselves and their current predicament. What the state officials view as illegal may be considered well within the bounds of acceptable behavior by local communities (Abraham and van Schendel 2005, 25). The distinction between the legal and illegal revolves around opposed cultural meanings attributed to the activities in question (ibid., 19). The overlapping of political, geographical, ecological, and historical understandings makes the borderlands of the Dibang Valley with China a space where the distinction between illegal and legal becomes blurred.

Depending on what side of the border one is on, "patriots" and "traitors" are defined. State agencies (i.e., forest department and Indian Army) and non-state agencies (e.g., corporations and NGOs) compete for this border space and are appropriating large portions of it. The Mishmi are caught in the middle of disputes between them, so they become partners, collaborators, victims, beneficiaries, or criminals, depending on which agencies need or do not need them at any given point in time. The role of the local Mishmi as informers disguised as hunters is a good example of illicit and licit categories as a contradiction within the state. The state both condones and approves hunting as a way to collect information on Chinese activities on the border. The Mishmi's knowledge of the area, their facial features, and their language makes it more feasible for them to do this job for the government than the staff of the Army or Intelligence Bureau, whose employees are often from outside the region. They bear very little physical resemblance to the local Mishmi and have limited knowledge of the terrain, which is absolutely essential for survival in the region. The risk is much higher for the state actors themselves undertaking borderland tasks than it is for Mishmi actors, whose "mongoloid" facial features help them get away with "spying." According to the Union Minister of Home Affairs, Kiren Rijiju (Minister of State), who is from Arunachal, the villagers near the Indo-Tibetan border can be trained to become informers. Rijiju states that "...the government would like to train villagers along the 3,500 km Indo-Tibetan border to provide information about the suspicious activity" (Kaul 2014).

The relationship of the state with the local people can be ambiguous at times. Mishmi's ethnic identity and their earlier trading links with their kin across the border, sometimes create anxiety among military agencies. The state not only looks at the indigenous population with some doubt but also scrutinizes even the researchers who visit these regions, mostly the lone researcher from outside Arunachal, such as the first author of this article. Another scholar, an ornithologist who is now a faculty member of the Wildlife Institute of India has surveyed extensively along the borders of Arunachal. He was tracked back to Mysore, where he worked for a NGO at the time, to verify his identity by government officials. An Indian doctoral student registered at University College London also had difficulties when the Indo-Tibetan Border Police[24] authorities questioned him about his work on camera traps, which he used to study tigers. He was viewed with deep suspicion, but the officials showed keen interest to know how the cameras work, their cost, how to procure them, and, more importantly, the strategic locations where the devices were placed.

Conclusion

After the 1962 war, the Government of India was very concerned about the loyalty of the people residing on the border, for they were seen as an "uncertain factor" in state-citizen relations (SINGH 2010, 68). It was felt then that since the hill people shared ethnic and racial ties with the people across the border, there was every possibility that they might side with their ethnic "neighbors" (SINGH 2010), a concern that the British also had during their period of colonial rule.

Mishmi people take pride in their dual purpose for visiting the borders: for hunting and for patrolling. The former is an illegal activity according to the state, while the latter is seen as very much legal and preferred by the locals as a livelihood option. Since the war, the region has entered into a new nationalist discourse of development as a priority of the state agenda, aimed at the "nationalization of the frontiers," as the political scientist Sanjib BARUAH puts it (2003). For the local people within and across the border, the agents of the state are both welcome and unwelcome, depending on who they are and what the purpose of their presence is. Although the borders are politically constructed and are drawn arbitrarily on maps created by human agents with various agendas, the situation on the ground for the local people on both sides of the border is different from the perception of borders as lines of separation and territorial control. Local people see the presence of state actors as an opportunity to acquire economic benefits during patrolling and as a controlling mechanism when the forest department bars tourists from entering their sanctuary without written permission.

During tense encounters, the Mishmi stress that they are "residents of India" too, but their very presence on the border also reminds state authorities about their ethnolinguistic linkages with their Chinese brethren across the border. Such encounters will only become more frequent when border regions such as the Dibang Valley become "cosmetically nationalized," to use BARUAH's (2003) term, through roads, dam constructions, and the establishment of protected areas. The border residents in question often find different and innovative ways to engage with state actors. Similarly, authorities in each administrative office involved use legal and political apparatuses to find ways to engage and control locals for effective administration on both sides of the Sino-Indian border.

In this article, we investigated how changes in the environment along the borders have affected the Mishmi community as a whole. We engaged changing

Mishmi perceptions of the borderlands within and against the historical perspective of India and China's entangled border history. While the borderlands are constantly under construction by India's development projects that are fueled by changes in China–India relations, the Mishmi living on the border also act as agents engaging in exchange through informal and fluid lived experience. Historians treat borders as a post-colonial phenomenon shaped by cumulative past events, whereas anthropologists define borders "as boundaries that separate social forms, peoples, and regions" (ALVAREZ 1995, 448). The Mishmi are thus, in this dual sense, both historical and anthropological agents.

Since the war between India and China, the borders have been shaped by nation-building exercises and development agendas that are often transnational. With globalization, international boundaries have taken on new geopolitical connotations (NEWMAN 2003). The building of roads indicates a change in Indian military thinking that has so far opposed developing roads near the border, in case the Chinese use them during a conflict for speedy movement inside Indian territory.

What is happening now in the Mishmi hills is quite similar to what happened a century ago: mapping, census taking, and military interests converge to impact upon the local populations. Several political officers from the Assam administration were posted in Sadiya, from where they conducted surveys of the Mishmi hills near the Indo-China border to assess the practicality of road construction, to build frontier posts, and to resolve inter-village disputes and rivalries (GODFREY 1940; WILLIAMS 1944; MAINPRICE 1945; ROUTLEDGE 1945). One of the fears of the British was that Mishmi people might end up becoming Chinese subjects. The British continued mapping the region until the time of India's independence, counting villages and assessing crop production through what they termed "hoe-tax." They even encouraged Mishmi hunters to grow vegetables and fruits (peaches and apples) and become peasants, by offering them seeds and teaching them how to maintain orchards. Agricultural officers were deputed, and new crops like potatoes were also introduced.

The end of British rule brought about a temporary conclusion to expeditions and missionary evangelism, since the northeastern tribal regions were closed off to all foreigners after the independence of India in 1947, at least temporarily. During the early years of the post-independence period, the area was opened only to official research carried out at the Tribal Research Institute, which was commissioned by the first prime minister, Pandit Jawaharlal Nehru, with the well-known anthropologist Verrier Elwin as its head. The Government of India's tribal studies network in the hills was mainly focused on bringing "development" to the frontier people without disturbing their culture (ELWIN 1959). However, these ideas of protection have changed over time in the post-Nehruvian era of liberalization, for the region is currently witnessing the construction of several hydro-electric and interstate road building projects (GOVERNMENT OF ARUNACHAL PRADESH 2005).

Ideas of development are reflected through the spread of road networks, the construction of dams, and also by the setting up of national parks and biosphere reserves that are presented to the public as "green modernity" progress through the colonization of nature. The surge of ideas relating to conservation and development in the region is rooted in the detailed but often biased descriptions by colonial missionaries, explorers, pundits, military officials, and botanists, whose resulting images of wildness were constructed through their textual descriptions found in the memoirs and travelogues they wrote and fortuitously left behind for contemporary researchers.

Because of the fieldwork performed by the first author in the valley of Dibang, this article contains more information from the Indian than Chinese side of the border. Ethnic minorities living along and across national borders are essentially challenging to study, due to their sensitive positioning. Doing research on such populations in Arunachal Pradesh, a disputed and restricted area on both sides, is even more difficult. Indeed, China and India impose the highest level of national security on this region. Both nations realize the huge significance of the area and its inhabitants. Researchers therefore face problems having research proposals approved and obtaining permits to carry out the work on site. They also encounter logistical issues, language problems, and find it frustratingly difficult to secure entry permits at the entry points of such sensitive sites along the disputed international borders straddling the Mishmi homelands in China and India. Moreover, there is also a shortage of surviving and accessible secondary resources for consultation.

Both China and India are competing to gain global prominence, but they continue to impose the highest level of security along their national borders. While the focus for both nations is on defense mechanisms, development, and trade links, the lives of the minority societies that live along these borders get marginalized and become somewhat irrelevant. We discussed one such community, the little-known transnational Mishmi. We hope that this research note, based on personal narratives and oral histories and supplemented with archival documents, conveys a sense of Mishmi social history through their stories that are otherwise likely to get lost as this small ethnolinguistic group gets sandwiched tighter and tighter between the two countries both competing for global superpower status, a new "great game" that continues to unfold in the shadow of low media exposure.

NOTES

1. There are several indigenous communities or ethnic minorities who share national borders with China. TAPP (2002) discusses minorities of China who live in Southeast Asia and CHAUDHURI (2013) provides insights into minorities living in India close to the international border with China.

2. We use pseudonyms for informants in order to protect their identities.

3. We are aware of the problematic nature of the term "tribe," which is why we have put it within quotation marks in this instance of first use. While the term is still used in India, thanks to British anthropological classification, the term is rarely, if ever, used in China, which built its classificatory system on the basis of Soviet anthropology. Instead, the term *minzu* 民族 (ethnic minority) is used for ethnic minority groups. See, for example MULLANEY and ANDERSON (2011) and HARRELL (2002). For the persistence of the concept of tribe in India, however, see BHATTACHARYA and BHATTACHARYA (2003), and for a reflection on the term's future, see GREGORY (2003).

4. It was 60 million US dollars supplied by the Asian Development Bank (ADB) for watershed development projects (i.e., flood management, water supply, and sanitation) for Arunachal.

5. See also T. K. Baruah (1988), T. K. Bhattacharjee (1983), D. S. Negi (1996).

6. Their Chinese name is *Dengren* 僜人 (Deng people) or *Dengbaren* 僜巴人 (Dengba people). They may also be known as "Idu Mishmi (Idu Lhoba)," "Digaru tribe (Taraon, Darang Deng)," or "Miju Mishmi (Kaman Deng)."

7. Because of a lack of information, we cannot definitively confirm whether the Deng speak the same language or dialect as the Mishmi.

8. The British came to Assam during the Anglo-Burmese war of 1824–26, after which Assam came under its rule (Bose 1979).

9. *Posa* is money or products offered to the hill tribes by the Ahom kings of Assam to prevent them from raiding the villages in the foothills and plains. *Posa* was greatly valued by the hill people. It came in the form of clothes, salt, and iron (Singh 2009). For every ten houses in the foothills, the hill people were entitled to receive a set of clothes, one *dao* (machete), ten heads of horned cattle, and four *seer*s of salt. *Seer* (Farsi *sihr*) is a traditional unit of mass and volume used throughout South Asia in the past. In India, the Standards of Weights and Measures Act (No. 89 of 1956, amended in 1960 and 1964) set it at 1.25 kg. However, it varies from state to state in India, existing in "old" and "new" forms.

10. Zayu often appears as Zayul Chu.

11. Village headmen were given woolen red coats by the British to signify the authority of the person and to represent the administration in the area concerned.

12. F. J. Monahan was the Secretary to the Chief Commissioner of Assam.

13. Sappers were soldiers who performed a variety of military engineering duties, such as bridge building, laying or clearing minefields, demolition, field defense, and general construction as well as road and airfield construction and repair.

14. A Fellow of the Royal Geographical Society, Angus Hamilton gave an account of the British military expeditions in the Mishmi Hills in 1911–1912.

15. Mishmi was also written as Mishmee in the colonial documents found in Indian and British archives.

16. All interviews were conducted in Hindi and English by the first author. Yaaku wrote her diary in Chinese, and the few pages left from her diary were translated into English by the second author.

17. Indian ethnic groups are known to have different names in China. Luo Yu is most likely one of the names the Chinese use for Mishmi.

18. Sanjib Baruah (2003) refers to *the Assam Tribune* article which mentions Yaaku's brother-in-law and the first author met him in Anini in 2013–2014. Sanjib Baruah (2003) also refers to this Mishmi man.

19. When the Mishmi speak of the Chinese, they could be referring either to the local Chinese, Tibetan hunters, or the Chinese Army.

20. This is one of India's paramilitary troops.

21. The Indian Army and the Indo-Tibetan Border Police jointly undertake border patrol duty, including Long Range Patrols, to get a sense of the international border's dynamics as well as to check on China's activities.

22. This expression is widely used by geographers. Cartographic aggression is a term by which a country describes any act by a neighboring country that shows part of its geographic area as its own territory. It is often used in the case of maps.

23. The Mehao Wildlife Sanctuary staff is responsible for manning this site. As such, there are no regular staff members residing within the Dibang Wildlife Sanctuary, according to the Management Plan of Dibang Wildlife Sanctuary (2010–2011 to 2014–2015).

24. The Indo-Tibetan Border Police force was created in 1962 in the wake of Sino-Indian war earlier that year. The force is deployed along the India's border with the Tibet Autonomous Region.

REFERENCES

ABRAHAM, Itty, and Willem van SCHENDEL
  2005   Introduction: The making of illicitness. In *Illicit Flows and Criminal Things: States, Borders, and the Other Side of Globalization*, Willem van Schendel and Itty Abraham, eds., 1–37. Bloomington and Indianapolis: Indiana University Press.

AISHER, Alexander
  2012   Coevolving with the landscape? Migration narratives and the environmental history of the Nyishi tribe in upland Arunachal Pradesh. In *Origins and Migrations in the Extended Eastern Himalayas*, Toni Huber and Stuart Blackburn, eds., 63–82. Leiden and Boston: Brill.
         doi: 10.1163/9789004228368_006

AIYADURAI, Ambika
  2012   Bird hunting in Mishmi hills of Arunachal Pradesh, north-eastern India. *Indian Birds* 7: 134–37.
  2016   'Tigers are our brothers': Understanding human–nature relations in the Mishmi Hills, northeast India. PhD dissertation, National University of Singapore.

ALVAREZ, Robert R. Jr.
  1995   The Mexican-US border: The making of an anthropology of borderlands. *Annual Review of Anthropology* 24: 447–70.

ANON.
  2008   Disquiet in Dibang. *Down to Earth*. May 15. http://www.downtoearth.org.in/coverage/disquiet-in-dibang-4539 (accessed 24 October 2015).

ANON.
  2014   *Yin zai Zangnan xiu 2,000 gongli gonglu jichang, ye yi xingcheng dui Jiefangju youshi* 印在藏南修2000公里公路机场, 也已形成对解放军优势 [India prepares for repairing a 2,000 km road in southern Tibet and already has advantages over the People's Liberation Army]. 环球时报 [*Global Times*] October 16 (accessed 3 December 2014).

ARPI, Claude
  2013   The so-called Chinese claims on Arunachal. *Claude Arpi*. http://claudearpi.blogspot.sg/2013/12/the-so-called-chinese-claims-on.html (accessed 3 December 2014).

BAILEY, F. M.
  1945   *China-Tibet-Assam, a journey, 1911*. Jonathan Cape: London.

BARAL, Kailash C.
  2009   Colonialism and ethnography: In search of an alternative mode of representation. *Man and Society: A Journal of North East Studies* VI: 83–94.

BARUAH, T. K.
  1998   The Idu Mishmis. Directorate of Research, Government of Arunachal Pradesh, Itanagar.

BARUAH, Sanjib
  2003   Nationalising space: Cosmetic federalism and the politics of development in northeast India. *Development and Change* 34: 915–39.
         doi: 10.1111/j.1467-7660.2003.00334.x

BASU, Dipak R., and Victoria MIROSHNIK

2012   China-India border dispute and Tibet. *Tōnan Ajia kenkyū nenpō* [*Southeast Asian Studies Annual Report*] 53: 43–51.

BHATTACHARJEE, P. C.

2002   Cross-country trade of Arunachal Pradesh in retrospect. In *Cross-Border Trade of North-East India: The Arunachal Perspective*, S. Dutta, ed., 33–41. Kolkata: Greenwich Millenium Press Ltd.

BHATTACHARYA, Kumkum, and Ranajit K. BHATTACHARYA

2003   Tribes: State of mind? *Journal of the Indian Anthropological Society* 38: 159–65.

BHATTACHARJEE, T. K.

1983   Idus of Mathun and Dri Valley. Directorate of Research, Government of Arunachal Pradesh: Shillong.

BHAUMIK, Subir

2009   *Troubled Periphery: Crisis of India's North East*. Los Angeles: Sage Publications. doi: 10.4135/9788132104797

BLACKBURN, Stuart

2005   The journey of the soul: Notes on funeral rituals and oral texts in Arunachal Pradesh, 'Die Riese der Seele: Bemerkungen zu Bestattungsritualen und oralen Texten in Arunachal Pradesh, Indien [*The journey of the Soul: Notes on funeral rituals and oral texts in Arunachal Pradesh*]', in Jan Assmann, Franz Maciejewski and Axel Michaels (eds.), in *Der Abschied von den Toten. Trauerrituale im Kulturvergleich*. Göttingen: Wallstein. https://www.soas.ac.uk/tribaltransitions/publications/file32490.pdf (accessed 31 October 2017)

BOSE, Manilal

1979   *History of Arunachal Pradesh*. New Delhi: Concept Publishing Company.

CHAUDHURI, Sarit K.

2008   Plight of the Igus: Notes on shamanism among the Idu Mishmis of Arunachal Pradesh, India. *European Bulletin of Himalayan Research* 32: 84–108.

2013   The institutionalization of tribal religion: Recasting the Donyi-Polo movement in Arunachal Pradesh. *Asian Ethnology* 72: 259–77. http://asianethnology.org/articles/230 (accessed 18 October 2017).

COOPER, Thomas Thornville

1873   *The Mishmee Hills: An Account of a Journey Made in an Attempt to Penetrate Tibet from Assam to Open New Routes for Commerce*. London: H.S. King.

DEPARTMENT OF ENVIRONMENT AND FOREST, GOVERNMENT OF ARUNACHAL PRADESH

2014   F. No 15-12/2014-NTCA. A proposal for a Tiger Reserve dated 28 May 2014.

DEURI, R. K.

1983   Ritual beliefs and practices of the Miju Mishmis of Lohit Valley. *Resarun* 9: 1–4.

DIKSHIT, Sandeep

2013   Arunachal archers with stapled visas prevented from leaving for China. *The Hindu*. October 13. http://www.thehindu.com/news/national/arunachal-archers-with-stapled-visas-prevented-from-leaving-for-china/article5226118.ece (accessed 22 December 2014).

DUTTA, Arnab P.
2008   Reservoir of dams: Arunachal Pradesh. *Down to Earth* 16: 32–39.

ELWIN, Verrier
1959   *A Philosophy for NEFA.* Shillong: Gyan Publishing House.
1964   *The Tribal World of Verrier Elwin: An Autobiography.* New Delhi: Oxford.

FEI Xiaotong 费孝通
1980   Guanyu woguo minzu shibie de wenti 关于我国民族识别的问题 [Ethnic identification in China]. *Zhongguo shehuikexue* 中国社会科学 [*Social Sciences in China*] 1: 94–107.

GAO, David
2015   Railways and the issue of Inner Line Permit in Arunachal Pradesh: Can the two function together? *Economic and Political Weekly* 50(8). http://www.epw.in/journal/2015/8/reports-states-web-exclusives/railways-and-issue-inner-line-permit-arunachal-pradesh (accessed 7 October 2016).

GODFREY, R. W.
1940   *Report on the Tour by the Political Officer, Sadiya Frontier Tract by the Lohit Valley to Rima.* London: British Library.

GOVERNMENT OF ARUNACHAL PRADESH
2005   *Arunachal Pradesh Human Development Report 2005.* Department of Planning, Government of Arunachal Pradesh.

GREGORY, Robert J.
2003   Tribes and tribal: Origin, use and future of the concept. *Studies in Tribes and Tribals* 1: 1–5.

GUHA, Ramachandra
1999   *Savaging the Civilized: Verrier Elwin, His Tribals, and India.* Chicago: The University of Chicago Press.

HAMILTON, Angus
1912   *In Abor Jungles: Being an Account of the Abor Expedition, the Mishmi Mission and the Miri Mission.* London: Eveleigh Nash.

HARRELL, Stevan
2002   *Ways of Being Ethnic in Southwest China.* Seattle: University of Washington Press.

HERIOT, Leo
1979   *The First Martyrs in Arunachal Pradesh: The Story of Frs. Krick and Bourry, Foreign Missionaries of Paris.* Bombay: Asian Trading Corporation.

HUBER, Toni
2012   Micro-migrations of hill peoples in northern Arunachal Pradesh: Rethinking methodologies and claims of origins in Tibet. In *Origins and Migrations in the Extended Eastern Himalayas,* Toni Huber and Stuart Blackburn, eds., 83–106. Leiden and Boston: Brill. doi: 10.1163/9789004228368_007

INSTITUTE OF ETHNOLOGY AND ANTHROPOLOGY,
CHINESE ACADEMY OF SOCIAL SCIENCES
1990   僜人社会历史与调查 *Dengren shehui lishi diaocha* [*Research on Deng's Society and History*]. Kunming: The Peoples Press of Yunnan.

JACOB, Jabin T.
2015   Arunachal Pradesh in the Sino-Indian boundary dispute: Constant claims, changing politics. In *Voices from the Border: Response to Chinese Claim over*

Arunachal Pradesh, Gurudas Das, C. Joshua Thomas, and Nani Bath, eds., 49–62. New Delhi: Pentagon Press.

Joshua Project
n.d. *Deng, Darang in China*. https://joshuaproject.net/people_groups/18436 /CH_(accessed 3 December 2014).

Kaul, Sanat
2014 Use locals to protect borders. *India Today*. August 8. http://indiatoday .intoday.in/story/sanat-kaul-kiren-rijiju-indo-tibetan-border-shyam -saran-mcmohan-line/1/376048.html (accessed 2 February 2015).

Kaulback, Ronald
1935 *Letter from Ronald Kaulback to Col. F.M. Bailey*. MSSEUR F157/252. London: The British Library.

Kingdon-Ward, Frank
1913 *Land of the Blue Poppy: Travels of a Naturalist in Eastern Tibet*. Cambridge: Cambridge University Press. doi: 10.1017/CBO9780511694134
1927 The Mishmi country. *The Geographical Journal* 69: 287–88. London: The Royal Geographical Society. doi: 10.2307/1782056

Kri, Hakraso
2008 *The Mishmis: An Introduction*. Tinsukia: The City Press.

Kumar, Manan
2014 PM to decide on constructing 2000 km strategic road in Arunachal Pradesh. *Daily News and Analysis*. November 5. http://www.dnaindia .com/india/report-pm-to-decide-on-constructing-2000-km-strategic- road-in-arunachal-pradesh-2032161 (accessed 2 February 2015).

Kurian, Nimmi
2014 *India-China Borderlands: Conversations beyond the Centre*. New Delhi: Sage Publications. doi: 10.4135/9789351507925

Lang Runfang 朗润芳 and Duoji Qiangba 强巴多吉
2000 Xiaoyi Chayu Dengbaren 小议察隅僜巴人 [Dicussing Chayu's Dengba People]. *Zhongguo Xizang* 中国西藏 [*China's Tibet*] 1: 37.

Li Jianwen 李建文
2008 "Di wushi ge: minzu "第五十七个" 民族 [The fifty-seventh minority]. *Qingnian Kexue* 青年科学 [*Youth Science*] 11: 41.

Lingi, Mite
2011 Call for concern on cultural endangerment in midst of changing time. *Reh Souvenir*, 15–16. Roing: Central Reh Celebration Committee.

Lyte, Charles
1989 *Frank Kingdon-Ward: The Last of the Greatest Plant Hunters*. London: John Murray.

Mainprice, Frederick Paul
1945 *Tour Diary of F.P. Mainprice, ICS, Assistant Political Officer, Lohit Valley, Nov 1943 - May 1945*. London: The British Library.

Maps of India
n.d. MapsofIndia.com, http://www.mapsofindia.com (accessed 6 June 2015).

McAfee, Kathleen Elaine
1999 Biodiversity and the Contradictions of Green Developmentalism. PhD dissertation, Berkeley: University of California at Berkeley.

McDuie-Ra, Duncan

2012   *Northeast Migrants in Delhi: Race, Refuge and Retail.* Amsterdam: Amsterdam University Press. doi: 10.26530/oapen_424531

Mene, Tarun

2011   Suicides among the Idu Mishmi tribe of Arunachal Pradesh. PhD dissertation, Itanagar: Rajiv Gandhi University,.

2013   Underestimation of suicides: A study of the Idu Mishmi tribe of Arunachal Pradesh. *Economic and Political Weekly* 48: 129–33.

Mills, James Philip

1952   The Mishmis of the Lohit Valley, Assam. *The Journal of the Royal Anthropological Institute of Great Britain and Ireland* 82: 1–12. doi:10.2307/2844036

Mishra, Charudutt, M. D. Madhusudan, and Aparajita Datta

2006   Mammals of the high altitudes of western Arunachal Pradesh, eastern Himalaya: An assessment of threats and conservation needs. *Oryx* 40: 29–35. doi: 10.1017/s0030605306000032

Mitchell, J. F.

1883   *Report (Topographical, Political and Military) on the North-East Frontier of India.* Calcutta: Superintendent of Government Printing.

Monahan, F. J.

1899   *Massacre at Mitaigaon, a Khamti Hamlet, and Proposals for an Expedition against the Bebejoya Mishmis.* 432 For./3332 P. Itanagar, Arunachal Pradesh: State Archives Office, Directorate of Research,.

Mullaney, Thomas, and Benedict Anderson

2011   *Coming to Terms with the Nation: Ethnic Classification in Modern China.* Berkeley: University of California Press.

Myers, Nyers, Russell A. Mittermeier, Cristina G. Mittermeier, Gustavo A. B. da Fonseca, and Jennifer Kent

2000   Biodiversity hotspots for conservation priorities. *Nature* 403: 853–58.

Negi, D. S.

1996   *A Tryst with Mishmi Hills.* New Delhi: Tushar Publications.

Newman, David

2003   On borders and power: A theoretical framework. *Journal of Borderland Studies* 18: 13–25. doi: 10.1080/08865655.2003.9695598

Noorani, A. G.

2011   *India-China Boundary Problem: 1846–1947, History and Diplomacy.* New Delhi and New York: Oxford University Press. doi: 10.1093/acprof:oso/9780198070689.001.0001

Pandit, Rajat

2014   Army kicks off raising new mountain strike corps against China. *The Times of India.* January 9. http://timesofindia.indiatimes.com/india/Army-kicks-off-raising-new-mountain-strike-corps-against-China/article-show/28571907.cms (accessed 6 June 2015).

Pulu, J.

1977   The bamboo and cane culture of the Idus. *Resarun* 3: 33–39.

1982   Folk songs of the Idu Mishmis. *Resarun* 9: 35–37.

RAHMAN, Mirza Zulfiqur
  2014   *Territory, tribes, turbines: Local community perceptions and responses to infra-structure development along the Sino-Indian Border in Arunachal Pradesh.* New Delhi: Institute of Chinese Studies.

REUTERS
  2015   China protests over Japan's comments on border dispute with India. *Reuters.* January 19. http://in.reuters.com/article/2015/01/19/china-japan-india-idINL4N0UY30320150119 (accessed 6 June 2015).

ROBB, Peter
  1997   The colonial state and constructions of Indian identity: An example on the northeast frontier in the 1880s. *Modern Asian Studies* 31: 245–83. doi: 10.1017/s0026749x0001430x

RONDO, Jonomo
  2011   Ethno-medicine: Tradition and practices of the Idus. *Resarun* 36: 80–84.

ROUTLEDGE, B. H.
  1945   *Tour Diary of B. H. Routledge, Sadiya Frontier, Dec 1945 – Dec 1946.* Mss Eur D1191/2. London: The British Library.

SARKAR, Jayant
  1987   *Society, Culture and Ecological Adaptation among Three Tribes of Arunachal Pradesh.* Calcutta: Ministry of Human Resource Development, Department of Culture, Government of India and Anthropological Survey of India.

SARMA, Rashmirekha
  2015   Disappearing dialect: The Idu-Mishmi language of Arunachal Pradesh (India). *International Journal of Intangible Heritage* 10: 62–72.

SAXER, Martin, and Juan ZHANG, eds.
  2016   *The art of neighboring: Making relations across China's borders.* Amsterdam: Amsterdam University Press and Chicago: University of Chicago Press.

SHARMA, Aman
  2014   Chinese troops training Pak Army near India-Pakistan border, BSF tells NSA Ajit Doval. *The Economic Times.* December 3. http://articles.economictimes.india-times.com/2014-11-15/news/56115065_1_bsf-chinese-troops-border-security-force (accessed 3 December 2014).

SHARMA, Rajeev
  2015   Modi in China: A high-octane reception muddied by CCTV's map of India. *Firstpost.* May 15. http://www.firstpost.com/world/modis-china-visit-high-octane-reception-muddied-cctv-map-2245418.html (accessed 19 May 2015).

SINGH, Bikash
  2014   Arunachal Pradesh now on railway map, train reaches Naharlagun, a town near capital Itanagar. *The Economic Times.* April 12. http://articles.economictimes.indiatimes.com/2014-04-12/news/49080232_1_harmuti-railway-map-arunachal-pradesh (accessed 12 July 2014).

SINGH, Deepak Kumar
  2009   *Stateless in South Asia: The Chakmas between Bangladesh and India.* New Delhi: Sage.

2010   Arunachalis' self-perceptions: Assertion and reconstruction of identity and ethnic nationalism. In *Stateless in South Asia*, ed. D. K. Singh, 180–220. New Delhi: Sage Publications. doi: 10.4135/9788132104940.n7

STEWART, Jules
2006   *Spying for the Raj: The pundits and the mapping of the Himalayas*. Phoenix Mill: Sutton Publishing.

TAPP, Nicholas
2002   In defence of the archaic: A reconsideraton of the 1950s ethnic classification project in China. *Asian Ethnicity* 3: 63–84.
doi: 10.1080/14631360120095874

TIMES OF INDIA
2014   India to fortify defence along China border, 54 new ITBP posts being planned in Arunachal. *The Times of India*. October 24. http://timesofindia.indiatimes.com/india/India-to-fortify-defence-along-China-border-54-new-ITBP-posts-being-planned-in-Arunachal/articleshow/36353494.cms (accessed 19 May 2015).

TNN
2013   Protest against Chinese incursion in Arunachal Pradesh. *The Times of India*. August 28. http://timesofindia.indiatimes.com/city/guwahati/Protest-against-Chinese-incursion-in-Arunachal-Pradesh/articleshow/22110499.cms (accessed 12 July 2014).

TSING, Anna
2005   *Friction: An Ethnography of Global Connection*. New Jersey: Princeton University Press.

VERTZBERGER, Yaacov
1982   India's border conflict with China: A perceptual analysis. *Journal of Contemporary History* 17: 607–31. doi: 10.1177/002200948201700403

WALLER, Derek J.
1990   *The Pundits: British Exploration of Tibet and Central Asia*. Lexington: The University Press of Kentucky.

WILLIAMS, J. H. F.
1944   *Tour Diary of J.H.F. Willaims Esq I.P. Political Officer, Sadiya Frontier Tract for the Months of Sept-Oct and Part of Nov 1944*. The British Library London.

WILLIAMSON, Noel
1910   *Report of Mr. Williamson, APO in Connection with His Work Carried Out in 1909-1910 in the Digaru-Miju Bridle Path and of His House in the Mishmi Hills to the Border of South-Eastern Tibet*. F/20 P of 1910. Itanagar: State Archives of Arunachal Pradesh.

YEH, Emily T.
2009   Greening western China: A critical review. *Geoforum* 40: 884–94. doi: 10.1016/j.geoforum.2009.06.004
2012   Transnational environmentalism and entanglements of sovereignty: The tiger campaign across the Himalayas. *Political Geography* 31: 408–18. doi: 10.1016/j.polgeo.2012.06.003

General

Raymond Silverman, ed., *Museum as Process: Translating Local and Global Knowledges*

Routledge, 2015. xvii + 303 pages. List of figures, notes, references, index. Paperback, US$49.95, ISBN: 978-0-415-66157-7. Hardback, US$150.00, ISBN: 978-0-415-66156-0. (E-book, ISBN: 978-1-315-76693-5.)

GLOBALLY, the museum as a cultural institution is in a period of radical change. From at least the late 1980s onward, curators, scholars, source communities, and viewing publics have been engaged in rethinking the nature of museum/community relationships. Attending to the imbalances of power (gendered, racial, ethnic, settler-colonial/indigenous, and so forth), a wide range of museum practitioners have begun to seek new modes of "collaboration involving museums defined broadly as collecting institutions (including archives), the communities that are represented in and by these institutions, and the individuals who mediate these encounters" (1). *Museum as Process* comprises an ethnographically rich, thoroughly reflexive series of accounts of these deeply collaborative ventures which, now in their third decade, have moved "beyond museums' most public face, their exhibitions, to reach into other museum components and roles" including the structuring of databases and classification systems, the remodeling of storage spaces to allow for religious and ceremonial treatment of the material objects, and the rethinking of the nature and processes of knowledge production and claims to authenticity (281).

As editor Raymond Silverman notes in the Introduction, the volume grew out of a yearlong lecture series "Translating Knowledge: Global Perspectives on Museum and Community" that Silverman organized at the University of Michigan in 2009–2010. One of the major points of inspiration for the lecture series was the work of Ivan Karp, long a leading voice in scholarly and praxis-based discourse on the changing nature of museums, the politics of representation, and the relationships between museums and communities (whether source communities, viewing publics, or a combination of both). True to its multidisciplinary origins, *Museum as Process* works at the intersection of museum studies, applied anthropology, and Indigenous studies, while bearing the strong imprint of postcolonial and subaltern theory tuned to the ends of a pragmatic, ethical engagement.

Silverman identifies three key ways in which the volume as a whole intervenes into this cluster of ongoing debates. First, he provides an overall framework for understanding the process of collaboration as one of "transcultural translation," a complex negotiation of meaning as "objects of knowledge" move across and are shared between different cultures and settings (3). Further, in a frank admission of the openendedness of the work, Silverman advocates for a thick description of the dynamics of museum-community collaboration, arguing that "messiness" is a positive sign, and that "there is much to be learned from failure" (2), the experience of which ideally provides guidelines and important clues toward further, more enhanced and equitable partnerships. Finally, in his framing essay, Silverman offers a defense of "slow museology" (3). The fundamental insight of the volume is that museums must come to terms with "multiple 'ways of knowing' that often meet and coalesce in the objects upon which various meanings have been inscribed. This applies to both material culture as well as intangible tradition, basically anything that can be objectified" (3). In what follows, I will center my comments on those chapters likely to be of most interest to the readers of this journal—that is, the chapters which deal with Asian and Pacific Islander cultures and communities—while also giving a sense of the volume as a whole.

The first seven chapters provide deeply textured accounts concerning repatriation: the process of returning, in some form or fashion, a living object to its source community. One particularly interesting feature of this section is the way in which several of the chapters grapple with questions of material versus digital repatriation. Several of the authors describe the co-creation of databases and Gwyneira Isaac's chapter caps off this opening section by problematizing economies of knowledge and heritage through a close consideration of museological circulations of Zuni material culture. A second, smaller grouping of three chapters describes the creation of community-based cultural centers, while a final section, also of three chapters, concerns exhibition projects. The closing chapter, by Ivan Karp and Cory Kratz, offers a critical summation, forwarding the idea of the "interrogative museum" as a processual space and an "interrogative attitude" as "one that will challenge—not overthrow, but challenge—the claims to authority that museums make" (294).

A core concept, developed across the volume as a whole, concerns the practice of decolonizing the museum. Aaron Glass's chapter ("Indigenous Ontologies, Digital Futures"), focuses on collections of Northwest Coastal Indigenous Peoples' cultural objects housed in Berlin and gives a fascinating account of how the construction of databases poses a "challenge to re-imagine… the terms of knowledge management so that multiple ways of knowing and being are encoded into the architecture of management systems themselves" (21). Glass provides extensive commentary on how his team grappled with encoding different cultural ontologies, taxonomies, and epistemologies into the digital database and, most crucially, fleshes out some of the ethical contours of "e-patriation" which he defines as "the transfer of tangible or intangible cultural patrimony (or heritage material) to its source community in the form of electronic or digital media" (23). As the authors of the next chapter (Bohaker, Ojiig Cobriere, and Phillips, writing on Anishinaabe cultural representations in Ontario museums) note, ideally such collaboration and co-creation transforms the database "from a passive repository of standardized information to a digital space in which new knowledge is generated, lost knowledge recovered, and both added back into a shared knowledge pool that can change and enrich understandings" of cultural heritage and history (61).

The next three chapters focus on similar attempts to decolonize knowledge, now moving the geographical focus to Asia. Jennifer Shannon describes a collaborative project between the University of Colorado Museum of Natural History and the National Taiwan Museum. A richly suggestive dialogue, the collaboration involved the sharing of knowledge, protocols developed through intentionally conducted trial-and-error, and techniques learned through working with Indigenous communities: the Navajo Nation, on the one hand, and the Paiwan, on the other. Howard Murphy's chapter on "Open Access versus the Culture of Protocols" concerns the interfaces of Aboriginal peoples and the Australian museum, offering an investigation of the ways in which "protocols of diplomacy and protocols of the digital age come together in the discourse of access and rights in images" (97). Joshua A. Bell, on the other hand, takes the digital conversation and turns it toward a consideration of fieldwork, knowledge management, and the mapping of cultural objects in the Purari Delta of Papua New Guinea. Bell's fascinating chapter explores the failures and pitfalls of visibility (photographs, GPS, sketches) as it comes into contact and conflict with embodied, memorial, and oral knowledge claims.

The penultimate chapter, Paul Tapsell's "*Ko Tawa*: Where Are the Glass Cabinets?" was, for me, the most exciting study in the volume. A detailed account of "the challenges facing museums seeking to translate indigenous knowledge into an exhibitionary context" (262), the chapter lays out the ways in which the creation of a Maori Values Team "set in motion… distinct procedures of curatorial management" such that material objects "became 'human' again" (265). Tapsell recounts the lengthy, collaborative process of knowledge co-creation, focused on Captain Gilbert Mair's collection of Maori *taonga* (defined as "any item, tangible or intangible, passed down from kin-ancestors/tribal knowledge base," 266). As a process, this exhibit revealed long-forgotten, crucially important messages and meanings embodied in the material objects. "By gifting associated guardian ancestors or *taonaga* to Mair as a colonial agent," Tapsell argues, "Maori tribal leaders were ceremonially petitioning the government (Crown) to recognize and honor its 1840 Treating of Waitangi promise to protect the tribes' leadership (*tino rangatiratanga*, absolute chieftainship) over their lands (*whenua*, placenta of Earth Mother), villages (*kainga*, *marae*-based communities) and resources (*toanga*)" (266).

There is some unevenness between the chapters, and the volume as a whole would have benefited from a more explicit framing of the sub-grouping of chapters. Eleven of the sixteen chapters (the first nine and the last two), for instance, focus on co-creation of knowledge with Indigenous communities. The remaining five chapters, however, while intriguing and exciting in their own ways, maintain a different focus. A more sharply-maintained interest on Indigeneity throughout, or a more robust editorial framing, would have articulated the ways in which Chapters 10-14 continue to develop the ideas and arguments developed in the first nine chapters and concluded in the final two. This would not have been too much of a stretch. As Ana Maria Theresa P. Labrador notes in her chapter on museums in southern Luzon, many of the social and cultural functions typically accorded to museums—communicating and exhibiting tangible and intangible heritage, providing opportunities for education and study, conserving material objects, and transmitting contextual and cultural information adhering to those objects—are performed by groups of people, "particularly among indigenous people" who may "share the responsibility of caring for sacred objects" and so forth (247).

Taken as a whole, the volume does an excellent job of accounting for the imperative to, the difficulties involved in, and the promise of "relocating authority" (12) such that the museum becomes a nexus of collaboration in which various knowledge systems, epistemologies, and value systems coexist and a variety of stakeholders each have access to, and differing valences of authority to speak about, living objects of material culture. Decolonizing the museum and creating a more symmetrical relationship between various stakeholders (most especially source communities from whom objects may have initially been taken or from whom objects may have been acquired inequitably) means asking a host of crucial questions. Museum professionals, applied anthropologists, Indigenous community organizers, and scholars in a range of fields (especially cultural anthropology, museum studies, Indigenous studies, and ethnography) will find this volume, the questions it asks, and the tentative answers it poses, of great interest. Its frank assessment and rich account of the promises, and rigorous demands, of collaborative knowledge creation are a gift to each of these fields.

Charlotte Eubanks
Penn State

Victoria Lindsay Levine and Philip V. Bohlman, eds., *This Thing Called Music: Essays in Honor of Bruno Nettl*
Lanham, Maryland: Rowman & Littlefield, 2015. xxvii + 507 pages. List of figures, list of tables, index. Hardback, $55.00/£37.95, ISBN: 978-1-4422-4207-4. eBook, $54.99/£37.95, ISBN: 978-1-4422-4208-1.

THIS EIGHTEENTH volume in the series *Europea: Ethnomusicologies and Modernities* (edited by Bohlman and Stokes) celebrates the multifaceted research fields of Bruno Nettl, and the man as a teacher, colleague, and friend, on the occasion of his 85th birthday. The nature of Bruno Nettl's research is all-encompassing as he is one of the few universally operating ethnomusicologists, who are becoming rare in recent times.

The editors, Bohlman and Levine, have organized the volume in six parts: "Communities of Music," "Intellectual History of Ethnomusicology," "Analytical Studies," "Historical Studies," "Issues and Concepts," and "Change, Adaptation, and Survival." This structuring implies that the editors may not have had in mind to put up a genuinely coherent volume, but rather to give former students, colleagues, and friends an opportunity to contribute. The parts are not mutually exclusive, and emphasize different perspectives of "this thing called music." The volume is widely inclusive and does not impose any disciplinary strictures on the contributors, although ethnomusicology somewhat stands out.

Each part consists of five to seven chapters that are diverse in their approaches and exemplary in their topics and academic quality—sticking largely to American views on musicology as a discipline within an English-speaking world. The volume contains 34 chapters, of which 90% are written by female contributors, reflecting an above-average distribution of successful female researchers in the field of musicology. Some contributors re-work preceding research outcomes, others take up new topics and issues. Many of the chapters take a look at the relationship between the respective author and Bruno Nettl; however, in so doing, save a few exceptions, the respective authors tend to reduce the effects of Nettl's research and teaching on their own experience of the discipline.

Part I, "Communities of Music," starts with an interesting chapter by Theresa Allison on medical humanities (3–14) reflected through observations in a nursing home—another emerging field of music research. This chapter is followed by Patricia Shehan Campbell writing on "Music in the Culture of Children" (15–27). Then comes Chris Goertzen's piece, with a rather local focus, on layers of identity, taking the Mississippi Choctaw Fair and Veteran's Day as an example (28–40). Margaret Sarkissian adds a rather auto-descriptive chapter on Malaccan Traditions (41–55) among or initiated by Portuguese descendants, followed by a more analytical approach in the last chapter in this part by Anna Schultz on performing translation in Jewish India (56–70). The communities introduced in this part are diverse and the chapters offer a wide range of resources available for further studies.

Part II is about the "Intellectual History of Ethnomusicology," which excludes discussions on technical and infrastructural preconditions of the discipline. However, the intellectuality is somewhat connected to these preconditions, and appears more or less in all chapters starting with Samuel Araújo on Brazil (73–89), followed by Zuzana Jurková on "Bohemian Traces in the World of Ethnomusicology" (90–101), and William Kinderman on Munich in the first half of the 20th century (102–12). These chapters are ambiguous in their interpretation of goals in gaining professional knowledge, as they show a certain tendency to superimpose national belongings and construction of narrow meta-identities that do not always correlate with the disciplinary contents of actually overcoming these identities. Nevertheless, they are important for the understanding of knowledge growth and the diversity of contemporary disciplinary thinking. Part II also consists of more general analysis, as provided in the following four chapters: Harry Liebersohn's "Western Civilization" (113–24); Daniel M. Neuman's general exposition of everything American musicologists reflect on and discuss (125–36); A. J. Racy's reflection, in a rather anecdotal narrative, on dealing with the Cairo Congress of Arab Music (1932), especially the recording project connected to it (137–50); and Anthony Seeger on keeping track of ethnomusicological knowledge (151–63). This last chapter is outstanding for its innovative approach that will help future studies in the field.

Part III, "Analytical Studies," consists of five chapters. They submit to a rather biased view on what analytical studies may deliver. While the first three chapters—Stephen Blum on "The Persian Radif and the Tajik-Uzbek Šašmaqom" (167–79), Robert Garfias on "The Saz Semaisi in Evcara by Dilhayat Kalfa and the Turkish Makam After the Ottoman Golden Age," and Orin Hatton on Gros Ventre Songs (196–208)—try to go beyond this narrow focus on music analysis, the fourth chapter by Lars-Christian Koch on "Permutation as a Basic Concept of Rāga Elaboration in North Indian Music" (209–38) is a somewhat auto-descriptive approach enriched with technological applications that Koch finally recommends in order to research "ethnic music" (235). However, North Indian researchers and/or musicians may have problems with this interpretation, as permutation is rather conceptually applied by musicians of the South Indian classical tradition. However, the two strong categories of classical music in India are barely reflected as "ethnic music," a questionable term even in other contexts.

The last chapter of this section is Albrecht Schneider's chapter, "Aspects of Sound Recording and Sound Analysis." This is quite an old contribution and is dedicated to general melographic issues that were discussed at the end of the 1990s. It is surprising that the author describes some music related technicalities given that they became outdated in a relatively short time.

Part IV of the volume, "Historical Studies," again presents a wider field open to a rich diversity of researchers. The chapters include Philip V. Bohlman on music's intimate moments, taking a composition of Viktor Ullmann as an example (241–54); Martha Ellen Davis on oral history, emphasizing biographical studies (255–66)—a very necessary chapter on historical studies in recent times; Beverley Diamond on Indian Residential Schools in Canada (267–79); Amnon Shiloah's re-worked article about music in the accounts of medieval Arab travelers (280–290); Gordon Thompson on working with the Beatles (291–301); and the inspiring chapter by Philip Yampolsky on "Commercial 78s" as a resource for future ethnomusicologists (302–14). Historical studies seem to be less burdened with ethnomusicological distrust, as they are seen as a complementary necessity. However, this conclusion gives rise to the perception among the researchers and editors who contributed to this volume of the discipline as being naturally in need of historical depth.

Part V takes a look at "Issues and Concepts." The most outstanding contribution to this topic is the chapter written by Marcello Sorce Keller on musical knowledge (366–77). This wonderful composition of thoughts makes the entire volume special. In contrast, the other chapters in Part V are overarching looks at a wide variety of folk-defined music and fieldwork-based experiences. They are written by Stefan Fiol on Indian Folk Music (317–29); J. Richard Haefer on O'odham story and song (330–41); Melinda Russell on College Folk Music classes (342–53); Gabriel Solis on Multi-Sited Ethnomusicology (354–65), who defends comparative musicology in an appealing way; and Thomas Turino on theory and models, who is concerned about academic clarity (378–90).

Part VI, "Change, Adaptation, and Survival," is seemingly comprised of those topics and issues that did not fit the other chapters, but are most closely related to topics Bruno Nettl was working on himself over a longer period of time. Charles Capwell writes on music, modernity, and Islam in Indonesia (393–405), which gives an overview by re-interpreting regional attitudes in performing arts using provocative terms such as "Islamic" and "Indonesian" in conjunction with "modernity". Other chapters show well-observed facts and careful conclusions, such as Charlotte J. Frisbie on Navajo oral traditions (406–18); Frederik Lau on new Chinese work songs (419–32)—who in some instances simplifies his subject matter; Yoshitaka Terada on fusion music in South India (433–46); Stephen Slawek on Cross-Cultural Collaborations in Hindustani Music (447–57)—some of which no longer seem fresh. In the last chapter, Victoria Lindsay Levine provides a very detailed contribution on re-researching the Duck Dance observed among diverse Woodlands peoples (458–70).

The volume includes a helpful classical index and the biodata of the contributors. The entire volume consists of 10 chapters that deal with Asian culture in a more or less detailed and focused way. Many chapters are interesting as parallel studies in an anthropology of music that includes a less rigid and more participatory approach to music research, in keeping with the fact that the volume is written and edited in honor of Bruno Nettl.

REFERENCE

BOHLMAN, Philip V. and Martin STOKES, eds.
  2003–2015   *Europea: Ethnomusicologies and Modernities.* Book Series, 18 vols. New York & London: Rowman & Littlefield.

Gisa Jähnichen
Shanghai Conservatory of Music

Jonathan Arnold, *Sacred Music in Secular Society*
Farnham: Ashgate, 2014. 188 pages. Hardcover, $153.00, ISBN: 9781409451709. Paperback, $40.95, ISBN: 9781409451716. eBook, $28.67, ISBN: 9781409451723. doi: 10.4324/9781315607368

SOME MIGHT SAY, possibly rhetorically, although when it comes to religion such beliefs can be firmly held, that there is a god-shaped hole somewhere inside each person, and that this explains why religion is such a persistent aspect of human life across the world. Others, rather than arguing that the human soul needs a god (or God), would prefer to champion the belief that it needs music, and that it is the affective nature of music that inspires faith in the supernatural—in other words, that music is an essential component of religion, or at the extreme point, music *creates* religion. Jonathan Arnold, the author of *Sacred Music in Secular Society*, is a Christian chaplain at a college at the University of Oxford, and would prefer to argue that music should serve religion, although his take is nuanced, not least because he recognizes the need to account for how music created for sacred purposes increasingly has a life as secular, concert repertoire as well as filling the airwaves from secular broadcasters. Arnold includes a smattering of psychology as he accounts for music's impact, although his choice of theory is highly selective and mixes theology with Eurocentric psychology. There is nothing wrong in this, but since my review is for an ethnological journal based in Asia, I need to explore what such a take can offer a broad readership.

Psychologists have long noted that the human body and its psyche reacts to musical stimuli, receiving them in the archipallium and through the limbic system, reacting instinctively, but then utilizing the "thinking" parts of the brain to interpret what is heard. Instinct is, of course, not readily open to reason, but processes of interpretation are socialized into us as part of a received culture. It is this that gives us the ability to apply reason to music. Music is the most plastic of arts, and therefore the most open to interpretation. But music can, remark SCHNECK and BERGER (2006, 71), drive the very organism that invents it, restoring balance, healing, and managing needs; the body can resonate with sound and, as many have argued, we can become "lost" in music. Even Charles Darwin believed that music (or singing) predated language in the development of humankind, but for two centuries the dogma of "art for art's sake" has blurred the need to identify meaning in music, at least when considering the Western art music canon. Where music and religion are considered to belong together, and where a distinction is made between sacred and secular music, then music is routinely taken to serve religion. At this point, reasoning and interpretation are duty bound to enter the fray: sacred music is held to interpret liturgy through programmatic tone painting, or by setting meaningful lyrics. In Europe, it is a commonplace that musicians are—or once were—required to serve their religious masters; the very word "performer" (or "professional musician") can be pejorative, something that religious leaders and institutions hold up as threatening the requirement to serve, *a priori*, the godhead. Today we can readily observe the challenges that this throws up: musicians typically want to perform at the highest possible level and proficiency, not least so they can stay ahead of competition and ensure their economic survival. Again, religious faith is not necessarily expected of those who provide sacred music, as those familiar with church organists know only too well.

Arnold, in observing and exploring all this, makes himself heavily reliant on interviews. He carefully chooses his informants from those in Britain who compose, perform, or exercise oversight for sacred music, both old and new, from the Western art canon. Key among them are Harry Christophers, founder and conductor of *The Sixteen*, a widely acclaimed choral group; Peter Phillips, founder and director of a second celebrated choral group, *The Tallis Scholars*; Francis Steele, formerly a professional bass member with both groups; Stephen Farr and James O'Donnell, directors of music at London churches; James MacMillan and Robert Saxton, well-known composers; writer and intellectual Roger Scruton; and former Archbishop of Canterbury (that is, head of the Anglican communion), Rowan Williams. Scruton is a research fellow at an Oxford college, while Williams is master of a Cambridge college; these are serious commentators, all sharing a common background. Another composer also appears, the late Jonathan Harvey, representing a European Buddhist perspective, the counterpart to the Jewish Saxton, but both fade from view after the first chapter as Christian apologetics become increasingly central.

The last decade has seen ethnomusicologists move toward focusing on individual musicians in a way that matches much anthropology, witnessed, say, in Helen Rees's edited *Lives in Chinese Music* (2009), Sara Le Menestrel's *Des vies en musique* (2012), or my own collaborative work with individual musicians in Korea, Kyrgyzstan, Nepal, and Zimbabwe (e.g., Howard 2011). There is, though, a greater sense of a shared enterprise in Arnold's text than in such ethnomusicological writing, and he allows those he talks with to lead, or to appear to lead, much of the theoretical discussion. The account hinges on the claim that composers in the past had solid Christian faith, but with Christianity now a choice in an increasingly secular society, composers who "out" themselves as Christians do so in deliberate and thoughtful ways. Certainly, European composers and many musicians in Renaissance and Baroque Europe had little choice but to be employed or commissioned by the church, and much the same applies to many religious institutions outside the European art tradition, but does this signal that the musicians held solid religious beliefs, or was their collaboration simply a reflection of the need to get on?

The limits that Arnold's Christian orientation imposes are essentially no different than those imposed by many music psychology texts: Western art music remains at all times the musical material *sine qua non*, and its components—rhythm, melody, harmony, dynamics, and structures—are what counts. Ethnomusicologists, including I suspect many of us who value the world we find beyond Europe and America, may well reject the particularity of much of his argument, but the primary issues are not uncommon: Who creates sacred music, and who, inside and outside the contexts of ritual, performs it? Who listens to it? How is it mediated in our technological age, and why does it persist in having such a prominent place within our secular constructions of culture? How can it survive into a future in which notions of "traditional" religion will always be challenged as pre-modern rituals lose their meaning and technological mediations increase? These questions form, albeit in disguised ways, the subject matter of the six chapters in Arnold's volume. The questions, though, are as valid for, say, the large rituals of East Asian Buddhism or Southeast Asian shamanism as they are for African spirit mediumship and the music of South Asian courts. Equally, giving pride of place to complex masses, and to the glorious antiphonal choral music of Europe's Renaissance and Baroque periods, encourages us to question the superficiality of populist music, wherever it is found and studied. In this volume, Theodor Adorno and the Frankfurt School's critiques of mass culture form the underpinning of the perspective, elaborated particularly by Roger Scruton in interview, but updated to include a rejection of New Age spiritualism as well as the tendency for more evangelical Christian churches to replace masses and complex settings of the liturgy with banal choruses that can be picked up and sung by anybody and everybody, endlessly and mindlessly, for seeming eons of time. Taken more broadly, the argument is that we should search for magnificence in the music of religious and cultural traditions and question whether scholarship should follow and reflect popular taste or, rather, seek to understand the ethereal qualities of music as art. This, certainly, is an argument that we should all consider, whatever religion and cultural tradition we work with.

REFERENCES

HOWARD, Keith and Saparbek KASMAMBETOV, eds.
　　2011　*Singing the Kyrgyz Manas: Saparbek Kasmambetov's Recitations of Epic Poetry.* Folkestone: Global Oriental. doi: 10.1163/9789004218048

LE MENESTREL, Sara (co-ordinateur)
　　2012　*Des Vies en Musique. Parcours d'Artistes, Mobilités, Transformations.* Paris: Éditions Hermann.

REES, Helen, ed.
　　2009　*Lives in Chinese Music.* Urbana and Chicago: University of Illinois Press.

SCHNECK, Daniel J., and Dorita S. BERGER
　　2006　*The Music Effect: Music Physiology and Clinical Applications.* London and Philadelphia: Jennifer Kingsley Publishers.

Keith Howard
SOAS, University of London

Viv Golding and Wayne Modest, eds., *Museums and Communities: Curators, Collections and Collaboration*

London: Bloomsbury Academic, 2013 (reprinted 2015). xvi + 290 pages. Hardcover, $99.95, ISBN: 978-0-85785-130-7. Paperback, $32.36, ISBN: 978-0-85785-131-4. e-book, $25.19, ISBN: 978-0-85785-132-1. doi: 10.5040/9781474215299

THIS BOOK, edited by Viv Golding and Wayne Modest, came to us about two decades after the canonical publication by KARP, KREAMER, and LAVINE (1992). While both books explore questions about the purpose of museums and the "publics" they serve, the twenty-three contributing authors to the present book (including museum professionals and museum studies faculty) offer interdisciplinary perspectives, experiences, and insights into the practical application of museum theory since the 1990s, sharing the joys, pains, successes, and failures they experienced in collaborating with communities.

While community collaboration has become relatively standard in exhibition and program development, it is a process with which museums still struggle. How we define community and engage with it, how we share "authority," and how we define "authentic" (as opposed to "tokenistic") collaborations remain challenges that this book attempts to tackle. Karp described "every society…as a constantly changing mosaic of multiple communities and organizations" (1992, 3). Precisely because of this constant change, the museum's ability to stay relevant depends on its ability to ride waves, and adapt to new methods and styles of communication as generations, demographics, and political climates change. Nearly all the authors of this collective work explicitly refer to the plurality of communities and their experiences, rejecting the notion of "culture" or "community" as bounded, pure, or homogenous.

Each chapter in the book's three parts offers a case study that responds to specific questions and offers critical evaluation of a project. The authors argue that interrogation of museum practice can guide practitioners to develop exhibitions that more authentically engage communities, recognize diversity of experience, and honor multicultural publics. Additionally, museums can confront difficult issues of social justice by critically examining practice and thoughtfully turning attention to communities (not because we have to, but because we want to). Museums can take a moral or political position and acknowledge injustices and abuses committed by wider institutions of power, perhaps offering communities validation and even healing. Doing so does not have to compromise expertise, or reliability of content, but it *does* require inclusion of multiple (not necessarily *opposing*) perspectives. The book, however, does not attempt to make the reader think the process is easy—sticky-note pads are simply not the answer to all our problems.

In Part I, "Community Matters," starting with Golding's Chapter 1, authors interrogate the meaning of "community." While raising some of the challenges associated with co-curation, collaboration, representation, and presenting diverse perspectives on an equal footing, authors ponder whether there exists a balance between dismissing the needs of diverse audiences and oversimplifying content for "lowest common denominator audiences" (25). The argument to work collaboratively with community is not without disagreement. Onciul (Chapter 5) makes the solid point that engagement is not necessarily the solution to representing complex issues faced by multifaceted communities. She asserts that engagement can be both beneficial *and* detrimental, and that it "does not grant integrity or validity" to exhibitions. While this is bold in the context of "new museology," it is truly important in considering difficult topics. Onciul builds on James Clifford's concept of the contact zone with her notion of an "engagement zone," and explores how power is negotiated and what is at stake for participants who enter complicated and capricious relationships.

The chapters in Part II, "Sharing Authority," interrogate the power and authority of museums assumed by the "new museology" (clearly defined by Hutchinson in Chapter 9). Recurring concerns in Part II include the techniques of representation, the politics of display, and the task of negotiating authority in different ways by different people. Authors (such as Exell) suggest that for certain topics, some visitors prefer the museum's authority over crowd-sourced information (another bold claim in the "new museological" turn), noting that some people lack confidence in exhibitions built on visitor opinions. Referencing Michael Frisch's notion of shared authority, Hutchinson promotes the idea that together scholarly authority and experiential authority underscore one another's agency, and she offers a more balanced view of the kinds of authority presented. Using equalized graphic techniques, she holds that different authorities (such as those of personal life experiences and historical facts) are given equal weight. Part III, "Audiences and Diversity," acknowledges heterogeneous experiences within communities. Also, while the museum's hegemonic authority is scrutinized, the hegemony of communities is also questioned. For example, in Chapter 13, Wood points to how dominant cultural values within communities can influence what museums do. She makes a good point, unique in the context of thinking about museum authority. Wood's project, "The Power of Children: Making a Difference" at the Indianapolis Children's Museum (presented in Chapter 13) brings civic engagement and social justice issues out of the "niche" museum. She attributes success to critical pedagogy, but makes clear the challenge of incorporating multiple experiences, beliefs, and knowledges into an exhibit that is essentially about racism. Chapter 14 likewise details challenges involved with exhibiting stories of racism, here as a commemoration of Britain's bicentennial of abolition. Despite the good intentions of the organizers and their genuine consultation with communities, the project did not reach a satisfactory conclusion. Readers are privileged by authors' exploration of practical issues that lead to what they conclude was a failure: the divide between community needs and museum goals, time limitations, the timing of community consultation in the exhibition development process, museum-held assumptions that representatives could speak for entire communities, and the lack of community understanding of how museums work.

An interview with Susan Pearce in the afterword is a particular highlight of the book. Pearce discusses the importance of physical and tactile elements in the museum experience, the difficulty of including complex, multiple perspectives in a single interpretive label, the (near) universality of material culture, and the 'wow' factor that objects can elicit. But while Pearce says she has always been open to sharing "authority," she critiques curators for their opposition. While this may be so for some, at this point in our discipline's history, most museum anthropologists, ethnologists, folklorists, and other curators with similar backgrounds have long understood the vital importance of (and found personal fulfilment in) collaborating with communities. Many mid- to late-career curators "grew up" on this theory, having been academically trained in the "new museology" twenty-plus years ago; sharing authority on some level is now perhaps somewhat naturalized. Happily, the book helps us wrestle with *how* to share authority and engage multicultural (and changing) communities in changing times.

I find few weaknesses in this book. While these chapters are inspiring, working with communities, asking for their participation, expertise, and personal experiences, and to co-produce exhibition content is demanding not only of staff time, but also of participants' time. We still lack guidance in compensating our "collaborators." Few people have the luxury these days to volunteer on such time-consuming projects. People work, have children, and are burdened with real-world responsibilities. When asking for communities to commit to working with us, if there is not a solid contract for consultation work, is authentic (not "tokenistic") collaboration equitable for communities?

Despite this insignificant shortcoming, this book is a significant contribution. Theoretical musings on museums and communities often fail to consider the very harsh realities of exhibition budgets, understaffed exhibition teams, unforgiving deadlines, and other constraints that don't allow for the "ideal." Much of the extant literature simplifies the effort and resources that go into engaged, democratic, participatory, community-centered exhibition development. These contributors nod to logistical complexities of the exhibition process and grant no illusion that collaboration is an easy feat or always successful, thus filling an important gap in museum studies literature. Additionally, practical application seen in these case studies transcends theoretical idealism regarding community engagement. Authors acknowledge that while issues of social justice need to be addressed by all museums, not every museum needs to tackle these issues in *every* exhibition, and museums should not be expected to deal with such issues in the same way. Finally, by interrogating the notion of "community" this book commands us to genuinely consider our multiple publics, the politics of recognition, and the impossibility of including all communities and all perspectives, and therefore to think about the implications of our choices. It also inspires us to move theories of multiculturalism into the public sphere, where more general populations can better understand that "community" involves "communities" and can perhaps more readily empathize with varying perspectives of important social issues, past, present, and future.

REFERENCE

KARP, Ivan, Christine Mullen KREAMER, and Steven LAVINE, eds.
  1992 *Museums and Communities: The Politics of Public Culture.* Washington: Smithsonian Institution Press.

Felicia Katz-Harris
Museum of International Folk Art

Peter van der Veer, *The Value of Comparison*
Durham: Duke University Press, 2016. ix + 192 pages. Notes, bibliography, index. Cloth, $79.95, ISBN: 978-0-8223-6139-8. Paperback, $22.95, ISBN: 978-0-8223-6158-9. doi: 10.1215/9780822374220

THE VALUE OF COMPARISON is an expanded version of a lecture Peter van der Veer gave as part of the Lewis Henry Morgan Lecture Series in 2013. It is a "reminder of the ethical responsibility of all those who study the human condition to subject their own categories and practices to continuous critique" (ix). Van der Veer presents an argument for the value of the comparative project in anthropology and historical sociology. He asserts that the comparative approach ought to be revitalized as a counterpoint to the "growing generalism in sociology and the expanding influence of cognitive universalism in the social sciences" (147).

While its theoretical depth and breadth covers the history of the comparative method, it is a highly accessible book that specialists and non-specialists alike will find thought provoking and engaging. The formatting makes for easier reading, as the unobtrusive endnotes do not distract. Van der Veer explores the current state of anthropological thought through a critique of what he describes as the "misplaced quest for generality" (vii). The main purpose of the book is stated as providing "an anthropological lens on historical material" (2). Van der Veer makes it clear that his project is to overcome the essentializing, ethnocentric narratives that arise through the assumptions of civilizational unity (7) by means of comparative description (3).

The book is divided into three sections: "The Fragment and the Whole," "Civilization and Comparison," and "Comparing Exclusion." Over six chapters, van der Veer argues for a comparative approach, which he asserts is anthropology's "starting point" (27), that can connect contemporary and past societies through connecting anthropology and history (2). Each section has two chapters, which provide valuable essays on rational choice theory, iconoclasm, urban poverty, sanitation, social exclusion, and the marginalization of mountain people.

The first chapter provides an argument for the comparative advantage of anthropology. It builds on Geertz's thick description, arguing that comparative, conceptual engagement with a fragment can allow for complex reflection of the underlying structures of our own and other societies (28). Van der Veer argues that the comparative approach is necessary to understand the common characteristics of shared, intimate, globalized spaces, where different worldviews and practices sometimes clash, and at other times, provide glimpses of hope for humanity's future, that enable penetrating insight through the opaqueness of totalizing attitudes founded upon "holistic" "ways of life," and a civilizational ethos that elides the "fragmented and contradictory realities people inhabit" (7). Anthropology, van der Veer asserts, can go deeper through a comparative understanding of social inequality, which might lead to social transformation (33). In the comparative project, van der Veer highlights the difference between caste and race, explaining that the former is an example of a hierarchical ideology, while the latter is an example of an egalitarian ideology (36). However, he argues that similar does not mean same (37).

The second chapter critiques economic models, exposing an explanatory weakness for their role in the sociology of religion (48). He focuses on Rational Choice Theory, and suggests that it is not a convincing explanatory model for the Indian religious market. Instead, in a post-Weberian push, the binary assumptions between rational/irrational expose all the more the assumptions of modernizing elites. While reliance upon such models might lead to static conceptualizations of the market and the state, they are in fact complex, dynamic, and culturally situated metaphysical entities (54).

The third chapter focuses on the othering process specific to keeping Muslims out of public and national spaces and discourses (79). It does this through comparing the concepts of civilization, civility, and civil society in India, China, and Western Europe. The biggest socio-cultural question posed in this chapter, and possibly in the whole book, is how to live amicably with all this diversity around us. Taylor's "secular age" is critiqued within the context of the axial age dyad of immanence and transcendence. Through comparison of the secular idea, we learn that it is a Western imposition, particularly on India, where it has a different meaning (65). However, the political cosmologies of China, India, and Western Europe balance on a set of ideals for cultural or national unification by othering Muslims and keeping them out.

The fourth chapter explores the afterlife of images, iconicity, and iconoclasm. Iconoclasm is regarded as the sovereign power of the state to arbitrarily decide its visible formation, social transformation, and how sacred cosmological space is consciously constructed as expressions of vigorous nationalisms (95). An Indian example is the construction of the Akshardham temple in New Delhi, which provides a physical example of the ideal, glorious present and future for India, where the sacred, political, quotidian, and commercial merge in a visual display of "ancient" spirituality and scientific modernity (101).

The third section compares exclusion. Chapter Five engages with the sociology of knowledge. It focuses on the dynamic relationships between nation-states and their frontier-borders, where ethnic-minorities are quite often found. Van der Veer highlights the relations that people in North-East India and South-West China have with their respective states. Here the historical sociological and anthropological method he promotes produces a startling clarity about complex issues. Moreover, he argues that neglect of historical circumstances combined with static representations of borders and the people that inhabit these regions further exacerbates the tensions between states and their ethnic minorities, which are often mined for tourist initiatives for their exotic and romantic peculiarities.

The final chapter explores the middle class and higher caste indifference to waste management and living conditions of the poor, and how this results in denial of good health and prosperous lives. Importantly, van der Veer argues that this is both a theoretical and a political problem. Like all the chapters in this book, the strength of this analytical approach lies in the ethnographic observations linked with historical comparisons of modernization and development, particularly between China and India.

In the short conclusion we are reminded that the value of the comparative project in anthropology and historical sociology needs to be revitalized to overcome the growing generalization found in the social sciences. Van der Veer urges a turn toward a post-Weberian/Durkheimian attitude, which he argues is better suited to conceptualizing the complex world within which we live by moving our framework beyond the limiting scope of Western modernity.

The value of this approach is that it does not privilege ethnocentrism nor anecdotal essentialisms.

Patrick McCartney
Australian National University

S. Brent Plate, ed., *Key Terms in Material Religion*
London: Bloomsbury, 2015. xvii + 284 pages. Hardback, $114.00, ISBN: 978-1-47259-546-1. Paperback, $35.95, ISBN: 978-1-47259-545-4. eBook, $26.99, ISBN: 978-1-47259-548-5. PDF eBook, $26.99, ISBN: 978-147259-547-8.

EMBODIMENT AND MATERIAL religion have been emergent topics of research in religious studies for the past two decades. However, when pushed to define what these terms *really* mean, these concepts devolve into "bodies" and "things." The ascendance of the concept of "embodiment" as an intellectual device to describe physical practices and matter in religious life and practice has, according to Plate, continued to hew to the tendency to privilege "mind over matter" (4). A materially centered understanding of embodiment underlies Plate's five-fold working definition of material religion, which is characterized by (1) scholarly investigations of the interchanges between humans and physical objects; (2) the role of the sensorium; (3) an awareness of both time and space; (4) moments of orientation (eating, singing) and disorientation (physical transformation of the body) of religious communities and individuals, and (5) religious laws and rules that train the body (4–7).

Key Terms in Material Religion originated as a special issue of *Material Religion: The Journal of Objects, Art and Belief* in 2011. Plate is the Managing Editor of this pioneering journal focusing on the place of material culture in religious life and practice, and he co-edited this special issue on "key terms" with the journal's editors Birgit Meyer (University of Utrecht), David Morgan (Duke University), and Crispin Paine (University College London). *Key Terms* includes the original nineteen essays from the special issue of *Material Religion* as well as an additional eighteen addressing a broad range of topics that cluster around the sensorium (aesthetics, body, emotion, food, masks, memory, prayer, sensation, smell, sound, taste, touch, vision, and words), space-place (city, maps, space), and material-object (body, brain-mind, collection, digital, display, dress, fetish-factish, icon (image), magic, medium, race, screen, sign, technology, and thing). As with most edited volumes that incorporate such a diversity of topics, the quality of these brief essays is inconsistent, and some are not as deft in drawing clear connections between Plate's five-fold definition of material religion and their field of study. Readers of this volume will find North American religions somewhat overrepresented, although some of the contributors do focus on Buddhist and Hindu traditions in Asia (for example, Inken Prohl on aesthetics, James McHugh on smell, Anita Patil-Deshmukh on maps, Wei-Cheng Lin on sign, and Rich Freeman on taste).

Many of the essays found in this special issue have been expanded and given more detail in the edited volume. The eighteen new contributions that have been added to the edited volume by emergent, mid-career, and senior scholars focus on traditional (aesthetics, dress, food) and unexpected dimensions (screen, technology, words) of material religion. The essays are arranged alphabetically rather than thematically, allowing considerable flexibility with how the book may be used for either research or teaching.

In the *Aesthetica*, published in 1750, Alexander Gottlieb Baumgarten defined "aesthetics" as the science of "sensual perception, the human memory, beauty, and the arts" (11). Taking Zen Buddhism as a lens through which to analyze the ways in which religious practitioners sensually experience and perceive material culture, Prohl argues for an understanding of aesthetics that moves beyond a simple equation of the term with beauty to one that returns to Baumgarten's more comprehensive definition. Through the rituals of Zen Buddhism, including temple ceremonies, *zazen*, the burning of incense, and other practices, which bring mind and body into alignment, Prohl defines aesthetics as "theorizing about the sensory experience of the world" (14).

Patil-Deshmukh's essay on maps begins with a dictionary definition of the meaning, "to map something," which is far less interesting than the image conjured by the statistic from the 2001 Census of India revealing 2.4 million places of worship located throughout the country (124–25). In 2012, the Municipal Corporation of Greater Mumbai (MCGM) created a two-tier system for the preservation of religious structures (pre- and post-1964 construction). Through the Partners for Urban Knowledge Action and Research (PUKAR) Barefoot Researchers initiative, these structures were mapped, and it was observed that in the slums (*cāḷs*), religious buildings (illegal or not) were "being guarded with great gusto under the pretext of worship, but underpinning the safeguarding was the desire for preservation of a sense of place" (127). This process of mapping described by Patil-Deshmukh reveals and gives voice to the economically disenfranchised and marginalized and indicates the strategic power that the "use of religious spaces as tools for asserting rights over land" can have as a negotiating tool.

McHugh's essay on "Smell" focuses on the use of "aromatic materials of worship," particularly camphor and civet oil, which is derived from the anal glands of small cat-like creatures related to mongooses at the Hindu temple dedicated to Lord Venkatkeshvara in Tirupati, Andhra Pradesh, India (209). The specialness of these scents, which are reserved exclusively for the adornment of the god, generates a sense of the mysterious and the uncertain: Are these scents real? How do we know what the scent *really* smells like (212)?

Freeman links aesthetics and Indic theories of taste, *rasa*, which as a means of observing "changing bodily states," emerged as one of the primary tropes in South Asia (240). The eight "flavors" of *rasa* aesthetics combined the savor of food with eroticism, and the "equally early assimilation of drama to a kind of ritual forum, a religious festival offered to please the gods, where dramaturgy was claimed as a 'fifth Veda'" (241). The eight flavors of *rasa* aesthetics, the tension between the erotic and the ascetic, was later systematized in the medieval tradition of intense emotional love and longing for the god in *bhakti* (*bhakti rasa*). The consumption of the "leftovers" of the food offerings made to temple gods and goddesses are known as *prasāda* ("grace"), which are consumed by devotees as a sign of utmost humility and devotion, rather than of potential food pollution (242).

A sign, according to Lin, is "vital and invocatory," and through semiotic theory we can understand how signs mediate between subject and that to which the sign refers, such as the object or image (202). Signs are invocatory and have a performative tendency that emphasizes their material nature, which points to divine presence. Lin notes that in "medieval Chinese Buddhism, radiant light, a chiming sound, a curing touch, and scented smell experienced unexpectedly served as signs of the divine presence, manifesting miraculously in response to the deserving believer for his/her accrued karma" (203). Signs accrue meaning to communities of interpreters, who change over time in different historical and social contexts.

This volume will be useful for introductory and advanced undergraduate courses in religious studies, anthropology, material culture studies, and art history. The essays are, for the most part, engagingly written and accessible. While there is no bibliography, each essay includes a brief list of suggested readings.

REFERENCE

MEYER, Birgit, David MORGAN, Crispin PAINE, and S. Brent PLATE, eds.
    2011   Special issue: Key words in material religion. *Material Religion: Journal of Objects, Art and Belief* 7: 4–162. doi: 10.2752/175183411X12968355481737

Karen G. Ruffle
University of Toronto

Michael Bull and Jon Mitchell, eds., *Ritual, Performance and the Senses*

London and New York: Bloomsbury Academic, 2015. 208 pages. Hardcover, $97.20, ISBN: 9780857854735. doi: 10.5040/9781474217712

THIS SATISFYING COLLECTION edited by Michael Bull and Jon Mitchell sets out to explore "the potential of combining cognitive/neuroanthropology, performance studies, and the anthropology of the senses to develop a new understanding of religious transmission" (1). And it achieves this admirably. The editor's introduction lays theoretical groundwork and sketches out the contents.

Chapter 1, "Ontology, Mimesis and Divine Intervention: Understanding Catholic Visionaries" by Mitchell, is a case study of divine intervention in Malta. To paraphrase the introduction, in January 2006, Angelik Caruana noticed that a statue of the Virgin Mary recently purchased by his wife began to weep tears of blood. He began to receive messages from the Holy Mother and built a shrine to her. In his weekly prayer meetings, he received visions and messages, fought demons and the devil, and experienced the pain of Christ's passion. The weekly sessions were published on YouTube. Caruana has a blog and has received wide media coverage. Mitchell does a wonderful job of describing the performer, his performances, and the broader cultural and social setting. His aim is "to understand not merely that this happens, but *how*: what are the processes that lead to visionary experiences of holy presence" (29).

In "Ritual Action Shapes Our Brains: An Essay in Neuroanthropology," Robert Turner argues that rituals have "the function of physically changing the brains of the participants, or maintaining such changes that have already taken place" (31), changes that can now be measured using magnetic resonance imaging. He begins with a definition of ritual and suggests that ritual persists "because it is useful" (33) in some way. MRI studies of the brains of twins show the importance of heredity and the ways in which the brain changes with age and experience, including the catchy observation that "neurons that fire together, wire together"—that is, repeated experiences bring about permanent linkages in our brains. "Learning a skill by repetition is now known materially to change our brains" (36). The suggestion is that ritual stimulates neurotransmitters to produce rewards, which we experience as happiness. Is this why ritual persists—because it makes us feel good? This chapter demands careful re-reading. We are used to images of meditating monks wired up to have their brain functions monitored. What seems to be missing here are MRIs of folk performing rituals.

Greg Downey opens his chapter, "The Importance of Repetition: Ritual as a Support to Mind," with a touching vignette of his elderly and increasingly infirm grandmother faithfully praying the Rosary, as she had done for many years. But why do people pray? This chapter employs a multi-pronged neuroanthropological approach to explore the role of "quiet, contemplative practice" such as silent prayer in religious practice. He argues that prayer functions as "a socially constituted technology of neurological self-manipulation, especially in times of stress, existential fear, or moral conflict" (47). In the section entitled "Prayer as Emotional Coping: A Neuroanthropological Perspective," Downing cites research that suggests prayer releases extra dopamine and that this offers an explanation of prayer's ability to soothe. In addition, he cites research that suggests prayer causes long-term changes in neural physiology, the ways in which our brains are wired. People who pray know that prayer makes them feel good, and this chapter goes some way to explain why.

The chapter on "Place-making in the 'Holy of Holies': The Church of the Holy Sepulcher, Jerusalem" by Trevor H. J. Marchand, is the result of a twelve-day observation of the supposed site of Jesus Christ's crucifixion and burial. It is based on observations and interviews with pilgrims, priests who officiate at the site, and the traditional Muslim caretakers. The author argues that "place-making," an individual's sense of place, is "grounded in the integral weave between mind, body, and environment" (63), but it is also shaped by emotional states. The surprising point made in this chapter is that the Church of the Holy Sepulcher is so crowded, so chaotic, and so contested that it seems impossible to get any real sense of the sanctity of the place. The senses are so heavily bombarded that it is impossible to achieve the "emotional state" in which one can experience the site's sanctity. Because this is the case, the author argues that spiritual connection with the site is only achieved once the pilgrims are safely home again. There they can relive their visit through photos, souvenirs, relics, and other memorabilia. This is an interesting suggestion, but the author could have offered more evidence in its support. That said, the chapter is worthwhile for its colorful thick description of a dysfunctional pilgrimage site.

On the banks of the Ganges River outside Benares in Northern India, a month-long performance of the story of Ram, the Ramlila, is held. This is the subject of "The Spaces and Places of Ramnagar Ramlila" by Richard Schechner. For the faithful who attend, the actors "become" the deities they act out, and the various site to which the performance shifts each day "becomes" a sacred pilgrimage site. This is much more than a performance, a play, or a show; it is a sacred ritual of great significance to actors and audiences alike. Schechner, the guru of performance studies, gives a long (36 page) scene-by-scene description of the event. I was surprised that there was not more performance theory at work here. It is certainly one of the best descriptions of the event that I have read, but it seemed to lack the analysis and theoretical perspective one might expect from Schechner.

In "'Inner Movement' between Practices of Meditation, Martial Arts, and Acting," Phillip B. Zarrilli takes a phenomenological approach to exploring the conscious states experienced in three "embodied practices": meditation, martial arts, and acting. It includes four case studies written in the first person, recounting various conscious states experienced in a range of exercises. This is not an easy chapter. It is likely that the current reviewer lacks the background knowledge to derive full benefit from it.

In "Exploring the Andean Sensory Model: Knowledge, Memory, and the Experience of Pilgrimage," Zoila Mendoza argues that different societies organize the senses differently, and that we need to understand a society through its "sensory model" in order to understand its practices. The chapter is a case study of a pilgrimage in the Peruvian Andes dedicated to the Señor de Qoyllorit'i (Lord of the Shiny Snow). Once a year, 40,000 to 50,000 pilgrims travel high in the mountains to view a picture of the Christ painted on a rock. This has been a sacred site since pre-Hispanic times. The chapter focuses on dance troupes who walk for three days and two nights for 85 miles to the continual accompaniment of flutes and drums, sustaining themselves by chewing coca leaves. The author argues that it is the unity of visual, auditory, and kinesthetic experience that makes pilgrimage valid and authentic. This is a lively and interesting chapter. Much of it is concerned with popular dance forms known as Chakiri Wayri and Wayri Ch'unchu—the reader is advised to view these performances on YouTube.

Contemporary psychology holds that perception "begins at the edge of the central nervous system (CNS) and is conditioned by the properties of the receptor organs" (153), that is to say, perception is a physical and chemical process. In his chapter, "Sensation and Transmission," David Howes argues convincingly for an "extended sensorium," a world in which our senses and perception are conditioned by specific cultural practices. He illustrates this with four sense-intensive case studies of religious experience: a cacophonous festival among the Ilahita Arapesh of Papua New Guinea, the worship of a Byzantine icon experienced through vision, the silence of a Quaker meeting, and the feeling of "Divine Touch" in Pentecostal traditions in Ghana.

In conclusion, this collection will be of interest to scholars engaged in the performative and phenomenological aspects of religious studies. It has an excellent bibliography and a good index. One minor irritation is that the notes for each chapter are gathered at the end of the volume.

At the outset, this volume suggests criteria by which it might be evaluated: "As an experiment in anthropological theory, it might be judged not according to the definitive answers it provides, but rather by the questions asked and avenues opened by combining cognitive, performative, and sensory studies of ritual" (10). In this it has certainly succeeded.

McComas Taylor
The Australian National University

Huib Schippers and Catherine Grant, *Sustainable Futures for Music Cultures: An Ecological Perspective*

Oxford: Oxford University Press, 2016. 392 pages. Hardback, $105.00, ISBN: 9780190259075. Paperback, $35.00, ISBN: 9780190259082. eBook, $14.39, ISBN: 0190259086. doi: 10.1093/acprof: oso/9780190259075.001.0001

Sustainable Futures for Music Cultures is the rare edited volume that hangs together tightly from beginning to end, and where each chapter is structurally and thematically closely connected to the others despite analyzing wildly disparate traditions. This may be in part because this well-curated volume is not the product of a conference panel, but of a long-term research project, funded by the Australian Research Council, that brought together experts on several music traditions from around the globe under the premise that music cultures are best viewed as ecologies, and that assessing the sustainability of a culture might benefit from this ecological perspective. To do this, the scholars established a single research protocol and analytic framework through which the ecology of each tradition might usefully be studied, and interviewed individuals involved at all levels of the music process—from instrument makers to teachers and beyond. The results were then disseminated not only in the form of this book, but also through a freely available website (soundfutures.org).

The case studies in *Sustainable Futures* were chosen to include both robust and endangered traditions. This diverse set of case studies ensures both enhanced comparability and, therefore, the enhanced opportunity to understand the building blocks of sustainability. Some of the traditions benefit from strong governmental support. Others require private patronage. Some are closely woven into the ritual and social life of strong communities; others struggle to maintain relevance in a changing world. Some have robust support and hope for intergenerational transmission in the near future, while others may be considered critically endangered. These diverse examples provide fertile ground for comparison.

The premise that music cultures are ecosystems required the researchers to view each tradition holistically. To make the ecosystem legible, each chapter focuses on a single case study that begins with an introduction to the tradition, followed by a systematic examination of the tradition's vitality in five domains: "systems of learning music," "musicians and communities," "contexts and constructs," "regulations and infrastructure," and "media and music industries." Each chapter also ends with a conclusion describing past and present sustainability efforts and assesses the tradition's future prospects.

The care that has gone into crafting this volume is evident from the opening pages, with a foreword by the inimitable Toni Seeger giving a sense of this volume's significant contribution. The body of the book opens with two introductory chapters. In Chapter 1, "Sound Futures: Exploring the Ecology of Music Sustainability," Huib Schippers introduces the concepts of sustainability, the ecological metaphor, the five domains (see above) around which the book is structured, and the format of the volume itself. In Chapter 2, "Music Sustainability: Strategies and Interventions," Catherine Grant then surveys the state of the field of sustainability, fleshes out the five domains in greater depth, and introduces some existing cultural sustainability initiatives around the world. Following this, readers are then treated to nine case studies, each based on the same set of questions asked of those involved in the given traditions. The traditions are, in order of their appearance: Ghanaian Ewe, Hindustani music, Central Australian Yawulyu/Awelye, Balinese Gamelan, Western opera, Amami Shimi Uta from Japan's Amami Islands, Korean SamulNori, Mexican Mariachi, and Vietnamese Ca Trù.

In the concluding chapter, the editors team up to describe how we might evaluate these case studies and their implications for theoretical and applied work in the field of cultural sustainability. In particular, they highlight the role of prestige in sustaining traditional practices. Prestige may motivate an individual to invest the considerable amount of time (and sometimes capital) necessary to learning a musical tradition. Prestige may also motivate private and governmental patronage and ensure continued audiences for a tradition. Nevertheless, the editors also caution that any findings should not be taken as a one-size-fits-all blueprint for sustainability but rather a set of guidelines for assessing traditions and their ecosystems.

This path-breaking book will be of interest to folklorists, anthropologists, and ethnomusicologists alike. The early chapters provide something of a primer on cultural sustainability and the ecological metaphor; the book's remaining, uniformly structured chapters are written in a fairly accessible style, which ensures that any individual chapter can be assigned for class reading at both undergraduate and graduate levels, while a group of chapters can also be assigned for comparative purposes. While I recommend the volume in its entirety, readers of *Asian Ethnology* might be interested in the Asia-focused case studies, including chapters on Balinese Gamelan, Hindustani music, Japanese Amami Shima Uta, Korean SamulNori, and Vietnamese Ca Trù traditions.

If there is a critique to be made of this incredible work, it is that the method for assessing a tradition's ecology does not seem to explicitly account for the role of other (especially non-musical) traditional forms that might either be in competition with or complementary to them. It stands to reason that such music-adjacent traditions within the same community may have important consequences for sustainability, particularly as it relates to cultivating competent audiences with interest in traditional forms. This in turn may affect the all-important prestige factor. Nevertheless, this minor quibble should not detract from the incredible value and contribution of *Sustainable Futures for Music Cultures*, and I am pleased to enthusiastically recommend this book.

Timothy Thurston
The University of Leeds

India

Kirin Narayan, *Everyday Creativity: Singing Goddesses in the Himalayan Foothills*

Chicago: University of Chicago Press, 2016. 256 pages. Notes, bibliography. Cloth, $75.00, ISBN: 9780226407425. Paperback, $25.00, ISBN: 9780226407562. eBook, $25.00, ISBN: 9780226407739.

IN THIS ENGAGING and lovingly crafted text, Kirin Narayan creates an entrée for readers into the world of women in Kangra, a community situated in the Indian Himalayan foothills, through the medium of singing. Narayan's premise is that women's singing practices in Kangra constitute acts of "everyday creativity." The practice of singing, Narayan asserts, "may not carry value through institutions, commoditization, or acclaim, and yet remains a form of well-being and even happiness for individuals and their immediate community" (xxi).

For more than two decades, Narayan has been engaged in scholarly conversation with a group of feminist South Asianist scholars regarding South Asian women's expressive practices as loci for articulation of women's views on their own lives and the world they inhabit. This work has done much to counter stereotypes of South Asian women as passive, accepting victims of patriarchy, revealing such women's points of view and structures of feeling on their own lives, as well as the societies and the sacred worlds they (re)create and resist. *Everyday Creativity*'s intervention into such discussions is through its emphasis on beauty and pleasure, with singing presented as a life-enhancing feature of individual and community life. Nonetheless, Narayan does not lose sight of the context of patriarchy, her premise being that "song offers a form of creativity accessible to people who might not control or own much else" (xx). One related function of singing—that it allows for the indirect expression and emotional processing of personal experience in the context of cultural restrictions on direct voicing—is also made evident throughout the book. In the words of one of Narayan's subjects, "You can't tell someone else what's in your heart. But if there's some pain then it comes right out of your mouth in the form of a song" (180).

While this is a book about songs and singing, for Narayan these phenomena are actually also a "pretext and a context" (219) for attending to more broadly philosophical and anthropological concerns such as the emergence of pleasure and beauty amid constraint and the weathering of change in individual and communal life. Listed in the University of Chicago Press's "Big issues in Music" ethnomusicology series, the text also speaks to what in his foreword Philip Bohlman identifies as a dearth of attendance to "smallness" in the field of music studies. An additional aim of the text is to offer songs as a resource that "extends and nuances our understandings of the Hindu tradition, taking it from the fraught domain of identity politics to loving acts of faith within and between households" (223). For readers in some fields, especially anthropology and feminist studies, this focus on smallness/the everyday/the domestic may not strike one as particularly groundbreaking, especially given women's exclusion from the halls of power and prestige and the responsibility for much of mundane life.

Eschewing standard ethnographic or anthropological expectations, Narayan foregoes most overt theoretical and analytical writing in this book, opting instead for a work that centers Kangra women's song texts, their own interpretive words, and Narayan's descriptive (non-typologizing) passages about particular women's joys and sorrows, manners and embodiments, and ways of relating with one another and the world around them. (Only occasionally, as when feminist forebears were given very short shrift, did this reader miss such recognizable academic discourse.) While Narayan uses words to draw the reader into her artfully evoked scenes, the several black and white photographs she includes enrich the sensibility further, visually bringing the women to life and also appearing to honor them—their strength, suffering, intelligence, generosity and joie de vivre. In both word and photo, Narayan also makes evident her own presence, depicting herself at times as bewildered, and at others as mirthful or vexed. These photos establish Narayan's intimacy with the singers, as well as—through older and newer images—the longevity of her connection with them. The result of these strategies is a rich, highly aesthetic text of thematic eddies and character development, by the end of which one *feels* as much as cognitively understands the social and psychological functions, the cultural work and artistry of singing, as well as the tenor of the lives of women in a particular historical-cultural-social location. One may gain a new appreciation more generally for the role of mundane forms of creativity in the flow of human life, as well.

In organizing her text into chapters, Narayan employs locally relevant plant metaphors, starting with a "base" (background) chapter, then four chapters focused on the "fruits" of singing (somewhat corresponding to women's life stages). In each such chapter, she highlights a particular individual singer, clustering songs thematically and according to their focus on particular deities or devotees. The final chapter is the "head," in which she reflects on what is to be learned overall from this tradition of singing. Frankly, I found I benefited little from this use of metaphor, which sometimes felt forced or became confusing (as when layers of metaphor multiplied) in what was otherwise a wonderfully crafted text.

Drawing for materials on her own ethnographic archive of recordings, field notes, and translations from years of visits in the community, Narayan is able simultaneously to portray a sustained tradition of singing and to depict the unfolding lives of women she has known across long periods of time (and in some cases has outlived), learning about their lives even as they tutored her in song. Following the instruction of her doctoral thesis advisor, Alan Dundes (also referencing Lila Abu-Lughod's work), Narayan makes much effort to elicit singers' own interpretations of their songs. Indeed, this investment in "oral literary criticism" is a hallmark of Narayan's scholarship that both remains relatively rare among folklorists and is much to be admired. Though sometimes thwarted in this effort, Narayan is still able to exhume singers' elided, partial, and/or coded comments for clues toward culturally resonant exegesis. While Narayan highlights singers' own interpretations of their songs and singing, she occasionally adds her own "feminist sense of how songs might offer additional routes to well-being beyond conventional goals" (219–20). She uses the soft linguistic touch of "wondering," for instance "if there might not be a frisson of pleasure in celebrating a goddess who made up her mind and then single-pointedly attained her heart's desires" (92), and "about the ways this song expressed the trauma of violence against girl children, cautioning perpetrators of a goddess's fury that could be unleashed to strike them" (118). These are examples of the stylized and unobtrusive way she incorporates cultural critique into the book.

While Narayan admits that everyday acts of creativity like singing do little to alter the difficult patriarchal and other circumstances (of health, material welfare, etc.) in which singers live, a central point of her book is to demonstrate that such acts "can help establish an inner way around or through hardship" by "gaining skills to establish one's own stamp on received practices; companionably messing about and playing with materials; finding the comfort of inner escape even in difficult times; and opening oneself to a sense of possibility" (xxiv). Such activity encompasses what Narayan means by "everyday creativity," corresponding to the Kangra concept of *sukinni* or *shauk*, "the enthusiastic zest that draws people to particular cultural practices not because they have to but because they want to" (224). While for some women singing is certainly characterized by such zest, Narayan notes that singing is also a form of ritual work necessary to the well-being of households and the community, a means by which women create bonds across households, and an accompaniment to various sorts of physical labor, "potentially transforming expected duty toward others into a space of personal flourishing" (149). In *Everyday Creativity*, Narayan also demonstrates that in their sung stories referencing the worlds encountered in the Sanskrit Puranas (sacred texts), women often shift the lens toward the perspectives of goddesses and female devotees, as well as to Kangra women's own concerns, bodies and landscapes, and structures of feeling.

From Narayan's opening words—"Who is that young girl listening from the courtyard outside?" (xvii)—the author places herself at the heart of the text and its project. She seems to have a dual aim in doing so: she wants the reader to know her positionality vis-a-vis the knowledge she is producing for us, and she wants to relate her own process of research and writing as itself a form of everyday creativity that has developed in the course of understanding the creative process of her Kangra interlocutors. By the end of the book, the reader realizes that alongside the subject of Kangra women's lives and singing, we have received a coming-of-age tale of Narayan's own ethnographer-self. In addition to the portrayal of herself as an "insider-outsider" ethnographer, we gain insights into the process of ethnography itself, with its initial half-understandings, social navigations, and cultural ambivalences. We also see just how dependent a researcher is on the particular relationships formed under particular and shifting conditions, exemplifying Donna Haraway's insight about partial and situational knowledge. By now, this technique of "reflexive" ethnographic writing is no longer new, but it is still appreciated and deftly carried out in this text.

Narayan points out that networks of women singers tend to be of the same caste or castes that interact socially. She notes further that because of her personal connections with upper-caste singers, they became her mentors. Unlike their younger counterparts, this older generation of high-caste women are among those who were "raised with the vision for a flourishing life located squarely within domesticity, child-rearing, and the nurturing of others" (224). Also, she states that it is upper-caste singers who hold cultural capital in relation to their singing, while those of stigmatized caste identities were more reluctant to share the songs associated with their communities. Unfortunately, due to these factors, her text therefore fails to address the frequent bias of ethnographic and other research in Hindu South Asia toward upper-caste experiences and perspectives. On the other hand, the book does attend to decades of change in material and cultural life as well as individual aging characters. Shifts toward greater literacy in national languages and English, and away from oral tradition and toward film, television, and social media, are now literally drowning out Kangra women's voices even at local ritual events, giving a particular urgency to Narayan's close attention to women's oral performances.

In the end, as Narayan has hoped, her "lingering over commentaries on songs in general and songs in particular" has indeed "conveyed [more than] a little of the beauty, value, and wisdom that singers perceive in them" (220), and given the reader pause as to the sources and expressions of joy, creativity, and wisdom in our own lives.

Coralynn V. Davis
Bucknell University

Michael Youngblood, *Cultivating Community: Interest, Identity, and Ambiguity in an Indian Social Mobilization*
Pasadena, CA: South Asian Studies Association, 2016. 324 pages. Paperback, $38.32, ISBN: 978-0-9834472-7-6.

CULTIVATING COMMUNITY is an intricately woven, careful analysis of an agrarian social movement in rural Maharashtra called Shetkari Samgathna (*śetkarī saṃgathnā*) written by an insider. Michael Youngblood deconstructs hegemonic prescriptions about successful social movements generated from without that are based on theoretical presuppositions that he terms "progressive solidification." He discusses the cultural significance of symbols that produce a hinge for multiple, interconnected layers, positing the movement's structural multivocality, to reveal sliding scales of converging interests within Shetkari Samgathna that produce meaning at the interstices of shared symbols. He proposes that this multiple and plural cultural imagery constitutes a medium of cohesive social action and leadership that allows for the formation of an alternative and mobilized social identity in rural Maharashtra.

The book describes how social identity encompassed by Shetkari Samgathna (often ritually expressed) charts anticolonial and postcolonial agitation when distinguishing between dual and juxtaposed imageries. The juxtaposition of a toiling and virtuous India (*bhārat*) that is ruled by a non-Brahmin figure titled the *balī rājā*, and exploited by a Brahminical India controlled by the black British or *kāḷe iṃgraz* reveals layered religious, social, and historical imagery to contest entitlement, privilege, and power.

The book is divided into six chapters. The first introductory chapter briefly describes Shetkari Samgathna and the role played by its leader Sharad Joshi, while outlining the image of an alternative, exploited farmer's India that is conceptualized as *bhārat* and *balī-rājya* (Bali's kingdom). Youngblood ponders the various theoretical and interpretative frameworks that can prove useful for understanding Shetkari Samgathna without running the additional risk of deploying too many assumptions, presuppositions, or textbook notions leading to progressive solidification. Identifying traps in theoretical presuppositions or progressive solidification, the author describes how movements are misunderstood as a narrow range of converging interests that provide voice to the most prominent ideology among participants, or more problematically erase the rationale of other participants, who are ideologically less empowered. Therefore, while agitating for higher prices constitutes an important Shetkari Samgathna demand, other demands create multiple variables of overlapping interests that are also constitutive of the movement, described as having a mass base of more than 500,000 participants. Exploring interpretive theories such as proctological theory and frames theory, Youngblood discards these as useful but nevertheless romantic and fixed within certain immovable assumptions that are notional of community life. Raising further questions about concepts such as, in his terms, "claste" (intersections between caste and class) or subalternity, the author discusses how the concentration on converging interests within such theories, disinvests the movement from the divergence of interests that he encountered during fieldwork. Instead, he prefers a sliding scale of interpretation that allows for interests to slide in opposing directions, as suggested by John and Jean Comaroff, along with Stanley Fish's concept of a dialogic community that theorizes the emergence of a social movement through communication.

The second chapter, "Contours of Community and Place," details the profile of Shetkari Samgathna, which is a linguistic and geographic Marathi social movement enjoying preponderance in the Marathwada and Vidarbha agrarian regions of rural Maharashtra. Participating villages, areas, and communities here are considered *balī-rājya* (or the kingdom of King Balī), which is central to the movement's characterization as exploited by Brahminical forces. This chapter concentrates on cultural symbols as important for mass rural, non-Brahminical, agrarian mobilization within Shetkari Samgathna. The author delineates the role of the *vārkarī sampradāya* (or the *bhakti* (devotion) of Vithoba at Pandharpur), the claiming of King Shivaji as a Shudra king by Shetkari Samgathna, and the significance of Jyotiba Phule's non-Brahmin movement that propels *balī-rājā* as the protagonist of the hard-working, poor, and exploited farmers of *balī-rājya*.

The third chapter, "The Field of Signs," describes Sharad Joshi's leadership of the movement, his communication of Shetkari Samgathna's agenda through written pamphlets, and the headquarters of the movement at Angarmaḷa. Furthermore, various symbols of interest that are central to the posters and materials used by the movement are analyzed. Youngblood discusses how the seemingly singular demand of "price" is multivocal and representational, since questions of wages among landless laborers are of paramount importance for the movement as well, in which price is transformed into a metaphor for control over rural livelihoods by outsiders. Youngblood further analyzes the self-referential figure of the farmer (*śetkarī*) as a "sign" for the agricultural community, despite differing landed interests, wherein agrarianism is united with the identity of *kaṣṭakarī* (one who toils). The denigration of agrarianism by Brahminical elites from western Maharashtra symbolized by Vaman (who according to Puranic myths, stamped on Bali and usurped his kingdom) becomes embroiled in a collective play of symbols that include the *śetkarī*'s *vāri* (pilgrimage) to Vithoba at Pandharpur, thus expressing a desire to reinstate King Shivaji's justice for *balī-rājya*.

While the interplay and mutual communication of symbols ensures inclusivity and the continuing unity of Shetkari Samgathna's ideal of liberation in the face of black colonization, it also ensures differentiation of interests within the movement, as shared symbols expand the canopy of experience among its participants. Youngblood "peels the onion," as he puts it, of the misperceived single-issue movement in chapter four,

"Dialogues of Interest and Identity", where he investigates how various diverse *śetkarī* interests and identities find place in the movement. These diverse interests are posited as a shifting set of hybrid identities that are exemplified by two case studies of Perugaon and Dorlapur villages, where the following interests are identified as important: SBP (*svataṃtra bhārat pakṣa*), a political platform for rural leaders; exposing corruption through the Q movement (quit corruption); and regional autonomy demands for Marathwada and Vidarbha. Other issues include women-led (*sītā śetī*) forms of alternative agriculture; registering women as property owners; promoting women's representation in village *pañcāyat*s; cooperative marketing schemes; land development companies; infrastructural demands; compensatory demands; and temperance initiatives. Finally, labor and Dalit (formerly "Untouchable") rights initiatives led to the declaration of participating villages as *baḷī-rājya gāv* (villages), consolidating rural and caste interests.

The fifth chapter, "Bali Will Rise: Dialogues of Interest and Identity, Continued," is concerned with the *baḷī-rājā* as the figurehead or protagonist-leader of the Shetkari Samgathna. The author discusses the *baḷī-rājā* as a symbol of rural Marathi subalternity, and he explores various textual references to Bali's defeat at the hands of Brahminical forces that result in Shetkari Samgathna's battle against Brahminism. The śetkarī's narrative and engagement with rituals, such as the *ghaṭasthāpanā* (jug establishment) during the Navaratri festival reflects claims of a victorious Bali's return to defeat a future Vaman. The ritual is described as explaining how the *śetkarī's* alliance with Bali results in the boycott of Brahminical victory, signified by Diwali festivities. The chapter explores how farmers burn effigies of Vaman to mark their anti-Diwali politics and uphold Bali as their *śetkarī* king, calling for an increase in *baḷī-rājya* villages, and intensifying their claim of Marathwada and Vidarbha as the *baḷī-rājya* domain. Finally, Shetkari Samgathna hails Sharad Joshi as a rural insider, venerating him as the mythical Bali, the anti-Brahmin demon king who is the leader of the movement.

Discussing cultural idioms surrounding Sharad Joshi's veneration in Shetkari Samgathna as an insider, a representative leader, and as Bali himself, the author provides field narratives that culturally characterize Sharad Joshi's leadership as strong, or as *śīl*, a leadership that is celebrated for its actions being consistent with opinion. Moving to his concluding chapter, Youngblood reflects on convergences between the nature of participation and the dialogic diversity of participants, just as he explores the relationship between perceptions of divergence between leaders and leadership. According to the author, Sharad Joshi's deification as Bali remains metaphoric for change within the movement, rather than a mark of the movement's success, wherein Joshi's projection as divine cements the cultural association between leadership and divinity, rather than a perception of leaders being supernatural.

Youngblood's anthropological analysis of agrarian mobilization in rural Maharashtra that intersects caste, class, and religious fervor with women's participation, all within the frameworks of nativist emancipation is quite unique and one of a kind. Academic enterprises about modern mobilization in rural Maharashtra, apart from studies such as QUACK's (2012), are indeed rare and refreshing. Youngblood declares his interests in analyzing social mobilization from the beginning pages of his book, where he reveals his research compulsions to lie in the increasing valence of social movements in modern global times, social movements that have been inadequately understood, such as the Arab Spring.

Youngblood's book is a tremendous pleasure to read. Yet although his subject is indeed rare, and though the book is well articulated, sensitive, and thoroughly analyzed, I wondered in the end, whether readers might not gain a deeper understanding of Marathi rural life through theories of emotional communities and emotive labor (PLAMPER 2010). This is especially so since the author uses physical concepts to describe the *śetkarī*'s experience of the movement, such as toil (*kaṣṭa*), labor (*majūr*), and sweat (*ghām*). The reward of understanding divergent interests through emotional experiences could only heighten the understanding of the movement as an emotional community with consenting and dissenting voices. I would deeply recommend this thoughtful and well-written book for an audience interested in rural and agrarian studies, global social movements and their underlying strategies of action for empowerment, and sociopolitical history and anthropology of Maharashtra in particular and India in general.

REFERENCES

PLAMPER, Jan
    2010   The history of emotions: An interview with William Reddy, Barbara Rosenwein, and Peter Stearns. *History and Theory* 49: 237–65.
QUACK, Johannes
    2012   *Disenchanting India: Organized Rationalism and Criticism of Religion in India.* New York: Oxford University Press.

Deepra Dandekar
Max Planck Institute for Human Development

Steven J. Rosen and Kaisori Bellach, *Avatar Art: Neo-Vedic Paintings Celebrating Life*
Los Angeles: The Bhaktivedanta Book Trust, 2016. 224 pages. Paperback, $15.95, ISBN: 978-91-7149-801-4.

When I first encountered the International Society for Krishna Consciousness (ISKCON) in the late 1960s, I was intrigued by their exotic appeal: the saffron dress, shaved heads, sandalwood *tilak*s, sweet scented incense, sandals, barrel drums and cymbals, etc. These certainly attracted others as well, but what has not really been discussed in any great detail in the sociological literature on conversion to ISKCON is the role that the movement's colorful art played in attracting people into its fold. Indeed, the paintings reproduced in virtually all official ISKCON publications draw on the indigenous Indian tradition of chromolithographs and poster art, documented by scholars such as Christopher PINNEY (2004) and Kajri JAIN (2007). However, virtually nothing has been written about ISKCON art until the book under review was published. It is therefore a unique document worth consulting for anyone interested in this Hindu devotional tradition in the diaspora.

Two longtime members of ISKCON are the authors of the book. As such, it represents a particular point of view, but it also provides a wealth of information for the non-initiated reader. It is not very clear to me if the book is intended for other ISKCON members or non-members, but the very brief introduction written by Rosen states at the outset that the book is "art as yoga and yoga as art" (8), by which he means viewing the paintings is a devotional act that is supposed to transport the physical viewer into the realm of spirit, as it does to the artist as well. Rosen proceeds to map out briefly the concept of *bhakti* (devotional) art, before his very short discussion of western spiritual art. He then delves into the development of spiritual art in India. From here on, we notice cthe emic (insider) perspective emerging, as Rosen solely emphasizes the importance of Vishnu in the origins of Hindu iconography before focusing specifically on the Krishna incarnation of Vishnu, who is so central to ISKCON theology.

These brief sections are written from a subjective perspective, without any standard documentation of sources, and will most certainly be contested by art historians and archaeologists. Nonetheless, Rosen then moves on to the arrival of ISKCON's founder in the west, Bhaktivedanta Swami Prabhupada, who wanted his translations of Vaishnavite texts "beautified" (18) with transcendental paintings. He thus discusses an early follower named Jadurani Devi, who graduated from an art school. She was one of the first to study with Prabhupada, when he gave her some Indian prints of Radha and Krishna, Sri Chaitanya, and Vishnu to reproduce. Once proficient in the art form and its philosophical background, she started training others at their New York headquarters. Soon thereafter, Prabhupada trained another woman named Govinda Dasi, who began painting at the San Francisco temple. In the late 1960s, the ISKCON Press set up shop in Boston, then moved to Brooklyn in the 1970s, and finally achieved maturity in Los Angeles. As a result, there are now a number of artists thriving as permanent members of the Bhaktivedanta Book Trust.

The book under review contains paintings by 26 painters from across the world, all of whom are members of ISKCON. The book is divided into three sections: "Avatars, Devas, Sages, and Demons," "The Life of Krishna," and "Sri Chaitanya." The format in each section is the same. First, there is a very brief written introduction to the section, followed by a one-page discussion on the left page and the corresponding painting on the right. The written sections are interpretations of the paintings, often including stories about the images included in any given painting. Unfortunately, the stories are retold, with no references to the textual sources from which they are culled.

Avatar Art is not an academic publication by any means, but it does serve as a primary document for anyone interested in learning more about the role that art plays in ISKCON. The images are also a feast for the eyes. It is thus unfortunate that the authors (editors, really) chose a 5½" x 8" format for the book. A larger "coffee table" type format would have been better to display the paintings, which are really the highlight of this book. Perhaps the authors wished to provide a compact pocket book that could easily be carried around by the book's owners. I would also have liked more information on the artists themselves: who are they, how did they come to ISKCON, what is their artistic background, etc.? The intention of the volume thus becomes quite clear. It is intended to highlight Krishna and the Vaishnavite mythology that surrounds him, which is not a bad thing. Yet I would have appreciated at least some semblance of scholarly rigor to balance out this attractive publication that is produced on high-quality glossy paper for the viewer's delight

REFERENCES

JAIN, Kajri
  2007   *Gods in the Bazaar: The Economies of Indian Calendar Art.* Durham, NC: Duke
         University Press. doi: 10.1215/9780822389736
PINNEY, Christopher
  2004   *Photos of the Gods: The Printed Image and Political Struggle in India.* London:
         Reaktion Books.

Frank J. Korom
Boston University

Aditya Malik, *Tales of Justice and Rituals of Divine
Embodiment: Oral Narratives from the Central Himalayas*
New York: Oxford University Press, 2016. 320 pages. Hardcover,
$105.00, ISBN 9780199325092.

WHAT GEOGRAPHERS call the Central Himalayan region, encompassing far western
Nepal and the Indian state of Uttarakhand, possesses an extraordinarily rich set of oral
and ritual traditions. While the population is massively Hindu, its Hinduism includes
its own divinities and sometimes divinized ancient kings and heroes who remain very
much part of regional imagination and practice. Throughout the area there are singer-
drummers who continually recreate a vast narrative corpus; and there is a variety of
ways to interact with the regional gods, often involving some form of embodiment of
divine beings in human vehicles, what the West has called possession. A distinctive in-
terlocking of these practices typifies the former kingdom of Kumaon, now the eastern
part of Uttarakhand. In Kumaon, as to some degree in Garhwal to its west, narration
and possession are bound together: rituals of divine embodiment take place under the
guidance of a narrating singer. These complex rituals, most often called *jāgar*, from
the verb "to wake" (also "stay awake" or "awaken"), are ways of interacting directly
with regional gods, and they are usually called for in cases of misfortune that can be
attributed to these gods. Some of them, particularly those involving the extremely
popular god Golu Dev (also called Goriya or Goll Jyu), are held in order to correct,
and sometimes to reveal, injustice. Golu Dev also has his own temples, and thousands
of written petitions requesting justice are to be seen on their walls. *Jāgar* rituals have
been described in a number of unpublished doctoral dissertations (e.g., QUAYLE 1981,
LEAVITT 1985, BERNÈDE 2004), articles, and book chapters (e.g., GABORIEAU 1975,
LEAVITT 1997), and parts of more general books about the folk literature and religion
of Uttarakhand (e.g., PĀNDE 1962). There is also a book on Golu Dev's temples and
petitions to him (AGRAWAL 1992). Aditya Malik's *Tales of Justice and Rituals of Divine Embodiment: Oral Narratives from the Central Himalayas*, however, is the first
book to explore the intersection of oral narrative, divine embodiment, and conceptions of justice. MALIK is a specialist on folk narration and ritual, author notably of a
transcription and richly contextualized translation of the Devnarayan legend and cult
in Rajasthan (2003, 2005). This book is particularly important because, for the most
part, the English-language literature on South Asian oral epics and other folk tradi-

tions (e.g., BLACKBURN and RAMANUJAN 1986, BLACKBURN, CLAUS et al. 1989) has left aside this tiny corner of the subcontinent.

I will go briefly through the chapters of the book, then offer some general comments. Since the book covers so many topics, these comments will have to be superficial.

Chapter 1, "The Presence of the Everyday," is organized upon the model that repeats throughout the book in other chapters: an alternation of presentation of the Kumaoni ethnography with, on the one hand, personal anecdotes, and on the other hand, discussions of broad themes: the nature of justice, the nature of everyday experience, and how to conceptualize possession. The discussions are often illuminating, although the relationship of the anecdotes to the rest is not always evident. The author gives a number of personal anecdotes, all illustrating the unknowability and vulnerability of life in this world, and in some cases, how these anecdotes intersect with the intercession of the god.

Chapter 2, "Temples, Travels, Territories," introduces the god Golu Dev, his legend, his temples, and stories of his travels to establish his temples. Comparisons are made to stories from other parts of South Asia which, like Golu's, tell of a queen who is younger than her co-wives, and whose child(ren) is taken away by jealous older queens; the child(ren) return triumphantly and the evil queen(s) is punished. In the Kumaoni case, Golū is today said to be an incarnation of Gaur Bhairav, the servant of the deity Shiva, which ties Golu into the Sanskritic pantheon.

Chapter 3, "Ideas of Justice," begins with interviews with shopkeepers at one of Golū's temples, and gives a series of cautionary tales about important justice-givers— British authorities and Indian District Magistrates—who were taught lessons by this or another god. The point here is that this divine justice is based on the immediate context, not on an abstract code.

Chapter 4, "Writing Intimacy," deals with the petitions left for Golū at his temple, with the discussion of some cases described in the petitions. While the discussion ranges over poetry, *bhakti* (devotion), Borges, and the nature of the everyday, the main point is the immediacy of concrete rather than abstract legality.

Chapter 5, despite its title "Alterity and Modernity," is chapter about possession. The author very fairly critiques tendencies to explain possession away as a delusion or a trick, while offering an important rethinking of possession as "relinquishment of control accompanied by a loss of self, memory, and identity, and rooted in an uncertainty with regard to agency and authority" (144). He identifies this "mixing of bodies and selves" with non-modern societies, particularly with the "non-duality" of Indian thought. This does not, it seems to me, take into account the epidemics of multiple personality that have periodically struck the modern West; the West, too, is probably less "modern" than it likes to think. The author also offers an argument for the predominance of women as possessed mediums. But there is a well-known difference between possession as an affliction and oracular possession of the kind associated with Golu: while it is most often young women who are possessed by ghosts and demons, oracular mediums can be either women or men, as the examples given in the chapter show.

Chapter 6, "Transformations," begins with epiphanies of Golu and the Goddess, following which the reader gets the impression that the author is moving toward a description of what actually happens in a *jāgar*. Unfortunately, no such description is offered. We hear, rather, about an auto accident the day after the *jāgar*, and then a discussion of the nature of the self, drawing on neuropsychology, Heidegger, and Advaita philosophy to argue that the experience of embodiment of the god in the medium is an overcoming of the difference between the experiencing self and the objectified self. What this does not answer, it seems to me, is how practices of embodiment such as those in the *jāgar* are different from, say, classical meditation, which by no means serves to embody a divine or demonic being.

The final chapter, "Dancers Dancing," gives stories about possessed mediums, and recounts the author's visit to a Golū Dev temple where a woman was possessed, apparently by the Goddess. The chapter concludes with a beautiful discussion of the nature of possession, raising what is certainly the key question this practice poses: what does it mean to live in a world in which one can "be another" (223)?

The book ends with an epilogue positing the universality of feelings of justice, and particularly, of injustice, arguing that reality emerges through language. As may be obvious from the comments, this reader is not convinced by the practice of jumping from ethnography to personal reminiscence to philosophical disquisition. But this is a stylistic question. There are more important issues that need to be addressed.

First, the language of the author's interaction with his subjects is not identified. In this part of the world, Hindi is the language of public and much private interaction, but in the rituals themselves, as far as I have been able to observe, the narratives and the gods' speeches are in Kumaoni. More information on the linguistic status of the author's observances and interactions would have been welcomed. Second, the book's references are primarily to Western sources for both ethnography and philosophy. There is nothing wrong with this in itself—indeed, it is standard practice in much writing about non-Western cultures. But there is a rich Hindi-language literature on Kumaoni folk religion that might have been cited. It should be said that the book does include a compelling discussion of the constraints and contradictions that face a non-Western but Western-trained scholar. Finally, the geography of Uttarakhand and its neighboring regions is often cited in the book, and plays an important role in the stories being presented. The reader gets lost among the hills, and the book, perhaps in a future edition, would greatly benefit from some maps.

These are quibbles concerning what is, in the end, a major and a highly welcome contribution to the study of oral traditions and religious practice in general, of South Asia in particular.

References

AGRAWAL, C.M.
 1992 *Golu Devata : The God of Justice of Kumaun Himalayas.* Almora: Shree Almora Book Depot.

BERNÈDE, Franck
 2004 Le jagar au Kumaon: musique, danse et rituels de possession dans l'Himalaya central. Doctoral Dissertation, École des Hautes Études en Sciences Sociales, Paris.

BLACKBURN, Stuart H., Peter J. CLAUS, et al., eds.
 1989 *Oral Epics in India.* Berkeley: University of California Press.

BLACKBURN, Stuart H., and A.K. RAMANUJAN, eds.
 1986 *Another Harmony: New Essays on the Folklore of India.* Berkeley: University of California Press.

GABORIEAU, Marc
    1975   La transe rituelle dans l'Himalaya central: folie, avatār, méditation. *Puruṣārtha* 2: 147–72.

LEAVITT, John
    1985   The Language of the Gods: Discourse and Experience in a Central Himalayan Ritual. Doctoral Dissertation, University of Chicago.

    1997   The language of the Gods: Poetry and prophecy in the central Himalayas. In *Poetry and Prophecy: The Anthropology of Inspiration*, John Leavitt, ed., 129–68. Ann Arbor: University of Michigan Press.

MALIK, Aditya
    2003   *Śrī Devnārāyaṇ Kathā: An Oral Narrative of Marwar.* New Delhi: South Asia Institute.

    2005   *Nectar Gaze and Poison Breath: An Analysis and Translation of the Rajasthani Oral Narrative of Devnārāyaṇ.* New York: Oxford University Press.

PĀNDE, Trilocan
    1962   *Kumāū̃ kā lok sāhitya* [Folk Literature of Kumaon]. Almora: Sri Almora Book Depot.

QUAYLE, Brendan
    1981   Studies in the Ritual Traditions of the Kumaon Himālaya. Doctoral dissertation, University of Durham.

John Leavitt
Université de Montréal

Brian Black and Laurie Patton, eds., *Dialogue in Early South Asian Religions: Hindu, Buddhist, and Jain Traditions*
Surrey, England: Ashgate, 2015. 278 pages. Hardcover, $122.00, ISBN: 978-1-4094-4012-3. Paperback, $40.95, ISBN: 978-1-4094-4013-0. eBook, $28.67, ISBN: 9781315576978. doi: 10.4324/9781315576978.

THIS WORK, while not technically the first volume to be released in Ashgate's new "Dialogues in South Asian Traditions" series, can nevertheless be taken as its flagship. A product of the Sammukham Project, which held workshops in Chicago in 2008 and Montreal in 2009, this volume collects essays organized around the theme of "dialogue" by eleven scholars of early Indian religions who participated in the workshops. As such, the book displays the typical strengths and weaknesses of edited volumes coming out of conferences. On the one hand, it brings into conversation—dialogue, if you will—a number of scholars whose work might not otherwise be found in the same place, providing a useful space for synergistic comparisons under the rubric of a common theme. On the other hand, the inevitable breadth of the unifying topic means that at times certain contributions can go off in quite tangential directions. In the case of this volume, a key example would be the chapter by Alf Hiltebeitel, whose contribution to the volume's theme at times feels subordinated to Hiltebeitel's career-long argument for the unitary authorship of the Mahābhārata.

The themes of conferences and workshops are often interpreted quite loosely by participants. Black and Patton do an excellent job, however, of providing a coherent framework to the different interpretations of the theme of "dialogue" in the way they organize the book. They divide the book into three parts, each including contributions that interpret "dialogue" in a particular way. The first part, "Dialogues Inside and Outside the Texts," includes essays that address "dialogue" in the most literal way, that is, actual dialogues between people that take place within early Indian religious texts. This section includes contributions by Laurie Patton on a dialogue between frogs in the *Ṛg Veda*, and Alf Hiltebeitel, Anna Aurelia Esposito, and Naomi Appleton on the use of dialogues as frame narratives in the epics, Jain literature, and Buddhist Jātaka literature, respectively. The second part, "Texts in Dialogue," addresses the way in which texts engage in "dialogue" with one another. It includes contributions by Douglas Osto on the dialogue that the Prajñāpāramitā Sūtras implicitly engage in with earlier Buddhist texts, Elizabeth M. Rohlman on intertextual dialogue among the Purāṇas, and Andrew J. Nicholson on the textual genres in which Indian philosophy appears. Finally, the third part, "Moving Between Traditions," explores the textual expressions of dialogues that took place in early South Asia between religious traditions. It includes contributions by Michael Nichols on dialogues between the Buddha and non-Buddhists, Jonathan Geen on dialogues justifying early renunciation in the Jain and Hindu traditions, Lisa Wessman Crothers on royal advising in the *Arthaśāstra* and Buddhist Jātakas, and Brian Black on the comparison of dialogues found in Hindu and Buddhist literature.

I will begin with two criticisms and then address the strengths of the book. The first criticism is relatively minor, but may prove an annoyance to some readers: the type, at least in the paperback version that I reviewed, is far smaller than is typical in academic books. In spite of the fact that I have not yet reached the age where I need reading glasses, I found it difficult to read. My more substantive critique, admittedly based on my own interests in dialogue in early South Asian religions, is that "dialogue" in this volume comes across as remarkably static. With a few notable exceptions, what we often get are "snapshots" of dialogue between characters in texts, between texts themselves, and between religious traditions, rather than a full sense of the *dialectical* and therefore fundamentally transformative nature of dialogue. I would like to have seen a fuller exploration not just of the way in which literary, textual, and institutional agents engage in dialogue, but of *the way in which dialogue brings those agents into being.*

Nevertheless, the creative application of the theme "dialogue" in different ways to the study of early South Asian religions gives us new eyes with which to see the textual traditions of early India and will surely lead to important insights in scholarship to come. All of the contributions to the volume provide the seeds of important insights, some of which—like the contributions of Naomi Appleton on the Jātakas and Brian Black on comparison of Buddhist and Brahmanical dialogues—have already been borne out in their other work. Two contributions that I felt were particularly innovative were those of Andrew Nicholson and Lisa Crothers. In Chapter 7, Nicholson makes the compelling argument that part of the reason that Western philosophers do not recognize Indian philosophy as philosophy is that Indian philosophy retains throughout its history a dialogic format that was once found in ancient Greek philosophy, but has since been abandoned in the professional discipline of philosophy in the West. In Chapter 10, Lisa Crothers engages in a fascinating comparative study of the *Arthaśāstra* and Buddhist Jātakas that explores the different ways in which they deal with the problematic figures of royal advisors and spies. Overall, this volume is the harbinger of exciting work to come—within the "Dialogues in South Asian Traditions" series, within the individual scholarship of the contributors, and within the field of South Asian religions as a whole.

Nathan McGovern
University of Wisconsin-Whitewater

Asko Parpola, *The Roots of Hinduism: The Early Aryans and the Indus Civilization*

Oxford: Oxford University Press, 2015. 384 pages. Hardback, $105.00, ISBN: 978-0-022690-9. Paperback, $36.95, ISBN: 978-0-19-022692-3. eBook, $19.24, ISBN: 978-0-19-022693-0. doi: 10.1093/acprof: oso/9780190226909.001.0001.

THE ROOTS OF HINDUISM is the fruit of some fifty years of research into the early history of India, research that has necessarily spanned the history, language, and culture of a vast expanse of regions west to Mesopotamia, and north-west to central Asia. It is a work of considerable and lasting importance, which will both inform and stimulate the field for decades to come. But the nature of its scope and vision, as well as its methodology, is such that some of its details, if not its conclusions, will inevitably attract specialists' criticism, and some will inevitably be refined by later scholarship. Nonetheless, we may state immediately that this work is required reading for any serious study of the issues with which it deals, and will demand serious consideration and reflection even by its critics. Only those misguided souls who cling to "the impossible hypothesis that the Vedic Aryans were indigenous to South Asia" (92) can fail to appreciate it, for it is a large nail in their coffin.

Asko Parpola participated in the famous recreation and recording of the Vedic fire sacrifice conducted by the Nambudri Brahmins in Kerala (at the initiative of Frits Staal). He is now Emeritus Professor of Indology and South Asian Studies at the University of Helsinki, and is known to us through an impressive corpus of articles—some 70 of which are listed here in the biography, which have principally examined, in forensic detail, the origins, beliefs, and practices of the Indo-European peoples in South Asia, and the vexed question of the identity and meaning of the Indus valley script, an issue on which no consensus exists.

Parpola's linguistic range embraces not only various forms of Sanskrit but also forms of Dravidian languages, such as Old Tamil. His methodology embraces both archaeology and historical linguistics, and it is unlikely that any relevant study, not the least written in Russian, has escaped his consideration. That breadth of expertise lends considerable authority to his conclusions when he moves from evidence to speculation, and while there is much here that we might consider proven, there is also much that is advanced as a thesis.

It is impossible in a short review to do justice to the range of scholarship in this work. But we might isolate his principal conclusions and historical narrative. The roots of Hinduism lie, according to this work, in the fusion of elements deriving from separate waves of Indo-European peoples with those of the Indus valley culture.

Speakers of Proto-Indo-European emerged from their early homeland in the Pontiac-Caspian steppes in southern Ukraine and southern Russia. It was in the south Uralic Sintashta culture around 2100 BCE that the horse-drawn chariot first appeared, a technological leap that allowed its peoples military supremacy over their neighbors. A detailed route for the coming of the Aryan languages to Central, West, and South Asia is then traced through the correlation of archaeology with linguistics. Pushing east and reaching South Asia by around 1900–1700 BCE, one East Iranian-speaking group, whose principal gods were the Aśvins and Mitra-Varuṇa, succeeded the Bactria and Margiana Archaeological Complex (BMAC) culture that stretched to Baluchistan, Persia, and even Syria. Taking over some of BMAC traditions, notably fortified settlements, this group formed the Yaz-1 culture in the latter half of the second millennium BCE.

A second wave of Proto-Indo-European speakers, who adopted horse-riding around 1500 BCE, formed the Androvono culture on the steppes between the Urals and the Altai. By its mature phase, when it centered on southern Turkmenistan, Uzbekistan, and northern Afghanistan, the Androvono culture had contact with both Mesopotamia and the Indus Valley and its elites were speakers of Indo-Iranian. The Androvonans, steppe pastoralists whose main god was Indra, moved east toward the Indus valley some 500 years after their predecessors. In the lands that are now Waziristan and south-eastern Afghanistan, they encountered the settled first wave of the Yaz-1 culture, peoples identified here with the *Dasas*, *Dasyus*, and *Paṇis*, who are described in the Rig Veda as the inhabitants of fortified cities destroyed by Indra. Those city dwellers had, by this time, absorbed deities such as Rudra from the Indus civilization, along with aspects of the traditions that emerged in the Atharvaveda.

Parpola proposes that the subsequent collation of the Rig Veda was made by the wave of Indra-worshipping Indo-Aryans, with its early core, the hymns of the "family books" II–VII later augmented by books I and VIII–X. They represent the contribution of the earlier wave that emerges more fully in the later Arthavaveda, which reflects the blending of the Indra-worshipping wave with the earlier culture that had taken on ideas from the Indus civilization. He is, however, largely silent on how the two processes of cultural merger occurred or the context in which they happened.

He does, however, advance a significant new refinement to our understanding of migratory "waves" of eastward movement into the sub-continent and their consequent Sanskrit literary association, concluding that a third significant wave of Indo-Aryan immigrants entered South Asia following the stabilization of Vedic/Brahmanical culture in the powerful Kuru kingdom. He identifies this wave with a new group of Iranian language speakers, associated in the archaeological record with megalithic graves and Black and Red Ware pottery remains, who travelled via Sindh, Gujarat, and Rajasthan around 800 BCE and took over the Kuru kingdom. This enables him to propose "a wholly new interpretation of the Mahābhārata war" (145) and that this third wave of immigrants stimulated a new literary genre, being represented in the Mahābhārata by the Pāṇḍavas (with their subsequent takeover of Sri Lanka represented in the Rāmayāna).

In the second section of the book, Parpola turns to a closer examination of the Indus Valley culture, necessarily beginning with the debate over the language represented by its 400 or so signs—noting that there have been more than 100 published claims to have deciphered that script since the 1920s (27). He concludes that as with the other most ancient scripts, it is "logosyllabic" and that without a "Rosetta stone" it cannot be completely deciphered. But he argues that while it is too early to be an Indo-Aryan language, it must have left its mark on Vedic languages and, rejecting Michael

WITZEL'S "Para-Munda" proposal (2005, 165), he concludes it is a proto-Dravidian language—more controversially, tracing among six examples of its mark on Vedic Sanskrit the word *oṁ*! Emphasising the importance of Old Tamil for the study of the Indus script in that it preserves archaic elements of Proto-Dravidian, he then advances a number of "translations" of Indus signs. To the non-specialist at least, some of these claims will seem tenuous, for example the otherwise apparently unsupported thesis that the sign of the grasping fig or *banyan* tree "could be a symbol for Rudra" (283). Nonetheless, his conclusions probably still represent the leading work on the subject.

This Indus-orientated section of *The Roots of Hinduism* does contain both a wealth of impressive scholarship and somewhat speculative claims for which available evidence is marshalled, rather than necessarily critically interrogated (albeit his footnoted articles often shed further light on these claims). Archaeological evidence that the Indus culture borrowed much from Mesopotamia rather than the reverse might, for example, have been problematized by a discussion of how ideas and goods may fail to leave an archaeological record rather than used to support a claim to west-east transmission. Similarly, while it is commonly suggested that the Indus civilization was ruled by Kings or Priest-kings (231), the claim is not proven, which problematizes the author's thesis that Vedic rites of kingship derived from Harappan royal rituals originally transmitted from West Asia.

The claim to connection between early sexualized rituals such as those of the early Vedic *vrātya*s and Tantrism, which in its fully developed form is much more than a millennium later, is particularly controversial (251), while the use of the similarly late Kālikā Purāṇa as evidence in discussion of the Indus culture is equally problematic— entirely different historical trajectories could be proposed to explain concordances. The same is true for any possible concordance between the Vedic Śambara and the much later Tantric deity Cakrasaṃvara. Such claimed transmissions over vast periods of time leave us with little alternative but to allow the rather unsatisfactory explanatory device of the "sub-stratum".

In emphasizing west-east migrations and transmissions, there are other possible formative influences on Hinduism that the author has chosen not to discuss. Given that many scholars assign them a role in the roots of Tantric ritual, one might wonder about the tribals, not least of the Himalayas, that engine of religious growth. Indeed, what of the *nāga*s, whose worshippers seem to form a pre-historic Pan-Asian religious understanding and whose watery homes should surely be factored into consideration of the significance of water bodies and sources in both Hinduism and the Indus Valley, with its famous bathing tanks. Parpola sees "folk religion" as descending from the Indus culture (as also Vedic cosmology and later yoga). But here again mono-directional agencies may be an oversimplification of ancient history.

Yet this is in its way a succinct work, advancing a complex series of explanatory models rather than exploring every possible option. It certainly does not claim to be the last work on the subject. Indeed, its aim is to stimulate further research, and it should achieve that aim. Its broad conclusions are immensely satisfying as an explanatory model, and while perhaps its utility is largely for the specialists who will engage with its conclusions for many years to come, it is written in a simple yet erudite style that should ensure that it is accessible to the advanced undergraduate.

REFERENCE

WITZEL, Michael
2005   Central Asian roots and acculturation in South Asia: Linguistic and archaeological evidence from western Central Asia, the Hindukush and northwestern South Asia for early Indo-Aryan language and religion. In *Linguistics, Archaeology and the Himan Past: Occasional Paper 1, ed.* Toshiki Osada, 87–211. Kyoto: Indus Project, Research Institute for Humanity and Nature.

A. C. McKay
International Institute for Asian Studies, Leiden

V. Ravi Vaithees, *Religion, Caste, and Nation in South India: Maraimalai Adigal, the Neo-Saivite Movement, and Tamil Nationalism 1876-1950*

New Delhi: Oxford University Press, 2015. 347 pp. Hardcover, Rs. 1645, ISBN 978-0199451814.

IN *Religion, Caste, and Nation in South India,* V. Ravi Vaithees explores the religious roots of Tamil nationalism and the Dravidian movement through a critical examination of the life and career of Maraimalai Adigal (1876–1950), whose life not only intersected with the pioneer figures in the neo-Śaivite and Dravidian movement but also who played a central role in consolidating the intellectual and cultural foundation for non-Brahmin Tamil nationalism and the Dravidian movement. The book advances the argument that it was the anti-Aryan, anti-Brahmin character of Tamil nationalism and the Dravidian movement to the Neo-Śaivite movement that was firmly grounded in ancient Tamil and bhakti poetry and Tamil Saiva Siddhanta tradition (14). In highlighting the neo-Śaivite revival that played a significant role in shaping the character of Tamil nationalism and the Dravidian movement, Vaithees at a larger lever questions the "logocentric" assumptions of cultural solidarity across heterogeneous people and invites his readers to appreciate the role of religion at the grassroots level.

The book is organized into an introduction, four chapters, and a conclusion. Through the introduction, the author provides the framework for the entire work demonstrating how anti-Aryan and anti-Vedantic imperatives informed the reimagining and reconstruction of a non-Brahmin Tamil nationalism. The first chapter, "Framing the Neo-Saivites Revival in Tamil Nadu," situates the neo-Saivite movement within its historical context discussing the various responses, intellectual, sociocultural, and religious, to the colonial impact and impacts of European Orientalists and Missionaries. Through the discussion of the life and contributions of various pioneers, it becomes obvious that there are two key intellectual developments that shaped and paved the way for the neo-Saivite revival movement: the philological researches of South Indian languages emphasizing the primacy of the Tamil language counter to Sanskrit and Indo-Aryan languages; and that Tamil Saivism and Saiva Siddhanta was the unique product of the Tamil Dravidians and not as an integral part of the Pan-Indian Hindu tradition (26-7). Importantly, it was the work and writings of early neo-Saivite pioneers that shaped the neo-Saivite revival, and the person who interacted with these figures and contributed towards the Saiva Siddhanta revival in the colonial public sphere was Maramalai Adigal.

Chapter two, "Maramalai Adigal and the Naveenar (Modernist) Saivite Revival in Tamil Nadu," closely examines the life and career of Adigal to reconstruct the Tamil neo-Saivite movement and to assert the central role Adigal played in forming the non-Brahmin Tamil nationalism and early Dravidian movement. In his inspirational essay, Tamil Nattavarum Melnattavarum (Tamils and the Westerners), Adigal critiques Brahmins and Brahmanical Hinduism. Apart from this, he was influenced by Christian theological works, especially of Cardinal Newman, which proved useful for Adigal's reinterpration of Saiva Siddhanta.

Chapter three, "Theorizing the Naveenar Saivite Revival: Reinscribing Religion as Nation," analyzes and theorizes the strategies with which Adigal's revival reinforced non-Brahmin Tamil religion and the formation of Tamil nationalism grounded in Saivism. The Naveenar and their Saivite contemporaries corroborates three things: first, the Saivite contemporaries were witness to the emergence of a movement from within their midst and influenced to some extent by the mid-1920s; second, the contemporaries understood these Naveenar's to represent a distorted Saiva tradition, not the "authentic" tradition; third, it reveals the strategies and methods through which Naveenar's reconfigured and re-inscribed Saivism as Tami nation with its own language, history, and in their re-imagination and redefining Tamilness as non-Brahmin, and in that process excluding the Tamil Brahmin (224).

Chapter four, "Forging a Tamil Nation: The Politics of Language, Race, Caste, and Gender," demonstrates how language, literature, and literary history was central to Adigal's reimagination, reconstruction, and historicization of the Tamil and his articulation of neo-Saivite movement as a "secular" non-Brahmin Tamil nationalism. Vaithees observes that Adigal's neo-Saivite movement had three objectives: conflating Tamil with Saivism and Tamil literature with Saiva literature; his reading ancient Tamil literature enabled him to reconstruct and historicize the Tamil and Saivite past; and he capitalizes on ancient Tamil literature as the ground for radically regenerating Tamil nationalism. These objectives transpired in his vision of caste, gender, and race in Tamil society as he envisioned a casteless society that was congruent with the progressive European thinkers of his days and promoted by mystical figures of Tamil-Saivite and Siddha traditions.

Despite the ambivalence in Adigal's vision of caste, gender, and race, he aspired to counter the extremely divisive hierarchical caste and gender discrimination in Tamil society of his time. Precisely, then, Adigal's reconfiguration, reinterpretation, and articulation of Tamil nation drawing from different literary sources was revolutionary. The concluding chapter, "The Promise and Legacies of Non-Brahmin Tamil Nationalism," Vaithees confirms that Adigal's reimagining and reconstructing of Tamil national consciousness was deeply steeped in Tamil Saivism and ancient Tamil literary tradition rather than in line with neo-Vedantic Hinduism. It becomes apparent from Adigal's life and contribution that the template for Tamil modernity was based on Christian missionary critique of Brahmanism and caste society. This study does not only present the layers of influences of European and Tamil thinkers that shaped the neo-Saivite movement, but also informs the new discourse on Tamil Language, literature, and literary history interspersed with neo-Saivite movement poses an ongoing challenge to the Dravidian movement.

Religion, Caste, and Nation in South India is a serious scholarly work that significantly contributes towards a historical understanding of the formation of the powerful non-Brahmin Tamil nationalism that plays a significant role in the cultural politics of the region. Vaithees inclusion of diverse literary sources and attention to details makes the volume a useful resource. Though the focus of the volume is the life and works of Maramalai Adigal, the study succeeds in providing insight into larger milieu concerning the construction of non-Brahmin Tamil nationalism and the neo-Saivite movement.

George Pati
Valparaiso University

Iran

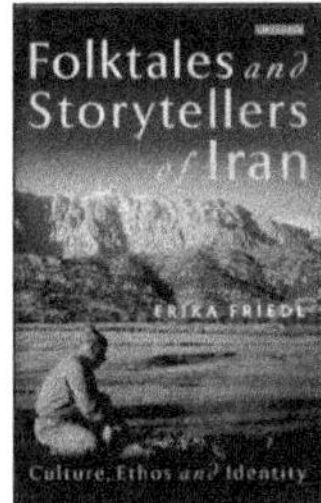

Erika Friedl, *Folktales and Storytellers of Iran: Culture, Ethos and Identity*
London and New York: I.B. Tauris & Co Ltd, 2014. 277 pages. Hardcover, $99.00, ISBN: 978-1780766690.

In 1969, folklorist Robert A. GEORGES cautioned fellow folklorists that the time had come to abandon the method of gathering and writing about folk tales common to the nineteenth and first half of the twentieth centuries, and develop a new methodology and lens to study them: "Nineteenth-century scholars came to regard stories as cultural artifacts and to conceive of them as surviving or traditional linguistic entities pervaded by meaningful symbols" (1969, 313–28). Instead of collecting and publishing the text, often with several variants, as was the general practice up until the 1970s, Georges suggested a more holistic approach, which he labeled "the storytelling event," in which he urged the folklore scholar to focus on all aspects of the event. In addition to furnishing the text and its meaning, he also urged the folklorist to report on the storyteller, the manner of telling, and the range of audience responses to the story. He concluded: "Data for studying storytelling events must be sought in natural field situations, and every attempt must be made to capture their wholeness....Only by attempting to study storytelling events holistically can we begin to appreciate their true significance as communicative events, as social experiences, and as unique expressions of human behavior" (327–28).

Georges's article has been influential beyond folklore, influencing dance studies, ethnomusicology, and anthropology, among other fields. To this day, folklorists and other gatherers of folk tales do not always follow Georges's sage advice, and both folklorists and amateur authors continue to publish uncontextualized collections of stories.

Anthropologist Erika Friedl, without mentioning Georges's article specifically, meticulously follows his advice in *Folktales and Storytellers of Iran* and provides us several texts, descriptions of storytellers and their lives, and how the tales relate to different worldviews and the lives of the people who listen to them in this rich study of the folk tales and storytellers in Boir Ahmad, a region of Luristan in southwestern Iran. Professor Friedl is well positioned to give us this illuminating view of the multiple ways in which the people of Boir Ahmad listen and respond to the tales, for she has spent over seven years doing field work in the region across the span of several decades, especially prior to the 1990s, during which time the lives of the people of the area materially improved. She has documented their lives in a series of books about the region (*The Women of Deh Kuh* (1991); *Children of Deh Kuh* (1997); as well as several articles). She confines the tales that she analyzes to this specific region and frequently comments when specific folk tales, motifs, or characters have wider Iranian meaning. She has translated the tales from Lori, the local language, related to Persian (Farsi), but significantly different from it.

Boir Ahmad is a mountainous region in which traditionally much of the population practiced transhumance, moving large flocks of sheep and goats from the winter quarters on the flatland areas to the summer quarters in the highlands and mountains, following the grass. It is a hard life, and poverty and hunger, which the older generations remember well, is a constant theme throughout the book and the tales. A recent YouTube recording shows the tribe on the move (https://youtu.be/JM8QHRC -MaYY; accessed 26 October 2017). The hunger and want that characterize the often harsh lives of the people of Luristan drive many of the plots and actors of the tales. For example, trying to obtain or steal food feature in many of the tales.

Friedl compares the folktales that she has gathered with collections by other authors, whom she consulted as she prepared the study. She has specifically avoided using trendy scholarly concepts and theories, and instead of providing us with a "scholarly interpretation" she focuses on the meaning these tales have for their local listeners and has organized her text to reflect this: "But even scholars who record tales in the field, close to ethnographic reality, tend to use folktales as texts to be analyzed in the framework of a theory such as, for example, psychoanalysis, structuralism, functionalism or feminism, ignoring the ethnographic context. The 'meaning' they are after transcends the meanings local people give the tales. This local meaning is my main interest. I aim to unite folktale texts with life as lived by the storytellers and their listeners" (2014, 1).

In this, she succeeds admirably. For example, several times she points out that readers should not read Freudian meanings into stories that might invite such an analysis, because the local people do not invest such meaning in the tales. As Friedl observes, and as I experienced when I lived in Iran, folklore and storytelling is still a living activity and a source of local identity construction and pride. Folklore is fairly recent form of scholarly study in Iran, which makes this collection and the information it brings to Iranian studies a valuable addition to the field of folklore and anthropology.

Above all, she notes that the tales do not take on an other-worldliness, even when peopled with fairies (*pari*), or demons (*div*), or animals that talk. The animals behave like they do in the real world: wolves kill, foxes are clever, dogs guard flocks and endure the beatings of their masters, snakes poison. It is the world of here, as Friedl stresses. The listeners recognize their world, the creatures in it, and their belief systems embedded in the tales. In part, the tales provide the cautionary message to always be aware of your surroundings.

In the organization of the book, Friedl provides several full-length tales, but due to concerns with space, and because of the repetitive quality of many of the tales, she more often gives us a condensed version, especially with the popular "string tales" type (also popular in folk songs), such as the mouse eats the cheese, the cat eats the mouse, the dog eats the cat, etc. In addition, she describes the tale collections that she uses, their strengths, and their weaknesses. Chapter 1 relates the biographies of a male and female storyteller, and how their sex and class affect the tales they favor and their actors' behavior.

In subsequent chapters she analyzes the content, motifs, and characters. In Chapter 2, Friedl notes that most tales "start within the family" (45). She specifically analyzes the positive or negative relations between brothers and sisters that often propel the plots. In Chapter 3, she analyzes specific female characters, many of which remain nameless. The most common female characters are Old Woman, Girl/Bride, Wife, and Mother. Chapter 4 focuses on the role of plants, both medicinal and as food, and animals. The people in the region are Shi'i Muslims, but as Friedl notes, "[c]onsidering this religious background the scarcity of religious themes and references to God and theology in the people's tales is noteworthy" (128).

Chapter 6 discusses "extra-human beings" such as fairies, jinn, and ghouls. She notes that, "[p]eople do not worship these beings. Rather, they try to keep a prudent distance from those that are potentially harmful, and try to ingratiate themselves with those who they think can help them" (155). Even in Tehran some people believed in *jenn* and *moshkel gosha* ("difficulty opener," meaning the power to help one in times of need, such as in passing an examination), for which they had to enact ritual-like behavior to succeed. Fate (*pishani neveshteh*, "written on the forehead") occurs in several tales, but the evil eye, widely believed in, is curiously absent. In her last chapter, Friedl states about the philosophy of everyday life, "[i]n Iran many historical processes and cultural influences left behind thought systems from which people now choose. Even Islam, the most strictly formulated philosophical system offers choices and validations for just about any kind of behavior. The tales reflect this wealth of options" (181).

I found her discussion of *zarangi*, which she describes as "implying cunning and the wisdom to choose the most successful strategy in any situation," as "perhaps the most controversial of ethical principles" (197–99). Yet, *zarangi* features in many of the tales because in a society of hunger and want, *zarangi* provides the actors with a recognizable trait from the local viewpoint, an admirable form of agency that permits the characters to capitalize on *bakht* (luck) when it appears. Clearly, the tribal people and peasants of the region admire and recognize this character trait.

For an understanding of the worldviews of a non-Western ethnic group and how they see their world through the telling of tales, I highly recommend this valuable study. I would recommend, also, that it be used in conjunction with Friedl's folk tale collection, with Lori and English texts (2007).

REFERENCES

GEORGES, Robert A.
1969   Toward an understanding of storytelling events. *Journal of American Folklore* 82: 31328. doi: 10.2307/539777

FRIEDL, Erika
1991   *The Women of Deh Kuh: Lives in an Iranian Village*. NY: Penguin Books.
1997   *Children of Deh Kuh: Young Life in an Iranian Village*. Syracuse: SUNY Press.
2007   *Folktales from a Persian Tribe*. Dortmund: Verlag für Orientkunde.

Anthony Shay
Pomona College

Japan

David Odo, *The Journey of "A Good Type": From Artistry to Ethnography in Early Japanese Photographs*
Cambridge, MA: Peabody Museum Press (Harvard University), 2015.
144 pages. Hardcover, $45.00, ISBN: 978-0-87365-408-1.

Photography was becoming widespread in the latter years of the nineteenth century just as Japan was making its modern entry in the world. That nation's brilliant culture and highly sophisticated artistry caught the attention of the Western world. Enthusiasts for everything Japanese invented the term *Japonisme* to explain the influence of Japanese art, fashion, and aesthetics on Western culture. Japanese art and artifacts, particularly Buddhist items, became all the rage. It is often said that every fashionable living room in late Victorian Boston and London had at least one authentic Japanese artifact. Thousands of tourists made the long journey to Japan to see the place for themselves.

By the middle of the Meiji period (1868–1912), beautifully hand-tinted photographic prints of Japanese people, temples, and landscapes were among its earliest and most popular exports. Famous European photographers such as Raimund von Stillfried and Felice Beato opened studios in Japan as early as the 1860s, soon to be followed by their Japanese protégés Kuichi Ichida and Kimbei Kusakabe and many others. Hundreds of their photographs, collected en masse by travelers from the Boston area, were donated to Harvard University's Peabody Museum of Archaeology and Ethnology, where curators archived them for their ethnographic content. The biggest photographic collection at the Peabody is that of William Sturgis Bigelow, a prominent archaeologist and collector of art.

Visual anthropologist David Odo, Research Curator of University Collections Initiatives at the Harvard Art Museums, and a Lecturer in the Department of Anthropology at Harvard University, has created this work, *The Journey of "A Good Type,"* as an examination of the Peabody's collection of Japanese photographs. He presents his work as an analysis of how these collections reflect the desires and preconceptions of makers and consumers alike, and the ethnographic interests of the people who collected them.

A reader may approach this elegant volume from several points of view. It is superficially a beautiful "coffee table" album of Japanese photographs from the Meiji era. And the illustrations here are indeed outstanding, especially the portraits of Japanese people of that period. But a deeper look gives the reader a fascinating ethnographic view of how photographers and collectors of these photographs wanted to view Japan. Odo sees this collection of early photographs of Meiji Japan as being more than mere art. The subjects of the photographs and the way the images are arranged in albums tell us much about how the people who took the pictures and those who assembled and/or bought the albums perceived Japan at the time. Looking at one photo of a supposed geisha, Odo writes:

The photograph teemed with tropes of Japaneseness: the woman's elaborate hairstyle, glossy with camellia oil and punctuated with four fanciful hairpins of exotic design; the kimono, lightly clutched with her right hand, falling in graceful folds;

and the shamisen, the lutelike instrument that was part of a geisha's stock in trade, held upright with her left hand. This photograph seemed to perfectly embody certain nineteenth-century Western ideas about Japan—and Japanese women in particular—as hyperfeminine, subservient, and somehow inscrutable. (xv–xvi)

Tourists and armchair "travelers" in the United States and Europe were fascinated by everything supposedly quaint and old in Japan. We can see how Westerners of the Victorian period imagined what Japan looked like. Oscar Wilde, once commenting on this phenomenon, quipped, "In fact the whole of Japan is a pure invention. There is no such country, there are no such people." Nevertheless, these tourists raced to Japan to see the true face of traditional Japan before it was destroyed by the driving force of modernization. They wanted to buy souvenirs of the bygone feudal society of Japan—thus the surge in interest in pictures of geisha and samurai, and supposedly "traditional scenes of courtesans and kendo fighters." However, when Japanese photographers began setting up their own studios, they focused on everything modern.

The result was a "dual market" for these photos and photo collections. One was of a modern industrializing Japan with locomotives, factories, and shipyards. The other, catering to tourists fascinated by Japan's "quaint" feudal past, created a very mythical Japan that they imagined, but which never really existed.

It is this imagined Japan that is the focus of this book. It seems that many Victorian-era tourists came with the goal of visiting an exotic land. Since most did not bring cameras of their own, they collected albums of photographs as souvenirs. These photos were available in various forms: in prepackaged, pre-bound albums; as loose photographs that could be ordered by the purchaser and bound on the spot; and as loose prints which the tourist could make into an album back home. The album pages showed Japanese people posing to fixed stereotypes—women as geisha, men as samurai, religious figures and a variety of very traditional laborers. Albums also included stereotypical scenery—Mount Fuji, cherry blossoms in full bloom, and requisite temples and shrines.

Odo examines in detail the cottage industries that grew up to support the mythical Japan that the tourists came to see. Studios hired artists to add colors to the photographs. The samurai class had been dispersed by the time photography gained a foothold in Japan, but photographers hired handsome models who dressed as samurai and posed for pictures. In the caption of a man dressed as a courtly samurai, Odo writes: "Though clearly meant to represent a warrior, the portrait was made after the samurai class had already been disempowered, so the model is not an actual samurai but rather appears in costume. He wears a wig of the by-then forbidden hairstyle of the former warrior class and has theatre-ready eyebrows" (34). Attractive women were hired to dress as geisha, and as Odo notes, most of the women hired to pose as geisha were in fact common prostitutes. Others posed as traditional laborers and even as old-fashioned doctors feeling the pulse of a beautiful young maiden. All this to fuel the highly lucrative tourist image of an exotic Japan that never really existed.

Odo introduces a section, "Vanishing Types," that focuses on the Victorian notion that when members of "advanced civilizations" encountered primitive peoples from other racial groups, the primitive "tribes" faced the genuine prospect of extinction. "It was a widely accepted notion that colonized people were in danger of being overwhelmed by colonial cultures, which brought with them various aspects of Western societies ranging from advanced technologies to diseases. As a result, non-Europeans were thought to be in danger of vanishing off the face of the earth" (51). The result was a drive to photograph as many of these peoples as possible—natives of Africa, South Seas Islanders, Native Americans, Australian aborigines, etc.—so that the world would not forget them after they were gone.

A market soon grew for photographs of these "primitive peoples," and in Japan there was a rush of photographers and amateur anthropologists to capture images of the Ainu. Odo's book has an interesting collection of pictures of tall bearded Ainu warriors, who seem to represent the quaint notion of the "noble savage." Odo suggests that such images played a key part in the move to "salvage" the remnants of endangered cultures. It was efforts such as these that created both the popular and scientific rationale for the collecting of early photographs taken in Japan in The Peabody Museum (75).

This book will appeal to scholars interested in Japanese history, visual anthropology, and the history of photography. There are some technical terms that might confuse the general reader, but the writing is clear and is greatly enhanced by the photography. The connoisseur of the history of photography would find this work of great interest.

Odo's *The Journey of "A Good Type"* presents a fascinating ethnographic study of how photography can be used to demonstrate how cultures view each other through the lens of a camera. The reader will come away with a much clearer understanding of how the Victorian world of the West perceived a Japan that, as Oscar Wilde noted, never really existed. The photographs included here are worth the price of the book alone. I am only disappointed that Odo did not include photographs by Japanese who wanted to portray their country as a rapidly modernizing nation.

Daniel A. Métraux
Mary Baldwin College

Laos

Holly High, *Fields of Desire: Poverty and Policy in Laos*
Singapore: National University of Singapore Press, 2014. (Challenges in Agrarian Transition in Southeast Asia Series) 232 pages. Paperback, $27.93, ISBN 978-9971-69-770-9.

HOLLY HIGH's subtle, thoughtful, and lively ethnography study, *Fields of Desire*, deals with an issue that intrigues observers of Laos and other developmentalist countries, albeit hardly being articulated: Why would locals keep engaging in development schemes even though they have repeatedly seen them fail? In order to answer it, High goes beyond the dichotomy between advocates and critics of development. Instead, she observes how farmers on a Mekong island in southern Laos deal with the promises of poverty reduction schemes offered to, or forced upon, them.

Her central theoretical notion is desire—mostly inspired by Jacques Lacan—as a drive that emerges from what is incomplete and missing in the operation of daily life. This gap between what is there and what is hoped for does not simply manifest as an aim to be attained in the future, but as a "delirium" of contradictory orientations that produces its own coherence and rationality, and thus, much of the dynamics of social life.

High excellently analyzes these contradictions and the way they play out in social life. The central contradiction that organizes all the others is the village's relationship with the state. On the one hand, the state portrays itself as, and is understood to be, caring and nurturing, a powerful provider of goods, services, and opportunities to escape poverty. On the other, people experience the state as demanding, corrupt, and non-reciprocal.

Chapter 2 explores this relationship from the perspective of the role of rice production and the function of mothers in the household. The rice harvest is seen as a product of human labor, but it also reciprocates by providing nourishment. The state, however, fails in comparison on the count of reciprocation. A similar tension applies to the border with Thailand, just across the river, equally a site of hope and danger. In the past, the village was involved in anti-communist insurgency and charting a border with Thailand. Today, the village is exposed to state rhetoric that constructs Thailand as a danger to Lao sovereignty; meanwhile, Thailand is the destination of much hopeful emigration, and remittances form a major source of income.

In chapter 5, High carefully criticizes the idea that the caring state is an illusion while the corrupt state is the truth. If that was the case, villagers could give up on the state entirely. But they do not. Official and private images of the state remain in a tense balance that shapes villagers' intimacy with the state. Chapters 5, 6, and 7 together detail the way poverty reduction schemes played out and failed in the village. High identifies a perennial misunderstanding of village dynamics on the side of the state. Operating on an image of village solidarity and mutual aid, the administration delegates services that are actually state services, such as infrastructure, to the village, expecting villagers to organize joint projects for their own improvement. However, as other scholars have pointed out, while villages are important in certain respects—e.g., in forming identity, influencing politics, and participating in ritual—production and wealth are usually a domestic matter. Mutual aid is based on household networks, not village solidarity, and is organized less in terms of efficiency than on the basis of its enjoyment and aesthetic value. Thus, the tension between these two levels of organization obstructs the translation of state demands into village reality. In particular, High narrates a World Bank project that was supposed to help all, but instead proved to be of benefit to none. True to her balanced approach, High avoids blaming any of the actors or portraying the project as laughable.

The final chapter links the case study to wider concerns of Southeast Asian social life. It argues that the village turns its outside world into an aspect of its core self—an idea inspired by Sahlins and Lacan, and crucial for the study of Southeast Asia. While the difference between inside and outside is of central importance for understanding the constitution of these communities, this same difference is paradoxically at the root of village's self-understanding. Understanding this seeming contradiction goes a long way to explain the dynamics of Southeast Asian community building.

One major quibble with this otherwise excellent book concerns its theoretical approach. Arguably, the book uses the notion of desire consistently and in a way that makes a wealth of ethnographic data meaningful. However, it is not unproblematic. Lacan comes with a baggage of psychoanalytical epistemology that anthropologists routinely ignore when applying his ideas. Indeed, when High states toward the end of the book that desire precedes structure, she moves closer to Freud than to Lacan, for whom desire emerges from the tension between signifier and signified, i.e. from structure. In the context of an ethnographic analysis, this raises the crucial issue of where the "self" that "desires" is located. Does a village somehow operate like a person? Is each of its members programmed to share in a kind of collective psychology? High carefully analyzes when villages are meaningful units (e.g., in politics) and when they are not (e.g., in production). However, the question—how the subject of desire is constituted—is left unanswered. An alternative would have been to reframe the subject matter, not in terms of self and desire but in terms of values and expectations, both terms pointing to the constitution of the social. In particular, value systems are by necessity contradictory and dynamic, and the situation High describes is in no way different.

Overall, this is one of the best books on Laos in English to be produced in the past few years. Its substantial insights into the contradictions and complexities of development might be inconvenient for anyone who desires quick answers and clear solutions. For that very reason, it is highly recommended not just for scholars interested in Laos and mainland Southeast Asia, but also for development experts.

Guido Sprenger
Heidelberg University, Germany

South Asia – General

Anshu Malhotra and Siobhan Lambert-Hurley, eds.,
Speaking of the Self: Gender, Performance, and Autobiography in South Asia
Durham and London: Duke University Press, 2015. 312 pages. Cloth, $94.95, ISBN: 978-0-8223-5983-8. Paperback, $26.95, ISBN: 978-0-8223-5991-3. doi: 10.1215/9780822374978.

This work is a panoramic compilation of ten essays that explore women's autobiographical writings from South Asia. The central argument of this book, fleshed out in an erudite stand-alone introduction, is that autobiographical writings articulate performing selves—not a priori, autonomous, and decontextualized givens. Performing selves, or more aptly performing bodies, are polysemic and relational—the locus of multiple, often conflicting identities. Premised on this idea, each essay unravels how "one can be a different person at separate times" (13), always imbricated with, informed by, and responding to varied social, historical, and religious contexts.

The understanding that autobiography is a male European prerogative, Rousseau's *Confessions* being the prototype, emerged in mid twentieth-century literary discourses "in response to the end of Empire, or out of fear for a new cultural relativism" (3). This book systematically debunks a cluster of implications of this persuasion: that women's autobiographies lack introspection, individuality, honesty, and linear narration; that they make for poor social documentation; that they are all too easily subsumed into dominant nationalist and imperial ideologies; and importantly, that they are self-deprecatory, apologetic, and aesthetically sub par.

The first section is comprised of essays by Sylvia Vatuk, Ritu Menon, Asiya Alam, and Shubhra Ray. Vatuk explores how Urdu fictional novels shaped Zakira Ghouse's sense of adolescent self. In her memoir composed in the 1950s, Ghouse retells her childhood passion for reading as a meticulous, even desperate search for women role models that granted imaginary mobility in a highly circumscribed and conservative household. Vatuk argues that contrary to displaying "structural features of femininity" (49), Ghouse's memoir is informed by her education in the Islamic Indo-Persian biographical tradition, and an acute awareness of possible audiences.

Menon explores what writing meant for Nayantara Sahgal across her long career as a public figure. Going beyond the private–public binary, Menon traces a "secret" (67) that undergirds the differences in Sahgal's memoirs. In the former, "the author's personal and political selves are a harmonious whole" (68), optimistic about the promises of a nascent Indian nation and middle-class conjugal respectability. Menon argues that the latter, read alongside Sahgal's personal letters and private interviews, is a "monument to a buried self" (70) that emerged and deceased in years of marital crisis between the publication of both volumes, and a simultaneous disillusionment with bourgeois aspirations.

Alam and Ray's essays foreground an important methodological assertion of this book. Autobiographical writings "must be viewed through a lens of multiplicity where it is composed of different styles of self-narration and is closely related to the contexts of production" (73). Both essays argue against the thesis that women's autobiographies, and therefore the personas they document, are uncritically subsumed into larger political ideologies. Alam reads Nazr Sajjad Hyder's personal letters, diaries and memoirs that were eventually serialised in Urdu magazines, and Ray reads Kailashbashini Debi's diary and personal letters, to reveal selves that negotiated reformist politics in colonial India. These negotiations are subtle (for instance, Hyder risked making her emotional life public to push against the presumed passivity of Muslim women, and Debi noted her reflections on instances of casteist hypocrisy in reformist Bengali households), but they are there nevertheless. The autobiographical self must, therefore, be sought in a "kaleidoscope of its genres and its contexts" (90) far beyond the conventional likes of a first-person monologue that celebrates public achievements and teleological consistency.

The second section has essays by Uma Chakravarti, Shweta Jha, and Afshan Bokhari. Chakravarti analyzes novels to understand how Partition is remembered by Pakistani women writers Mumtaz Nawaz, Zaheda Hina, and Khadija Mastur. Why does violence not find mention in representations of violent pasts? Chakravarti argues that an emergent collective biography can be read in autobiographical accounts portrayed through fictional characters; the lack of explicit violence in narratives that are pervaded by it leads to "a cathartic release of the congealed emotions of a generation," (138) ultimately healing public archives of Partition memories.

Jha and Bokhari's essays explore how architectural monuments could also be understood as public announcements of selves. Mah Laqa Bai (1767–1824), courtesan in a princely court of Hyderabad, authored *ghazals* and patronized an *ashurkhana* (termporary prayer house). Doing so, Jha argues, gave her public memory a distinct religious connotation. In addition to being a courtesan, Mah Laqa Bai is thus remembered as "a pious women... as a patron, a regal woman of talent and honor" (157). Bokhari's essay discusses how Jahanara Begam, daughter of Mughal emperor

Shah Jahan, established her public memory in the Timurid-Mughal patrilineal history. Jahanara used masculine modes of self-expression to sustain Mughal sovereignty and advance Shah Jahan's imperial agenda. Importantly, Jahanara also patronized building mosques and *khanaqahs*, and composed the Sufi treatises *Munis al-arvah* (1940) and *Risalah-i-Sahibiyah* (1641). In addition to being a Mughal Princess (often considered incidental to the Empire's achievements), Jahanara established herself as a devout Sufi in her own right. Mah Laqa Bai and Jahanara Begam's public personas are preserved in both texts and monuments—together, they represent stories that consolidate reminiscent, agential selves.

The third section is comprised of essays by Anshu Malhotra, Siobhan Lambert-Hurley, and Kathryn Hansen. Each essay explores the intersections between gender and religion in autobiographical writings, and cumulatively they illustrate persevering selves (otherwise theorized as subordinate, subaltern, or mute). Malhotra and Lambert-Hurley closely analyze two texts, *Ik Sau Sath Kafian* by Piro (d. 1872), and *The Heart of a Gopi* by Raihana Tyabji (1901–1975). Why did Piro write about her move from a brothel to Guru Gulabdas's religious establishment, and why did Muslim-born Tyabji write of her 'mystic' encounters with Lord Krishna as a *gopi*? These questions, Malhotra and Lambert-Hurley poignantly suggest, can be addressed in light of the literary and devotional histories that endow Piro and Tyabji's "individual experiences with a kind of validity not achievable otherwise" (241). Contrary to "displaying an obsession with novelty and autonomy" (207), a presumed characteristic of 'good' autobiographies, Piro and Tyabji's texts borrow "cultural practices and mental habits that belonged to an earlier episteme" (206). The authors deploy recurring tropes, literary conventions, and religious themes not for lack of better options or creativity; instead, their attempt is to be remembered through familiarity, in societies that are by and large hostile to their life decisions.

Hansen's essay discusses autobiographies authored by male actors Jayshankar Sundari and Fida Husain, who performed as women. Their writings reveal a "doubled performativity" (256), through public and on-stage personas. Hansen argues that the very act of writing functioned to bust the commonly held belief that theatre actors are shallow and immoral; Sundari and Husain asserted their "self-regard, self-mastery, and self-determination" (277) as artists and individuals on the fringes of social normativity.

Speaking of the Self is relevant across academic disciplines, particularly South Asian studies, religion, comparative literature, history, gender, and performance studies. The sheer diversity of primary material included, crisp writing style, and careful treatment of issues relating to gender, performance, and autobiography make for an accessible, theoretically insightful, and delightfully engaging academic work.

Rohini Shukla
Columbia University

Ajaya Kumar Sahoo and Gabriel Sheffer, eds., *Diaspora and Identity: Perspectives on South Asian Diaspora*

London: Routledge, 2014. 184 pages. Hardcover, $160.00, ISBN: 9780415825443. Paperback, $54.95, ISBN: 9781138850712. eBook, $16.49, ISBN: 9781315540481.

A workable definition of diaspora (a Greek term meaning "scattering"), originally standing for the "dispersion" of the Jews following their Babylonian captivity, designates "a group that recognizes its separatedness based on common ethnicity/nationality, lives in a host country and maintains some kind of attachment to its home country or homeland" (Lahneman 2005, 7). As Pascale Herzig has it, the concept of diaspora "offers an alternative way of thinking about transnational migration and ethnic relations in contrast to those that rely on 'race' and 'ethnicity'" (2006, 96–97). The origin of Indian (South Asian) diaspora, a burgeoning influential phenomenon in world culture, harks back to the subcontinent's incorporation into the British Empire, and the dispersal in the nineteenth century of many of its inhabitants from mostly the northern part of the country as indentured laborers to the Empire's possessions in the Indian Ocean, South Sea islands, the Caribbean Sea, Southeast Asia, and South Africa. Following World War II and subsequently decolonization, the dispersal (voluntary emigration) of Indian labor and professionals has been a nearly global phenomenon. Indians and other South Asians provided labor in the reconstruction of war-torn Europe, particularly, the United Kingdom and the Netherlands; in more recent years unskilled labor from South Asia has been the main force in the transformation of the physical landscape of much of the Middle East.

Ajaya K. Sahoo and Gabriel Sheffer's edited volume *Diaspora and Identity* contains ten chapters that are reprints of the articles published in the *Journal of South Asian Diaspora* (2009–2012), also edited by Dr. Sahoo. All the chapters are well researched and expertly written, and their different perspectives notwithstanding, deal with the complex nodal conundrum of the diasporic South Asians holding on to their homeland traditions, which they are prompted to readjust, recreate, and negotiate with a view to coping with their hostland's cultural dominance. Yet this conflicting exchange does not degenerate into culture war, but a working, albeit occasionally precarious, compromise.

Over 30 million people from India, Pakistan, Bangladesh, Nepal, Sri Lanka, Bhutan, and the Maldives constitute the South Asian diaspora inhabiting the globe outside of their homelands. They are diverse in terms of language, religion, and social structure, but by assiduously using collective mobilization and communication technology they have created transnational communities, thereby contributing significantly to the politics, economy, and culture of their hostlands.

Dibyesh Anand shows the ways in which diasporas can achieve subjectivity as an ethical position in order to challenge the bounded community of nation-states. Modern day diasporas, a large collective of people with shared ethnic markers of identity, may harbor political allegiance to their homeland while continuing to reside in their hostland. Thus, their individual subjectivity is marked by an ambiguity in that they practice "a politics of identification" instead of their ethnicity and identity (13).

Bandana Purkayastha discusses how new global forces such as companies with global reach market cultural products like clothing, art, music, films, books, and cosmetics among South Asian target groups by appealing to their fundamental identities (27).

Pnina Werbner demonstrates how the diasporic Muslims of Britain, formerly considered non-threatening and relatively benign—their anti-Western and celebratory cultural rhetoric notwithstanding—have come recently under suspicion and accusations following suicide bombings on the London underground, and revelations of aborted conspiracies that they have been responsible for the failure of multiculturalism practiced in the country. The author believes that multiculturalism discourse is not "really about 'culture,'" (36) but about, in her neologism, "multiculturalism-in-history" (46–47). Thus, multiculturalism, imbricated in religion, began with the Rushdie affair, following the publication of *The Satanic Verses* (46). She concludes her essay by positing how the so-called "failure of multiculturalism" led the Muslim leaders of Britain toward "utilising the national platform of their own ethnic press, [and how this] has carved out a space of civility in which the responses of these leaders to expositions of their alleged extremism are expressed passionately and yet rationally" (58).

Rusi Jaspal and Adrian Coyle interview twelve second-generation Asians (SGA), focusing on the role of language in their identity formation. The authors subject their data to qualitative thematic analysis and formulate four superordinate themes: "Mother tongue and self," "A sense of ownership and affiliation," "Negotiating linguistic identities in social space," and "The quest for a positive linguistic identity." Participants expressed a desire for self-definition as Asian, but also a cautious concern about SGA monolingual in English as a possible loss of status among the diaspora Asians as whitewashed browns (77). The authors suggest careful intervention for sensitizing the SGA toward the pros and cons of monolingualism and bi-/multilingualism.

Laura Hirvi's case study of "The Sikh Gurdwaras in Finland" focuses on the role of the *gurudvārā* ("gate of the guru"), a Sikh religious institution, functioning as an agent negotiating, maintaining, and transmitting immigrants' identities. Her fieldwork conducted in metropolitan Helsinki leads her to comment on the question of identity among the Sikhs of Finland, who prefer to identify themselves as Indians (83). The author concludes that her fieldwork conducted during summer 2009 revealed that some of the Sikhs in Finland have formed a group with the intention of setting up their own separate worship gatherings (92).

In Herzig's study on the placement of identity among South Asians in Kenya, we note how intra-ethnic relations (in 1989 approximately 90,000 Asians, the majority of them Gujaratis and Punjabis from India, including some of the latter ethnic group from Pakistan), more specifically networking, form a key to successful social mobility. The Asians in Kenya are mainly concentrated in the urban centers, including Nairobi, where community associations and services have been developed, each with its own place of worship and its own schools. It should be understood, Herzig observes, that "South Asians in Kenya are not a monolithic ethnic group, but they are differentiated by religion and region of origin—the so-called communities" (102). However, the post–World War II and post-independence decades witnessed the gradual replacement of the communal networks by social networks. However, the established Asians have developed a specific East African identity. As one of Herzig's interviewees, an aging Hindu woman in Nairobi, averred: "I don't know to which community I belong. My father was a Brahmin, my mother a Kshatriya, both from Gujarat. Their families disowned them, that's the reason why they came to Kenya. I married a Punjabi Hindu, an Arya Samajist. I do not identify myself with any Community. If you asked my sons, they would say I'm a Kenyan—full stop!" (101).

In her "Trajectory of Social Mobility: Asian Indian Children Coming of Age in New York City," Rupam Saran investigates the intergenerational (upward or downward social mobility of individuals in relation to their parents) and intragenerational (changes in social position in one's lifetime). This task calls for dealing with four major issues: first, to determine the extent the current challenges in the US economy (economic depression since 2007) hinder their upward social mobility; second, how parental cultural, social, and human capitals contribute to their children's social mobility; third, what is the relationship between intragenerational and intergenerational mobility within the Asian Indian context; and fourth, how the second generation (and 1.5 generation) youth take advantage of parental cultural capital, and their counsels of benefiting from their two worlds: the traditional culture of their community, and the Western culture and education of their hostland. As Saran reports, "[s]econd-generation youths in this study expressed that 'the best of both worlds' was a normal thing for them and 'it was their way of life'" (131). Although the job situation has deteriorated due to the recession, and the consequent anti-immigration attitude has been gaining ground, the select young participants in Saran's study are, reportedly, "trying to do their best by reworking two worlds. Their success comes from their location between two cultures and their profound creativity to bridge the differences of two cultures" (133).

The ability of the Asian Indian youth of New York to tread successfully between the two cultures at home and in the outer world works to their advantage in the same way as for their Canadian counterparts in the Greater Toronto Area, in balancing between cultural moral constraints at home and pursuing their social and intimate cross-gender relationships in social space free from parental control and constraints. Their successful strategy owes to their expert use of computer-mediated communication (CMC), as we learn from an interesting study by three Canadian scholars, Arshia U. Zaidi, Amanda Couture, and Eleanor Maticka-Tyndale in "The Power of Technology: A Qualitative Analysis of How South Asian Youth Use Technology to Maintain Cross-Gender Relationships." The three researchers acknowledge their use of a psychological theory of uses and gratification (U&G) to explicate the goal-oriented motives of the CMC users. They clearly articulate these motives: "building relationships, keeping connected with partners, discreet communication, initiating relationships, easing potentially uncomfortable discussions and…communicating when face-to-face interaction is not possible" (143).

P. Pratap Kumar examines the role of caste identity in the Tamil- and Telegu-speaking South Asian diaspora in the West Indies and the UK. The Indians arrived in South Africa as indentured laborers from Madras and Calcutta during 1860 and 1870. By the end of the first generation, the practice and proliferation of using caste names as last names became widespread, by way of demonstrating one's social status through one's name, either for ritual purposes (priesthood) or for marriage purposes. As Kumar observes, "South Asian Hindu society is basically hierarchical in nature structured around caste and its institutions. So, it is obvious that the first-generation Indians in South Africa naturally tried to display the social behavior that they were used to" (162) by staying within their respective subcaste or *jāti* system. But the South African situation, where there was a shortage of requisite numbers of the same *jāti* group to exchange marriage partners and perform priestly functions, led to frequent violations of the *jāti* regulations. Hence, by the middle of the twentieth century, the *jāti* became obsolescent, yielding the pride of place to more universal affiliations such as language-based groupings, such as "Tamil," "Telegu," or "Gujarati." Yet the memory and mystique of the *jāti* persist to this day. As Kumar concludes, even the present generation of South African Hindus continue to "display their caste name as part of their last name or discreetly acquire caste names if they came from lower order caste groups" (167–68).

While acknowledging the undoubted excellence of this anthology, I am disappointed with the editors' exclusion of studies on the rising popularity of Indian religion (Hinduism), cuisine, and couture (for example, Desai 2003 and Chowdhury 2000). The exertions of the Ramakrishna Mission, the Hare Krishna movement, and the Hindu gurus (since the advent of the handsome and ebullient Swami Vivekananda) have made remarkable inroads into the Judeo-Christian West. Thanks to the diasporic South Asians, especially in the UK and US, Hindu festivals such as *Diwali* (*dīpāvalī*) and *Holi* have become widely popular, drawing enthusiastic participation by the native populace of the hostlands. The influential academic scholarly web post RISA (Religion in South Asia) has been a wonderful, creative, and critical global forum of discussions, debates, deliberations, and dialogue on mainline Hinduism, Buddhism, Islam, as well as the esoteric cults and tribal religions. Inclusion of these topics in the book under review would have vastly enhanced its scope and enriched the quality of its contents.

REFERENCES

CHOWDHRY, Prem
    2000   *Colonial India and the Making of Empire Cinema: Image, Ideology and Identity.* Manchester: Manchester University Press.

DESAI, Jigna
    2003   *Beyond Bollywood: The Cultural Politics of South Asian Diasporic Film.* New Delhi: Routledge. doi: 10.4324/9780203643952

LAHNEHAM, William J.
    2005   *Impact of Diaspora Communities on National and Global Politics: Report on Survey of the Literature.* College Park: University of Maryland Press.

Narasingha P. Sil
Western Oregon University

Anastasia Piliavsky, ed., *Patronage as Politics in South Asia*

Cambridge University Press, 2014. xiv + 469 pages. List of illustrations, bibliography, index. Hardback, $120.00, ISBN: 9781107056084. eBook, $96.00, ISBN: 9781316156681. doi: 10.1017/CBO9781107296930.

If, as Tim Ingold (1992, 696) writes, "Anthropology is philosophy with the people in," political anthropology is political theory with people's lived experiences, evaluations, and expectations in. What better way, indeed, to understand "the political" in South Asia (or anywhere) than listening to and observing those variously engaged in it? *Patronage as Politics in South Asia* does just that. In doing so, its editor and contributors recognize how—high-flying political philosophies and theories notwithstanding—democracy (and political life more widely) is simply a set of social relations: an arrangement between persons concerning governance and political authority and their discrepant roles and expectations in it. Anastasia Piliavsky poses in her incisive introduction, "what is democratic representation if not a social relation?" (29). If the form and meaning of social relations diverge from one society to the next, so, consequently, does the social substance of democracy. That democratic politics and lifeworlds are everywhere socially enmeshed and reworked into historically evolved contexts, moral values, and cultural circumstances is an observation many liberal theorists, and their ventriloquists, find difficult to accept, even perceive. But this book's sixteen essays (preceded by a foreword by John Dunn and an introduction by Anastasia Piliavsky) jointly show postulated models of modern, liberal democracy and of the "good political life" are just that: normative models and "as if systems" that superficially abstract that which cannot be abstracted from the pre-existent moral and political gloss of the land. "The land," here, is South Asia, a place, in all its diversities and complexities, that increasingly claims central stage in the study of our modern political condition.

Anthropologists, John Beattie (1964, 12) argued long ago, should study two things: first, those social relations that are "standardized, institutionalized, and so characteristic of the society being investigated," and, second, the ideas and values associated with these social relationships. In South Asia, it is patron–client relationships that make one such characteristic practice and value. It is the history, persistence, and moralities of patronage in South Asian political life that this book engages, through both historical and ethnographic excursions. Even as the contributors (wisely) refrain from adopting a single definition of patronage and variously celebrate, criticize, and convict its many manifestations, they all agree that patronage remains etched—as a value, idiom, practice, and critique—at the heart of South Asian political life. They also agree that patronage is best approached as a "living moral idiom" (4) that operates in a complex moral multiverse in which "relational principles" (13) and values of munificence, mutual dependencies, and "hierarchical reciprocity" (366) create political bonds and loyalties that last.

While not everyone may agree with Anastasia Piliavsky that "in the social sciences patronage has had its day" (4), many ethnographers do document relations of patronage in their work, or even in the academic settings in which they write (Peacock 2016). Patronage politics certainly finds no place in normative, Weberian projections of what modern, liberal democracy should look like; votes, after all, should not be bartered, and impersonal governance should supersede clientelistic exchanges, while politicians are expected to behave as *servants* of the public good, not as powerful patrons who provide and protect their devotee voters. This position has its adherents among mostly middle- and upper-class citizens in South Asia, but less so among the poorer, more vulnerable sections of the society, for whom patronage, in its many forms and guises, is coterminous with politicians and politics. It is the very moral framework, as most of the chapters variously conclude, through which they engage in politics, formulate their political demands, and evaluate their political representatives. Put differently, patronage, across South Asia, is not a dying remnant of a pre-modern past, soon to be swallowed by India's new modernity, but nourishes a contemporary political sociality and structure of political morals that are at once historically traceable and contested, but also scripted and evaluated afresh. Besides delving into the moral depths of patronage, the authors also, both explicitly and implicitly, use the study of patronage as a stepping stone leading to other questions, such as South Asian manifestations and meanings of the public good, political ideology, public sphere, political representation, and even corruption. These are fundamental fields of inquiry, into which sets of insights are offered.

In South Asia, "patronage politics" is everywhere just around the corner, both in the past and present. A tour around the region, as this book offers, shows this. In traditional Tibet, to start with, the polity took the form of a governmental diarchy between the "preceptor-donee" and ruler and lay donors, although it is not always clear, as Seyfort Ruegg (chapter 2) shows, whether the vocabulary of patronage does justice to this relation, or, for that matter, "who 'patronises' whom?" (69). Traveling south and bypassing Nepal (to which, unfortunately, no chapter is devoted), we arrive in northern India where Beatrice Jauregui (chapter 10) invites us into a police *thana* to show how the production of First Information Reports (FIRs), central to India's legal system, are often not the result of legal-rational proceedings but subject to interpersonal relations of exchange, negotiations, and protection, with police officers operating both as patrons and clients, depending on the context and actors involved. Also in northern India, we find that elected representatives are perceived—and manifest themselves—as "politician-kings" and "patron-protectors" (283), whose political clout hinges on their ability to protect (organizing violence if they must) and provision their followers, who, in turn, look upon their political representatives as "extraordinary kin" (283). Voters express their affection for (and reliance on) their political leaders in an idiom of caste competition and belonging, shared blood, and substantive bonds of divine kinship that trace back to Hindu gods, deities, and mythologies (Lucia Michelutti, chapter 12).

Heading westward and entering Bangladesh we meet "political bullies," or *mastans*, criminalizing street-level political life. They engage in muscular political brokerage, racketeering, politically motivated crime, and violence, and derive legitimacy and protection from the patronage they receive from political parties, which now and then rely on these "political bullies" to navigate the murkier and violent sides of Bangladeshi politics (Arild Engelsen Ruud, chapter 13). Moving south, we first learn about "remnants of patronage" among the Valaiyar community in Tamil Nadu, whose sense of history, place, and identity is traced and articulated through narratives of past royal patronage they received in the form of titles, land grants, and temples (Diane Miles, chapter 3). Also in South India, in Kerala, we learn about the (im)moralities of brokers who use their social "connectedness" (366) to help prospective labor migrants to jobs in the Gulf. While these brokers like to think of themselves as munificent and claim to be involved in community development, their fees are often hefty, their motivations selfish, and they occasionally cheat. All the same, most would-be migrants continue to prefer these informal networks of mediation, often immersed into relations of kith and kin, over the formal channels provided by the bureaucracy and other state-sponsored organizations (Filippo Osella, chapter 16).

Continuing our journey westward we are introduced to "political fixers" in Gujarat, who are employed both by the poor, to help them access the state and its resources, and by elected politicians, who use them to "facilitate clientelistic exchanges" (197) and to win votes (Ward Berenschot, chapter 8). Entering Rajasthan, we find that politicians relate to their constituents as donors do to donees, making a hierarchical political arrangement that, in some ways, traces back to the so-called Jajmani system. Voters' political preferences, Anastasia Piliavsky (chapter 6) shows ethnographically, are contingent on a politician's commitment and capacity to act as a benevolent patron whose duty it is to "provide." A pervasive idiom of "feeding and eating" (160) forms the moral basis for political relations, both literally through lavish election feasts, and metaphorically by politicians "getting things done" (174) for their voters. Both ways, "feeding and eating" is not merely transactional but generative of the lasting bonds and loyalties politicians need to win elections. Further westward, and crossing the India–Pakistan border, Nicolas Martin (chapter 14) emphasizes patronage's darker sides, as in the Pakistani Punjab clientelistic exchanges that "reinforce existing power structures and undermine popular freedoms" and are "integral to processes of dispossession" (343). In addition to the chapters mentioned above, this volume carries contributions by Mattison Mines, Sumit Guha, David Gilmartin, Lisa Björkman, Pamela Price (with Dusi Srinivas), Steven Wilkinson, and Hildegard Diemberger (constraints of space prevent me from discussing these chapters individually), each of which variously engage practices, moral principles, and paradoxes of patronage.

A few years ago Rajeev Bhargava (2010, 56) lamented that "a critical tradition of political theory does not exist in India." Most political treatises, he lamented, remain derivative from concepts and categories that emerged from the so-called "West." In the current search for India-centric (and South Asian) political theory and thought, scholars would do well to take careful note of this volume and include in their canons presently "under-construction" the histories, politics, and moralities of patronage. While patronage is many things, this volume shows convincingly how in South Asia it is not a field of moral aberration but has its own moral sense, historical trajectories, rules, rewards, and drawbacks. Relations of patronage will, of course, continue to evolve and change. Yet, as a moral frame and political praxis, patronage is probably there to stay in South Asia, certainly for the foreseeable future, and this collection of essays therefore contributes greatly to capturing the character of contemporary political life in South Asia.

REFERENCES

Beattie, John
1964   *Other Cultures: Aims, Methods, and Achievements in Social Anthropology.* London: Routledge. doi: 10.4324/9780203985069

Bhargava, Rajeev
  2010   *What is Political Theory and Why Do We Need It.* Delhi: Oxford University Press.
Ingold, Tim
  1992   Editorial. *Man,* New Series 27: 693–96.
Peacock, Vita
  2016   Academic precarity as hierarchical dependence in the Max Planck Society. *Hau: Journal of Ethnographic Theory* 6: 95–119. doi: 10.14318/hau6.1.006

Jelle J. Wouters
Royal Thimphu College, Bhutan

Tibet

Shokdung, *The Division of Heaven and Earth: On Tibet's Peaceful Revolution.* Trans. Matthew Akester
London: C. Hurst & Company, 2016. xliii + 162 pages. Paperback, $19.95, ISBN: 978-1-84904-6770.

The 2008 so-called "Peaceful Revolution in the Year of the Earth Rat," also known as the "3.14 Incident," was a turning point in Sino-Tibetan relations. Marking the fiftieth anniversary of violent protests in Amdo, and coinciding with the Beijing Olympics, it revealed that decades of development and integration had not assuaged Tibetan sentiments. In fact, the protests that followed the 2008 Revolution renewed discussions of independence within the Tibetan Autonomous Region of China (TARC). Many consider the period to be one of a Tibetan national awakening. Shokdung's *Division of Heaven and Earth* was written at the height of these developments and has emerged as one of TARC's most contentious political commentaries. Compared to the tenth Panchen Lama's *Petition in 70,000 Characters* (1962), its bold assertions and distinctly Tibetan prose provide a rare glimpse into an emerging intellectual scene in the People's Republic of China.

Shokdung (pseudonym; Tragya) argues that Buddhism, namely the doctrine of emptiness and no-self, contributed to the decline of the Tibetan polity. Citing Tibet's "history of repeated capitulation, sectarian conflict, priest–patron alliances and closure to the outside world," he asserts that Buddhist influences stunted notions of the individual, sovereignty, and territory needed to advance nation-states. Tibet could not achieve true autonomy until it reconciled its Buddhist heritage with modernity. In this background, Shokdung views the 2008 protests as a pivot away from this precedent. Advocating "freedom and rights in practice as well as in thought [and theory]," the Peaceful Revolution had adapted secular ideologies to justify political freedom.

While the book itself is not divided into general sections, it helps to imagine its four chapters as falling into two sections that expand upon the mentioned premises. The first section explores the author's powerful, emotive response to the events of 2008 in three chapters: "Joy," "Sorrow," and "Fear." Embellished with Buddhist analogies and proverbs, this section provides a coherent, albeit controversial, thesis fashioned in the style of Tibetan Buddhist commentaries. The first chapter on "Joy" bemoans the suffering of Tibetan communities since the Cultural Revolution but celebrates the fact that, through suffering, Tibetans have discovered their political agency. In the second chapter on "Sorrow," Shokdung elaborates upon political repression that followed the Peaceful Revolution. The third chapter on "Fear" comments on its aftermath, including both misconceptions about Tibetan terrorists and violent nationalism among Han Chinese. The second section then provides a way forward from these conditions based on the author's experiences. Of note, Shokdung suggests that Gandhian *satyāgraha* (Tib. *denpe utsuk*), or non-violent protest, is a possible method for maintaining political momentum in the Chinese context.

The book merits distinction from political scientists and scholars of modern China for its subaltern and intersectional analyses of modern Tibet. Texts of this nature seldom receive attention outside of the region, particularly those that maintain their Tibetan character. Matthew Akester's lucid translation upholds Shokdung's poetics and presents his philosophical discussions in accessible English. It will prove to be a valuable resource for those interested in subaltern studies as well as social movements in the PRC.

Despite its indigenous value, *The Division of Heaven and Earth* has several shortcomings that are addressed forthright by Hurst Publications in the foreword and preface. These include overt, functionalist claims on the development of Tibetan society. For instance, Shokdung states that "the Tibetan psychology is a primitive one, in which many characteristics of pre-civilized peoples can be seen," and that "[Tibetans are] primitive people still in the clutches of an old-world psychology of demons and spirits." Those familiar with South-Central Asia will quickly understand that these arguments are the product of regional education systems. Shokdung was largely self-educated in political science; many available and accessible texts in this area cater to a hierarchy of civilizations. Even with these conditions in mind, however, Western readers may disparage other claims such as the following: "Tibetans have not so far made contributions to world historical progress, political, economic, cultural or, in short, human development." Francoise Robin in his foreword to the book comments on this at length, elaborating upon Shokdung's inability to understand that "religion is not an obstacle to modernity but a feature of it."

Despite some tenuous claims, *The Division of Heaven and Earth* will undoubtedly provoke discussion on a wide variety of subjects, ranging from anthropology and religion to political theory and philosophy. I suggest that readers be familiar with the 2008 events, at least generally, before attempting to engage with Shokdung's arguments. The author greatly downplays crimes perpetrated by Tibetans against non-Tibetan business owners during the protests. Also, his assessments are indeed subaltern, even radical, in many respects. The book could easily be paired with Emily Yeh's *Taming Tibet* (2013) for a more holistic perspective on state space and power struggles that led to the Peaceful Revolution.

REFERENCE

YEH, Emily T.
  2013   *Taming Tibet: Landscape Transformation and the Gift of Chinese Development.* New York: Cornell University Press.

Alexander R. O'Neill
Duke University

CONTRIBUTORS

Ambika AIYADURAI is Assistant Professor of Anthropology at Indian Institute of
Technology Gandhinagar. She completed her PhD thesis in Anthropology
from the National University of Singapore. Her thesis focused on the politics
of wildlife conservation in the Mishmi hills of Arunachal Pradesh, Northeast India. She is trained in both natural and social sciences with a dual masters' degree in Wildlife Sciences from Wildlife Institute of India (Dehradun)
and Anthropology, Environment and Development from University College
London (UK). Her research interest is to understand people-nature relations
and how the local and global forces shape these relations leading to collaborations and contestations among different interest groups. She has published
on the issues of biodiversity conservation and indigenous communities in
national and international journals.

Shenshen CAI completed her PhD in contemporary Chinese culture studies with
the School of Humanities at Griffith University. She has broad research interests in contemporary Chinese literature, film, theatre, and folklore studies.
She currently works as a lecturer with Swinburne University of Technology
in Australia, teaching Chinese and Chinese culture-related courses. She has
recently published articles in *Portal Journal of Multidisciplinary International Studies, East Asia: An International Quarterly, Journal of International Women's Studies,* and *New Zealand Journal of Asian Studies.*

Deepra Dandekar is a researcher interested in religious studies and gender studies. Her doctoral research explored childlessness and its ritualization in rural
Maharashtra, resulting in her first book *Boundaries and Motherhood: Ritual and Reproduction in Rural Maharashtra* (Zubaan, Delhi, 2016). She
co-edited with Torsten Tschacher *Islam, Sufism and the Everyday Politics
of Belonging in South Asia* (Routledge, 2016). She has recently translated a
nineteenth-century Marathi novel on Christian conversion that is under publication with the AAR Series of Religion in Translation, Oxford University
Press. She currently works as a researcher on "Migration and Exclusion" at
the Max Planck Institute for Human Development in Berlin.

Coralynn V. DAVIS is Professor of Women's and Gender Studies and Anthropology
and Faculty Director for Academic Civic Engagement at Bucknell University
(Lewisburg, PA). Her initial work in Nepal focused on issues of women's
development and tourism, while her more recent scholarship examines Maithil

women's folktales and storytelling practices. She has published numerous articles in peer reviewed journals and a monograph *Maithil Women's Tales: Storytelling on the Nepal-India Border* (University of Illinois Press, 2014).

Charlotte EUBANKS is Associate Professor of Comparative Literature, Japanese, and Asian Studies at Penn State. She is the author of *Miracles of Book and Body: Buddhist Textual Cultures in Medieval Japan* (University of California Press, 2011) and is completing a monograph on twenthieth-century Japanese visual culture. She also serves as Associate Editor at the journal *Verge: Studies in Global Asias*, where she is co-editing a special issue on Indigeneity.

Keith HOWARD is Professor of Music at SOAS, University of London. He has written and edited nineteen books, including *Korean Musical Instruments: A Practical Guide* (Se-Kwang Music Publishing Company, 2015) and *Music as Intangible Cultural Heritage: Policy, Ideology and Practice in the Preservation of East Asian Traditions* (Routledge, 2012). He has been a regular broadcaster on Korean affairs for BBC, ITV, Sky, NBC, and others.

Gisa JÄHNICHEN is currently teaching and researching at Shanghai Conservatory of Music on ecomusicology and the performing arts of Southeast Asia. Her recent publications include *Studies on Musical Diversity: Methodological Approaches* (Universiti Putra Malaysia Press, 2011), *Studies on Music and Dance Cultures in Laos* (Books On Demand, 2013), and numerous journal articles. She is chief editor of Studia Instrumentorum Musicae Popularis (New Series), a Study Group book series of the International Council for Traditional Music.

Felicia KATZ-HARRIS is the senior curator and curator of Asian and Oceanic Folk Art at the Museum of International Folk Art (Santa Fe). Her publications include *Inside the Puppet Box* (2010) on *wayang kulit*, and she curated major exhibitions on Japanese kites, material religion in Asia, and Javanese shadow puppets, which won an American Alliance of Museums award for "Overall Excellence in Exhibitions."

Frank J. KOROM is Professor of Religion and Anthropology at Boston University and co-editor of *Asian Ethnology*.

Terence LANCASHIRE currently teaches in the Department of Human and Social Sciences at Osaka Ohtani University. He has written various articles on Japanese music and folk performing arts, and has published *Gods' Music: The Japanese Folk Theatre of Iwami Kagura* (Florian Noetzel, 2006) and *An Introduction to Japanese Folk Performing Arts* (Ashgate, 2011; Routledge, 2016).

John LEAVITT is a professor in the Department of Anthropology, Université de Montréal. His fields of interest are publishing and analyzing epic and oracular texts from the central Himalayas, the relationship between language and culture, Indo-European comparative mythology, identity and performance among Hindu immigrants in Canada.

Claire Seungeun LEE Claire Seungeun Lee is Assistant Professor of Chinese Studies at Inha University and affiliated with the University of Massachusetts Boston.

She has worked in the educational, media and legal sectors in Hong Kong, Shanghai, Taipei and Seoul, and, latterly, for the China Regional and Provincial Research Team at Korea Institute for International Economic Policy, one of the leading think tanks in South Korea. Her research areas include cultural, economic, and digital sociology, international migration and borderscapes, and the interdisciplinary study of Asian societies, with her primary concern being an investigation of the complex connections between China and its neighboring countries throughout the Asia region.

Mu LI, is an assistant professor in folklore at Southeast University in China. His research interest is Chinese diasporic folklore. His publications include "Chinese Restaurants' Interior Decor as Ethnographic Objects in Newfoundland" (*Western Folklore*, 2016); "Negotiating Chinese Culinary Traditions in Newfoundland," (*Digest* 2014); "Jewish Activities on Christmas: An Online Case Study," (*Voices* 2011).

Patrick McCARTNEY is currently a Visiting Fellow at the Australian National University and a Post-doctoral Scholar at the University of Kyoto. His work focuses at the intersection of the utopian aspirations of global yoga and ethno-nationalism, and uses an interdisciplinary analytical framework that focuses on the politics of imagination, the economics of desire, the sociology of spirituality, and the anthropology of religion. His publications include "Politics beyond the yoga mat: Yoga fundamentalism and the 'Vedic Way of Life'" (*Global Ethnographic*) and "Utopian symmetries: Reflections on future worlds and transglobal yoga (*The Journal of the International Society for the Interdisciplinary Study of Symmetry*).

Nathan McGOVERN is Assistant Professor in the Department of Philosophy and Religious Studies at the University of Wisconsin-Whitewater. His research focuses on problematizing the boundary between Buddhism and Hinduism, with a particular interest in ancient India and modern Thailand. He has published in the *Journal of Southeast Asian Studies* and the *Journal of the International Association of Buddhist Studies*. He is currently working on a book, *The Snake and the Mongoose: The Emergence of Identity in Early Indian Religion*, forthcoming with Oxford University Press.

A. C. McKAY is the author of a number of works on the history and culture of the Indo-Tibetan Himalayas. His most recent publication is *Kailas Histories: Renunciate Traditions and the Construction of Himalayan Sacred Geography* (Brill, 2015).

Daniel A. MÉTRAUX is Professor Emeritus and Adjunct Professor of Asian Studies at Mary Baldwin University. He has written extensively on modern Japanese and East Asian history and religion. His most recent publication is *How Journalists Shaped American Foreign Policy: A Case Study of Japan's Military Seizure of Korea in 1905* (Edwin Mellen Press, 2017). His current research focuses on the Wakamatsu Tea and Silk Colony Farm, the first Japanese settlement of Japanese in North America in 1869.

Muhammad A. Z. MUGHAL is Assistant Professor of Cultural Anthropology at

King Fahd University of Petroleum & Minerals, Saudi Arabia. He received his PhD in Anthropology from the University of Durham, UK in 2014. He is affiliated with the University of Durham as Honorary Research Fellow. His research interests include time, space, social change, globalization, environment, and Pakistan. He has widely published on these issues in different international journals and reference volumes.

Alexander O'NEILL is a Graduate Candidate at Duke University's Nicholas School of the Environment. His research centers on sustainable development in South-Central Asia, namely the role of local communities in natural resource management. He has spent several years working in both public and private sectors in the region, including as a David L. Boren Scholar (Kathmandu, Nepal) and Fulbright-Nehru Research Scholar (Sikkim, India).

George PATI is an Associate Professor of Theology and International Studies in the College of Arts and Sciences at Valparaiso University, IN. His primary research and teaching interests lie in historical study of South Asian religions, languages, and cultures, with special emphasis on Hinduism and Malayalam language and literature. Recent publications include "Nambūtiris and Ayyappan Devotees in Kerala," in *Contemporary Hinduism*, ed. P. Pratap Kumar, 204–16 (Durham, UK: Acumen, 2013).

Karen G. RUFFLE is Associate Professor in the Department for the Study of Religion at the University of Toronto. She specializes in Indo-Persian Shi'ism. Her research and teaching interests focus on devotional texts, ritual practice, and Shi'i material practices in South Asia. Her first book was *Gender, Sainthood, and Everyday Practice in South Asian Shi'ism* (University of North Carolina Press, 2011). She is currently working on her second book, tentatively titled *Somatic Shi'ism: The Body in Deccani Shi'i Material Religion and Ritual Practice*.

Sudipta SEN is a historian of late Mughal and early British India and the British Empire. His work has largely focused on the early history of British expansion in India. He is the author of *Empire of Free Trade: The English East India Company and the Making of the Colonial Marketplace* (1998) and *Distant Sovereignty: National Imperialism and the Origins of British India* (2002). His forthcoming book *Ganga: The Many Pasts of an Indian River* is an exploration of the idea of a cosmic, universal river at the interstices of myth, historical geography and ecology.

Anthony SHAY is Associate Professor of Dance and Cultural Studies in the Department of Theatre and Dance at Pomona College in Claremont, California. He is the author of six monographs, the latest of which is *The Dangerous Lives of Public Performers: Dance, Sex and Entertainment in the Middle East* (Palgrave Macmillan, 2014). He is currently writing a book about Igor Moiseyev and the Moiseyev Dance Company, the first state-supported folk dance company in the world.

Rohini SHUKLA is a graduate student at the Department of Religion, Columbia University. Her research interests are religions in South Asia, bhakti, gender and sexuality studies, performance studies, Indian philosophy and Marathi literature.

Narasingha P. Sil retired from Western Oregon University in 2011 as Professor Emeritus of History. He has published numerous monographs, scholarly articles, book reviews, and encyclopedia, including *William Lord Herbert of Pembroke (c. 1507–1570): Politique and Patriot* (Edwin Mellen Press, 1988), and *Crazy in Love of God: Ramakrishna's Caritas Divina* (Susquehanna University Press, 2009).

Guido Sprenger is Professor of Social Anthropology at the Institute of Ethnology, University of Heidelberg. He is the author of *Die Männer, die den Geldbaum fällten* (Lit Verlag, 2006) and co-editor of *Animism in Southeast Asia* (2016).

McComas Taylor is Associate Professor and Reader in Sanskrit at the ANU College of Asia and the Pacific. His research lies at the intersection of contemporary critical theory and classical Sanskrit narrative literature. He published The Fall of the Indigo Jackal (SUNY Press, 2007) and more recently Seven Days of Nectar: Contemporary Oral Performance of the Bhagavatapurana (Oxford University Press, 2016).

Timothy Thurston is currently lecturer in Chinese Studies at the University of Leeds and Research Associate at the Smithsonian Institution, Center for Folklife and Cultural Heritage. His research examines ethnic minority languages and cultures in contemporary China with an emphasis on Tibet. His articles have been published in *Asian Ethnology, Asian Ethnicity, Asian Highlands Perspectives*, and *CHINOPERL: The Journal of Chinese Oral and Performance Literature*. Articles are also forthcoming in *Journal of Folklore Research, and Journal of Asian Studies*.

Jelle J. P. Wouters is a faculty member in the Department of Social Sciences, Royal Thimphu College, Bhutan. He has conducted ethnographic and historical research among the upland and tribal Naga in India's Northeast, and his research focuses on Naga political lifeworlds, vernacular manifestations of democracy, and the development state. His recent publications include: "Sovereignty, integration or bifurcation? Troubled histories, contentious territories and the political horizons of the long lingering Naga Movement" (*Studies in History*, 2016) and "Polythetic democracy: tribal elections, bogus votes, and political imagination in the Naga uplands of Northeast India" (*Hau: Journal of Ethnographic Theory* 2015).